WORSHIP IN THE EARLY CHURCH

WORSHIP IN THE EARLY CHURCH

An Anthology of Historical Sources

Volume One

Lawrence J. Johnson

A PUEBLO BOOK

Liturgical Press Collegeville, Minnesota

www.litpress.org

A Pueblo Book published by Liturgical Press

Cover design by David Manahan, OSB

Excerpt (1), *Qaddish*: translated, with permission of the publisher, from *Enchiridion Euchologicum Fontium Liturgicorum*, ed. E. Lodi (Rome: Centro Liturgico Vincensian), p. 19. Copyright © 1979.

Excerpts (2, 3, 5, 6), *Qiddush for Sabbaths and Feasts, Birkat ha-mazon, Shemaʾ Yiśraʿel and Its Blessings, Shemoneh Esre*: translated, with permission of the publisher, from *Prex Eucharistica*, ed. A. Hänggi and I. Pahl, Spicilegium Friburgense 12 (Fribourg: Editions Universitaires), pp. 5–7, 9–12, 35–39, 41–54. Copyright © 1968.

Excerpt (4), *Passover Haggadah*: from *The Passover Haggadah*, ed. N.N. Glatzer (New York: Schocken Books), pp. 17–109. Copyright © 1953, 1969. Reprint permission requested.

Excerpt (33-A), Inscription of Pectorius: from *Infant Baptism in the First Four Centuries*, by J. Jeremias, trans. D. Cairns (Philadelphia: The Westminster Press), p. 42. Copyright © 1962. Reprinted by permission of SCM Press in London.

Library of Congress Cataloging-in-Publication Data

Johnson, Lawrence J., 1933–
    Worship in the early church : an anthology of historical sources / Lawrence J. Johnson.
        p.   cm.
    "A Pueblo book."
    Includes index.
    ISBN 978-0-8146-6197-0 (v. 1) — ISBN 978-0-8146-6198-7 (v. 2) — ISBN 978-0-8146-6199-4 (v. 3) — ISBN 978-0-8146-6226-7 (v. 4)
    1. Worship—History—Early church, ca. 30–600.   2. Church history—Primitive and early church, ca. 30–600. I. Title.
    BV6.J64   2009
    264.00937—dc22
                                       2009035344

Contents

Abbreviations

SCRIPTURE

Acts	Acts of the Apostles	Joel	Joel
Amos	Amos	John	John
Bar	Baruch	1 John	1 John
Cant	Canticle of Canticles	2 John	2 John
1 Chr	1 Chronicles	3 John	3 John
2 Chr	2 Chronicles	Jonah	Jonah
Col	Colossians	Josh	Joshua
1 Cor	1 Corinthians	Jude	Jude
2 Cor	2 Corinthians	Judg	Judges
Dan	Daniel	1 Kgs	1 Kings
Deut	Deuteronomy	2 Kgs	2 Kings
Eccl	Ecclesiastes	Lam	Lamentations
Eph	Ephesians	Lev	Leviticus
Esth	Esther	Luke	Luke
Exod	Exodus	1 Macc	1 Maccabees
Ezek	Ezekiel	2 Macc	2 Maccabees
Ezra	Ezra	Mal	Malachi
Gal	Galatians	Mark	Mark
Gen	Genesis	Matt	Matthew
Hab	Habakkuk	Mic	Micah
Hag	Haggai	Nah	Nahum
Heb	Hebrews	Neh	Nehemiah
Hos	Hosea	Num	Numbers
Isa	Isaiah	Obad	Obadiah
Jas	James	1 Pet	1 Peter
Jdt	Judith	2 Pet	2 Peter
Jer	Jeremiah	Phil	Philippians
Job	Job	Phlm	Philemon

Prov	Proverbs	2 Thess	2 Thessalonians
Ps/Pss	Psalms	1 Tim	1 Timothy
Rev	Revelation	2 Tim	2 Timothy
Rom	Romans	Titus	Titus
Ruth	Ruth	Tob	Tobit
1 Sam	1 Samuel	Wis	Wisdom
2 Sam	2 Samuel	Zech	Zechariah
Sir	Sirach	Zeph	Zephaniah
1 Thess	1 Thessalonians		

PERIODICALS AND BOOKS MOST FREQUENTLY CITED

AB	*Analecta Bollandiana* (Brussels, 1882ff.).
ABR	*American Benedictine Review* (Atchison, KS, 1950ff.).
AC	*Antike und Christentum* (Münster, 1929–50).
AER	*American Ecclesiastical Review* (Washington, D.C., 1889–1975).
Altaner (1961)	B. Altaner, *Patrology*, trans. H.C. Graef, 2nd ed. (New York, 1961).
Altaner (1966)	B. Altaner, *Patrologie. Leben, Schriften und Lehre der Kirchenväter*, 6th ed., rev. A. Stüber (Freiburg/Basel/ Vienna, 1966).
Altaner (1978)	B. Altaner, *Patrologie. Leben, Schriften und Lehre der Kirchenväter*, 8th ed., rev. A. Stüber (Freiburg/Basel/ Vienna, 1978).
ALW	*Archiv für Liturgiewissenschaft* (Regensburg, 1950ff.).
Amb	*Ambrosius* (Milan, 1925–60).
ANF	A. Roberts and J. Donaldson, eds., *The Ante-Nicene Fathers: Translations of the Writings of the Fathers down to A.D. 325* (New York, 1885, 1926).
Ant	*Antonianum* (Rome, 1926ff.).
APB	*Acta Patristica et Byzantina* (Praetoria, 1990ff.).
ApT	*Apostolic Tradition.*
Assem	*Assembly* (Notre Dame, 1974ff.).
AThR	*Anglican Theological Review* (New York, 1918ff.).
Aug	*Augustinianum* (Rome, 1961ff.).
AugMag	*Augustus Magister*, Congrès international augustinien (Paris, Sept. 21–24, 1954). Vols. I and II: *Communications*; vol. III: *Acts.*
BALAC	*Bulletin d'ancienne littérature et d'archéologie chrétienne* (Paris, 1911–14).

Bardenhewer (1908)	O. Bardenhewer, *Patrology: The Lives and Works of the Fathers of the Church*, trans. T.J. Shahan (Freiburg i. B./ St. Louis, 1908).
Bardenhewer (1910)	O. Bardenhewer, *Patrologie* (Freiburg i. B., 1910).
Bardenhewer (1913)	O. Bardenhewer, *Geschichte der altkirchlichen Literatur*, 5 vols. (Freiburg i. B./St. Louis, 1913–32).
Bardy (1929)	G. Bardy, *The Greek Literature of the Early Christian Church*, trans. Mother Mary Reginald, Catholic Library of Religious Knowledge 2 (St. Louis, 1929).
Bardy (1930)	G. Bardy, *The Christian Latin Literature of the First Six Centuries*, trans. Mother Mary Reginald, Catholic Library of Religious Knowledge 12 (St. Louis, 1930).
Bautz	F.W. Bautz, ed., *Biographisch-bibliographisches Kirchenlexikon* (Hamm Westf., 1970ff.).
BCE	*Bulletin du comité des études* (Paris, 1953–70).
Bib	*Biblica* (Rome, 1920ff.).
BLE	*Bulletin de littérature ecclésiastique* (Toulouse, 1899ff.).
Bouyer	L. Bouyer, *Eucharist: Theology and Spirituality of the Eucharistic Prayer* (Notre Dame, 1968).
BT	*The Bible Today* (Collegeville, 1962ff.).
BVC	*Bible et vie chrétienne* (Brussels/Paris, 1953–68).
CA	*Cahiers archéologiques* (Paris, 1945ff.).
Campbell	J.M. Campbell, *The Greek Fathers*, Our Debt to Greece and Rome series (New York, 1929).
CATH	G. Jacquemet, ed., *Catholicisme*, 9 vols. (Paris, 1947ff.).
CB	*Collationes Brugenses* (Bruges, 1896–1954).
CC	*La Civiltà Cattolica* (Rome, 1850ff.).
CCL	*Corpus Christianorum, Series Latina* (Turnhout, 1954ff.).
CE	*Catholic Encyclopedia*, 13 vols. + index (New York, 1907–14).
CH	*Church History* (Chicago and Tallahassee, 1932ff.).
CHECL	F. Young, L. Ayres, and A. Louth, eds., *The Cambridge History of Early Christian Literature* (Cambridge, 2004).
ChQ	*Church Quarterly Review* (London, 1875–1968).
Chr	*Christus* (Paris, 1954ff.).
CollMech	*Collectanea Mechliniensia* (Mechlin, 1927–70).
ComL	*Communautés et liturgies* (Ottignies, 1975ff.).
Con	*Concilium* (Glen Rock, NJ, etc., 1965ff.).
Courtonne	Y. Courtonne, ed., *Saint Basile: Lettres*, 3 vols. (Paris, 1957, 1961, 1966).
CPG	M. Geerard and F. Glorie, eds., *Clavis Patrum Graecorum*, 5 vols. (Turnhout, 1974–87).

CPGS	M. Geerard and others, eds., *Clavis Patrum Graecorum Supplementum* (Turnhout, 1998).
Cph	*Classical Philology* (Chicago, 1906ff.).
CPL	E. Dekkers and A. Gaar, eds., *Clavis Patrum Latinorum*, 3rd ed. (Turnhout/Steebrugge, 1995).
CR	*The Clergy Review* (London, 1931–87).
CRI	*Comptes-rendus de l'Académie des Inscriptions et Belles Lettres* (Paris, 1857ff.).
Cross	F.L. Cross, *The Early Christian Fathers* (London, 1960).
CS	*Chicago Studies* (Mundelein, IL, 1962ff.).
CSEL	Corpus Scriptorum Ecclesiasticorum Latinorum (Vienna, 1866ff.).
CV	G.M. Diez, *Concilios visigóticos e hispano-romanos* (Barcelona/Madrid, 1963).
DACL	F. Cabrol and H. Leclercq, eds., *Dictionnaire d'archéologie chrétienne et de liturgie*, 15 vols. (Paris, 1913–53).
DCA	W. Smith, ed., *A Dictionary of Christian Antiquities*, 2 vols. (London, 1876–80).
DCB	W. Smith and H. Wace, eds., *A Dictionary of Christian Biography, Literature, Sects and Doctrines*, 4 vols. (London, 1877–87).
DDC	R. Naz and others, eds., *Dictionnaire de droit canonique*, 7 vols. (Paris, 1935–65).
DDCon	P. Palazzini, ed., *Dizionario dei Concili*, 6 vols. (Rome, 1963–67).
DEC	N.P. Tanner, ed., *Decrees of the Ecumenical Councils* (London/Washington, D.C., 1990).
Deiss	L. Deiss, *Springtime of the Liturgy: Liturgical Texts of the First Four Centuries* (Collegeville, 1979).
DGA	P.-P. Joannou, ed., *Disciplina Generale Antique* (Rome, 1962).
DHGE	A. Baudrillart, ed., *Dictionnaire d'histoire et de géographie ecclésiastiques* (Paris, 1912ff.).
DictSp	M. Viller and others, eds., *Dictionnaire de spiritualité ascétique et mystique* (Paris, 1937ff.).
Did	*Didache*
Didas	*Didascalia Apostolorum*
Di Sante	C. di Sante, *Jewish Prayer: The Origins of the Christian Liturgy*, trans. M.J. O'Connell (New York, 1991).
Div	*Divinitas* (Vatican City, 1957ff.).
Dix	G. Dix, *The Shape of the Liturgy*, 4th ed. (Westminster, 1949).
DLW	J.G. Davies, ed., *A Dictionary of Liturgy and Worship* (New York, 1972).
Dolbeau	F. Dolbeau, ed., *Vingt-six sermons au peuple d'Afrique / Augustin d'Hippone; retrouvés à Mayence*, Collection des études augustiniennes, Série Antiquité 147 (Paris, 1996).
DPAC	A. di Berardino, ed., *Dizionario Patristico e di Antichità Cristiane*, 3 vols. (Marietti, 1983–88).

DR	*Downside Review* (Bath, England, 1800ff.).
DT	*Divus Thomas* (Fribourg i. S., 1871–1953).
DTC	A. Vacant, E. Mangenot, and E. Amann, eds., *Dictionnaire de théologie catholique*, 15 vols. (Paris, 1903–50).
DV	*Dieu vivant* (Paris, 1945–55).
EC	P. Paschini and others, eds., *Enciclopedia Cattolica*, 12 vols. (Vatican City, 1949–54).
ED	*Euntes Docete* (Rome, 1948ff.).
EEC	A. di Berardino, ed., *Encyclopedia of the Early Church*, trans. A. Walford, with a foreword and bibliographic amendments by W.H.C. Frend, 2 vols. (New York, 1992).
EEChr	E. Ferguson, ed., *Encyclopedia of Early Christianity*, 2 vols., 2nd ed. (New York, 1997).
EgT	*Eglise et théologie* (Ottawa, 1970–99).
Elbogen (1962)	I. Elbogen, *Der jüdische Gottesdienst in seiner geschichtlichen Entwicklung*, 4th ed. (Hildesheim, 1962).
Elbogen (1993)	I. Elbogen, *Jewish Liturgy: A Comprehensive History*, trans. R.P. Scheindlin (Philadelphia/New York, 1993).
EO	*Echos d'Orient* (Paris, 1897–1942).
EOr	*Ecclesia Orans* (Rome, 1984ff.).
EphL	*Ephemerides Liturgicae* (Rome, 1887ff.).
ERP	*Etudes religieuses, philosophiques, historiques, et litteraires* (Paris, 1888–1940).
EstAg	*Estudio Teologico Augustiniano* (Valladolid, Spain, 1973ff.).
Et	*Etudes* (Paris, 1897ff.).
ETL	*Ephemerides Theologicae Lovanienses* (Louvain, 1924ff.).
ETR	*Etudes théologiques et religieuses* (Montpellier, 1926ff.).
ExpT	*The Expository Times* (Edinburgh, 1889ff.).
FF	*France franciscaine* (Lille, 1912–29).
FLDG	Forschungen zur christliche Literatur- und Dogmengeschichte (Mainz/Paderborn, 1910–38).
Folia	*Folia. Studies in the Christian Perpetuation of the Classics* (Worcester, MA, 1959–79).
FThSt	Freiburger theologische Studien (Freiburg i. B., 1910ff.).
FZPT	*Freiburger Zeitschrift für Philosophie und Theologie* (Fribourg i. S., 1954ff.).
GCS	Die griechischen christlichen Schriftsteller der ersten (drei) Jahrhunderte (Berlin, 1897ff.).
Goodspeed	E. J. Goodspeed, *A History of Early Christian Literature*, rev. and enl. R. Grant (Chicago, 1966).
GOTR	*Greek Orthodox Theological Review* (Brookline, MA, 1954ff.).
Greg	*Gregorianum* (Rome, 1920ff.).

Hamell   P.J. Hamell, *Handbook of Patrology* (New York, 1968).
Hänggi   A. Hänggi and I. Pahl, *Prex Eucharistica: Textus e Variis
                Liturgicis Antiquioribus Selecti (Fribourg i. S., 1968).
Harp   *Harp: A Review of Syriac and Oriental Studies* (Kerala, India,
                1987–2000).
Hefele   C.J. Hefele, *Histoire des conciles d'après les documents originaux*,
   (1905)   trans. H. Leclercq, 11 vols. (Paris, 1905–52).
Hefele   C.J. Hefele, *A History of the Councils of the Church: From the
   (1871)   *Original Documents*, trans. W.R. Clark and H.N. Oxenham,
                5 vols. (Edinburgh, 1871–96).
HS   *Hispania sacra* (Madrid, 1948ff.).
HThR   *Harvard Theological Review* (New York, 1908–9; Cambridge,
                MA, 1910ff.).

Idelsohn   A.Z. Idelsohn, *Jewish Liturgy and Its Development* (New York,
                1967).
IER   *Irish Ecclesiastical Record* (Dublin, 1864–1968).
Imp   *Impacts: Revue de l'Université catholique de l'Ouest* (Angers,
                1967ff.).
Ire   *Irénikon* (Amay, 1926ff.).
Ist   *Istina* (Paris, 1954ff.).
ITQ   *Irish Theological Quarterly* (Dublin, 1906–22; Maynooth, 1951ff.).

Jasper   R.C.D. Jasper and G.J. Cuming, *Prayers of the Eucharist: Early
                and Reformed*, 3rd rev. ed. (Collegeville, 1992).
JBL   *Journal of Biblical Literature* (Boston/New Haven, 1890ff.).
JECS   *Journal of Early Christian Studies* (Baltimore, 1993ff.).
JEH   *The Journal of Ecclesiastical History* (London, 1950ff.).
Jeremias   J. Jeremias, *Die Abendmahlsworte Jesu*, 3rd. ed. (Göttingen,
   (1960)   1960).
Jeremias   J. Jeremias, *The Eucharistic Words of Jesus*, trans. N. Perrin
   (1966)   (London, 1966).
JL   *Jahrbuch für Liturgiewissenschaft* (Münster, 1921–41).
JLH   *Jahrbuch für Liturgie und Hymnologie* (Kassel, 1955ff.).
JQR   *The Jewish Quarterly Review* (London, 1889–94; New York,
                1896–1908).
JR   *The Journal of Religion* (Chicago, 1921ff.).
JThSt   *The Journal of Theological Studies* (London, 1900–1905; Oxford,
                1906–49; n.s. 1950ff.).
JucL   *Jucunda Laudatio* (Milan, 1963ff.).
Jurgens   W.A. Jurgens, *The Faith of the Early Fathers*, 3 vols. (Collegeville,
                1970–79).

Kat   *Katholik: Zeitschrift für katholische Wissenschaft und kirchliches
                Leben* (Mainz, 1821–89).

Labriolle (1947)	P.C. de Labriolle, *Histoire de la littérature latine chrétienne*, 3rd rev. ed. (Paris, 1947).
Labriolle (1968)	P.C. de Labriolle, *History and Literature of Christianity from Tertullian to Boethius*, trans. H. Wilson, History of Civilization (New York, 1968).
LAC	*L'Ami du clergé* (Langres, France, 1888–1968).
Latomus	*Latomus. Revue d'études latines* (Brussels, 1937ff.).
Lau	*Laurentianum* (Rome, 1960ff.).
Leigh-Bennett	E. Leigh-Bennett, *Handbook of the Early Christian Fathers* (London, 1920).
LJ	*Liturgisches Jahrbuch* (Münster, 1951ff.).
LMD	*La Maison-Dieu* (Paris, 1945ff.).
LMF	*Le messager des fidèles* (Mardesous, 1884–89).
LNPF	P. Schaff and H. Wace, eds., *A Select Library of Nicene and Post-Nicene Fathers of the Christian Church* (repr. Grand Rapids, 1951ff.).
LO	Lex Orandi (Paris, 1944–71).
LQF	Liturgiegeschichtliche Quellen und Forschungen (Münster i. W., 1918–39).
LThPh	*Laval théologique et philosophique* (Quebec, 1970–82).
LTK	W. Kasper and others, eds., *Lexikon für Theologie und Kirche*, 11 vols., 3rd ed. (Freiburg i. B., 1993–2001).
LV	*Lumière et vie* (Bruges, 1951–60).
LWP	*Liturgical Week Proceedings, North American*
LwQF	Liturgiewissenschaftliche Quellen und Forschungen (Münster i. W., 1919–2005).
LXX	Septuagint
Mansi	J.D. Mansi, ed., *Sacrorum Conciliorum Nova et Amplissima Collectio*, 31 vols. (Florence, 1759–98).
Mel	*Melto. Melta. Recherches orientales* (Kaslik, Liban, 1965–69).
Millgram	A.E. Millgram, *Jewish Worship* (Philadelphia, 1971).
MilS	*Milltown Studies* (Dublin, 1978ff.).
Mnem	*Mnemosyne: Bibliotheca classica Batava* (Leyden, 1852ff.).
MRR-1	J. Jungmann, *The Mass of the Roman Rite: Its Origins and Development (Missarum Sollemnia)*, trans. F.A. Brunner, 2 vols. (New York, 1951).
MRR-2	J. Jungmann, *The Mass of the Roman Rite: Its Origins and Development (Missarum Sollemnia)*, trans. F.A. Brunner, rev. C.K. Riepe (New York, 1959).
MS	*Mediaeval Studies* (Toronto, 1939ff.).
MSR	*Mélanges de science religieuse* (Lille, 1944ff.).
Mus	*Le Muséon* (Louvain, 1882–1916, 1921ff.).

NCE	*New Catholic Encyclopedia*, 14 vols. + index (New York, 1967) + 3 supplementary vols. 16–18 (1974–89).
NCES	*New Catholic Encyclopedia, Second Edition*, 15 vols. (Detroit/ Washington, D.C., 2003).
NDSW	P.E. Fink, ed., *The New Dictionary of Sacramental Worship* (Collegeville, 1990).
Not	*Notitiae* (Rome, 1965ff.).
NRTh	*Nouvelle revue théologique* (Tournai, 1869–1913, 1920–39, 1945ff.).
NTes	Novum Testamentum (Leiden, 1956ff.).
NTS	New Testament Studies (London, 1954ff.).
NWDLW	J.G. Davies, ed., *The New Westminster Dictionary of Liturgy and Worship* (Philadelphia, 1986).

OC	Oriens Christianus (Wiesbaden, 1931–39, 1953ff.).
OCA	Orientalia Christiana Analecta (Rome, 1935ff.).
OCP	*Orientalia Christiana Periodica* (Rome, 1935ff.).
ODCC	F.L. Cross, *The Oxford Dictionary of the Christian Church*, 3rd ed., ed. E.A. Livingstone (New York, 1997).
Oesterley (1911)	W.O.E. Oesterley, *The Religion and Worship of the Synagogue*, 2nd ed. (London, 1911).
Oesterley (1925)	W.O.E. Oesterley, *The Jewish Background of the Christian Liturgy* (Oxford, 1925).
OLZ	*Orientalische Literaturzeitung* (Berlin, 1909ff.).
OrSyr	*L'Orient syrien* (Paris, 1956ff.).
OstkSt	*Ostkirchliche Studien* (Würzburg, 1952ff.).

ParL	*Paroisse et liturgie* (Bruges, 1946–74).
PB	*Pastor Bonus* (Trier, 1889–1943).
PEA (1894)	A.F. von Pauly, *Paulys Real-encyclopädie der classischen Altertumswissenschaft* (Stuttgart, 1894–1919).
PEA (1991)	H. Cancik and H. Schneider, eds., *Der neue Pauly. Enzyklopädie der Antike* (Stuttgart, 1991ff.).
PG	J.P. Migne, *Patrologia Graeca*, 162 vols. (Paris, 1857–66).
PhW	*Philologische Wockenschrift* (Leipzig, 1881–1940).
PL	J.P. Migne, *Patrologia Latina*, 221 vols. (Paris, 1844–64).
PLS	J.P. Migne, *Patrologiae Cursus Completus. Series Latina Supplementum*, ed. A. Hamman (Paris, 1958ff.).
PO	*Parole de l'Orient. Melto dmadnho* (Kaslik, Lebanon, 1970ff.).
PP	*Parole et pain* (Paris, 1964–73).
PrO	*Présence orthodox* (Paris, 1967–81).
PrOChr	*Proche-orient chrétien* (Jerusalem, 1951ff.).

QL	*Questions liturgiques* (Louvain, 1970ff.).
QLP	*Questions liturgiques et paroissiales* (Louvain, 1919–69).

Quasten	J. Quasten, *Patrology*, 4 vols. (Westminster, MD, 1962ff.). (Vol. 4, 1986, is a translation of vol. 3 of *Patrologia*, ed. A. di Berardino.)

RAC	*Rivista di Archeologia Cristiana* (Rome, 1924ff.).
RACh	*Reallexikon für Antike und Christentum*, ed. T. Klauser (Leipzig, 1950ff.).
RAM	*Revue d'ascétique et de mystique* (Toulouse, 1920–71).
RAp	*Revue pratique d'apologétique* (Paris, 1905–21).
RAug	*Recherches augustiniennes* (Paris, 1958ff.).
RB	*Revue bénédictine* (Maredsous, 1890ff.).
RBibl	*Revue biblique internationale* (Paris, 1891ff.; n.s. 1904ff.).
RBPh	*Revue belge de philologie et d'histoire* (Brussels, 1922ff.).
RCF	*Revue du clergé francais* (Paris, 1894–1920).
RCT	*Revista catalana de teología* (Barcelona, 1976–88, 1990ff.).
RDC	*Revue de droit canonique* (Strasbourg, 1951ff.).
REAug	*Revue des études augustiniennes* (Paris, 1955ff.).
REF	*Revue d'histoire de l'Eglise de France* (Paris, 1910ff.).
REG	*Revue des études grecques* (Paris, 1888ff.).
REJ	*Revue des études juives* (Paris, 1880ff.).
REL	*Revue ecclésiastique de Liège* (Liège, 1905–67).
RELA	*Revue des études latines* (Paris, 1923ff.).
Res	*Résurrection* (Paris, 1956–63).
ResQ	*Restoration Quarterly* (Abilene, TX, 1957ff.).
RET	*Revista española de teología* (Madrid, 1940ff.).
RevAgusEsp	*Revista augustiniana de Espiritualidad* (Calahorra, Spain, 1960–79).
RevAug	*Revue augustinienne* (Louvain, 1901–10).
RevSR	*Revue des sciences religieuses* (Strasbourg, 1921ff.).
RHE	*Revue d'histoire ecclésiastique* (Louvain, 1900ff.).
RHL	*Revue d'histoire et de littérature religieuse* (Paris, 1896–1922).
RHPR	*Revue d'histoire et de philosophie religieuses* (Strasbourg, 1921ff.).
RIT	*Revue internationale de théologie* (Berne, 1893–1910).
RivAM	*Rivista di Ascetica et Mistica* (Florence, 1956ff.).
RL	*Rivista Liturgica* (Turin, 1914ff.).
Rocz	*Rocznik theologico-kanoninczne* (Lublin, Poland, 1949–90).
RPLH	*Revue de philologie, de littérature et d'histoire anciennes* (Paris, 1845–47; n.s. 1877–1926; 3. s. 1927ff.).
RQ	*Römische Quartelschrift für christliche Altertumskunde* (Freiburg i. B., 1887ff.).
RQH	*Revue des questions historiques* (Paris, 1866–1939).
RR	*Revue réformé* (Saint-Germaine-en-Laye, France, 1950ff.).
RRel	*Review for Religious* (St. Louis, 1942ff.).

RSPT   *Revue des sciences philosophiques et théologiques* (Paris, 1907ff.).
RSR   *Recherches de science religieuse* (Paris, 1910ff.).
RT   *Revue thomiste* (Paris, 1924–65).
RTAM   *Recherches de théologie ancienne et médiévale* (Louvain, 1969ff.).
RTL   *Revue théologique de Louvain* (Louvain, 1970ff.).
RTP   *Revue de théologie et de philosophie* (Lausanne, 1921ff.).
RUO   *La revue de l'Université d'Ottawa* (Ottawa, 1931–87).

Sal   *Salesianum* (Turin, 1939ff.).
SC   *Scuola Cattolica* (Milan, 1902ff.).
SCA   Studies in Christian Antiquity (Washington, D.C., 1941–85).
ScE   *Science et esprit* (Montreal, 1928ff.).
SChr   Sources chrétiennes (Paris, 1941ff.).
SCJ   *Second Century: Journal of Early Christian Studies* (Abilene, TX, 1981–92).
Scr   *Scripture* (London, 1969–75).
SE   *Sacris Eruditi* (Bruges, 1948ff.).
SJT   *Scottish Journal of Theology* (Edinburgh, etc., 1948ff.).
SM   *Studia Monastica* (Barcelona, 1959ff.).
SP   *Studia Patristica: Acts of the International Conventions of Oxford* (TU) (Berlin, 1957ff.).
SPMed   Studia Patristica Mediolanensia (Milan, 1974ff.).
ST   *Studi e Testi* (Rome, 1900ff.).
StC   *Studia Catholica* (Nijmegen, 1924–60).
Steidle   B. Steidle, *Patrologia: seu Historia Antiquae Litteraturae Ecclesiasticae, Scholarum Usui Accommodata* (Freiburg i. B., 1937).
StGKA   Studien zur Geschichte und Kultur des Altertums (Paderborn, 1907ff.).
STh   *Studia Theologica* (Lund, 1947ff.).
StLit   C. Jones and others, eds., *The Study of Liturgy*, rev. ed. (New York, 1992).
StP   *Studia Patavina* (Padua, 1954ff.).
Strack   H.L. Strack and P. Billerbeck, *Kommentar zum Neuen Testament aus Talmud und Midrasch,* vol. iv/i, 2nd ed. (Munich, 1956).
StudEnc   *Study Encounter* (Geneva, 1965–76).
StudLit   *Studia Liturgica* (Rotterdam, 1962ff.).

TD   *Theology Digest* (St. Louis, 1953ff.).
Theol   *Theology* (Norwich, England, 1976ff.).
ThGl   *Theologie und Glaube* (Paderborn, 1909ff.).
ThQ   *Theologische Quartalschrift* (Stuttgart/Tübingen, 1831–1928; various places, 1929ff.).
ThStKr   *Theologische Studien und Kritiken* (Gotha, 1828–42).
Tixeront J. Tixeront, *A Handbook of Patrology*, trans. S.A. Raemers (London/St. Louis, 1947).

Tra	*Traditio: Studies in Ancient and Medieval History, Thought, and Religion* (New York, 1943ff.).
TRE	G. Krause and G. Müller, eds., *Theologische Realenzyklopädie* (Berlin, 1976ff.).
TS	*Theological Studies* (Baltimore/Woodstock, 1940ff.).
TU	Texte und Untersuchungen zur Geschichte de altchristlichen Literatur (Berlin, 1882ff.).
TV	*Theologia Viatorum: Jahrbuch der kirchlichen Hochschule Berlin* (Berlin, 1948/49–1979/80).
TZ	*Theologische Zeitschrift* (Basel, 1945ff.).
VC	*Vigiliae Christianae* (Amsterdam, 1947ff.).
VerC	*Verbum Caro* (Taizé, France, 1947–69).
VetChr	*Vetera Christianorum* (Bari, 1964ff.).
VS	*La Vie Spirituelle* (Paris, 1919ff.).
WEC	L. Johnson, ed., *Worship in the Early Church: An Anthology of Historical Sources*, 4 vols. (Collegeville, 2009).
Werner	E. Werner, *The Sacred Bridge: The Interdependence of Liturgy and Music in Synagogue and Church during the First Millennium* (London/New York, 1959).
Wor	*Worship* (Collegeville, 1952ff.; formerly *Orate Fratres*, 1926–51).
Wright (1928)	F.A. Wright, ed., *Fathers of the Church: Tertullian, Cyprian, Arnobius, Lactanius, Ambrose, Jerome, Augustine: A Selection from the Writings of the Latin Fathers* (London, 1928).
Wright (1932)	F.A. Wright, *A History of Later Greek Literature from the Death of Alexander in 323 B.C. to the Death of Justinian in 545 A.D.* (London, 1932).
WSt	*Wiener Studien: Zeitschrift für klassische Philologie* (Vienna, 1879ff.).
ZAW	*Zeitschrift für die alttestamentliche Wissenschaft* (Berlin/New York, 1881ff.).
ZKG	*Zeitschrift für Kirchengeschichte* (Gotha, 1877–1930; Stuttgart, 1931ff.).
ZkTh	*Zeitschrift für katholische Theologie* (Innsbruck, 1877–1940; Vienna, 1947ff.).
ZNeW	*Zeitschrift für die neutestamentliche Wissenschaft und die Kunde der älteren Kirche* (Giessen/Berlin/New York, 1900ff.).
ZNW	*Zeitschrift für Missionswissenschaft* (Münster, 1911–37).
ZTK	*Zeitschrift für Theologie und Kirche* (Tübingen, 1891ff.).
/	= "or," e.g., 543/554
[ ]	Textual material supplied by translator of the original source or by the present editor/translator

Introduction

Recent decades have witnessed numerous Christian denominations reforming and renewing their communal worship structures. Well before such a venture occurred, there took place, mainly though not exclusively in Europe, a scientific study of the early development of the Church's common prayer, a study that continues today. Both professional and amateur historians have applied and are applying their expertise to this important task, for understanding the past is not merely an intellectual exercise but offers one of the all-important keys for understanding the present.

Yet many students of worship have but little direct contact with the great literary heritage that witnesses the way Christians lived their liturgical life during the early ages of Christianity. Often a person's acquaintance with the primitive Church's written documentation is only by way of citations in end- or footnotes. Frequently access to the excellent English language collections of early source material is limited, since these are for the most part found only in the libraries of theological schools and major universities. The same is true of texts related to particular subjects, e.g., initiation. Furthermore, a large amount of pertinent material has simply not appeared in English. Texts in Latin, Greek, and other languages— apart from their inherent problems for many students of the liturgy—are no less difficult to obtain.

The four volumes of the present series aim to present a selection or thesaurus (representative, to be sure) of a wide selection of source material illustrating the growth of the Church's common prayer, in both East and West, from its Jewish roots down to the end of the sixth century. Included are texts from homilies, dogmatic and spiritual treatises, letters, monastic rules, church orders, prayer formulas, conciliar and synodal legislation, inscriptions, and the like. The subject matter is not only sacramental celebration but also the liturgical year, the times of the day for personal or group prayer, music and song, the physical arrangement of the church building, times for fasting (considered to be so closely allied with prayer), veneration of the martyrs, liturgical roles, decorum within and without the church, etc.

The user of these volumes fortunate enough to have access to a major theological library may well profit from the references to patristic and other manuals, as well as from the bibliography of pertinent periodical articles and treatises.

In a few cases the most recent edition of a text was, for various reasons, unavailable to me. Also, several texts initially intended to appear in this work are, in fact, not included since a particular volume could not be obtained.

It should be noted that, unless otherwise indicated, the enumeration of the psalms follows the Hebrew.

All cited texts have been translated by the present editor from the source indicated ("Translated from . . .") or are taken from a preexisting translation ("Translation from . . .").

A note on format

Each subhead (author, anonymous document, synods, etc.) is assigned an identification number, which is usually followed by a letter indicating a particular work of an author or a particular synod.

The internal enumeration of paragraphs usually corresponds to that of the edition from which the text was translated. Marginal numbers, running sequentially, are assigned to paragraphs of the text.

Cross-references are indicated by the abbreviation for *Worship in the Early Church*, i.e., WEC, followed by the volume number and then either the subhead number in bold text (e.g., WEC 1:**17** or WEC 1:**27-B**) or else the marginal paragraph number (e.g., WEC 1:244).

There are three types of footnotes: daggers, letters, and numbers. Daggered notes indicate the sources from which translations have been made, lettered notes contain explanations for words and phrases used in the text, and numbered notes indicate scriptural references.

* * *

No work of this kind can reach completion without the encouragement and assistance of many people. And thus I must express my gratitude to Mr. Peter Kearney for sharing his expertise in Latin and Hebrew. To the Rev. James Challancin, a priest of the diocese of Marquette, Michigan, and a former professor of liturgy, for his many words of encouragement. To the staff (especially Jessica) of the Escanaba, Michigan, Public Library for such gracious assistance in procuring by means of interlibrary loans ever so many volumes from libraries throughout the country. To the whole publishing team at Liturgical Press and especially to Stephanie Lancour, my copy editor, whose careful reading of the text has saved me from any number of embarrassing moments. And especially to my wife, Marlene Winter-Johnson, not only for her patience throughout this endeavor but especially for the numerous hours in researching materials found in the library of The Catholic University of America and in that of the University of Notre Dame, as well as for helping to prepare the work's manuscript for publication.

Chapter I

Jewish Texts. Home and Synagogue

1. *QADDISH*[†]

The *qaddish* (kaddish), a term deriving from the Aramaic word *qadosh*, meaning "holy," is a prayer of sanctification whereby God's holiness is proclaimed, his power is praised, and his consolation and peace are requested. The history of the text is complex. According to some commentators the most important and original section of the prayer is the response, "Let his great . . ." The formula has variations according to its use, whether prayed by a group studying the Talmud (called "the scholar's *qaddish*"); whether concluding a structural element, e.g., the *tefillah* in the synagogue liturgy (the first mention of its synagogue use dates from about the sixth century); or whether used in the cemetery for the burial of a loved one (the mourner's *qaddish*), the latter practice dating from thirteenth-century Germany. It has been suggested that the first two petitions of the Lord's Prayer may have been inspired by the *qaddish*.

Deiss 17–19 * Idelsohn 84–88 * Di Sante 19–23, 171–73 * Millgram 153–57 * Oesterley (1925) 72–73, 151–52

J.J. Petuchowski and M. Brocke, eds., *The Lord's Prayer and Jewish Liturgy* (London and New York, 1978).

    May his great Name be magnified and sanctified in the world which   1
he created according to his will; may his kingdom rule and redemption
take seed; may he lead his Messiah into your paths during your days and
through the life of the whole house of Israel, doing so quickly and soon,
and let them say Amen.

    Response: Let his great Name be blessed forever and for all eternity.   2

    May it be blessed, praised, made known, exalted, elevated, and honored; and may the blessed Name of the Holy One be above all blessings   3
and hymns, praises and consolation that are given in the world. Amen.

    May your prayer be accepted and your petitions be efficacious, joined to   4
the prayer of the whole house of Israel, before our Father in heaven.

[†] Translated (with adaptations) from E. Lodi, *Enchiridion Euchologicum Fontium Liturgicorum* (Rome, 1979) 19.

5   May it bring for us heaven, great peace, help, redemption, abundance, life, fullness, health, consolation, freedom, healing, propagation, for you, for us, and for the whole house of Israel, unto life and peace, and let them say Amen.[a]

2. QIDDUSH FOR SABBATHS AND FEASTS[†]

Each week on Friday, once the table has been covered with a handsome cloth, the mother of the family places two loaves upon it, and then the wine, a cup, and two candles that she lights at the appropriate time. Afterwards, the father of the family, having returned from the evening synagogue service, says the blessing, the *Qiddush* (*kiddush*), namely, the domestic rite by which the Sabbath and feast days are consecrated to God.

This ceremony, with roots perhaps going back to the fifth century B.C., contains three blessings or *berakoth*: the first over the wine, the second praising God for the Sabbath, and a third over the bread.

Deiss 5–6 * Di Sante 154–57 * Elbogen (1962) 107, 110–12 * Jeremias (1960) 20–23 * Jeremias (1966) 26–29 * Millgram 297–99 * Oesterley (1911) 374–83 * Oesterley (1925) 79–81

I. Elbogen, "Eingang und Ausgang des Sabbats nach talmudischen Quellen," in *Festschrift zu Israel Lewy's siebzigstem Geburtstag* (Breslau, 1911) 173–87.

1. Blessing over the wine

6   *First, the head of the family, taking the cup of wine in his right hand, reads Genesis 1:31b–2:3; he does so standing and with eyes upraised.*

(*In a low voice*) And evening and morning were made (*then in a loud voice*) on the sixth day. Thus heaven and earth and all their ornaments were completed. And on the seventh day God completed the work he had done; and God rested on the seventh day from all the work he had accomplished. And he blessed it on the seventh day and sanctified it because on this day he ceased from all his work, a day God created for this purpose.

7   *Having asked permission from the honored guests and looking toward the cup, he says the blessing over it; our lords, teachers, and doctors approve.*

O Lord our God, blessed are you, King of the universe; you created the fruit of the vine.

8   *And he adds this blessing for sanctifying the Sabbath day or the feastday:*

Blessed are you, O Lord our God, King of the universe. By your commandments you sanctified us, took great delight in us, and give us the holy Sabbath as an inheritance, doing so out of love and kindness to be a memorial of the works of your creation. Wherefore this is a day of holy

---

a. Omitted in the *qaddish* for mourners.

† Translated from Hänggi 5–7.

convocations,[1] a memorial of the exodus out of Egypt. You chose and
sanctified us above all peoples, and in love and goodness you gave us the
holy Sabbath as an inheritance. Blessed are you, O Lord, for making holy
the Sabbath.

All present then receive some wine from the cup to drink, doing so after the   9
father of the family.

2. Blessing over the bread

The father of the family begins, his hand being placed on what covers the   10
bread. When he comes to the words "bring forth," he uncovers the loaves of bread
[lèhèmisnèh]; then, when he comes to the word "bread," he holds the loaves up
and then places them on the table.

Blessed are you, O Lord our God, King of the universe. You bring forth
bread from the earth.

Having finished the blessing, he breaks one of the loaves and takes some for   11
himself and distributes a portion to the others, enough for the whole meal, which
is then eaten.

3. Zemirot

They eat the meal, prolonging it as they rejoice and sing the zemirot.[a]   12

3. BIRKAT HA-MAZON[†]

For the pious Jew the daily meal shared with family members was the
focal point of the individual's prayer to and praise of God. Thus it is no
surprise that the prayer formulas connected with this meal are among the
most venerable of the Jewish heritage of worship texts.

The meal begins with a very short blessing known as the *birkat ha-motsi,*
whose text, taken from Psalm 104:14, thanks God for bringing forth bread
from the earth.

It is at the conclusion of the meal that the most cherished blessing,
known as the *birkat ha-mazon* (*mazon* = "food"), occurs. After an initial dialogue (called the *birkat ha-zimmun*) three (now four) prayers of blessing
are said: the first (the *birkat ha-zan*) blesses the Creator who provides food
for all creation; the second (the *birkat ha-ʾarets*) gives thanks for the land,
the covenant, and the Law; the third (the *birkat Ierušalayim*) intercedes on
behalf of Jerusalem and the house of David; the fourth blessing (the *birkat
ha-tov we-ha-metiv*) brings the prayer to an end.

As to the dates of these formulas, many believe that the first and second
are the oldest, the third perhaps going back to the second century before

---

a. *Zemirot*: hymns and songs not coming from the psalter but found in the ritual
books for Friday and Saturday.

1. See Lev 23:3.

† The proposed primitive text of the *Birkat ha-mazon* is translated from Finkelstein's article listed below. All else is translated from Hänggi 8–12.

Christ, with the fourth being added after the destruction of the temple in the second century after Christ.

Included below are the formulas proposed by A.L. Finkelstein[a] as original, as well as more developed, forms of these texts coming from the ninth and tenth centuries. It should be noted that the prayers allow for embolisms or insertions on certain feasts.

Bouyer 78–83 * Deiss 6–9 * Di Sante 145–50 * Hänggi 8–12 * Jasper 10–11 * Millgram 293–95

L. Finkelstein, "The Birkat Ha-Mazon," JQR 19 (1928–29) 211–62. * G. Dix, *The Shape of the Liturgy*, 4th ed. (Westminster, 1949) 50–56, 214–25. * B. Fraigneau-Julien, "Elements de la structure fundamentaler de l'eucharistie. I. Bénédiction, anamnèse et action de grâces," RevSR 34 (1960) 35–61. * J. Heinemann, *Prayer in the Period of the Tanna'im and the Amora'im: Its Nature and Its Patterns* (Jerusalem, 1964) 31, 37–39, 49, 73, 102, 138, 180. * L. Ligier, "De la cène de Jésus à l'anaphore de l'Eglise," LMD, no. 87 (1966) 30–33, 50–51; also in RL (1966) 503–6, 521–22.

13   *When the meal is finished, Psalm 137, "By the rivers of Babylon," is said on ordinary days, and on the Sabbath and feasts there is Psalm 126, "When the Lord delivered Sion from captivity." Then one of those reclining at table (A.), designated because of that person's dignity, begins the "birkat ha-zimmun," the blessing of invitation, namely, the invitation to bless God, to which the others (R.), reclining, respond.*

14   1. *Birkat ha-zimmun*
A. My lords, let us bless.
R. May the Name of the Lord be blessed now and forever.
A. With the approval of our lords, teachers, and doctors, let us bless what we eat of his (*If there are ten who are reclining, he says*: ". . . let us bless our God that . . ." *and he adds other names, if there are a hundred or a thousand, etc.*).
R. May he be blessed (*if fitting*: our God) that we may eat of his gifts and live from his goodness.
A. May he be blessed (*if fitting*: our God) that we may eat of his gifts and live from his goodness.
R. May he be blessed, and may his name be blessed.

15   2. *Birkat ha-mazon*
With two hands he holds the cup of wine and, when he begins the blessing, he takes it with his right hand, raising it a little. When he says the second part, he mixes the cup with water.

---

a. See "The Birkat Ha-Mazon," *Jewish Quarterly Review* 19 (1929) 243–59.

a) Text proposed by A.L. Finkelstein as original.

1. *Birkat ha-zan* (*Blessing of the one who nourishes*)   16
   Blessed are you, O Lord our God, King of the universe. You feed the whole world with goodness, kindness, and mercy. Blessed are you, O Lord, for you feed the universe.

2. *Birkat ha-ʾarets* (*Blessing of the earth*)   17
   O Lord our God, we give thanks to you because you have given to us a desirable earth [that we might eat of its fruits and be filled with its goodness]. Blessed are you, O lord our God, because of the earth and because of food.

3. *Birkat Ierušalayim* (*Blessing for Jerusalem*)   18
   O Lord our God, have mercy on your people Israel and upon your city Jerusalem and upon Sion the dwelling place of your glory and of your altar and your sanctuary.
   Blessed are you, Lord, the builder of Jerusalem.[b]

b) Liturgical Recensions

According to the Seder Amram (*9th century*)	*According to the Seder Rav Saadja* (*10th century*)	
1. Blessed are you, O Lord our God, King of the universe, for you nourish the whole world with your goodness, kindness, and mercy; you give bread to all flesh, because you nourish and feed all things and provide food for all creatures. Blessed are you, O Lord, for you nourish the universe.	1. Blessed are you, O Lord, our God, King of the universe, for you nourish us and the whole world with goodness, grace, kindness, and mercy. Blessed are you, O Lord, for you nourish the universe.	19
2. We give thanks to you, Lord, our God, because of the land—desirable, good, and widespread—which you loved and gave to our fathers as an inheritance and because of your covenant which you have placed in our flesh, and because of the Law which you have given us, and because of the life, kindness, grace, and food, which you provide for us.	2. We give thanks to you, O Lord our God, because you have given us as an inheritance the land—desirable, good, and widespread—together with the covenant and the Law, life and food.	20

---

b. Finkelstein conjectures that the primitive text had only three blessings.

Here occurs the embolism used on Hannukah and Purim.	*Here occurs the embolism used on Hannukah and Purim.*
And, O Lord our God, for all these things we thank you and bless your Name. May your Name be blessed continually forever and ever. Blessed are you, O Lord, because of the earth and because of the food.	For all these things we thank you and bless your Name forever and ever. Blessed are you, O Lord, because of the earth and because of food.
3. O Lord our God, have mercy on Israel your people, on your city Jerusalem, and on Sion, the dwelling place of your glory and of the kingdom of the house of David your Anointed One, and on the great and holy abode called by your Name. [our Father, our King] our shepherd, our nourisher, our feeder, our sustenance, quickly free us from our difficulties. Nor do you [Lord, our God] allow us to be without the gifts of flesh and blood, of which duties are few and insults are many: because we trust in the great and fearful name of your holiness. And may Elias and the Messiah, the son of David, come in our lifetime and quickly restore the kingdom of the house of David [our Anointed One] to its place and may he rule over us [because] you alone [are] and save us for your Name's sake. And have us ascend into its middle, and gladden us in it, and console us in Sion, your city.	3. O Lord, our God, have mercy on Israel your people, on your city Jerusalem, on your sanctuary, on your dwelling place, on Sion the dwelling place of your glory, and on the great and holy abode where you can be called by your Name. Restore the kingdom of David to its place and build up Jerusalem quickly.
Here occurs the embolism "Yaʾalèh we-yavo.	*Here occurs the embolism "Yaʾalèh we-yavo.*
Blessed are you, O Lord, who builds Jerusalem. Amen.	Blessed are you, O Lord, who builds Jerusalem. Amen.

21

4. Blessed are you, O Lord our God, King of the universe, our Father, our King, our Redeemer, our protector, our Creator; the ruler of our souls, our holy one, the holy one of Jacob, the good and kind king, who does good to us day after day; he enriches us and will forever enrich us with grace, kindness, mercy, and with all that is good.	4. Blessed are you, Lord, our God, King of the universe, God, our Father, our King, our Creator, our Redeemer, the good and kind King, who day after day takes care to do good for us in many different ways and who enriches us with grace, kindness, spirit, mercy, and with all that is good.	22

4. PASSOVER HAGGADAH[†]

The Hebrew word *Haggadah* literally means a "telling," a "narrating," a "recital." In one sense it refers to the "telling" of the events connected with the passage of the Jewish people out of Egypt. In another sense the word is applied to the book or instruction manual detailing the steps to be followed during the meal—called the *Seder* (Aramaic for "order") Meal—which commemorated or celebrated this deliverance.

The texts used come from various time periods and represent various literary genres, e.g., selections from the Hebrew Scriptures, explanations from Jewish literature, prayers, blessings, etc. Some elements are of a late origin, composed after the destruction of the Jerusalem Temple in 70 A.D. by the Romans. Other elements belong to an earlier tradition, one originating before the time of Christ. It was in the ninth century that the Haggadah began to appear in Jewish prayer books, whereas the first separately printed Haggadah date from Spain (ca. 1482) and Italy (1505). Well over four thousand such books, often beautifully decorated, have come down to us.

Historically, the Passover Haggadah exists in various versions or traditions, often reflecting the country of use, e.g., Spain, Germany, Italy, etc. Although the basic framework remains the same, precise details of the prayer texts and the ritual gestures vary depending on particular religious and ethnic traditions. Today, rabbis encourage adapting the service to contemporary situations, and as a result there are feminist Haggadahs, military Haggadahs, children's Haggadahs, even atheist Haggadahs.

Oesterley (1925) 157–93 * Millgram 301–13 * Hänggi 13–34

H.L. Strack, Pesahim, *Der Mischnatrakat Passafest mit Berücksichtigung des Neuen Testaments und der Jetzigen Passafeier der Juden* (Leipzig, 1911). * H.L. Strack and P. Billerbeck, *Kommentar zum Neuen Testament aus Talmud und Midrasch* IV/1 (Munich,

---

[†] Translation (with modifications) from *The Passover Haggadah. With English Translation, Introduction, and Commentary based on the commentaries of E.D. Gold-schmidt*, ed. Nahum N. Glatzer, revised edition (New York, 1953, 1969). Headings in < > are supplied by the present editor.

1956) 41–76. * L. Finkelstein, "The Oldest Midrash: Pre-Rabbinic Ideals and Teachings in the Passover Haggadah," HThR 31 (1938) 291–317. * L. Finkelstein, "Pre-Maccabean Documents in the Passover Haggadah," HThR 33 (1942) 291–332; 30 (1943) 1–38. * S. Stein, "The Influence of Symposia Literature on the Literary Form of the Pesah Haggadah," *The Journal of Jewish Studies* 8 (1937) 13–44. * E.D. Goldschmidt, *Die Pessach Haggada* (Berlin, 1937). * T.H. Gastner, *Passover: Its History and Traditions* (New York, 1949). * E.D. Goldschmidt, *The Passover Haggadah: Its Sources and History* (Jerusalem, 1960; Philadelphia, 1961). * A. Yaari, *Bibliography of the Passover Haggadah from the Earliest Printed Edition to 1960* (Jerusalem, 1960). * J. Jeremias, *Die Abendmahlsworte Jesu* (Göttingen, 1960) 35–83, 229–46. * H. Kosmala, *Hebräer – Essener – Christen. Studien zur Voggeschichte der frühchristlichen Verkündigung* (Leiden, 1959) 174–91, 393–97. * K. Kosmala, "'Das tut in meinem Gedächtnis,'" NTes 4 (1960) 81–94. * L. Ligier, "L'hymne christologique de Philippiens 2:6–11, la liturgie eucharistique et la bénédiction synagogale 'Nishmat kol hays,'" *Analecta Biblica* 18 (1963) 63–74. * L. Ligier, "L'action de grâces de la communion et la 'Birkat Ha-Shir' de la Pâques," PrOChr 13 (1963) 99–111. * J.B. Segal, *The Hebrew Passover: From the Earliest Times to A.D. 70*, London Oriental Series 12 (London, 1963). * L. Ligier, "De la cène de Jesus à l'anaphore de l'Eglise," LMD, no. 87 (1966) 7–49; RL, n.s., 4 (1966) 480–522. * E. Le Déaut, *La nuit pascale: essai sur la signification de la Páque juive à partir du Targum d'Exode XII:42* (Rome, 1963). * J.B. Segal, *The Hebrew Passover* (London and New York, 1963). * J. Sloan, trans., *The Passover Haggadah, with English translation; Introduction and Commentary, Based on the Commentaries of E.D. Goldschmidt*, ed. N.N. Glatzer (New York, 1979). * L.A. Hoffman and D. Arnow, eds., *My People's Passover Haggadah*, 2 vols. (Woodstock, VT, 2008).

THE QIDDUSH

23 *The first cup of wine is prepared, and the father of the family recites the Sanctification (qiddush).*[a]

24 Blessed are you, O Lord our God, creator of the fruit of the vine.

25 Blessed are you, O Lord our God, king of the universe, who chose us from every people and exalted us among every tongue and sanctified us by his commandments. With love you have given us, O Lord our God, holidays for gladness, festivals and seasons for rejoicing, this day of the festival of unleavened bread, the season of our deliverance, a holy convocation in remembrance of the departure from Egypt. For us have you chosen, and us have you sanctified from all the people. And the holidays of your sanctification you have given us, with gladness and joy to inherit. Blessed are you, O Lord, who sanctifies Israel and the seasons.

26 Blessed are you, O Lord our God, king of the universe, who has kept us alive, who sustained us, and who enabled us to reach this season.

27 *The first cup of wine is drunk in a reclining position.*

28 *Pitcher, basin, and towel are offered to the participants in the Seder to wash their hands, though without saying the usual blessing over the washing of hands.*

---

a. *Qiddush*: namely, "blessing."

The father of the family dips some celery or other vegetable in salt water (or vin- 29
egar) and then offers a piece of the vegetable to each participant. The following
blessing is spoken before eating the karpas.

Blessed are you, O Lord our God, king of the universe, who creates the   30
fruit of the earth.

The father of the family breaks in two the middle of the three wafers of unleavened 31
bread on the platter, wraps up the larger half in a cloth, and sets it aside for the
afikoman.
The father of the family removes the shankbone (zeroa) and the egg from the plat- 32
ter; those sitting near him lift up the platter and all recite:

<THE BREAD OF POVERTY>

This is the bread of poverty which our forefathers ate in the land of   33
Egypt. Let all who are hungry enter and eat; let all who are needy come to
our Passover feast. This year we are here; next year may we be in the Land
of Israel. This year we are slaves; next year may we be free men.
The platter is put back on the table, and the second cup of wine is poured. The 34
youngest child or another participant asks the four questions.

THE FOUR QUESTIONS

Why does this night differ from all other nights? For on all other nights   35
we eat either leavened or unleavened bread; why on this night only unleavened bread?

On other nights we eat all kinds of herbs; why on this night only bitter   36
herbs?

On all other nights we need not dip our herbs even once; why on this   37
night must we dip them twice?[b]

On all other nights we eat either sitting up or reclining; why on this   38
night do we all recline?

<INTRODUCTION TO THE STORY OF THE EXODUS>

The head of the family and all the participants recite the reply.   39
We were Pharaoh's slaves in Egypt, and the Lord our God brought   40
us forth from there with a mighty hand and an outstretched arm. And if
the Holy One, blessed be he, had not brought our forefathers forth from
Egypt, then we, our children, and our children's children would still be
Pharaoh's slaves in Egypt. So, even though all of us were wise, all of us
full of understanding, all of us elders, all of us knowing in the Torah, we
should still be under the commandment to tell the story of the departure
from Egypt. And the more one tells the story of the departure from Egypt,
the more praiseworthy he is.

---

b. The reference to the "double dipping" is obscure.

<DISCUSSION BETWEEN SCHOLARS
ON THE IMPORTANCE OF THE PASSOVER>

41   A tale is told of Rabbi Eliezer, Rabbi Joshua, Rabbi Eleazar ben Azariah, Rabbi Akiba, and Rabbi Tarfon, who once reclined together at Bene
Berak telling about the departure from Egypt all night, until their disciples
came to them and said, "Masters, the time has come to read the morning
shema."c

42   Rabbi Eleazar ben Azariah said: "Lo, I am like a man of seventy years,
yet I never understood why the story concerning the departure from
Egypt should be recited at night until Ben Zoma interpreted it so. So it is
said, 'That you may remember the day when you came forth out of the
land of Egypt all the days of your life.'1 Had it been written 'the days of
your life,' it would have meant the days only; but 'all the days of your life'
means the nights as well." The other sages explain the verse differently:
"Had it been written 'all the days of your life,' it would have meant this
world only; 'all the days of your life' means that the times of the Messiah
are included as well."

THE FOUR SONS

43   Blessed be the Omnipresent, blessed be he, who gave the Torah to his
people Israel.

44   The Torah has four children in mind: one, intelligent; a second, wicked;
a third, simple; and a fourth, a child that does not yet know how to ask.

45   What does the intelligent child say, "What mean the testimonies, and
the statutes, and the ordinances which the Lord our God has commanded
you?"2 And you instruct him in the precepts of the Passover, to wit,
"One may not conclude after the Pascha meal (by saying), 'Now to the
entertainment!'"

46   What does the wicked child say, "What is this service to you?"3 "To
you," and not to him. Since he removes himself from the group, and so
denies God, you in return must set his teeth on edge and answer him:
"It is because of that which the Lord did for me when I came forth from
Egypt."4 "For me," not for him. Had he been there, he would not have
been redeemed.

47   What does the simple child say? "What is this?" And you shall say to
him, "By strength of hand the Lord brought us out from Egypt, from the
house of bondage."5

48   And with him who does not know how to ask you must open and begin
yourself. "And you shall tell your son in that day, saying, It is because of
that which the Lord did for me when I came forth out of Egypt."6

---

c. *Shema*: see WEC 1:5.
   1. Deut 16:3.   2. Deut 6:20.   3. Exod 12:26.   4. Exod 13:8.   5. Exod 13:14.
6. Exod 13:8.

<TELLING THE STORY ON THE EVE OF THE PASSOVER>

"And you shall tell your son . . .": It might have been thought that the 49
telling should begin on the first day of the month [of Nisan]: therefore
the text teaches us "in that day." But since it says, "in that day," we might
have thought that we should begin while it is still day; therefore the Scripture also teaches us "because of that." You could not say "because of *that*"
if it were not referring to the time when unleavened bread and bitter herbs
were lying before you.

<ANOTHER INTRODUCTION TO THE PASSOVER STORY>

In the beginning our fathers were idolaters, but now the Omnipresent has 50
drawn us to his service, as it is said, "And Joshua said to all the people: 'Thus
says the Lord, the God of Israel: Your fathers dwelt of old time beyond the
River, even Terah, the father of Abraham and the father of Nahor; and they
served other gods. And I took your father Abraham from beyond the River,
and led him throughout all the land of Canaan, and multiplied his seed,
and gave him Isaac. And I gave to Isaac, Jacob, and Esau; and I gave to Esau
Mount Seir, to possess it; and Jacob and his children went down into Egypt.'"[7]

Blessed is he who keeps his promise to Israel, blessed is he. For the 51
Holy One, blessed be he, premeditated the end of the bondage, thus
doing that which he said to Abraham in the covenant between the sections: "And he said to Abram, 'Know for certain that your seed shall be a
stranger in a land that is not theirs, and shall serve them; and they shall afflict them four hundred years; and also the nation, whom they shall serve,
will I judge; and afterward shall they come out with great substance.'"[8]

The participants lift up their cups of wine and say: 52

And it is this promise which has stood by our fathers and by us. For 53
it was not one man only who stood up against us to destroy us; in every
generation they stand up against us to destroy us, and the Holy One,
blessed be he, saves us from their hand.

The cups are put back on the table. 54

<THE PASSOVER STORY>

Go forth and learn what Laban, the Aramean, sought to do to Jacob, our 55
father. While Pharaoh decreed death only for the male children, Laban
sought to uproot all.

For it is said, "An Aramean would have destroyed my father, and he 56
went down into Egypt and sojourned there, few in number; and he became there a nation, great, mighty, and populous."[9]

"And he went down into Egypt," compelled by the word of God. "And 57
sojourned there,"[10] teaching us that Jacob did not go down to Egypt to

---

7. Josh 24:2–4.   8. Gen 15:13–14.   9. Deut 26:5.   10. Gen 15:13–14.

settle but to sojourn there. As it is said, "And they said to Pharaoh, 'To
sojourn in the land are we come; for there is no pasture for your servants'
flocks; for the famine is sore in the land of Canaan. Now therefore, we
pray to you, let your servants dwell in the land of Goshen.'"[11] "Few in
number," as it is said, "Your fathers went down into Egypt with threescore
and ten persons; and now the Lord your God has made you as the stars
of heaven for multitudes."[12] "And he became there a nation," teaching us
that the Israelites were distinguishable there. "Great and powerful": as it
is said, "And the children of Israel were fruitful and increased abundantly,
and multiplied, and grew exceedingly strong; and the land was filled with
them."[13] "And populous": as it is said, "I caused you to increase even
as the growth of the field. And you did increase and grow up, and you
came to excellent beauty; your breasts were fashioned, and your hair was
grown; yet you were naked and bare."[14]

58   "And the Egyptians considered us evil; they afflicted us and laid upon
us hard bondage."[15]

59   "And the Egyptians considered us evil": as it is said, "Come let us
deal wisely with them lest they multiply, and it come to pass that, when
there befalls us any war, they also join themselves to our enemies, and
fight against us, and get them up out of the land."[16] "And afflicted us":
as it is said, "Therefore they did set over them taskmasters to afflict them
with their burdens. And they build for Pharoah store-cities, Pithom and
Raamses."[17] "And laid upon us heavy bondage": as it is said, "And the
Egyptians made the children of Israel to serve with rigor."[18]

60   "And we cried unto the Lord, the God of our fathers, and the Lord
heard our voice and saw our affliction, and our toil, and our oppression."[19]

61   "And we cried to the Lord, the God of our fathers": as it is written,
"And it came to pass in the course of those many days that the king of
Egypt died; and the children of Israel sighed by reason of the bondage,
and they cried, and their cry came up to God by reason of the bondage."[20]

62   "And the Lord heard our voice": as it is said, "And God heard their
groaning, and God remembered his covenant with Abraham, with Isaac
and with Jacob."[21] "And saw our affliction." This is enforced marital continence. As it is said, "And God saw the children of Israel, and God knew."[22]
"And our travail." This is the sons, as it is said, "Every son that is born
you shall cast into the river, and every daughter you shall save alive."[23]
"And our oppression." This is the vexation of which it is said, "Moreover I
have seen the oppression wherewith the Egyptians oppress them."[24]

63   "And the Lord brought us forth out of Egypt with a mighty hand, and
with an outstretched arm, and with great terribleness, and with signs and
with wonders."[25]

---

11. Gen 47:4.   12. Deut 10:22.   13. Exod 1:7.   14. Ezek 16:7.   15. Deut 26:6.
16. Exod 1:10.   17. Exod 1:11.   18. Exod 1:12–13.   19. Deut 26:7.   20. Exod 2:23.
21. Exod 2:24.   22. Exod 2:25.   23. Exod 1:22.   24. Exod 3:9.   25. Deut 26:8.

"And the Lord brought us forth out of Egypt," not by the hands of an   64
angel, and not by the hands of a seraph, and not by the hands of a messenger, but the Holy One, blessed be he, himself, in his own glory and in his
own person. As it is said: "For I will go through the land of Egypt in that
night and will smite all the firstborn in the land of Egypt, both man and
beast; and against all the gods of Egypt I will execute judgments: I am the
Lord."[26]

"For I will go through the land of Egypt in that night." I and not an   65
angel. "I will smite all the firstborn in the land of Egypt." I and not a seraph. "And against all the gods of Egypt I will execute judgments." I and
not a messenger. "I am the Lord." I am he and no other.

"With a mighty hand." This is the blight, as it is said, "Behold the   66
hand of the Lord is upon your cattle which are in the field, upon the
horses, upon the asses, upon the camels, upon the herds, and upon
the flocks; there shall be a very grievous blight."[27] "And with an outstretched arm." This is the sword, as it is said, "Having a drawn sword
in his hand stretched out over Jerusalem."[28] "And with great terribleness." This is the revelation of the Divine Presence, as it is said, "Or has
God assayed to go and take him a nation from the midst of another nation, by trials, by signs, and by wonders, and by war, and by a mighty
hand, and by an outstretched arm, and by great terrors, according to all
that the Lord your God did for you in Egypt before your eyes?"[29] "And
with signs." This is the rod of Moses, as it is said, "And you shall take
in your hand this rod, wherewith you shall do the signs."[30] "And with
wonders." This is the blood, as it is said, "And I will show wonders in
the heavens and in the earth, blood, and fire, and pillars of smoke."[31]

Another explanation is: "A mighty hand" makes two, "an outstretched   67
arm" makes two, "and with great terribleness" makes two, "and with
signs" makes two, "and with wonders" makes two. These make up the ten
plagues which the Holy One, blessed be he, brought upon the Egyptians
in Egypt, and they are these: blood, frogs, lice, beasts, blight, boils, hail,
locusts, darkness, the slaying of the firstborn. Rabbi Judah made a mne-
monic (out of the first letters of the Hebrew words for the plagues), thus:
DeTZaKh AdaSH BeAHaB.

THE TEN PLAGUES

Rabbi Jose the Galilean said: "Whence do we learn that the Egyptians   68
were smitten with ten plagues in Egypt and were smitten with fifty plagues
on the Sea? With regard to Egypt, what does it say? 'Then the magicians said
to Pharoah: This is the finger of God.'[32] And with regard to the sea, what
does it say? 'And Israel saw the great hand which the Lord laid upon the
Egyptians, and the people feared the Lord, and they believed in the Lord and

---

26. Exod 12:12.   27. Exod 9:3.   28. 1 Chr 21:16.   29. Deut 4:34.   30. Exod 4:17.
31. Joel 3:3.   32. Exod 8:17.

in his servant Moses.'[33] With how many were they smitten where it says one finger? Ten plagues. We can say from this that in Egypt they were smitten with ten plagues while at sea they were smitten with fifty plagues."

69   Rabbi Eliezer said: "Whence do we learn that each and every plague that the Holy One, blessed be he, brought upon the Egyptians in Egypt was the same as four plagues? For it is said, 'He sent forth upon them the fierceness of his anger, wrath, and indignation, and trouble, a legation of messengers of evil.'[34] 'Wrath' makes one, 'indignation' two, 'trouble' three, 'a legation of messengers of evil' four. You can say from this that they were smitten with forty plagues in Egypt, and at sea they were smitten with two hundred plagues."

70   Rabbi Akiba said: "Whence do we learn that each and every plague that the Holy One, blessed be he, brought upon the Egyptians in Egypt was the same as the five plagues? For it is said: 'He sent forth upon them the fierceness of his anger, wrath, and indignation, and trouble, a legation of messengers of evil.'[35] 'The fierceness of his anger' makes one, 'wrath' two, 'indignation' three, 'trouble' four, 'a legation of messengers of evil' five. You can say from this that they were smitten with fifty plagues in Egypt, and at sea they were smitten with two hundred and fifty plagues."

<A POEM PRAISING GOD'S BENEFITS TO ISRAEL>

71   How many are the claims of the Omnipresent upon our thankfulness!
        Had he taken us out of Egypt
            but not executed judgments on them,
        We should have been content!
    Had he executed judgements on them,
            but not upon their gods,
        We should have been content!
    Had he executed judgements on their gods,
            but not slain their firstborn,
        We should have been content!
    Had he slain their firstborn,
            but not given us their substance,
        We should have been content!
    Had he given us their substance,
            but not torn the Sea apart for us,
        We should have been content!
    Had he torn the Sea apart for us,
            but not brought us through it dry,
        We should have been content!
    Had he brought us through it dry,
            but not sunk our oppressors in the midst of it,

---

33. Exod 14:31.   34. Ps 78:49.   35. Ibid.

We should have been content!
Had he sunk our oppressors in the midst of it,
    but not satisfied our needs in the desert for forty years,
  We should have been content!
Had he satisfied our needs in the desert for forty years,
    but not fed us manna,
  We should have been content!
Had he fed us manna,
    but not given us the Sabbath,
  We should have been content!
Had he given us the Sabbath,
    but not brought us to Mount Sinai,
  We should have been content!
Had he brought us to Mount Sinai,
    but not given us the Torah,
  We should have been content!
Had he given us the Torah,
    but not brought us into the Land of Israel,
  We should have been content!
Had he brought us into the Land of Israel,
    but not built us the House of his choosing,
  We should have been content!

Then how much more, doubled and redoubled, is the claim the Omni- 72a
present has upon our thankfulness! For he did take us out of Egypt, and
execute judgments on them, and judgments on their gods, and slay their
firstborn, and give us their substance, and tear the Sea apart for us, and
bring us through it dry, and sink our oppressors in the midst of it, and satisfy our needs in the desert for forty years, and feed us manna, and give
us the Sabbath, and bring us to Mount Sinai, and give us the Torah, and
bring us into the Land of Israel, and build us the House of his choosing to
atone for all our sins.

PASSOVER SACRIFICE, UNLEAVENED BREAD, AND BITTER HERBS

Rabban Gamaliel used to say, "Whoever does not make mention of the 72b
following three things on Passover has not fulfilled his obligation: namely,
the Passover Sacrifice, unleavened bread, and bitter herbs."

The Passover Sacrifice which our fathers used to eat at the time when 72c
the Holy Temple still stood—what was the reason for it? Because the Holy
One, blessed be he, passed over the houses of our fathers in Egypt. As it is
said: "It is the sacrifice of the Lord's passover, for that he passed over the
houses of the children of Israel in Egypt when he smote the Egyptians and
delivered our houses. And the people bowed the head and worshiped."[36]

---

36. Exod 12:27.

72d   *The father of the family lifts up the matzot, showing them to the participants.*

73   The matzah which we eat, what is the reason for it? Because the dough of our fathers had not yet leavened when the King over all kings, the Holy One, blessed be he, revealed himself to them and redeemed them. As it is said: "And they baked unleavened cakes of the dough which they brought forth out of Egypt, for it was not leavened; because they were thrust out of Egypt, and could not tarry, neither had they prepared for themselves any victual."[37]

74   *The father of the family lifts up the bitter herbs, showing them to the participants.*

75   These bitter herbs we eat, what is the reason for them? Because the Egyptians made the lives of our forefathers bitter in Egypt. As it is said: "And they made their lives bitter with hard service, in mortar and in brick, and in all manner of service in the field; in all their service, wherein they made them serve with rigor."[38]

IN EVERY GENERATION

76   In every generation let each man look on himself as if *he* came forth out of Egypt.

77   As it is said: "And you shall tell your son in that day, saying, It is because of that which the Lord did for me when I came forth out of Egypt."[39] It was not only our fathers that the Holy One, blessed be he, redeemed, but us as well did he redeem along with them. As it is said: "And he brought us out from thence that he might bring us in, to give us the land which he swore unto our fathers."[40]

<AN INVITATION>

78   Therefore we are bound to thank, praise, laud, glorify, exalt, honor, bless, extol, and adore him who performed all these miracles for our fathers and for us. He has brought us forth from slavery to freedom, from sorrow to joy, from mourning to holiday, from darkness to great light, and from bondage to redemption. Let us then recite before him a new song: Alleluia.

79   *The cups are put back on the table.*

THE HALLEL: FIRST PART[d]

80   Alleluia. Praise, O servants of the Lord . . . (Psalm 113)
When Israel came forth out of Egypt . . . (Psalm 114:1–8)

BLESSING FOR REDEMPTION

81   *The participants lift up their cups of wine and say:*

---

d. *Hallel*: the "praise" psalms, namely, Psalms 113–18.
37. Exod 12:39. 38. Exod 1:14. 39. Exod 13:8. 40. Deut 6:23.

Blessed are you, O Lord, our God, King of the universe, who redeemed   82
us and who redeemed our fathers from Egypt, and has brought us to this
night, to eat thereon unleavened bread and bitter herbs. So, Lord our God
and God of our fathers, bring us to other festivals and holy days that come
toward us in peace, happy in the building of your city and joyous in your
service. And there may we eat of the sacrifices and the paschal offerings,
whose blood will come unto the walls of your altar for acceptance. Then
shall we give thanks to you with a new song, for our redemption and the
liberation of our soul. Blessed are you, O Lord, Redeemer of Israel.

Blessed are you, O Lord our God, King of the universe, creator of the   83
fruit of the vine.

The second cup of wine is drunk in a reclining position.   84

The participants wash their hands and say the following blessing: 85

Blessed are you, O Lord our God, King of the universe, who sanctified   86
us with his commandments and commanded us concerning the washing
of hands.

The father of the family breaks pieces from the upper and middle wafers and dis-   87
tributes them; the following blessings are recited:

Blessed are you, O Lord our God, King of the universe, who brings   88
forth bread from the earth.

Blessed are you, O Lord our God, King of the universe, who sanctified   89
us with his commandments and commanded us concerning the eating of
unleavened bread.

The matzah is eaten in a reclining position.   90

The father of the family dips some bitter herbs in the haroset and offers a piece to   91
each participant. The following blessing is spoken before eating the bitter herbs:

<THE MEAL>

Blessed are you, O Lord our God, King of the universe, who sanctified   92
us with his commandments and commanded us concerning the eating of
bitter herbs.

The father of the family breaks the bottom matzah, puts some bitter herb sandwich-   93
fashion between two pieces of matzah. The following is recited before eating:

In memory of the Temple, according to the custom of Hillel.[e]   94

Thus did Hillel when the Holy Temple still stood: he used to combine   95
unleavened bread and bitter herbs and eat them together to fulfill that
which is said, "They shall eat it with unleavened bread and bitter herbs."[41]

The Seder platter is removed. At this point the Seder meal is eaten.   96

After the meal the Seder platter is again placed on the table. The matzah which   97
has been set aside for afikoman[f] is distributed among the Seder company.

---

e. *Hillel*: a famous rabbi who lived 30 B.C.–9 A.D.

f. *Afikoman*: the final eating of the matzah.

41. Num 9:11.

98   *Before Grace the third cup is filled. If three or more men are present, the following introductory phrases are recited. If ten or more are present, the words in brackets are also recited. (Grace is customarily preceded by the singing of Psalm 126.)*

<BIRKAT HA-MAZON>

99   *The master of the Seder:*
      Gentlemen, let us say the blessing.

100   *The participants:*
      May the Name of the Lord be blessed from now unto eternity.

101   *The master of the Seder:*
      Let us bless Him [our God] of whose food we have eaten.

102   *The participants:*
      Blessed be he [our God] of whose food we have eaten and through whose goodness we live.

103   *All:*
      Blessed are you, O Lord our God, King of the world, who feeds the entire world in his goodness, with grace, loving kindness, and compassion. He gives bread to all flesh, for his mercy is forever. And through his great goodness food has never failed us, and may it never fail us, for his great Name's sake. For he feeds and sustains all, and does good unto all, and prepares food for all his creatures which he did create. Blessed are you, O Lord, who feeds all.

104   Let us give thanks to you, O Lord our God, because you have given our fathers to inherit a pleasant land, goodly and broad, and because you have brought us forth, O Lord our God, from the land of Egypt and redeemed us out of the house of slaves; and for your covenant which you have sealed in our flesh; and for your Torah which you have taught us; and for your laws which you have informed us; and for the life, grace, and mercy which you have graciously given us; and for the eating of the food with which you feed and sustain us continually, every day, at all times and at every hour. And for all this, O Lord our God, we give thanks to you and give blessing to you; blessed be your name in the mouth of each living thing forever, continually. As it is written: "And you shall eat and be satisfied, and bless the Lord your God for the good land which he has given you."[42] Blessed are you, O Lord, for the land and for the food.

105   Take pity, O Lord our God, on Israel, your folk, and on Jerusalem, your city, and on Zion, the habitation of your glory, and on the kingdom of the House of David, your anointed, and upon the great and holy House over which your name is called. Our God, our Father, shepherd us, feed us, maintain us, sustain us, and ease us. Ease us, O Lord our God, speedily from all our troubles. And let us not be needing, O Lord, our God, gifts at the hands of flesh and blood, or their loins, but only at your hand, that is

---

42. Deut 8:10.

full and open, holy and broad, so that we be never ashamed or disgraced
at all.

Our God and God of our fathers, may there rise, and come, and come   106
unto, be seen, accepted, heard, recollected and remembered, the remembrance of us and the recollection of us, and the remembrance of our
fathers, and the remembrance of Jerusalem, your holy city, and the remembrance of all your people, the house of Israel. May their remembrance
come before you, for rescue, goodness, grace, mercy, and compassion, for
life and for peace, on this the Festival of Unleavened Bread.

Remember us, O Lord our God, thereon for good, and recollect us   107
thereon for a blessing, and save us thereon to live. And with word of
salvation and compassion spare us and be gracious with us; have compassion on us and save us—for to you are our eyes, for you are a God gracious and compassionate.

And build Jerusalem, the sacred city, speedily in our days. Blessed are   108
you, O Lord, who builds in his compassion Jerusalem. Amen.

Blessed are you, O Lord our God, King of the universe, O God, our Father,   109
our King, our Mighty One, our Creator, our Redeemer, our Maker, our Sacred
One, the Sacred One of Jacob, our Shepherd, the Shepherd of Israel, the King,
who is good and does good to all, he who every day did, does, and will do
good to us. He has favored, he favors, he will favor us forever: for grace, for
mercy, and for compassion and for ease, rescue, and success, blessing and
salvation, consolation, maintenance and sustenance, and compassion and life
and peace, and all that is good; may he not let us lack of all that is good.

<THE COMPASSIONATE ONE>

The Compassionate One—may he reign over us forever and ever.   110
The Compassionate One—may he be blessed in the heavens and on the
earth.
The Compassionate One—may he be lauded throughout all the generations, and glory in us forever and for all eternity, and be honored in us
forever and ever.
The Compassionate One—may he sustain us with honor.
The Compassionate One—may he break our yoke from off our neck and
may he lead us upright to our land.
The Compassionate One—may he send much blessing to us in this house
and to this table from which we have eaten.
The Compassionate One—may he send Elijah, the prophet (may he be remembered for good) to us that he may bring us good tidings of salvations
and consolations.
The Compassionate One—may he bless the master of this house, and the
mistress of this house, and their household and their seed and all they
have, us and all we have. As our fathers, Abraham, Isaac, and Jacob were
blessed in all, of all, all—so bless us altogether with a perfect blessing, and
let us say, Amen.

On high, may the merits of their case and ours be pleaded successfully, that it may become a guardian of peace. And may we bear away a blessing from the Lord and righteousness from the God of our salvation. May we find grace and good favor in the eyes of God and man.
The Compassionate One—may he cause us to inherit a day that is all good. The Compassionate One—may he find us worthy of the days of the Messiah and of the life of the world to come.
"A tower of salvation is he to his king; and he shows mercy to his anointed, to David and to his seed for evermore."[43] He who makes peace in his high places, he shall make peace for us and for all Israel, and say to you, Amen.

111   "O fear the Lord, you his holy ones; for there is no want to them that fear him."[44]
"The young lions do lack and suffer hunger; but they that seek the Lord want not any good thing."[45]
"O give thanks to the Lord, for he is good, for his mercy endures forever."[46]
"You open your hand, and satisfy every living thing with favor."[47]
"Blessed is the man who trusts in the Lord, and whose trust the Lord is."[48]
"I have been young and now am old; yet I have not seen the righteous forsaken. Nor his seed begging bread."[49]
"The Lord will give strength to his people; the Lord will bless his people with peace."[50]

112   *The participants lift up their cup of wine and say:*
Blessed are you, O Lord our God, King of the universe, Creator of the fruit of the vine.

113   *The third cup of wine is drunk while in a reclining position.*
[. . .]

<CONCLUSION OF THE HALLEL>

114   *The fourth cup is filled and the Hallel recital concluded.*
Not to us, O Lord, not to us . . . (Ps 115:1–11)
The Lord has been mindful of all . . . (Ps 115:12–18)
I love that the Lord should hear . . . (Ps 116:1–9 and 116:10–11)
How can I repay to the Lord . . . (Ps 116:12–18)
Praise the Lord, all you nations . . . (Ps 117)
Give thanks to the Lord, for he is good . . . (Ps 118)
[. . .]

THE BREATH OF EVERY LIVING THING

115   The breath of every living thing shall bless your name, O Lord our God, and the spirit of all flesh shall glorify and exalt your memory, our King,

---

43. 2 Sam 22:51; Ps 18:50.   44. Ps 34:19.   45. Ps 34:10.   46. Ps 118:1.   47. Ps 145:16.
48. Jer 17:7.   49. Ps 37:25.   50. Ps 29:11.

forever. From the eternity of the beginning to the eternity of the end, you are God, and except for you we have no redeeming and saving king, a king who is liberating and delivering, provident and compassionate each time we are afflicted with trouble and distress.

We have no king but you, O God of the first things and the last, God of all creatures, the Lord of all generations, who is lauded with many songs of praise, who conducts his universe with mercy and his creatures with compassion. The Lord slumbers not nor sleeps. It is he who awakens the sleeping, and rouses the slumbering, and makes the dumb converse, and loosens the bound, and steadies the falling, and straightens the bent.   116

To you alone do we give thanks. Though our mouth were full of song like the sea, and our tongue of rejoicing like the multitude of its waves, and our lips of praise like the breadth of the horizon, and our eyes were shining like the sun and the moon, and our hands were spread like the eagles of the sky, and our feet light as the hinds—we should never thank you enough, O Lord our God and God of our fathers, and to bless your name, for one of the thousands of thousands and myriads of myriads of the good you have done with our fathers and us.   117

From Egypt you have redeemed us, O Lord our God, and from the house of slaves ransomed us, in famine fed us, and in plenty provided us, from the sword saved us, and from the pest delivered us, and from evil and serious illness lifted us. Till now your compassions have helped us, and your mercies have not deserted us; and may you never, O Lord our God, desert us. Therefore, the limbs that you have distributed among us, and the spirit and breath that you have blown into our nostrils, and the tongue which you have placed in our mouths—they shall give thanks and bless, and extol, and glorify, and exalt, and reverence, and sanctify, and crown your name, our King.   118

For every mouth shall give thanks to you, and every tongue shall swear to you, and every knee shall kneel to you, and every stature bow before you, and all hearts shall fear you, the inward parts and reins shall sing to your name. As it is written, "All my bones shall say, 'Lord, who is like unto you, who deliver the poor from him that is too strong for him, yea, the poor and the needy from him that spoileth him?'"[51]   119

Who is like you, and who is equal to you, and who is comparable to you, the God who is great, mighty, and awesome, God most high, master of heaven and earth? We shall praise you, and laud you, and glorify you, and bless your holy name. As it is said, "Bless the Lord, O my soul; and all that is within me, bless his holy name."[52] God, in the might of your power, great in the glory of your name, mighty forever, and awesome in your awesome acts. King, who sits on a high and exalted throne!   120

---

51. Ps 35:10.   52. Ps. 103:1.

121   Dweller in eternity—High One and Holy One is his name. And it is
written, "Rejoice in the Lord, O you righteous. Praise is comely for the
upright."[53] In the mouth of the upright shall you be praised, in the words
of the just shall you be blessed, in the tongue of the pious shall you be exalted, and in the midst of the holy shall you be hallowed.

122   And in the assemblies of the myriads of your folk, the house of Israel,
in joyful song your name will be glorified, our King, in every generation.
For such is the duty of all created things to you, O Lord our God and God
of our fathers, to give thanks, to praise, laud, glorify, extol, honor, bless,
exalt, and commend more than all the words of the songs and praises of
David the son of Jesse, your servant, your anointed one.

123   Praised be your name forever, our King, God the King, great and holy
in heaven and on earth. For unto you are becoming, O Lord our God and
God of our fathers, song and praise, adoration and chant, power and
dominion, victory, greatness, and strength, fame and glory, sanctity and
sovereignty, blessings and thanksgivings from now until forever. Blessed
are you, O Lord, God and King, who are mightily praised, God of thanksgivings, Lord of wonders, who chooses song and psalm, King, God, the
life of the world.

124   *The participants lift up their cups of wine and say:*
Blessed are you, O Lord our God, King of the universe, Creator of the
fruit of the vine.

125   *The fourth cup is drunk while reclining. The following final blessing is then
recited.*

\<FINAL BLESSING\>

126   Blessed are you, O Lord our God, King of the universe, for the vine and
for the fruit of the vine, for the yield of the field and for the land, pleasant,
goodly and broad which you favored and gave as an inheritance to our
fathers, to eat of its fruit and to be sated with its goodness. Have pity, O
Lord our God upon Israel, your people, upon Jerusalem, your city, upon
Sion, the dwelling of your glory, upon your altar and upon your dwelling
place. And build Jerusalem, the city of holiness, speedily and in our days
and bring us up into its midst, and cause us to rejoice in its rebuilding; let
us eat its fruit and be sated with its goodness and bless you for it in holiness and purity. And make us rejoice upon this Festival of Unleavened
Bread. For you, O Lord are good and do good to all. And we shall thank
you for the land and for the fruit of the vine. Blessed are you, O Lord, for
the land and for the fruit of the vine.

\<A WISH FOR THE FUTURE\>

127   Next year in Jerusalem!

---

53. Ps 33:1.

5. *SHEMA꜄ YIŚRA꜄EL AND ITS BLESSINGS*[†]

Prayed twice each day (morning and evening), whether privately or in the synagogue, the core of the *Shema꜄ Yiśra꜄el* is a continuous reading from three books of the Torah. Morning prayer begins with two blessings and concludes with one blessing, whereas in the evening there are two concluding blessings. This prayer, at least in its essentials, appears to date from the pre-Christian era.

Two blessings begin the morning prayer: the *birkat yotser*, which focuses on God as the maker of light; the *birkat ahaval*, which recalls God's love shown in the gift of the Torah.

The very heart of the prayer, the *Shema꜄ Yiśra꜄el* (= "hear"), consists of at least one (usually three) biblical passage. The first (Deut 6:4–9) begins with what have been called the most important words of Judaism, namely, "Hear, O Israel, the Lord is our God, the Lord is one," and proceeds to list the most important commands God has given his people. The second passage (Deut 11:12–21) recalls the happy consequences of following God's will. The third passage (Num 15:37–41) speaks of making tassels to remind one of the Lord's will and includes a divine self-description in light of the Exodus event.

After the reading of the *Shema꜄ Yiśra꜄el* comes the blessing *emet we-yatsibh* ("True and firm"), recalling how God's words are lasting and how God has liberated the people from Egypt. The text concludes with praising the God "who redeems his people Israel," and thus in the vernacular this blessing is known as the "blessing of redemption."

Bouyer 58–70 * Di Sante 49–78 * Elbogen (1962) 16–26, 511–15 * Hänggi 35–39 * Millgram 96–101 * Oesterley (1911) 364–68 * Oesterley (1925) 2, 42–51, 121–25 * Werner 5–8

M. Liber, "La récitation du Schéma et des bénédictions," REJ 57 (1908) 161–93; 58 (1909) 1–22. * L.J. Liebreich, "The Invocation to Prayer at the Beginning of the Yozer Service," JQR 39 (1948–49) 285–90, 407–12. * A. Baumstark, *Liturgie comparée: principes et méthodes pour l'étude historique des liturgies chrétiennes*, 3rd ed., Ire 7 (Chevetogne, 1953) 56–58, 65, 73. * S. Gandz, "The Benediction over the Luminaries and the Stars," JQR 44 (1953–54) 305–25. * A. Baumstark, *Comparative Liturgy*, rev. B. Botte, ed. F.L. Cross (Westminster, MD, 1958). * C.P. Price, "Jewish Morning Prayers and Early Christian Anaphoras," AThR 43 (1961) 153–68. * D. Flusser, "Sanktus und Gloria," in *Abraham unser Vater. Juden und Christen im Gespräch über die Bibel* (Leiden/Cologne, 1963) 129–52. * J. Heinemann, *Prayer in the Period of the Tanna꜄im and the Amora꜄im: Its Nature and Its Patterns* (Jerusalem, 1964) 37, 41, 61–84, 106, 146–51, 172. * A. Mirsky, "An Ancient Example of the Yotzer Prayer," in *Third World Congress of Jewish Studies, Jerusalem 25th July–1st August 1961* (Jerusalem, 1963) 134ff. * L.J. Liebreich, "The Benediction Immediately Preceding and the One Following the Recital of the Schema," REJ 125 (1966) 151–65.

[†] Translated from Hänggi 35–39 where only the formulas for morning prayer are given.

1. *Yotser* [a]

128   Blessed are you, O Lord our God, King of the universe, forming the light and creating the darkness,[1] making peace and creating the universe, with mercy giving light to the earth and to those dwelling upon it, and in your goodness daily renewing the works of creation.

129   "How wonderful are your works, Lord. You did all things with wisdom: the earth is full of your creatures."[2] O sublime King, he alone is from then: wonderful, magnificent, exalted from "days of old."[3]

130   God of the universe, your mercies are multitude, have mercy on us. Ruler of our strength, rock of our refuge, shield of our salvation, our refuge.

131   Blessed God, great in wisdom, arranged and made the rays of the sun; he formed what is good for the glory of his Name. The towers of his soldiers are his holy ones. They always exalt God; they narrate the glory of the all-powerful one and his holiness. O Lord our God, you are because of the splendor of the works of your hand and because of the stars of the light which you made. They highly prize you. Sèlah.

132   May you be blessed, our rock, our King, our Redeemer, the Creator of the holy ones. May your Name be glorified forever, our King, the maker of the holy ones. All these stand over the universe and together loudly pronounce with reverence the words of the living God and the King of the universe. All of them are chosen, all are elect, all are all-powerful, and all with awe and trembling do the will of their Creator. All open their mouths in holiness and purity, singing a melody; they bless, glorify, praise, and adore the holy King and proclaim the Name of God who is the powerful King, great and to be feared, for he is holy. And all, one to another, take upon themselves the yoke of the heavenly kingdom and devote themselves to proclaiming the holy God, the Creator, doing so with peace of soul, with refined speech; and with holy sweetness all together respond and say with awe:

133   "Holy, holy, holy is the Lord of hosts: the whole earth is full of your glory."[4]

134   And Ophanim and the holy Hayyot[b] with loud roaring rise up [before the Seraphim]. From opposite sides they say, Blessed be "the glory of the Lord from its place."[5]

135   They sing melodies to the blessed God, to God the King, living and eternal; they sing songs and utter praise. He alone does wonderful deeds; he brings about new things; he rules those who do battle; he sows justice; he makes healthy things bloom; he creates healing; he is awesome to praise; he is the God of wonders.

---

a. The Hebrew for "forming."

b. Ophanim and Hayyot: two classes of heavenly beings who in Jewish thought assist in watching over and supporting the throne of God.

1. See Isa 45:7. 2. Ps 104:24. 3. Deut 32:7. 4. Isa 6:3. 5. Ezek 3:12.

In his goodness he daily renews the works of his creation, as is said,   136
[Give thanks to him] "who made the great lights because his mercy endures forever."[6]

Let a new light shine upon Sion, and may all of us soon be made wor-   137
thy of his light.

Blessed are you, O Lord, for you create the luminaries.   138

2. *Ahabhah Rabbah*[c]

O Lord, our light, you have loved us with much love. Great and abun-   139
dant is the kindness you have shown to us. Our Father and our King, have
mercy on us and teach us because of our fathers who trusted in you and
whom you taught the commandments of life.

Our Father, kind father, you are full of compassion. Have mercy on us.   140
Grant that our hearts might understand, know, hear, learn, teach, serve,
do, and fulfill in love all the teachings of your Law. Open our eyes with
your love; bind our hearts to your commandments; and bring together
our hearts in love and in awe of your Name so that we may never be reproached for eternity.

Because we trust in your holy Name that is great and wondrous, let us   141
rejoice and be glad because of your salvation. Lead us back in peace from
the four corners of the world, and have us enter our land as a free people
because you are the saving God, the God who has chosen us from among
all peoples and tongues, who has led us to your holy Name so that in love
we might freely confess you and your unity.

Blessed are you, O Lord, for you chose your people Israel in love.   142

3. *Shemaʾ Yiśraʿel*

Deuteronomy 6:4–9   143
Deuteronomy 11:13–21
Numbers 15:37–41

4. *Emet We-yetsibh*[d]

True and strong, impartial and stable, just and faithful, beloved and   144
cherished, pleasing and agreeable, awesome and majestic, upright and
welcome, good and beautiful, such is your word to us forever and ever.

Indeed the God of the universe is our King, who is the rock of Jacob, the   145
shield of our salvation. From generation to generation he endures and his
Name remains unchanged for eternity. His words are living and stable,
ever faithful and desirable. As they were for our fathers, so they are also
for us, for our children, for our generation and for all generations of the
seed of Israel his servants. From the first age to the last ages your word

c. The Hebrew for "with great love."
d. The Hebrew for "true and strong."
6. Ps 136:7.

is good, enduring forever and ever; it is truth and fidelity, a law that will always endure.

146   Truly you are the Lord our God and the God of our fathers, our King, the King of our fathers, our Redeemer, the Redeemer of our fathers, our Creator, the rock of our salvation, our liberator, our Savior. Your name exists from eternity; there is no God other than you.

147   O Lord our God, you redeemed us from Egypt and freed us from the house of slavery. You killed all their firstborn, but you redeemed your firstborn; you divided the Red Sea and drowned the proud; you had the chosen ones pass through it "and the waters covered their adversaries, not one of them remaining."[7] Therefore the chosen ones glorified and exalted you and offered melodies, songs, praises, blessings, and thanksgivings to you, the King, the living and eternal God, the God who is high and exalted, great and highly revered, who humbles the proud and raises up the humble, who leads out the captives, frees the poor, helps the needy, and responds to the people when they cry out to him.

148   Give praise to God on high: he is blessed and is to be blessed. Moses and the children of Israel joyfully sang a song to you, and all said: "Who among the gods is like you, O Lord? Who is like you, for you are great in holiness, revered because of your praiseworthy deeds, and doing wonderful things?"[8] The redeemed raised up a new song to your Name; on the seashore they were one in confessing and proclaiming your kingdom, saying, "The Lord will reign forever and ever."[9]

149   O rock of Israel, rise up so as to help Israel and free Judah and Israel according to your promise, O Redeemer. The Lord of hosts is your name, the holy one of Israel.

150   Blessed are you, O Lord, for you free Israel.

6. *SHEMONEH ESRE* (THE EIGHTEEN BLESSINGS)[†]

The *Shemoneh Esre*, namely, the eighteen (nineteen) blessings that are recited three times a day (morning, afternoon, and evening), is the principal part of pious Jews' daily prayer. Since they are prayed while one is standing, these blessings are also known as the *amidah*, from the word *amad*, meaning to "stand." They are also called the *tefillah*, meaning "Prayer," since they are considered "the" prayer of Judaism.

    As to the structure of the *Shemoneh Esre*, the prayer begins with three blessings whose theme is praise of God. These are followed by twelve (thirteen) intermediate petitions, each ending with a short blessing. The number of petitions differs according to various recensions since blessing fourteen (IERUŠALAYIM) is in some traditions divided into two requests, thus resulting in thirteen petitions that in turn result in nineteen blessings

7. Ps 106:11.   8. Exod 15:11.   9. Exod 15:18.
† Translated from Hänggi 41–43.

in all. Concluding the prayer are three final blessings having the theme of gratitude and thanksgiving.

A certain flexibility is characteristic of the *Shemoneh Esre*. Embolisms may be added: for example, the *kaddish* with its "Holy, holy" before the third blessing; also a request for rain added within the ninth blessing, etc. Furthermore, the petitions are not recited on the Sabbath and on feasts. And when prayed in the synagogue, the blessings are said twice: first all together and silently, then aloud with the leader adding any appropriate embolisms (i.e., insertions).

No different than numerous other prayer forms, the *Shemoneh Esre* is the result of a long historical development and growth. Many hands were at work. For example, the three introductory and the three final blessings go back to the pre-Christian era. On the other hand, blessings twelve (LA-MEŠUMADIM) and fourteen (IERUŠALAYIM) can be dated after the destruction of the Temple in 70 A.D. This prayer has come down to us in two main recensions, that of Palestine and that of Babylon (e.g., that of the *Seder Rev Amran*).

Bouyer 70–78, 121–35, 197–99 * Deiss 9–14 * Di Sante 78–112 * Elbogen (1962) 27–72, 515–23 * Hänggi 40–54 * Millgram 101–8 * Oesterley (1911) 362–64 * Oesterley (1925) 54–67, 127

K. Kohler, "The Origin and Composition of the Eighteen Benedictions," *Hebrew Union College Annual* 1 (1924) 387–425. * A. Marmorstein, "The Amidah of the Public Fast Days," JQR 15 (1924–25) 409–18. * L. Finkelstein, "The Development of the Amidah," JQR 16 (1925–26) 1–43, 127–70. * L. Finkelstein, "La Kedouscha et les bénédictions du Schema," REJ 93 (1932) 1–26. * A. Marmorstein, "The Oldest Form of the Eighteen Benedictions," JQR 34 (1943–44) 137–59. * M. Liber, "Structure and History of the Tefilah," JQR 40 (1949–50) 331–57. * L.J. Liebreich, "The Intermediate Benedictions of the Amidah," JQR 42 (1951–52) 423–26. * F.C. Grant, "Modern Study of the Jewish Liturgy," ZAW 65 (1953) 59–77, especially 61–72. * H.L. Strack and P. Billerbeck, *Kommentar zum Neuen Testament aus Talmud und Midrasch* IV/1, 2nd ed. (Munich, 1956) 208–49. * S. Zeitlin, "The Tefillah, the Shemoneh Esreh: An Historical Study of the First Canonization of the Hebrew Liturgy," JQR 54 (1963–64) 208–50. * J. Heinemann, *Prayer in the Period of the Tannaʾim and the Amoraʾim: Its Nature and Its Patterns* (Jerusalem, 1964) 29–47, 138–48.

Palestinian Recension

O Lord, open my lips, and my mouth will proclaim your praise.[1]   151

1. [ABHOTH] *Barukh attah*[a]
Blessed are you, O Lord our God [and the God of our fathers, the God   152
of Abraham, the God of Jacob],[b] the God who is great, powerful, and

---

a. The title in brackets is the name given to the blessing at the time of the Mishnah; the word or words in italics are the blessing's initial words in Hebrew.

b. Text in brackets appears to have been added to the original version at a later time.

1. Ps 51:15.

revered, the God most high, the Lord of heaven and earth, our shield
and the shield of our fathers, the God who increases our faithfulness [in
every generation].
Blessed are you, O Lord, for you are the shield of Abraham.

2. [GHEBHUROTH] *Attah ghibor*

153 You are powerful, [humbling the proud], strong, [judging tyrants,] living
forever, raising the dead, bringing back the wind, pouring forth the dew.
154 You nourish the living and give life to the dead; [in a twinkling of an eye
you have salvation issue forth its shoots].
Blessed are you, O Lord, for you bring the dead to life.

3. [QEDUŠAH] *Qadoš attah*

155 You are holy, and your Name is to be revered.
156 There is no god other than you.
Blessed are you, O Lord holy God.

4. [BINAH] *Hannénu*

157 Our Father, you present us with the knowledge [which is] from you to-
gether with the understanding and discernment that comes from your
Law.
Blessed are you, O Lord, who graciously give us knowledge.

5. [TEŠUHBHAH] *Hašbhénu*

158 Lord, convert us to you, and we will be converted.
"Renew our days as of old."[2]
Blessed are you, O Lord, for you are pleased by our converting.

6. [SELIHAH] *Selah*

159 Father, forgive our sins against you. Purge [and remove] our sins from before your eyes [because your mercies are many].
Blessed are you, O Lord, for you pardon many times.

7. [GHE'ULLAH] *Re'eh*

160 Father, look upon our affliction, take up our cause.
You redeem us because of your Name.
Blessed are you, O Lord, for you redeem Israel.

8. [REPHU'AH] *Repha'enu*

161 O Lord our God, cure us from the troubles of the heart [and keep dejection
and groaning away from us] and apply medicine to our wounds.
Blessed are you, O Lord, for you cure the sick among your people Israel.

9. [BIRKAT HA-ŠANIM] *Barékh*

162 O Lord our God, bless this year for us [so that all the fruits of the earth
may be abundant. Make the year of our redemption arrive soon.]

---

2. Lam 5:21.

May dew and rain fall upon the surface of the earth. Fill the world with   163
the treasures of your goodness. [And bless the work of our hands.]
Blessed are you, O Lord, for you bless the years.

10. [QIBBUTS GALUYOTH] *Teqa*
May the trumpet sound loudly for our freedom, and lift high the standard   164
for the gathering of our captives.
Blessed are you, O Lord, for you gather the exiles [of your people] Israel.

11. [MIŚPAT] *Hašibhah*
"Make our judges what they once were, our counselors what they for-   165
merly were."[3] And may you alone rule over us.
Blessed are you, O Lord, for you love righteousness.

12. [LA-MEŠHUMADIM] *La-mešumadim*
May there be no hope for the apostates.   166
And quickly [in our days] destroy the kingdom of pride. [And may all our
enemies and all heretics suddenly perish, and "may they be blotted out of
the book of the living and not be written among the just."[4]
Blessed are you, O Lord, for you humble the proud.

13. [LA-TSADIQIM] *ʿAl gere ha-tsedeq*
May your mercies move over the proselytes of justice.   167
Give us a [good] reward with those who do your will.   168
Blessed are you, O Lord, for you increase trust for the righteous.

14. [IERUŠALAYIM] *Rahèm*
O Lord our God, have mercy [in the fullness of your mercies on behalf of   169
Israel your people and] toward Jerusalem [and toward Sion, the dwelling place of your glory, and toward your sanctuary and your house,] and
toward the kingdom of David, the One Anointed with your justice.
Blessed are you, O Lord, the God of David [the Anointed One], the God
[who builds Jerusalem].

15. [TEFILLAH] *Śhema*
O Lord our God, hear our prayer [and have mercy on us] because you are   170
a gracious and merciful God.
Blessed are you, O Lord, for you hear our prayers.

16. [ABHODAH] *Retseh*
O Lord our God, may you be pleased to dwell on Sion.   171
May your servants serve you in Jerusalem.   172
Blessed are you, O Lord, for we will reverently serve you.

---

3. Isa 1:26.   4. Ps 69:28.

17. [HODAAH] *Modim anahnu lakh*

173   O Lord, we give thanks to you, [for you yourself are the Lord] our God [and the God of our fathers].

174   We do so because of all your benefits, [for your kindness and mercies by which you have enriched us and] which you have bestowed on us and on our fathers before us. [When we said, "Our feet have strayed, O Lord, your mercy will aid us."][5]

175   Blessed are you, O Lord.

176   It is good to give you thanks.

18. [ŠALOM] *Sim Šalom*

177   Grant your peace to Israel [and to your city and to your inheritance]. Let all of us together bless the Lord, the giver of peace; you are blessed.

---

5. Ps 94:18.

Chapter II

Subapostolic Texts

7. THE *DIDACHE* OR *THE TEACHING* OF *THE TWELVE APOSTLES*[†]

In 1873 P. Bryennios, the Greek Orthodox Metropolitan of Nicomedia, discovered at the Monastery of the Holy Sepulcher in Constantinople a codex, written in 1067, containing among other writings a Greek text entitled *The Teaching of the Twelve Apostles* or *The Lord's Teaching to the Gentiles through the Twelve Apostles*, this latter designation also occurring in the manuscript and believed by some to be the original title. Since its publication in 1883 the document, commonly known as the *Didache*, the Greek word for teaching or instruction, has been the object of intense scholarly investigation and discussion. A collection of ethical principles, liturgical directives, and instructions regarding the life of the community, the *Didache* is the earliest example of what are called church orders, namely, early collections of church law and discipline.

Not a homogenous and unified whole, the document is a compendium that relies on previous sources and has undergone the workings and revisions of an editor (or editors). For example, chapters I–VI form a short catechesis on ethical behavior and are based on an earlier and, as many believe, Jewish work designed for Gentile converts to Judaism. It outlines the Two Ways of moral behavior, namely, the Way of Life (I–IV) and that of Death (V). It has been suggested that the editor, to adapt this earlier text for Christian usage, made certain additions to the primitive form, for example, 1.3–II.1, among others. Although scholars agree that much revision occurred and that various layers or blocks exist within the text's final redaction, there are differences of opinion as to the precise nature and extent of the editorial process.

As is true of most early church orders, the editor of the *Didache* remains anonymous, although most probably being a Judeo-Christian living in Egypt, Palestine, or—as is most commonly believed—western Syria. Whereas parts of the document certainly have a very early origin, scholars are divided as to the date of the final redaction, some placing it in the first century and even as early as 60 A.D., others assigning it to the early or mid-second century, and still a few others opting for a third-century date.

[†] Translated from *La doctrine des douze apôtres. Didaché*, ed. and trans. W. Rordorf and A. Tuilier, SChr 248 (Paris, 1978).

Prior to the 1873 discovery of the manuscript in Constantinople, the *Didache* was known only by name and through various quotations in works by authors like Clement of Alexandria, Origen, and Athanasius, the latter saying it was used for the instruction of catechumens. So useful and revered was the document that it served in edited form as the basis of Book VII of the *Apostolic Constitutions* (WEC 2:77).

CPG 1: nos. 1735ff. * Altaner (1961) 50–54 * Altaner (1966) 79–82 * Bardenhewer (1908) 19–22 * Bardenhewer (1910) 18–20 * Bardenhewer (1913) 1:76–86 * Bardy (1929) 53–54 * Cross 8–11 * Goodspeed 11 –13 * Hamell 24–25 * Jurgens 1:1–6 * Quasten 1:29–39 * Steidle 268 * Tixeront 19–21 * CATH 3:747–49 * CE 4:779–81 * DACL 4.1:772–98 * DDC 4:1210–18 * DictSp 3:860–62 * DPAC 1:947–48 * DTC 1.2:1680–87 * EC 4:1562–65 * EEC 1:234–35 * EEChr 1:328–29 * LTK 3:207–8 * NCE 4:859 * NCES 4:736 * ODCC 478–79 * PEA (1894) 5.1:392–94 * PEA (1991) 3:538 * RACh 3:1009–13 * TRE 8:731–36

RECENT EDITIONS/TRANSLATIONS
J.-P. Audet, *La Didaché: Instruction des apôtres*, Etudes bibliques (Paris, 1958). [Provides a complete revised text and a fresh survey of all the textual evidence with full notes and related materials.] * W. Rordorf and A. Tuilier, *La Doctrine des Douze Apôtres (Didaché)*, SChr 248 (Paris, 1978); includes a critical text with introductions and notes. * A. Milavec, *The Didache: Text, Translation, Analysis, and Commentary* (Collegeville, 2003).

GENERAL COMMENTARIES/STUDIES
J. Daniélou, "Une antique liturgie judéo-chrétienne," *Cahiers sioniens* 4 (1950) 293–303. * A. Vööbus, *Liturgical Traditions in the Didache*, Eesti Usuteadlaste Selts Paguluses 16 (Stockholm, 1968). * S. Giet, *L'énigme de la Didaché* (Paris, 1970). * F.E. Vokes, "The Didache—Still Debated," ChQ 3:1 (July 1970) 57–63. * F. Hawkins, "The Development of the Liturgy: The Didache," in StLit, 55–57. * C.N. Jefford, ed., *The Didache in Context: Essays on Its Text, History, and Transmission*, Supplements to Novum Testamentum 77 (Leiden and New York, 1995). * J.A. Draper, ed., *The Didache in Modern Research* (Leiden and New York, 1996). * K. Niederwimmer, *The Didache: A Commentary*, Hermeneia—A Critical and Historical Commentary on the Bible (Minneapolis, 1998). * H. van de Sandt and D. Flusser, *The Didache: Its Jewish Sources and Its Place in Early Judaism and Christianity* (Minneapolis, 2002). * M. Del Verme, *Didache and Judaism: Jewish Roots of an Ancient Christian-Jewish Work* (New York, 2004). * A. Milavec, *The Didache: Faith, Hope, and Life of the Earliest Christian Communities* (New York, 2005).

BAPTISM
T. Klauser, "Taufe in lebendigem Wasser! Zum religions-und kulturgeschichtlichen Verständis von Didache 7, 1–13," in *Pisciculi F.J. Dolger dargeboten* (Münster, 1939) 157–64; repr. in JAC *Ergänzungsband* 3 (1975) 177–83. * B. Neunheuser, *Baptism and Confirmation* (St. Louis, 1963) 54–55. * G. Saber, "Le baptême chrétienne dans la 'Didachè' ou 'Instruction des Apôtres'" (in Arabic), Melto. Melta. *Recherches orientales* 4, no. 1 (1968) 126–40. * E. Ferguson, "Baptism from the Second to the Fourth Century," ResQ 1 (1957) 185–97. * W. Rordorf, "La baptême selon la Didachè," in *Mélanges liturgiques offerts au R.P. Dom Bernard Botte* (Louvain, 1972) 499–509. *

R. Pillinger, "Die Taufe nach der Didache Philologisch-archäologische Untersuchung der Kapitel 7, 9, 10 und 14," WSt, n.s., 9 (1975) 152–60. * R.S. Ascough, "An Analysis of the Baptismal Ritual of the Didache," StudLit 24:1 (1994) 201–13. * A.H.B. Logan, "Post-Baptismal Chrismation in Syria: The Evidence of Ignatius, the 'Didache' and the Apostolic Constitutions," JThSt, n.s., 49 (1998) 92–108.

EUCHARIST
P. Batiffol, "L'Eucharistie dans la Didaché," *Revue biblique internationale*, n.s., 2 (1905) 58–67. * J. Réville, "Les origines de l'Eucharistie (messe-Sainte-Cène)," RHE 56 (1907) 1–56, 141–96. * G. Klein, "Die Gebete in der Didache," *Zeitschrft für die neutestamentliche Wissenschaft* 9 (1908) 132–46. * Hans Lietzmann, *Messe und Herenmahl*, Arbeiten zur Kirchengeschichte 8 (Bonn, 1926) 230–38. * A. Greiff, *Das älteste Paschalritual der Kirche, Didache 1–10 und das Johannesevangelium*, Johanneische Studien 1 (Paderborn, 1929). * H.J. Gibbins, "The Problem of the Liturgical Section of the Didache," JThSt 36 (1935) 373–86. * R.D. Middleton, "The Eucharistic Prayers of the Didache," JThSt 37 (1935) 259–67. * A. Arnold, *Der Ursprung des christlichen Abendmahles* (Freiburg i. B., 1937). * R.H. Connolly, "Agape and Eucharist in the Didache," DR 56 (1937) 477–89. * M. Dibelius, "Die Mahl-gebete der Didache," ZNW 37 (1938) 32–41. * G. Dix, "Primitive Consecration Prayers," *Theology. Journal of Historic Christianity* 37 (1938) 261–83. * J. Jungmann (1951), vol. 1, 11ff. * Jungmann (1959) 6ff. * C.F.D. Moule, "A Note on Didache IX.4," JThSt, n.s., 6 (1955) 240–43. * H. Riesenfeld, "Das Brot von den Bergen: zu Didache 9, 4," *Eranos* 54 (1956) 142–50. * C.F.D. Moule, "A Reconsideration of the Context of *Maranatha*," NTS 8 (1960–61) 307–10. * L. Clerici, *Einsammlung der Zerstreuten; liturgiegeschichtliche Untersuchung zur Vol- und Nachgeschichtliche der Fürbitte für die Kirche in Didache 9, 4 und 10, 5*, LQF 44 (Münster, 1966). * M. Decroos, "Die eucharistische liturgie van Didache IX en X," *Bijdragen* 28 (1967) 376–98. * L. Bouyer, *Eucharist: Theology and Spirituality of the Eucharistic Prayer* (Notre Dame, 1968) 115–19. * J. Betz, "Die Eucharistie dans la Didaché," ALW 11 (1969) 10–39. * W. Rordorf, "The *Didache*," in W. Rordorf and others, *The Eucharist of the Early Christians* (New York, 1978) 1–23. * A. Verheul, "La prière eucharistique dans la Didachè," QL 60 (1979) 197–207. * J.W. Riggs, "From Gracious Table to Sacramental Elements: The Tradition-History of Didache 9 and 10," SCJ 4 (1984) 83–101. * B. Grimonprez-Damm, "Le 'sacrifice eucharistique' dans la 'Didaché,'" RevSR 64 (1990) 9–25. * J.-M. van Cangh, "Le déroulement primitif de la Cène," RBibl 102 (1995) 193–225. * W. Rordorf, "Die Mahlgebete in 'Didache' Kap. 9–10: Ein neuer 'status quaestionis,'" VC 51 (1997) 229–46. * A. Verheul, "La prière eucharistique dans la Didaché," QL 80 (1999) 337–47. * W. Rordorf, "Tà 'ágia toîs 'agíois," Ire 72 (1999) 346–63. * J. Schwiebert, *Knowledge and the Coming Kingdom: The Didache's Meal Ritual and Its Place in Early Christianity*, Library of New Testament Studies 373 (London, 2008).

FORGIVENESS OF SIN
J. Hoh, *Die kirchliche Busse im zeiten Jahrhundert* (Breslau, 1932) 103–11. * B. Poschmann, *Paenitentia Secunda* (Bonn, 1940) 88–97. * W. Rordorf, "La rémission des péchés selon la Didaché," Ire 46 (1973) 283–97.

OTHER TOPICS
E. Ferguson, "The Ministry of the Word in the First Two Centuries," ResQ 1 (1957) 21–31. * J. Gribomont, "'Ecclesiam Adunare': un écho de l'Eucharistie africaine et de la 'Didachè,'" RTAM 27 (1960) 20–28. * A. Vööbus, "Regarding the Background of

the Liturgical Traditions in the Didache," VC 23 (1969) 81–87. * E. Ferguson, "Ordination in the Ancient Church," ResQ 5 (1961) 17–32, 67–82, 130–46. * S. Gero, "The So-Called Ointment Prayer in the Coptic Version of the Didache: A Re-Evaluation," HThR 70 (1977) 67–84. * A. de Halleux, "Les ministères dans la Didaché," Ire 53 (1980) 5–29. * V. Balabanski, *Eschatology in the Making: Mark, Matthew, and the Didache*, Monograph Series, Society for New Testament Studies 97 (Cambridge and New York, 1997). * M. Slee, *The Church in Antioch in the First Century CE: Communion and Conflict*, Journal for the Study of the New Testament, Supplement Series 244 (London and New York, 2003).

178   I.1. There are two ways: one is the way of life; the other is that of death. And there is a great difference between them. 2. The way of life is this: First, love the God who made you;[1] then love your neighbor as yourself;[2] and whatever you do not desire to be done to you, do not do to another.[3] 3. This is the teaching of these words: Bless those who curse you, pray for your enemies, and fast for those who persecute you.[4] For what merit is there in loving those who love you? Do not even the pagans do this?[5] Love those who hate you, and you will not have an enemy. 4. Refrain from carnal[6] and bodily desires. If anyone strikes you on the right cheek, turn the other[7] and you will be perfect; if anyone forces you to go one mile, go also a second with that person;[8] if anyone takes your cloak, give this person your tunic as well.[9] If anyone takes what belongs to you,[10] do not ask for it back, not even if you can. 5. Give to each person who asks and request nothing back.[11] For the Father desires that we share his gifts with all. Happy the person who gives according to the commandment, for such a one is without reproach. Woe to the person who takes; certainly if one takes because of need, an account will be given of the reason and purpose for taking it. Placed in prison, such a person will be examined about what was done and will not depart [prison] until the last penny is paid.[12] But on this subject it has also been said: May your alms sweat in your hands till you know to whom you are giving.

179   II.1. The second commandment of the teaching is: 2. You are not to murder,[13] you are not to commit adultery,[14] you are not to molest children, you are not to commit fornication, you are not to steal,[15] you are not to perform magic and sorcery,[16] you are not to kill a baby by an abortion or kill it after birth. You are not to desire your neighbor's goods;[17] 3. you are not to swear falsely[18] or to bear false witness.[19] You are not to slander,[20] and

---

1. See Deut 6:5; Sir 7:30; Matt 22:37.   2. See Lev 19:18; Matt 22:39.   3. See Tob 4:15; Matt 7:12; Luke 6:31.   4. See Matt 5:44; Luke 6:28.   5. See Matt 5:46–47; Luke 6:32–33.   6. See 1 Pet 2:11.   7. See Matt 5:39; Luke 6:29.   8. See Matt 5:41. 9. See Matt 5:40; Luke 6:29.   10. See Luke 6:30.   11. See Matt 5:42; Luke 6:30. 12. See Matt 5:26; Luke 12:59.   13. See Exod 20:13; Deut 5:17.   14. See Exod 20:14; Deut 5:18.   15. See Exod 20:15; Deut 5:19.   16. See Deut 18:10.   17. See Exod 20:17; Deut 5:21.   18. See Zech 5:3, LXX; Matt 5:33.   19. See Exod 20:16; Deut 5:20. 20. See Exod 21:16, LXX.

you are not to bear malice.[21] 4. You will not be double-minded or double-tongued since deceit is the snare of death.[22] 5. Your speech is not to be false or vain but turned into deeds. 6. You should not be greedy nor rapacious nor hypocritical; nor malicious nor proud; and you are not to plan evil against your neighbor. 7. You are not to hate anyone; but you shall admonish some, pray for others, and still others you will love more than your own soul.

III.1. My child, avoid all that is evil and everything resembling evil.   180
2. Be not angry since anger leads to murder; be neither jealous nor quarrelsome nor irascible, for all this causes murders. 3. My child, do not hand yourself over to lust since this leads to fornication; avoid obscene speech and indiscreet glances, for all this results in adultery. 4. My child, do not give yourself to omens since this leads to idolatry, nor to witchcraft, to astrology, or to purifications. Refuse to see [and hear] these things since all this gives rise to idolatry. 5. My child, do not lie since lying leads to thievery; do not be avaricious nor taken with vain glory since all this results in thefts. 6. My child, do not grumble since this leads to blasphemy; be neither arrogant nor malicious since all this engenders blasphemy. 7. On the contrary, be meek, for the meek will inherit the earth.[23] 8. Be patient, merciful, kind, peaceful, good, and ever fearing the words you have heard.[24]
9. Do not exalt yourself and allow your soul to become insolent. Do not attach your soul to the arrogant but keep company with the just and the humble. 10. Receive whatever happens as good, knowing that nothing takes place without God.

IV.1. My child, day and night remember the one who speaks God's word   181
to you.[25] Honor such a person as the Lord, for the Lord is present where his authority[26] is preached. 2. Daily seek out the company of the saints in order to rest[27] upon their words.[28] 3. Create no dissension but reconcile those who are at odds with one another. Judge with justice and, when correcting sins, show favor to no one.[29] 4. Be not anxious as to whether something will happen or not. 5. Do not stretch out your hand to receive, and do not close it when giving.[30] 6. If you have anything by the work of your hands, give it for the redemption of your sins. 7. Do not hesitate to give, and give without murmuring, for you know who will grant a fitting reward in return.[31] 8. Turn not away from the needy,[32] but share all your goods with one another and do not say that these are your own; for if you are sharers in immortality, you should be all the more so in perishable things. 9. Do not withdraw your hand from your son or daughter, but teach them from infancy the fear of God.[33] 10. Do not with bitterness

---

21. See Zech 7:10; 8:17.   22. See Tob 14:10; Ps 18:5; Prov 14:27, LXX; 21:6.
23. See Matt 5:5; Ps 37:11.   24. See Isa 66:2.   25. See Heb 13:7.   26. See 2 Pet 2:10; Jude 8.   27. See Sir 6:28; 51:26ff.; Matt 11:28ff.   28. See Sir 6:34–36.   29. See Deut 1:16ff.; Sir 4:9; Prov 31:9.   30. See Deut 15:7ff.; Sir 4:31.   31. See Prov 19:17.
32. See Sir 4:5.   33. See Ps 34:11; Prov 19:18; Eph 6:4; Col 3:21.

command your male or female servants who hope in the same God lest they no longer fear God who is above both of you[34] because he comes to call, not according to appearance, but those for whom he has prepared the Spirit. 11. But you who are servants are to submit to your masters, as to an image of God, with respect and fear.[35] 12. Hate all impiety and all that displeases the Lord.[36] 13. Never abandon the commandments of the Lord, but keep what you have received, neither adding nor taking away from it.[37] 14. Confess your sins in the assembly,[38] and do not go to pray with a bad conscience. This is the way of life.

182   v.1. This is the way of death. First, it is evil and full of cursing: murders, adulteries, lusts, fornications, thefts, idolatries, magic, sorceries, robberies, false witnessing, hypocracies, duplicities, fraud, pride, malice, arrogance, covetousness, obscene speech, jealousy, impudence, haughtiness, boastfulness. 2. Persecutors of good people, enemies of truth, those who love lies and ignore the reward of justice, are attached neither to good nor to a just judgment; they desire not what is good but what is evil; being strangers to meekness and patience, they love vanity and seek to be rewarded; they pity not the poor; they have no concern for the afflicted, and they know not their Creator.[39] Murderers of children, they corrupt the work of God; they turn away from the needy and oppress the afflicted; they defend the rich and unjustly judge the poor; they are completely sinful. May you, my children, be kept from all of these.

183   vi.1. Take care that no one causes you to stray from this way of teaching since such a person teaches you without God. 2. If you are able to carry the full yoke of the Lord,[40] you will be perfect; but if not, do what you can. 3. As to food, bear what you are able but resolutely abstain from meat offered to idols[41] since this is to worship dead gods.

184   vii.1. Regarding baptism, baptize as follows: after having given [as an instruction] all these things [just mentioned], "baptize in the name of the Father and of the Son and of the Holy Spirit,"[42] doing so in running water. 2. But if you have no running water, baptize in other water; if you cannot in cold water, then in warm water. 3. But if you have neither, pour water three times on the head in the name of the Father and of the Son and of the Holy Spirit. 4. And let the baptizer, the person to be baptized, and others who are able to do so, fast before the baptism; bid the person to be baptized to fast for one or two [days] beforehand.

185   viii.1. Do not let your fasts be with the hypocrites. They, in fact, fast on the second day [Monday] and on the fifth day [Thursday] of the week; but you are to fast on the fourth day [Wednesday] and on the Preparation Day [Friday]. 2. Do not pray as the hypocrites.[43] But as the Lord has commanded you in his Gospel, pray as follows,

---

34. See Lev 25:43; Sir 7:20ff.; 33:30ff.   35. See Eph 6:5ff.; Col 3:22ff.   36. See Wis 9:10ff.   37. See Deut 4:2; 13:1.   38. See Sir 4:26, LXX.   39. See Deut 32:18.   40. See Matt 11:29–30.   41. See Acts 15:29.   42. Matt 28:19.   43. See Matt 6:5.

"Our Father in heaven,
hallowed be your name;
your kingdom come;
your will be done on earth as it is in heaven.
Give us today our daily bread;
forgive us our debts as we also forgive our debtors.
And lead us not into temptation
but deliver us from evil.[44]
For to you is the power and the glory forever."[a]

3. Pray in this manner three times a day.

IX.1. Regarding the Eucharist, give thanks as follows.[b]   186
2. First for the cup:
"We give you thanks, our Father,
for the holy vine of David, your servant,
whom you have revealed to us through Jesus, your servant.
Glory be to you forever."
3. Then for the broken bread:
"We give you thanks, our Father,
for the life and the knowledge
which you have given us through Jesus, your servant.
Glory be to you forever.
4. As this broken bread, scattered over the mountains,
was gathered together to be one,
so may your Church be gathered together in the same manner
from the ends of the earth into your kingdom;

---

a. This concluding formula is found in numerous, though not in the oldest, scriptural manuscripts. Used as an ending for two other prayers in the *Didache* (IX and x), the phrase is found first in Syrian liturgical texts and then in Byzantine usage, where the word "kingdom" is inserted before "power and glory."

b. No sections of the *Didache* have engendered more discussion and more divergent opinions than chapters IX and x. Whereas there is general agreement that chapter XIV describes in rudimentary fashion the Sunday celebration of the community's Eucharist, questions are raised about chapters IX and x. Are both eucharistic in our sense of the word? And if so, would these refer to small domestic Eucharists as distinct from those celebrated by the whole community on Sunday? Or does chapter IX refer to some type of Christian meal or agape, whereas chapter x describes what we would designate as the Eucharist? Or do both chapters IX and x concern prayers said at the agape? What is certain is that the texts contain strong Jewish elements, with themes reminiscent of Jewish meal prayers. Although arguments can be adduced on almost all sides of the question, a common opinion today appears to be that these texts are table prayers said at a domestic celebration of the Eucharist proper. Nonetheless, one suspects that definitive answers will continue to elude us.

44. See Matt 6:9–13; Luke 11:2–4.

for to you are the glory and the power
through Jesus Christ forever."
5. Let no one eat or drink of your Eucharist except those who have been
baptized in the name of the Lord; for it was in regard to this that the Lord
said, "Do not give what is holy to the dogs."[45]

187   x.1. After you have been filled, give thanks as follows:
2. "We give you thanks, holy Father,
   for your holy name
which you have made to dwell
   in our hearts,
and for the knowledge, the faith, and the immortality
which you revealed to us
   through your servant Jesus.
Glory be to you forever.
3. "Almighty Lord, you have created all things
   for the sake of your name.[46]
You have given all food and drink for refreshment
   so that they may give you thanks.
But to us you have given spiritual food and drink and eternal life
   through [Jesus] your servant.
4. "For everything we thank you
   because you are powerful.
Glory be to you forever.
5. "Lord, remember your Church; deliver it from all evil
   and perfect it in your love.
Gather this sanctified Church from the four winds[47]
   into the kingdom you have prepared for it.
For to you belong the power and the glory forever.
6. "May grace come, and may this world pass away.
Hosanna to the God of David.[48]
If anyone is holy, let him come;
   if anyone is not, let him do penance.
   Maranatha."[c]
7. Allow the prophets to give thanks as they wish.

---

c. This term transliterates into Greek the Aramaic, which, depending on word
division, can have two meanings. The early fathers understood the term as a credal
declaration, "The Lord has come," namely, as in the Aramaic *Maran Atha* (see 1 Cor
16:22). On the other hand, when the Aramaic is divided as *Marana Tha*, the expression is an eschatological prayer in expectation of the parousia, "O Lord, come" or
"Come, Lord Jesus" (see Rev 22:20).

45. Matt 7:6. 46. See Wis 1:14; Sir 18:1; 24:8, LXX; Rev 4:11; Isa 43:7. 47. See Matt
24:31. 48. See Matt 21:9, 15.

XI.1. If anyone comes to teach you all that was said above, receive him.   188
2. But if the teacher undertakes to teach another doctrine so as to destroy
[these things], do not listen; but if one teaches in order to increase justice
and knowledge of the Lord, receive such a one as [you would] the Lord.
3. As to the apostles and the prophets, act as follows in accord with the
Gospel. 4. May every apostle who comes to you be received as the Lord.
5. But he is to remain for only one day and—should there be need—for
the following day; if he remains three days, he is a false prophet. 6. Upon
departing, the apostle is to receive nothing other than some bread until he
reaches his next lodging; if he requests money, he is a false prophet.
7. You are not to test any prophet who speaks under the inspiration of the
Spirit, nor are you to judge him. For every [other] sin will be forgiven, but
this sin will not be.[49] 8. Not every person who speaks under the inspiration of the Spirit is a prophet, but only those who imitate the Lord. The
false prophet and the true prophet are recognized by their behavior.
9. Every prophet who orders a meal to be served under the inspiration of
the Spirit will abstain from it; but if he does not, he is a false prophet.
10. And every prophet who teaches the truth but does not put into practice what is taught is a false prophet. 11. And every prophet who is proven
and true and who acts in view of the mystery of the Church in the world
but who does not teach others to do what he does is not to be judged by
you, for God will judge. This, in fact, is how the ancient prophets acted.
12. But whoever, under the inspiration of the Spirit, says to you, "Give me
some money or something else," do not listen to this person; but if someone asks you on behalf of others who are in need, let no one judge.

XII.1. Let everyone who comes in the name of the Lord[50] be received; but   189
after testing them you will know them, for you will know what is true and
what is false. 2. If the one who comes is a traveler, give help to the best of
your abilities; but this person is to remain with you for only two or three
days, if it is necessary. 3. If some wish to stay with you and have a trade,
let them work and eat. 4. But if they have no trade, intelligently provide
the means so that a Christian may not live among you in idleness. 5. If
they do not wish to do so, they traffic in Christ. Beware of these.

XIII.1. But every true prophet who wishes to settle among you is de-   190
serving of food.[51] 2. Likewise the true teacher himself, like the worker, is
worthy of food.[52] 3. Therefore take the first fruits of the winepress and of
the harvest and of cattle and of sheep and give them to the prophets, for
these are your high priests. 4. And if you have no prophet, give them to
the poor. 5. If you make bread, take the first fruits from it and give them
according to the commandment. 6. Likewise, when you open a jug of wine
or of oil, take the first fruits from it and give them to the prophets. 7. From

---

49. See Matt 12:31.   50. Matt 21:9; Ps 118:26.   51. See Matt 10:10; 1 Cor 9:13ff.;
1 Tim 5:18.   52. Ibid.

your money, from your garments, and from all your goods, take the first fruits as seems best to you and give them according to the commandment.

191   XIV.1. And on the Lord's Day[d] gather to break bread and to give thanks, after having confessed your offenses[53] so that your sacrifice may be pure. 2. But let no one who has a difference with a comrade join you till they are reconciled so that your sacrifice not be defiled.[54] 3. For this is what the Lord said, "In every place and time let there be offered to me a pure sacrifice for I am a great king, says the Lord, and my name is revered among the nations."[55]

192   XV.1. Appoint for yourselves bishops and deacons worthy of the Lord, gentlemen, not seekers after money, those who are truthful and proven, for they serve you in the ministry of prophets and teachers. 2. And so do not despise them, for they are honored among you like the prophets and teachers. 3. Reprove one another, not in anger but in peace as you find in the Gospel. And let no one speak to any person who has done harm to another, nor is such a one to hear a word from you before doing penance.[56] 4. But offer your prayers, your alms, and all you do according to the Gospel of our Lord.[57]

193   XVI.1. Watch over your life; may your lamps not be extinguished, and may your loins not be ungirded.[58] But be ready, for you do not know the hour when our Lord will come.[59] 2. Come together frequently in order to seek what is fitting for your souls since the whole time of your faith will profit you nothing if, at the end, you have not obtained perfection. 3. In these last days false prophets and corrupters will multiply; sheep will be turned into wolves; and love will be changed into hatred.[60] 4. For as lawlessness increases, people will hate one another, persecute, and betray,[61] and the deceiver of the world will appear as a son of God.[62] He will do signs and wonders.[63] The world will be delivered into his hands, and he will commit iniquities as have never been done since the beginning of the world.[64] 5. Then all created people will come to the fire of testing.[65] Many will be scandalized[66] and perish; but those who endure in their faith will be saved[67] by him who is [made] accursed. 6. And then the signs of truth will appear. First, the sign spread out in the sky. Then the sign of the sound of the trumpet.[68] And then the third, the resurrection of the dead,[69]

---

d. The Greek here reads *Kata kuriakn de kuriou,* literally "On the Lord's Day of the Lord," this redundancy perhaps showing that the term "Lord's Day" had already become standard at the time of the *Didache's* final redaction. This is the oldest use of the designation outside Revelation 1:10. The term is analogous to "the Lord's Supper," namely, the day that commemorates Jesus.

53. See Jas 5:16.   54. See Matt 5:23ff.   55. Mal 1:11, 14.   56. See Matt 5:22–26; 18:15–35.   57. See Matt 6:2–18.   58. See Luke 12:35.   59. See Matt 24:42, 44; Mark 13:35; Luke 12:40.   60. See Matt 24:11ff.   61. See Matt 24:10.   62. See 2 Thess 2:4; 2 John 7.   63. See Matt 24:24.   64. See Joel 2:2; Dan 12:1; Mark 13:19.   65. See Zech 13:8ff.   66. See Matt 24:10.   67. See Matt 10:22; 24:13.   68. See Matt 24:31; 1 Cor 15:52; 1 Thess 4:16.   69. See Matt 24:30–31.

7. yet not of all people but as has been said, "The Lord will come and all the holy ones with him."[70] 8. Then the world will see the Lord coming upon the clouds of heaven . . .[71]

8. CLEMENT OF ROME

Clement of Rome is generally accepted as Peter's third successor, thus being the fourth bishop of Rome.

CPG 1: nos. 1001ff. * Altaner (1961) 99–102 * Altaner (1966) 45–47 * Bardenhewer (1908) 25–28 * Bardenhewer (1910) 23–26 * Bardenhewer (1913) 1:98–113 * Bardy (1929) 26–27 * Bautz 1:1048–49 * Casamassa 35–77 * Cross 11–13 * Goodspeed 7–11 * Hamell 26–27 * Jurgens 1:6–13 * Leigh-Bennett 1–8 * Quasten 1:42–53 * Steidle 11–13 * Tixeront 10–12 * CATH 2:1183–85 * CE 4:12–17 * DACL 3:1872–1902 * DCB 1:554–59 * DHGE 12:1089–93 * DictSp 2.1:962–63 * DPAC 1:712–14 * DTC 3.1:48–54 * EC 3:1809–11 * EEC 1:181 * EEChr 1:264–65 * LTK 2:1227–28 * NCE 3:926–28 * NCES 3:773–75 * ODCC 360–61 * PEA (1894) 4.1:13–20 * PEA (1991) 3:28–29 * RACh 3:188–97 * TRE 8:113–20

Th. Schermann, *Griechische Zauberpapyri und das Gemeinde- und Dankgebet im I. Klemensbrief*, TU 34, 2b (Leipzig, 1909). * J. Brinktrine, *Der Messopferbegriff in den ersten zwei Jahrhunderten*, FthSt 21 (Freiburg i. B., 1918) 68–76. * A. Baumstark, "Trishagion und Qeduscha," JL 3 (1923) 18–32. * L.M.A. Haughwout, "Church Organization according to Clement," AThR 6 (1923–24) 273–84. * J. Marty, "Etude des textes cultuels de prière conservès par les 'Pères apostoliques,'" RHPR 10 (1930) 99ff. * U. Wilcken, *Mitteilungen aus der Würzburger Papyrussammlung, Nr. 3: Ein liturgisches* Fragment (3. Jahrh.), AAB, phil.-hist. Klasse, no. 6 (Berlin, 1934) 31–36. * G. Bardy, "Le sacerdoce chrétien d'après les pères apostoliques," VS 53 (1935) 1–28. * E. Barnikol, "Die vorsynoptische Auffassung von Taufe und Abendmahl im I. Clemensbriefe," *Theologische Jahrbücher* 4 (1936) 77–80. * J. Quasten, *Monumenta Eucharistica et Liturgia Vetustissima* (Bonn, 1937) 327–34. * B. Poschmann, *Paenitentia Secunda* (Bonn, 1939) 112ff. * W.C. van Unnik, "1 Clement 34 and the 'Sanctus,'" VC 5 (1951) 204–48. * E. Ferguson, "The Ministry of the Word in the First Two Centuries," ResQ 1 (1957) 21–31. * E. Ferguson, "Ordination in the Ancient Church," ResQ 5 (1961) 17–32, 67–82, 130–46. * O. Koch, "Eigenart und Bedeutung des Eschatologie im theologis hen Aufriss des 1. Clemensbrief," *Theophania* 17 (Bonn, 1964) 56–64. * G. Konidaris, "De la prétendu divergence des formes dans le régime du christianisme primitif: ministres et ministères du temps des apôtres: la mort de s. Polycarpe," Ist 10 (1964) 59–92. * R. Padberg, "Gottesdienst und Kirchenordnung im (ersten) Klemensbrief," ALW 9 (1965–66) 367–74. * C. Riggi, "La liturgia della pace nella 'Prima Clementis,'" Sal 33 (1971) 31–70, 205–61. * M. Jourjon, "Remarques sur le vocabulaire sacerdotal dans la 1 Clementis," in *Epektasis: Mélanges patristiques offerts au Cardinal Daniélou* (Paris, 1972). * E. Ferguson, "'When You Come Together': 'Epi to auto' in Early Christian Literature," ResQ 16 (1973) 202–8. * G. Blond, "Clement of Rome," in W. Rordorf and others, *The Eucharist of the Early Christians* (New York, 1978) 24–47. * E.W. Fisher, "'Let Us Look upon the Blood of Christ' (1 Clement 7:4)," VC 34 (1980) 218–36. * J. Fuellenbach, *Ecclesiastical Office and the Primacy of Rome: An Evaluation of Recent*

---

70. Zech 14:5.   71. See Matt 24:30.

Theological Discussion of First Clement, Studies in Christian Antiquity 20 (Washington, D.C., 1980). * A. Faivre, "Naissance d'un laïcat chrétien: les enjeux d'un mot," FZPT 33 (1986) 391–429. * S. Légasse, "La prière pour les chefs d'Etat: antécédents juda-ïques et témoins chrétiens du premier siècle," NTes 29 (1987) 236–53. * H.O. Maier, *The Social Setting of Ministry as Reflected in the Writings of Hermas, Clement, and Igna-tius*, diss. (Waterloo, Ont., Canada, 1991).

8-A. Letter to the Corinthians[†]

Although this work does not bear his name, ancient and reliable sources attribute the Letter to the Corinthians to Clement. The date of its composition is commonly given as 96/98 A.D., although the argument has been made that the letter was written as early as 80 A.D. The abundance of Old Testament citations may indicate that the author came from a strongly Jewish background.

The occasion of the letter was strife in the city of Corinth, where, for one reason or another, ministers were being deposed from office. Clement, whether on his own initiative or having been asked, wrote to the Corinthians in the name of the Roman Church. Calling the faithful to repentance, the bishop of Rome insisted that there be due order in all things, especially those pertaining to ministry, presumably liturgical ministry. We may surmise that Clement's intervention was successful since, we are told, his letter was customarily read in Corinth during divine services.

194   7. Beloved, we write you not only to warn you but also that we may remember. We are in the same arena, and the same combat awaits us.[1] Let us leave behind vain and useless cares and conform ourselves to the wonderful and venerable norms of our tradition. Let us look at what is good, what is pleasing, what is acceptable in the sight of him who made us.[2] Let us gaze upon the blood of Christ and know how precious that blood is to his Father, the blood that was shed for our salvation, the blood that has prepared the whole world for the grace of repentance. Let us travel back through all generations and learn that in generation to generation the Lord has allowed penance to all who desire to return to him. Noah preached repentance and those who listened to him were saved. Jonah preached destruction to the Ninevites who, repenting of their sin, appeased God by their prayers[3] and were saved even though they were strangers to God.

195   8. Through the Holy Spirit the ministers of God's grace have spoken of doing penance. And the Lord of all things has himself spoken of penance, doing so with an oath: "As I live, says the Lord, I desire not the death of sinners but that they live."[4] And to help us better understand he adds:

[†] Translated from *Epître aux Corinthiens. Clément de Rome*, ed. and trans. J. Jaubert, SChr 167 (Paris, 1971) 110ff.

1. See Phil 1:30; Heb 12:1; 1 Tim 6:12; 2 Tim 3:7.   2. See 1 Tim 2:3; 5:4.   3. See Jonah 3:4–10; Matt 12:41; Luke 11:32.   4. Ezek 18:23; 33:11.

"Repent, O house of Israel, of your iniquity. Tell the children of my people, 'Even though your sins extend from the earth to heaven, and even though they be redder than scarlet and blacker than sackcloth,[5] if you return to me with all your heart and say "Father," I will hear you as I do a holy people.'"[6] Elsewhere he says, "Wash and purify yourselves. Remove from my sight the wickedness of your souls; put an end to your evil-doings; learn to do good; seek after justice and free the oppressed; do what is right to the fatherless, and do justice to the widow. Come, then, let us discuss, says the Lord. And even though your sins be like crimson, I will make them as white as the snow; and if they are like scarlet, I will make them white as wool. And if you agree to hear me, you will taste the good things of the Lord. But if you do not hear me, the sword will devour you. The mouth of the Lord has spoken these things."[7] The Lord's almighty will has determined these things since he wills that all who love him should repent.

40. Since these things are evident to us, and after having studied the depths of divine knowledge,[8] we should methodically do what the Lord has commanded us to carry out at determined times. He has ordered that the offerings and the [liturgical] services[a] take place not randomly or in a disorderly fashion but at appropriate times and hours. Where and by whom he desires these things to be done, he himself has decided by his own supreme will so that everything be done rightly according to his good pleasure and that they confirm to his will. So it is that those who make their offerings at the appointed times are pleasing and blessed, for they do not err in obeying the Lord's prescriptions. For the high priest has been assigned his proper functions; the priests have their own places; the Levites have their special services. The laic[b] is bound by the prescriptions proper to the laity.

41. May each of you, brethren, give thanks to God in the rank proper to each, doing so with a correct conscience, with dignity, not violating the rules determined for each person's ministry. Brethren, it is not in every place that sacrifices are offered, whether perpetual or votive, whether sin offerings or those of guilt,[9] but only in Jerusalem. And even in Jerusalem they are not offered in any place whatsoever, but on the altar before the temple, after a careful examination of the victim by the high priest and the ministers mentioned above. Those who act contrary to God's will deserve the punishment of death. You see, brethren, the higher the knowledge for which we are deemed worthy, the greater the danger to which we are exposed.

196

197

---

a. The Greek word here and in similar instances is *leitourgia*, namely, "public service."

b. The first use of this word in Christian literature.

5. See Isa 50:3; Rev 6:12.   6. A compact quotation from an unknown apocryphal Ezechiel.   7. Isa 1:16–20.   8. See Rom 11:33; 1 Cor 2:10.   9. See Exod 29:38–42; Num 28:3–8; Lev 4:3ff.

198   42. The apostles received the Gospel for us through Jesus Christ the
Lord, who was sent by God. Christ comes from God, the apostles come
from Christ; both orderly arrangements flow from the will of God. Having
received instruction, filled with confidence by our Lord Jesus Christ's resurrection, strengthened by God's word, and with the complete assurance
of the Holy Spirit, the apostles went forth proclaiming the good news that
God's Kingdom was at hand. They preached throughout the countryside
and in the cities, and they appointed the first fruits [converts], whom they
tested[10] by the Spirit in order to make them bishops and deacons for those
who would believe. There was nothing novel here because much earlier
Scripture somewhere spoke of bishops and deacons, "I will establish their
bishops in righteousness and their deacons in faith."[11]

199   44. The apostles also knew, through our Lord Jesus Christ, that there
should be no dispute concerning the ministry of the bishop. For this
reason the apostles, having received a perfect knowledge of the future,
appointed those [ministers] mentioned above, and afterwards they established the rule that after the death of those whom the apostles appointed,
other approved men should succeed them in their [liturgical] ministry.
And so these men who had been appointed by the apostles or appointed
afterwards by other eminent men with the approval of the whole Church,
who have blamelessly served the flock of Christ, doing so with humility,
peacefully, and with dignity—and for a long time receiving the testimony
of all—these men, we believe, are not justly deposed from their [litur-
gical] ministry. It is no small sin on our part if we eject from the episcopacy those who without blame and in holiness have presented [to God]
the offerings. Blessed are presbyters who have finished their journey and
whose life has come to a fruitful and perfect end; they need not fear being
removed from the place assigned them. For we see that some of them, in
fact, despite their good behavior, you have removed from the functions
they exercised with honor and beyond reproach.

200   59. [. . .][c] We request with continual prayer and supplication that the
Creator of the universe keep intact the number which has been counted of
his elect[12] throughout the world because of his beloved child Jesus Christ
our Lord, through whom he called us from darkness to light,[13] from ignorance to the knowledge of the glory of his name. [May we, Lord,] hope
in your name which is the beginning of all creation; you have opened the
eyes of our heart[14] so that we may know you; you alone[15] are the Most
High in the highest heavens and the Holy One among the holy ones.[16]
You humble the arrogance of the proud,[17] you bring down the designs of

---

c. It has been suggested that the following prayer has its origins in the liturgy,
perhaps being a formula used in Rome or in Egypt.
    10. See 1 Tim 3:10; Titus 1:5–8; 1 Tim 3:2–7.   11. Isa 60:17, but the Scripture here says
nothing about deacons.   12. See Rev 6:11; 4 Esdr 4:36.   13. See Isa 42:16; Acts 26:18;
2 Pet 2:9.   14. See Eph 1:18.   15. See John 17:3.   16. See Isa 57:15.   17. See Isa 13:11.

the nations,[18] you raise up the humble and humble the exalted,[19] you enrich and you impoverish,[20] you kill and you bestow life,[21] you are the sole benefactor of spirits and the God of all flesh,[22] you probe the depths,[23] you observe the things we do,[24] you assist those in danger and save those in despair,[25] you are the creator and overseer of all spirits,[26] you multiply the nations on the earth and have chosen from among them all those who love you through Jesus Christ your beloved child through whom you have instructed, sanctified, and honored us.[27] Lord, we ask you to be our help and protector.[28] Save those among us who are in tribulation; uplift those who have fallen; show yourself to those in need; heal the sick, lead back those of your people who wander away,[29] feed the hungry, free prisoners, raise up the weak,[30] give courage to the timid. Do this so that all nations may know that you alone are God,[31] that Jesus Christ is your child, and that "we are your people, the sheep of your pasture."[32]

60. By your deeds you have made manifest the eternal arrangement of the world. Lord, you created the world; you are faithful through all generations.[33] You are just in your judgments, wonderful in power and majesty, wise when creating things and intelligent when strengthening them, good in what is visible and gracious to those who trust you. You are merciful and compassionate.[34] Forgive our iniquities and injustices, our sins and our omissions. Remember not the sin of your servants, both men and women, but cleanse us with your purifying faith[35] and direct our steps[36] so that we may walk in holiness of heart[37] and that we may do what is good and pleasing to you[38] and to those who govern us. Yes, Lord, may your countenance shine upon us[39] for good is peace, that we may be protected by your powerful hand[40] and that we might be delivered from all sin by your uplifted arm,[41] that you might deliver us from all who unjustly hate us.[42] Grant peace and harmony to us as well as to all who live in this world, as you have given these to our ancestors when they piously called upon you with faith and truth,[43] so that we might obey your all-powerful and glorious name as well as obey our leaders and rulers on earth. 201

61. Lord, by your magnificent and inexpressible power you have given them royal power so that we might acknowledge the glory and honor you have given them and, being subject to them, may not oppose your will. Lord, give them health, peace, harmony, and stability so that they without 202

---

18. See Ps 33:10.   19. See Job 5:11; Isa 10:33; Ezek 17:24; 21:31.   20. See 1 Sam 2:7.   21. See Deut 32:39; 1 Sam 2:6; 2 Kgs 5:7.   22. See Num 16:22; 27:16.   23. See Dan 3:55.   24. See Esth 5:18.   25. See Jdt 9:11.   26. See Amos 4:13; Job 10:12. 27. See John 12:26; 17:17.   28. See Ps 118:14.   29. See Ezek 34:16.   30. See Job 4:4. 31. See 1 Kgs 8:60; 2 Kgs 9:19; Isa 37:20; Ezek 36:23; John 17:3.   32. Ps 79:13. 33. See Deut 7:9.   34. See Joel 12:13; Sir 2:11.   35. See John 17:17.   36. See Pss 40:3; 119:133.   37. See 1 Kgs 9:4.   38. See Deut 6:18; 12:25, 28; 13:19; 21:9.   39. See Num 6:25; Pss 31:17; 66:2; etc.   40. See Isa 51:16; Wis 5:16; etc.   41. See Deut 4:34; 5:15; etc. 42. See Pss 18:18; 106:10; etc.   43. See Ps 145:18.

harshness may exercise the authority you have given them. Heavenly Lord and king of the ages,[44] you give glory to the children of men; you give honor and power over earthly things. Lord, guide their decisions according to what is good and pleasing in your sight so that by piously exercising in peace and mildness what you have granted them they may find your graciousness. You alone can bring about these and greater things. We thank you through Jesus Christ the high priest and protector of our souls, through whom you receive glory and majesty now and for all generations and for all ages. Amen.

9. IGNATIUS OF ANTIOCH. LETTERS

According to Origen (WEC 1:**43**), Ignatius, who refers to himself as *Theophorus*, namely, the "God-bearer," was the second bishop of Antioch, the successor of Saint Peter; Eusebius (WEC 2:**81**), however, says that Ignatius was the third bishop of this city, following Euodius, Peter's successor. At any rate, during the reign of the emperor Trojan (98–117), Ignatius was arrested, placed under the guard of ten soldiers, and was being taken to Rome for execution. On the way he wrote seven letters, which rank among the most precious gems of early Christian literature.

Stopping at Smyrna (modern Izmir, a port city in what is now western Turkey), Ignatius was visited and offered encouragement by the bishops of Ephesus, Tralles, and Magnesia (all in what is today western Turkey). To each he gave a letter for their respective congregations. Additionally, he wrote to the church at Rome, requesting its members not to intercede with the authorities on his behalf. The Roman military contingent and its prisoner continued on to Troas. While there he wrote three letters, one to the faithful at Philadelphia (today Alasehir in western Turkey), another to the church at Smyrna, and a third to Polycarp, the bishop of Smyrna, a port city known today as Izmir in western Turkey. Although contemporary witness is lacking, tradition indicates that the holy bishop of Antioch did indeed reach Rome, where he was martyred, being the victim of attacks by wild beasts in the Coliseum.

These seven letters, so eloquent and so full of spiritual and theological insight, have come down to us in three collections or recensions: e.g., the short and earliest recension; the long recension—dating from the fourth century and incorporating various interpolations and containing spurious material; and the Syriac abridgment of three of Ignatius's letters. There was a time when some scholars doubted the authenticity of these seven letters, due to their witness of a very well-organized form of ordained church leadership and especially the prominent role accorded to the bishop. Today, however, there is almost universal agreement that the letters are indeed genuine.

---

44. See Tob 13:7, 11; 1 Tim 1:17.

CPG 1: nos. 1025ff. * Altaner (1961) 106–9 * Altaner (1966) 47–50 * Bardenhewer (1908) 30–35 * Bardenhewer (1910) 27–32 * Bardenhewer (1913) 1:119–46 * Bardy (1929) 55–57 * Bautz 2:1251–55 * Casamassa 103–54 * Cross 15–18 * Goodspeed 13–20 * Hamell 28–30 * Jurgens 1:17–26 * Quasten 1:63–76 * Steidle 13–14 * Tixeront 13–16 * CATH 5:1190–92 * CE 7:644–47 * DACL 7.1:67 * DCB 3:209–23 * DHGE 25:684–86 * DictSp 7.2:1250–66 * DPAC 2:1743–45 * DTC 7.1:685–713 * EC 6:1598–99 * EEC 1:404–5 * EEChr 1:559–60 * LTK 5:407–9 * NCE 7:353–54 * NCES 6:310–12 * ODCC 817–18 * PEA (1991) 5:924–26 * TRE 16:40–45

A. Scheiwiler, *Die Elemente der Eucharistie in den ersten drei Jahrhunderten*, FLDG 3, no. 4 (Mainz, 1903) 17–26. * J. Brinktrine, *Der Messopferbegriff in den ersten zwei Jahrhunderten*, FThSt 21 (Freiburg i. B., 1918) 76–84. * J. Vieujan, "La doctrine de s. Ignace d'Antioche sur l'Eglise," REL 26 (1934/35) 254–58. * P. Batiffol, *L'Eucharistie, la présence réelle et la transubstantion*, 9th ed., Etudes d'histoire et de théologie positive, 2nd series (Paris, 1939) 39–50. * J. Quasten, *Monumenta Eucharistica et Liturgica Vetustissima* (Bonn, 1935–37) 334–36. * D.C. Lusk, "What Is the Historic Episcopate? An Inquiry Based upon the Letters of Ignatius of Antioch," SJT 3 (1950) 255–77. * G. Jouassard, "Aux origines du culte des martyrs dans le christianisme: S. Ignace d'Antioche," RSR 39 (1951/52) 362–67. * E. Ferguson, "The Ministry of the Word in the First Two Centuries," ResQ 1 (1957) 21–31. * H. Koester, "Geschichte und Kultus im Johannesevangelium und bei Ignatius von Antiochien," ZTK 54 (1957) 56–69. * E. Ferguson, "Ordination in the Ancient Church," ResQ 5 (1961) 17–32, 67–82, 130–46. * O. Perler, "Eucharistie et unité de l'église d'après s. Ignace d'Antioche," in *XXXV Congreso Eucaristico International* (Barcelona, 1962) 244–49. * J. Colson, "Le rôle du presbytérium et de l'évêque dans le contrôle de la liturgie chez s. Ignace d'Antioche et le rôle de Rome au IIe siècle," ParL 47 (1965) 14–24. * W.L. Dulière, "Un problème à résoudre: l'acceptation du sang eucharistique par les premiers chrétiens juifs," STh 20 (1966) 62–93. * M. Jourjon, "La présidence de l'eucharistie chez Ignace d'Antioche," LV 16 (1967) 26–32. * J.F. McCue, "Bishops, Presbyters, and Priests in Ignatius of Antioch," TS 28 (1967) 828–34. * M. Thurian, "L'organisation du ministère dans l'église primitive selon s. Ignace d'Antioche," VerC 81 (1967) 26–38. * G. Saber, "La conception baptismale de s. Ignace d'Antioche," Mel 5 (1969) 177–96. * A. Vilela, "Le presbyterium selon s. Ignace d'Antioche," BLE 73 (1973) 161–86. * R. Johanny, "Ignatius of Antioch," in W. Rordorf and others, *The Eucharist of the Early Christians* (New York, 1978) 48–70. * R. Gryson, Les "lettres" attribuées à Ignace d'Antioche et l'apparition de l'épiscopat monarchique," RTL 10 (1979) 446–53. * T. Marsh, "The History of the Sacramental Concept," MilS 3 (1979) 21–56. * B. Dupuy, "Aux origines de l'épiscopat: le corpus des lettres d'Ignace d'Antioche et le ministère d'unité," Ist 27 (1982) 269–77. * D. Dufrasne, "S. Ignace d'Antioche: l'Eglise une dans le Père commun," ComL 66:4 (1984) 349–55. * F. Bergamelli, "Nel Sangue di Cristo: la vita nuova del cristiano secondo il martire s. Ignazio di Antiochita," EphL 100 (1986) 152–70. * R.F. Stoops Jr., "If I Suffer . . . Epistolary Authority in Ignatius of Antioch," HThR 80 (1987) 161–78. * L. Wehr, *Arznei der Unsterblichkeit: die Eucharistie bei Ignatius von Antiochien und im Johannesevangelium*, Neutestamentliche Abhandlungen, n.s., 18 (Münster, 1987). * A. Brent, "The Relations Between Ignatius and the Didascalia," SCJ 8 (1991) 129–56. * J.E. Lawyer Jr., "Eucharist and Martyrdom in the Letters of Ignatius of Antioch," AThR 73 (1991) 280–96. * A. Pettersen, "The Laity—Bishop's Pawn? Ignatius of Antioch on the Obedient Christian," SJT 44 (1991) 39–56. * A.H.B. Logan, "Post-Baptismal Chrismation in Syria: The Evidence of Ignatius, the 'Didache' and the Apostolic Constitutions," JThSt, n.s., 49 (1998) 92–108.

9-A. To the Ephesians[†]

203   Ignatius, also called Theophorus, sends best wishes for pure joy in Jesus Christ to the Church at Ephesus[a] in Asia, a Church deserving of congratulations, blessed as it is. [. . .]

204   III. [. . .] Since love does not allow me to be silent in regard to you, I am anxious to exhort you to walk in accord with God's thinking. For Jesus Christ, our inseparable life, is the thought of the Father, just as the bishops, appointed throughout the whole world, are in the thought of Jesus Christ.

205   IV. And so it is fitting for you to walk in accord with the thinking of your bishop, something you are already doing. Your presbyterate, justifiably honored and worthy of God, is in harmony with the bishop like strings with a harp; and so, in the unity of your affection and in the harmony of your love, you sing of Jesus Christ. May each one of you also become a choir so that in the harmony of your unity, taking the keynote from God in unity, you may sing with one voice through Jesus Christ a hymn to the Father so that he might hear and recognize you by your good works, like members of his Son. And so it behooves you to be inseparable and united so as to participate in God at all times.

206   V. If, in fact, in so short a time I have become so attached to your bishop—an attachment that is not human but spiritual—how much more do I congratulate you for being so deeply united to him, just as the Church is united to Christ and Christ is to the Father so that all things be in perfect unity. Be not deceived. If someone is not within the sanctuary, that person is deprived of the "bread of God."[1] For if the prayer of two people together has such power,[2] how much more has that of the bishop and the entire Church. Those who do not come to the common gathering have already shown pride and have judged themselves, for it is written that "God opposes the proud."[3] And so let us take care not to oppose the bishop so that we may be submissive to God.

207   VI. The more we see the bishop being silent, the more we should reverence him; for it is necessary that we receive the person whom the master of the house sends to administer his house[4] just as we would receive the one who sent this person.[5] And so it is clear that we are to look upon the bishop as if he were the Lord himself. [. . .]

[†]All letters translated from *Lettres. Ignace d'Antioche . . .*, 3rd rev. edition, ed. and trans. Th. Camelot, SChr 10 (Paris, 1958).

a. Ephesus: today Küçükmenderes on the Aegean Sea.

1. John 6:33.   2. See Matt 18:20.   3. Jas 4:6; 1 Pet 5:5; see Prov 3:34.   4. See Luke 12:42; Matt 24:45.   5. See Matt 10:40.

XIII. Make an effort, then, to gather more frequently in order to thank 208
God [celebrate the Eucharist?] and give praise. For when you gather often,
Satan's powers are overthrown, and his destructive work is destroyed by
the unity of your faith. [. . .]

XVIII. [. . .] Our God Jesus Christ was carried in the womb of Mary ac- 209
cording to the divine plan [and was born] from the seed of David[6] and
from the Holy Spirit. He was born and was baptized in order to purify the
water by his passion.

XX. [. . .] I will [send additional explanations] especially if the Lord re- 210
veals to me that each of you in particular and all of you together, through
grace that comes from his name, gather together in the same faith and in
Jesus Christ "who descended from David according to the flesh,"[7] Son of
Man and Son of God, so that you gather out of obedience to the bishop
and to the presbyterate, in perfect unity, breaking the same bread which is
the medicine of immortality, an antidote so that one does not die but lives
forever in Jesus Christ.

9-B. To the Magnesians[a]

Ignatius, also called Theophorus, to the church which is blessed with 211
the grace of God the Father in Jesus Christ our Savior, in whom I greet this
church at Magnesia by the Meander. I wish it all joy in God the Father and
in Jesus Christ.

III. It is fitting that you not take advantage of your bishop's youthful 212
age but, because of the power of God the Father, show him all respect. I
know, in fact, that your holy presbyters have not taken advantage of his
youthfulness, but like those who are wise in God, they yield to him, not to
him but to the Father of Jesus Christ who is the bishop of all. [. . .]

IV. And so we should not merely bear the name of Christian but also be 213
one. There are some who always refer to the bishop but act completely
apart from him. It seems to me that such people do not have a good conscience, in that their gatherings are neither legitimate nor in conformity
with the Lord's commandment.

VI. [. . .] I implore you, attempt to do everything in harmony with God 214
and under the presidency of the bishop who takes the place of God, the presbyters taking the place of the council of the apostles, and the deacons, who
are so dear to me, being entrusted with the ministry of Jesus Christ who before time was with the Father and who in these last days has appeared. Follow God's ways, all of you; respect one another; do not regard your neighbor
according to the flesh; but always love one another in Jesus Christ. Let there
be nothing among you that can divide you, but unite yourselves to the
bishop and to those who preside as an image and lesson of incorruptibility.

---

a. Magnesians: residents of Manisa or Manissa in western Turkey.
6. See John 7:42; Rom 1:3; 2 Tim 2:8.   7. Rom 1:3.

215   VII. Just as the Lord did nothing, whether by himself or by his apostles, apart from the Father[1] with whom he is one, so neither are you to do anything without the bishop and the presbyters. Do not try to convince yourselves that what you do on your own is acceptable, but do everything in common: one prayer, one supplication, one mind; one hope in love,[2] in irreproachable joy, that is, Jesus Christ to whom nothing is preferable. Come together, all of you, as one temple of God, around one altar,[3] around one Jesus Christ who has come from the one Father and who remained one in him and who has gone on to him.[4]

216   IX. If, therefore, those who lived in the former order of things have come to a new hope, no longer observing the Sabbath but the Lord's Day, the day when our life was raised up by him and by his death (although some deny this) and if through this mystery we have received the faith, this is why we hold fast in order to be found as [true] disciples of Jesus Christ, our only teacher—how then can we live without him since even the prophets, being his disciples by the Spirit, awaited him as their teacher? [. . .]

9-C. To the Trallians[a]

217   II. When you submit to the bishop as if to Jesus Christ, I do not see you living according to human standards but according to Jesus Christ who has died for you so that, believing in his death, you might escape death. And so it is necessary—as is your present practice—to do nothing without the bishop. Also submit yourselves to the presbyterate as if to the apostles of "Jesus Christ our hope"[1] in whom we expect to live forever. It is also necessary that the deacons, being servants[2] of the mysteries of Jesus Christ, be pleasing to all in every way. For they are not servants of food and drink but servants of the Church of God.[3] And so they are to avoid like fire all reason for reproach.

218   III. Likewise, let all respect the deacons as we would Jesus Christ; also the bishop who is the image of the Father; and the presbyters like God's council and like the assembly of the apostles; without these we cannot speak of the Church. [. . .]

9-D. To the Philadelphians[a]

219   IV. Take care, then, to participate in the one Eucharist, for there is only one flesh of our Lord Jesus Christ, and only one cup to unite us with his blood,

---

1. See John 5:19, 30; 8:28.   2. See Eph 4:4-6.   3. See Heb 13:10.   4. See John 8:42; 13:3;16:28.

a. Trallians: residents of Tralles (today Aydin) on one of the slopes of Mount Messogis in western Turkey.

1. 1 Tim 1:1.   2. See 1 Cor 4:1.   3. See ibid.

a. Philadelphians: residents of what today is Alasehir in western Turkey.

and one altar, just as there is one bishop with the presbyterate and the deacons, my fellow servants. And so whatever you do, do in the name of God.

9-E. To the Smyrnians[a]

VI. [. . .] Consider those who have a different opinion concerning the   220
grace of Jesus Christ which has come to us; see how they are opposed to
the mind of God. They have no concern for charity, nor for widows, nor
for orphans, nor for the oppressed, nor for those in prison or for those
who have been set free, nor for the hungry or the thirsty.

VII. They abstain from the Eucharist and from prayer because they do   221
not confess that the Eucharist is the flesh of our Savior Jesus Christ,[1] the
flesh which suffered for our sins and which the Father in his goodness has
raised from the dead. And so those who refuse the "gift of God"[2] die in
their disputes. [. . .]

VIII. All of you are to follow the bishop just as Jesus Christ follows his   222
Father, and you are to follow the presbyterate as you would the apostles;
regarding the deacons, respect them as you would God's law. Let no
one do anything apart from the bishop which pertains to the Church.
May there be only one legitimate Eucharist, namely, that done under the
bishop or whomever the bishop has committed it. Wherever the bishop
appears, there the people are to be; just as where Christ Jesus is, there is
the Catholic Church.[b] Without the bishop's permission it is not allowed to
baptize or to hold an agape, but whatever he approves is also pleasing to
God. Thus all that you do will be "sure and steadfast."[3]

9-F. To Polycarp of Smyrna

Although this is a personal letter to the bishop of Smyrna, part of the text
is addressed to the community at large.

V. [. . .] It is also proper that men and women who marry do so with the   223
consent of the bishop so that their marriage take place according to the Lord
and not according to passion. May all things be done for the honor of God.

VI. Be close to the bishop so that God also be close to you. I offer my life   224
for those who submit to the bishop, to presbyters, to deacons; may I share
with them in God. Work together, fight together, struggle, sleep, arise,
because you are God's stewards,[1] members of God's household, God's servants.[2] [. . .] May your baptism remain as your shield; your faith as your
helmet; your love as your spear; your patience as your armor. [. . .]

---

a. Smyrnians: residents of what today is the port city of Izmir in western Turkey.
b. This is the first use in Christian literature of the term "Catholic (i.e., "universal") Church."
1. See Luke 22:19.   2. John 4:10.   3. Heb 6:19.
1. See Titus 1:7.   2. See ibid.; 1 Cor 4:1.

9-G. To the Romans

225   VII. [. . .] I desire not corruptible food nor the delights of this life; what I desire is the "bread of God,"[1] which is the flesh of Jesus Christ who was of the seed of David;[2] and for drink I desire his blood, which is incorruptible love.

10. PASTOR HERMAS

According to the Muratorian Canon (end of second century), Hermas was the brother of the Roman bishop Pius I, who served as bishop of Rome ca. 140–ca. 154. From the writing of Hermas himself we know that he was a freed slave, a prosperous farmer who fell upon hard times, a husband whose wife had a loose tongue, a father whose children apostatized and denounced him. Further, due to several Hebraisms found in his writing, there is reason to believe that Hermas was of Jewish descent or at least taught by Jewish instructors. Well respected in antiquity, he is considered to be one of the "Apostolic Fathers."

CPG 1: no. 1052 * Altaner (1961) 84–88 * Altaner (1966) 55–58 * Bardenhewer (1908) 38–43 * Bardenhewer (1910) 107–11 * Bardenhewer (1913) 1:557–78 * Bardy (1929) 28–29 * Bautz 2:759 * Casamassa 191–216 * Cross 23–29 * Goodspeed 30–34 * Hamell 32–34 * Jurgens 1:32–38 * Quasten 1:92–105 * Steidle 284 * Tixeront 23–27 * CATH 5:667–69 * CE 7:268–71 * DACL 6.2:2265–90 * DCB 2:912–21 * DictSp 7.1:316–34 * DPAC 1:1197–98 * DTC 6.2:2268–88 * EEC 1:377 * EEChr 1:521–22 * LTK 4:1448–49 * NCE 6:1074 * NCES 6:785–86 * ODCC 760 * PEA (1894) 8.1:722–25 * PEA (1991) 5:420–21 * RACh 14:682–701 * TRE 15:100–108

A. d'Alès, "La discipline pénitentielle d'après le Pasteur d'Hermas," RSR 2 (1911) 105–39, 140–65. * A. Vanbeck, "La pénitence dans le Pasteur d'Hermas," RHL, n.s., 2 (1911) 389–403. * A. d'Alès, *L'Edit de Calliste, étude sur les origines de la pénitence chrétienne* (Paris, 1914) 52–113. * G. Rauschen, *Eucharist and Penance* (St. Louis, 1913) 155–59. * J. Hoh, *Die kirchliche Busse im zeiten Jahrhundert* (Breslau, 1932) 10–34. * J. Schümmer, *Die altchristliche Fastenpraxis,* LQF 27 (Münster, 1933) 124ff., 135ff., 138ff. * J. Svennung, "Statio = 'Fasten,'" ZNW 32 (1933) 294–308. * B. Poschmann, *Paenitentia Secunda* (Bonn, 1939) 134–205. * R.C. Mortimer, *The Origins of Private Penance in the Western Church* (Oxford, 1939). * R. Joly, "La doctrine pénitentielle du Pasteur d'Hermas et l'exégèse récente," RHE 147 (1955) 32–49. * E. Ferguson, "Baptism from the Second to the Fourth Century," ResQ 1 (1957) 185–97. * B. Neunheuser, *Baptism and Confirmation* (St. Louis, 1964) 62–63. * B. Poschmann, *Penance and the Anointing of the Sick* (St. Louis, 1964) 26–35. * S. Giet, "Pénitence ou repentance dans le Pasteur d'Hermas," RDC 17 (1967) 15–30. * J. Massingberd Ford, "A Possible Liturgical Background to the Shepherd of Hermas," *Revue de Qumrân* 6 (1967–69) 531–51. * P. Henne, "Le péché d'Hermas," RT 90 (1990) 640–51. * H.O. Maier, *The Social Setting of the Ministry as Reflected in the Writings of Hermas, Clement, and Ignatius* (Waterloo, Canada, 1991). * P. Henne, "La pénitence et la rédaction du 'Pasteur' d'Hermas," RBibl 98 (1991) 358–97. * C. Osiek, *Shepherd of Hermas: A Commentary* (Minneapolis, 1999).

---

1. John 6:33.   2. See John 7:42; Rom 1:3.

10-A. The "Shepherd" of Hermas[†]

Belonging to a literary genre that is called "apocryphal apocalypses," *The Shepherd* consists of three large sections: Visions (five chapters); Precepts or Mandates (twelve chapters); Parables or Similitudes (ten chapters, the ninth parable being an addition to the original work), this division being more external than logical. Numerous imaginary objects and characters appear in this lengthy work: e.g., a matron constantly growing younger and representing the Church, which is also symbolized by a mystical tower under construction whose stones are Christians and which is entered through the waters of baptism; a shepherd representing the angel of penance. A whole cast of characters is encountered: saints and sinners, apostles and martyrs, various classes of clerics good and bad, etc.

The text, originally written in Greek, appears to date from more than one period and may be the result of combining two different works, one by Hermas, the other by an anonymous author. *The Shepherd* was held in high esteem, especially in the East, where some Christian communities even read the book during the liturgical assembly.

The author focuses on the necessity of penance, an established practice that is offered to all after baptism. A person enters the Church through baptism; a person reenters the Church through penance. Normally given only once, penance is available to all, and yet whoever falls a second time can be saved only "with difficulty" (see Man IV-3). Little is said about reconciliation itself. A theological point of interest concerns the author's Christology. The term "Logos" or the name "Jesus Christ" is never used; it is always "Son of God" or "Lord." Curiously, the Holy Spirit seems to be identified with the "Son of God" before the Incarnation.

Vis I-1. My master sold me to a certain Rhoda in Rome. Many years later I met her again and began to love her as a sister. Some time afterwards, I saw her bathing in the Tiber River; extending my hand, I drew her up out of the water. Seeing her beauty, I said to myself, "I would be a happy man if I had a wife of such beauty and character." I merely thought about this, nothing more. Later, while walking toward Cumes, I was reflecting on the greatness, beauty, and power of God's deeds. Continuing on, I fell asleep. The Spirit took hold of me and led me through a pathless place where no one could walk since it was located in a rocky ravine. I crossed the river which was there and came to a plain where I fell down on my knees and began to pray to God to whom I confessed my sins. As I was praying, the heavens opened and I saw the lady whom I had desired. Greeting me from above, she said, "Greetings, Hermas." I looked at her and said, "My lady, what would you have me do?" She answered, "I was lifted up so that before the Lord I might accuse you of your sins." I said to her, "Are you now my denouncer?" "No," she said. "Listen to what I

226

[†] Translated from *Le pasteur. Hermas*, trans. and ed. R. Joly, SChr 53 (Paris, 1958).

will now tell you: God who dwells in the heavens,[1] who created all things from nothing, and who has multiplied and increased all things[2] because of his holy Church, is angry with you since you have sinned against me." I answered, "Sinned against you? In what way? When did I ever utter an unseemly word? Did I not always hold you in the highest esteem? Did I not always respect you as a sister? Why, my lady, do you falsely accuse me of sin and impurity?" She smiled and said, "Desire for sin has risen in your heart. Do you not believe that the just sin when an evil desire springs up in the heart? Sin exists here, and it is great," she said, "for the righteous have righteous thoughts. It is by reason of righteous thoughts that the glory of the just increases in the heavens, allowing the Lord to show mercy for all that the righteous do. But those whose thoughts are not righteous bring death and captivity upon themselves, especially upon those whose hearts are set on the things of this world, who rejoice in their riches, and who fail to look ahead to future happiness. They will be sorry in that they lack hope and have despaired of themselves and of their life. But you are to pray to God, who will heal your sins,[3] those of your whole household, and those of all the holy ones."

227   Vis I-2. After she had said all this, the heavens closed and I, deeply troubled and afflicted, said to myself, "If this sin is counted against me, how can I obtain salvation? How can I propitiate God in regard to my sins which are so great? What words can I use so that the Lord might be merciful to me?" While reflecting on all this, I saw in front of me a large white chair, made of wool. An elderly woman came, resplendent in garb and holding a book in her hands. She sat down alone and greeted me, "Good day, Hermas." And I, in distress and in tears, said to her, "Good day, my lady." Then she said to me, "Hermas, why are you so sad whereas formerly you were patient, calm, and always smiling? Why are you now so downcast and without cheer?" I replied, "Because a very good woman has said that I have sinned against her." And she said, "Far be this from a servant of God! Nonetheless, perhaps a desire for her has entered your heart. Such a desire, when held by a servant of God, brings about sin, for it is an evil and wicked wish in a complete and already well-tested spirit to desire something evil, and especially if it is Hermas, a temperate person who keeps himself from every evil desire and is full of perfect simplicity and great innocence.

228   Vis III-2. "Now what have they endured?" I asked. "Listen," she said, "blows, prison, great tribulations, the cross, wild beasts, all for the Name of God. This is why, in the holy place, division on the right is reserved for these and for all who suffer for God's name. The others are placed on the left. But for these two groups—those sitting on the right and those on the left—there are the same gifts, the same promises. Yet only those sitting on the right will enjoy a certain glory. You desire to be seated on the

---

1. See Ps 2:4; 123:1.   2. See Gen 1:28; 8:17.   3. See Deut 30:3.

right with these, but your sins are numerous. You have to be purified from them, and all those who have not doubted will be purified of all their sins up to this day." After saying this, she wanted to depart. But throwing myself at her feet, I implored by the Lord that she grant me the vision she had promised. Once again she took my hand, raised me up, and seated me on the left. She sat at the right. Lifting up a splendid rod, she said to me, "Do you see something great?" "My lady, I see nothing," I replied. She said, "Lo, do you not see before you a large tower with shining square stones being built upon the waters?" It was being built square by six young men who had come with her. Many other men brought stones to it, some stones coming from the bottom of the water, others from the land, and they handed these to the six young men who took them and were building. The stones taken from the deep were placed in the building exactly as they were since these were polished and fitted exactly with the other stones. The stones were so joined together that their joining could not be detected, and thus the tower appeared to have been fashioned from one stone. A different fate awaited the stones that were taken from the earth: some were rejected by the young men; some were fitted into the building; others were broken into pieces and thrown a distance from the building. Many other stones lay around the tower. These the young men did not use in the building. Some of these stones were mildewed; others were cracked; others were too short; others were white and round and yet not fit for use in the tower's construction. I saw other stones thrown far from the tower and, falling onto the road where they did not remain, rolled to a pathless place. Others I saw falling into the fire and burning there, and still others falling close to the water and yet not capable of being rolled into the water even though they desired to do so.

Vis III-3. Having shown me these things, she wanted to depart. I said to her, "My lady, for what purpose have I seen these things if I do not know their meaning?" She responded, "You are intent to learn everything possible pertaining to the tower." "Yes, my lady," I said, "in order to tell it to my brethren, to make them happy and by hearing these things to have them know God in all his glory." Her reply, "Many will hear. But having heard, some will rejoice; others, on the other hand, will weep. Yet even these last, if they pay attention and repent, will likewise rejoice. Listen, then, to the parables of the tower, for I will reveal all things to you; only pester me no longer in regard to the revelations since these will end. Nevertheless, you will not cease requesting me about them, for you are insatiable. I am the tower you see being constructed; I am the Church, which you once saw and now see. Ask what you will regarding the tower, and I will reveal it to you so that you may rejoice with the holy ones." I said, "My lady, now that you have judged me worthy to reveal all to me this one time, reveal it." She said to me, "What can be revealed to you will be revealed. Only let your heart be turned toward God and may you doubt nothing concerning what you have seen." I asked her, "My lady, why is

229

the tower built upon the waters?" She replied, "Previously I told you this, and yet you are curious concerning what has been written. Listen, then, as to why the tower is built upon the waters: because your life is and will be saved by water. The tower was erected by the word of the omnipotent and glorious Name, and it is maintained through the invisible power of the Master."

230   Vis III-5. "Listen now concerning the stones that are in the building. They are square and white and fit exactly with each other. These are the apostles, the bishops, the teachers, and the deacons, those who have walked in the holiness of God and who with purity and holiness have exercised their service as bishop, teacher, deacon, on behalf of God's chosen; some have already died whereas others are still living. They have always agreed with one another, kept the peace among themselves, and have listened to each other. Because of this their joinings fit together in the construction of the tower." "But who are the stones that have been taken from the depths of the water, those placed in the building and fitting together with the stones previously placed in the tower?" "These are the ones who have suffered for the name of the Lord." "And the others, those taken from the arid earth, I would like to know who they are, my lady." She answered, "Those going into the building without being cut square are those whom the Lord has approved because they have walked in the right way of the Lord and have perfectly observed his commandments." "And who are those that are being brought and placed in the building?" "They are the ones who are young in the faith and are faithful; the angels admonish them to do good since no evil has been found in them." "Who are those that are rejected and cast away?" "These are the ones who have sinned and who desire to do penance; therefore they were not cast a far distance from the tower; if they repent, they will be helpful for its construction. Those, then, who are inclined to repent, if they do so, will be made strong in the faith provided that they now repent while the tower is still under construction. But if the building is completed, there will be no place for them; they will be rejected; their only advantage will be to rest close to the tower."

231   Man IV-1. "I order you," he [the shepherd] said, "to preserve purity and never let it enter your heart to think of another man's wife nor commit fornication nor do any such sin. Should you do so, you commit a great sin. Now always remember your own wife and you will never sin. If these desires arise in your heart, you will sin; and if there are other thoughts that are just as evil, you commit sin. For this desire in a servant of God is a great sin. But if you commit this evil deed, you prepare death for yourself. Take care; refrain from this desire, for where holiness resides, there iniquity is not to enter the human heart." I said to him, "Sir, allow me to ask several questions." "Speak," he said. "Sir, if a man has a wife who believes in the Lord and if he discovers that she is adulterous, is it a sin for the husband to live with her?" He answered, "As long as he is ignorant of this, he commits no sin; but if he learns about this woman's sin and if she persists

in adultery rather than repents, by living with her the man shares in her sin and participates in her adultery." I said, "Sir, what is the husband to do if the woman persists in this passion?" "He is to send her away," he replied, "and remain by himself. But if, after having sent away his wife, he marries another, he also commits adultery."[4] And I said to him, "But what if the woman who has been put away should repent and desire to return to her husband, is he not to receive her?" And he replied, "To be sure, the husband sins if he does not take her back and brings a great sin upon himself, for he must receive her who has sinned and who repents, but not often. For the servants of God there is only one penance. It is in view of penance, then, that the husband is not to marry again. In this matter husband and wife are treated in the same fashion. Adultery does not only consist in defiling the flesh; it also occurs when someone lives as do the heathens. Therefore, if a person persists in this conduct without repenting, leave that person and cease to live with him or her. Otherwise you share in that individual's sin. This is why you were commanded to remain single, men and women alike, so that penance be possible." He continued: "And so my intent is not to facilitate such sins but that the sinner may sin no more. As to previous sins, there is someone who can bring healing, namely, he who has the power to do all things."

Man IV-3. "Sir," I said, "I have further questions." "Speak," he replied. 232 "I understand that certain teachers have said that there is no other penance than that of the day when we went down into the water and received the remission of our past sins." His response: "What you have heard is exact and indeed true. Whoever has received the pardon of sins is not, in fact, to sin again but rather to remain in holiness. Since you are now inquiring diligently into all things, I will also explain this, without giving occasion of error to those who will believe or have just lately come to believe in the Lord. Those who already believe as well as those who shall believe have no repentance for their sins; they have the remission of their former sins. And so the Lord instituted penance only for those who have been called before these last days. The Lord knows hearts, and knowing beforehand he knew human weakness and the numerous designs of the devil, who desires to harm God's servants and to inflict evil upon them. The Lord took pity on his creature and instituted penance and granted that I direct it. And so I say to you that if anyone, tempted by the devil, should sin after this important and solemn calling, this person may repent only one time. Should he or she sin time and time again, even if he or she repents, penance will be unprofitable and only with difficulty will that person live." I said to him, "Life has returned to me after this detailed information, for now I know that I will be saved if in the future I sin no more." And he said, "You will be saved together with all those who observe these commandments."

---

4. See Matt 5:32; 19:9; Mark 10:11; 1 Cor 7:11.

233   Par viii-6. After the shepherd had examined the branches of all, he said
to me, "I told you that this tree was living. You see how many repented
and were saved." "I see, Sir," I replied, "So that you might know how
great and glorious is God's mercy, he has also given his Spirit to those
who are worthy of doing penance." "Why then, Sir," I asked, "have not
all done penance?" "Those whom the Lord has seen about to purify their
hearts and ready to serve him completely, these he has allowed to repent.
As to those whose deceit and perversity he saw and who were ready to
repent only out of hypocrisy, he has not allowed these to do penance so
that they cannot again blaspheme his Law." I said to him: "Sir, explain to
me now something about those who gave up their branches, what kind of
persons they are, and something about their dwelling place, so that when
they hear this, those who believed and have received the seal and have
broken it and did not keep it whole, may understand what they are doing
and repent; may they receive a seal from you and glorify the Lord because
he took pity on them and has sent you to renew their spirits." "Listen," he
said, "those whose branches were found to be withered and worm-eaten
are the apostates, traitors to the Church, who by their sins blasphemed the
Lord and who are ashamed of his name which was invoked over them.[5]
These, therefore, are lost to God. You see that none among them has done
penance although they heard the words that at my command you spoke
to them. Life has thus departed from them. Those who gave up the green
and undecayed branches are also near them, for they were the hypocrites
who introduced heterodox teachings and who subverted the servants
of God, and especially those who had sinned, preventing these servants
from doing penance by convincing them with their false teachings. And so
these have a hope of repenting. You see that many among them have already done penance from the time when you spoke my commandments to
them. There are still others who wish to repent. Those who have not done
penance have already lost their lives;[6] and as many of them as repented
have become good, and their dwelling was placed within the first walls;
and some of them even ascended into the tower. You see, then, that repentance assures life to sinners; failing to repent brings death."

234   Par viii-8. "As to those who gave up their half-green and half-parched
branches, these are the ones who are engrossed in worldly affairs and
cling not to things that are holy. Therefore half of them are alive and the
other half are dead. But there are many who, having heard my commandments, have done penance and have their dwelling place in the tower.
Some others stood apart and did not repent. For the sake of their affairs
they blasphemed and denied the Lord. Thus by their sins they have lost
life. Many were doubtful. These still have an opportunity to do penance if
they act quickly, and their dwelling place will be within the tower. If they

---

5. See Acts 15:17; Jas 2:7; Gen 48:16; etc.   6. See Matt 10:39; Luke 9:24; 17:33;
John 12:25.

delay doing penance, they will dwell within the walls. But if they do not do penance, they also will have lost their lives. As to those who handed over their branches that are two-thirds withered and one-third green, they are the ones who have denied in various ways. Many of them have done penance and have gone on to dwell inside the tower. Many have definitely rebelled against God and have certainly lost life. Some among them have hesitated and caused dissension; penance is possible for them if they act quickly and do not persist in their pleasures. But if they continue on in their present conduct, they obtain death for themselves."

Par VIII-11. Having finished explaining all the branches, he [the shepherd] said to me, "Go and tell all to do penance, and they will live for God, for the Lord took pity and sent me to offer penance to all even though some of them are not worthy of salvation because of their deeds. But the Lord is patient[7] and desires that those called by his Son be saved." I said to him, "Sir, I hope that after having heard these words, all will do penance. I am persuaded that each person, being fully aware of his or her actions and fearing God, will do penance." His reply: "All who repent from the bottom of their hearts will, as noted above, repent and cleanse themselves from their evil deeds and not increase their sins. These will receive the Lord's healing of their previous sins provided that they have no hesitation concerning the commandments, and if they will live for God. But all those who increase their sins and walk in the passions of this world will condemn themselves to death. You are to walk according to my precepts and you will live for God." Having shown and explained all this, he said to me, "The rest I will make clear to you in a few days."

Par IX-16. "Explain more," I said. He [the shepherd] answered, "What more do you seek?" "Sir," I replied, "why did the stones that have borne these spirits ascend from the bottom of the water for use in constructing the tower?" "They had to rise up from the water to receive life since they could enter the kingdom of God[8] only by rejecting the death that was their former way of life. Those who died also received the seal of the Son of God and entered God's kingdom.[9] Before bearing the name of the Son of God, a person is dead; but after receiving the seal, a person rejects death and receives life. The seal is the water. They descend into the water as those who are dead and come out as those who are alive. To these also this seal was preached and they used it to enter the kingdom of God."[10] "Sir," I said, "why did the forty stones also go up with them after having already received the seal?" His reply: "Because these apostles and teachers who had preached the name of the Son of God, after they fell asleep in the strength and faith of the Son of God, also preached to those who fell asleep before them and who themselves had given them the seal which they preached. And so they went down with them into the water and then came up from it. But these went down alive in order to come out of it alive

235

236

---

7. See 2 Pet 3:9.   8. See John 3:5.   9. Ibid.   10. Ibid.

whereas those who died before them descended while dead and came up alive. With the help of the apostles and teachers they were made to live and came to know the name of the Son of God. This is why they ascended with them and were fitted with them into the building of the tower where they found a place without being chiseled; for they fell asleep in righteousness and great purity. All that was lacking was the seal. You have the explanation of these facts also." "Yes, sir," I said.

237   Par ix-26. [The shepherd continued]: "Believers coming from the ninth mountain, which was full of reptiles and wild beasts and which is the cause of human death, are the following: those with spots are the deacons who exercise their office badly, having stolen the subsistence of widows and of orphans and who enriched themselves with the resources they had received for assisting others. If they persist in this evil desire, they are already dead and there is no hope of life for them. Yet if they convert and piously fulfill their ministry, they shall be able to live; those with scabs are those who have denied their Lord and have failed to return to him, but like the wasteland and the desert and no longer clinging to the servants of God they live alone and lose their life.[11] A vine left within a hedgerow withers from neglect; evil weeds choke it. In time it becomes wild and so is useless to its owner; people like these, yielding to despair, become useless in the eyes of the Lord. Yet they can still do penance if they have not renounced the Lord from the bottom of their hearts, but if someone has denied the Lord from the bottom of the heart, I do not know whether or not that person can live. Nor do I say that in these days one can deny and receive penance, for salvation is impossible for one who shall now deny his Savior. As to those who have denied in the past, penance seems possible. If, then, some are about to do penance, let them do so quickly before the tower is completed. Otherwise, they will be killed by the women. The chipped stones are the deceitful and the slanderers. The wild beasts that you saw on the mountain poison people and cause them to die by means of their venom; in like manner the words of such people poison others and cause their death. These, then, have nothing more than a diluted faith because of their conduct. Some have done penance and have been saved. Others of this kind can be saved if they repent. Failing to do so, they will die. [. . .]

11. *ODES OF SOLOMON*[†]

Mentioned as early as the sixth century and existing only in fragments till the early twentieth century, the *Odes of Solomon* is a collection of forty-two religious hymns. Originally composed in either Greek or Syriac, the poems seemingly date from the late second century. It is debated whether

---

11. See Matt 10:39; Luke 9:24; 17:33; John 12:25.
† Translation (adapted) from *The Odes and Psalms of Solomon*, vol. 2, ed. R. Harris and A. Mingana (Manchester, London, and New York, 1920) 219, 356.

their origins are Jewish, Christian, or Jewish yet having a Christian context. No less debated is their relationship to Gnosticism. And although there are allusions to baptism, there is no reason to assume that the poems were used within or had any direct relationship to the initiatory process.

CPG 1: no. 1350 * Altaner (1961) 63–64 * Altaner (1966) 97 * Bardy (1929) 47–48 * Cross 190 * Goodspeed 84–87 * Quasten 1:160–68 * Tixeront 62–63 * CATH 1:696 * CE 14:137 * CHECL 166–67 * DACL 12.2:1903–21 * DictSp 11:602–8 * DPAC 2:2456–57 * EC 10:70 * EEC 2:609–10 * EEChr 2:824–25 * LTK 7:972–73 * NCE 2:402–3 * ODCC 1516

A. Harnack, ed., *Ein jüdisch-christliches Psalmbuch aus dem ersten Jahrhundert* (*Odes of Solomon*, now first published from the Syriac version by J. Randel Harris, 1909), translated from the Syrian by Johannes Flemming; edited and published by Adolf Harnack, TU 35, no. 4 (3rd ser., vol. 5, no. 4) (Leipzig, 1910). * P. Batiffol and J. Labourt, "Les odes de Solomon, une oeuvre chrétienne des environs de l'an 100–200," RBibl 21 (1910) 483–500, 22 (1911) 5–59, 161–97; published as one volume (Paris, 1911). * C. Bruston, "Les plus anciens cantiques chrétiens: les Odes de Salomen," RTP 1 S. 44 (1911) 465–97. * E.C. Selwyn, "The Feast of Tabernacles, Epiphany, and Baptism," JThSt 13 (1911–12) 225–49. * M. Franzmann, *The Odes of Solomon: An Analysis of the Poetical Structure and Form*, Novum Testamentum et Orbis Antiquus 20 (Freiburg i. S., 1952). * K. Gamber, "Die Oden Salomons als frühchristliche Gesange beim heiligen Mahl," OstkSt 15 (1966) 182–95. * J.H. Charlesworth, *The Odes of Solomon, Edited, with Translation and Notes* (Oxford, 1973). * B. McNeil, "A Liturgical Source in 'Acts of Peter' 38," VC 33 (1979) 342–46. * V. Saxer, "'Il étendit les mains à l'heure de sa Passion': la thème de l'orant-te dans la littérature chrétienne des IIe et IIIe siècles," Aug 20 (1980) 335–65. * D.E. Aune, "The Odes of Solomon and Early Christian Prophecy," NTS 28 (1982) 435–60. * M. Pierce, "Themes in the 'Odes of Solomon' and Other Early Christian Writings and Their Baptismal Character," EphL 98 (1984) 35–59. * D. Cerbelaud, "Un Dieu d'eau et de vent: l'Esprit Saint dans les 'Odes de Salomon,'" VS 148 (1994) 311–19. * E. Azar, *Les Odes de Salomon: Présentation et traduction*, Sagesses chrétiennes (Paris, 1996). * E. Engelbrecht, "God's Milk: An Orthodox Confession of the Eucharist," JECS 7 (1999) 509–26. * M. Lattke, *Oden Salomos: Text. Uebersetzung, Kommentar*, Novum Testamentum et Orbis Antiquus 41 (Fribourg i. S., 1999).

11-A. Ode 4

5. [. . .] For one hour of your Faith   238
Is more precious than all days and years.
6. For who is there that shall put on your grace and be injured?
7. For your seal is known,
And your creatures are known to it.
8. And the hosts possess it,
And the elect archangels are clad with it.
9. You have given us your friendship;
It was not that you were in need of us;
But that we are in need of you.

10. Distil your dews upon us;
and open your rich fountains that pour forth to us milk and honey. [. . .]

11-B. Ode 27

239   1. I expanded my hands: and I sanctified [them] to my Lord:
For the expansion of my hands is his sign.
2. And my expansion
Is the upright wood.

12. POLYCARP OF SMYRNA

Although little is known of his long life, Polycarp appears to have been an important bishop in the mid-second century. According to Irenaeus (WEC 1:**15**), Polycarp was instructed by the apostles and spoke with many Christians who had seen Christ. At any rate, toward the end of his life he visited Rome, where he discussed with Anicetus, bishop of that city (ca. 154–ca. 166), the proper date for observing the Christian Pasch. Anicetus defended the Roman custom of observing it on Sunday whereas Polycarp held to the Asian or Quartodeciman practice. Though no agreement was reached, they remained friends. After his return to Smyrna (today Izmir in Turkey), Polycarp was arrested for being unwilling to renounce the faith and consequently suffered martyrdom (ca. 155/156).

CPG 1: nos. 1040ff. * Altaner (1961) 110–12 * Altaner (1966) 50–52 * Bardenhewer (1908) 35–38 * Bardenhewer (1910) 32–34 * Bardenhewer (1913) 1:146–56 * Bautz 7:809–15 * Casamassa 155–75 * Cross 19–21 * Goodspeed 16–17 * Jurgens 1:28–30 * Leigh-Bennett 18–23 * Quasten 1:76–82 * Steidle 14–15 * Tixeront 16–17 * CATH 11:595–97 * CE 12:219–21 * DCB 4:423–31 * DictSp 12.2:1903–8 * DTC 12.2:2515–20 * EC 9:1670–71 * EEC 2:701 * EEChr 2:933–34 * LTK 8:404–5 * NCE 11:535–36 * NCES 11:464–65 * ODCC 1306 * PEA (1894) 21.2:1662–93 * PEA (1991) 10:62–63 * TRE 27:25–28

G. Bardy, "Le sacerdoce chrétien d'après les pères apostoliques," VS 53 (1935) (1)–(28). * G. Konidaris, "De la prétendu divergence des formes dans le régime du christianisme primitif ministres et ministères du temps des Apôtres à la mort de s. Polycarpe," Ist 10 (1964) 59–92.

12-A. Letter to the Philippians[†]

The Christians residing in the city of Philippi in Greece wrote to Polycarp and asked for copies of the letters that Ignatius of Antioch (WEC 1:**9**) had written during his journey to Rome. Polycarp granted their request and enclosed this "cover letter." The theory has been advanced that the present text is actually the combination of two letters: chapter thirteen being

---

[†] Translated from *Lettres. Ignace d'Antioche . . .*, 3rd rev. edition, ed. and trans. Th. Camelot, SChr 10 (Paris, 1958) 182–85.

the original letter that accompanied the Ignatian letters; chapters one to twelve being of later origin, perhaps ca. 135, with chapter fourteen serving as postscript. Yet not all agree with this conjecture.

v.2. Likewise, the deacons are to be beyond reproach before the face of his justice; they are to be servants of God and of Christ, not of other human beings. They are not to be slanderers, not to be double-tongued, not to be lovers of money; may they be chaste in all things, compassionate, zealous, walking according to the truth of the Lord, who was the servant of all. [. . .]   240

vi.1. The presbyters are to be compassionate, showing mercy to all; they are to bring back those who stray; they are to visit all the sick, not neglecting the widow, the orphan, the poor. But they are always to think of doing good before God and the people.[1] They are to refrain from all anger, respect of persons, and unjust judgments. They are to keep themselves far from love of money. They are not to be quick in ascribing evil to anyone. They are not to be severe in judging others, knowing that all of us are under a debt of sin. [. . .]   241

13. *MARTYRDOM OF POLYCARP*[†]

This account was written at the request of the church at Philomelium in Phrygia by a certain Marcion not long after the death of Polycarp (WEC 1:**12**). It is the first document to use the term "martyr" to designate a person who gives up his or her life for the faith.

CPG 1: no. 1045 * Altaner (1961) 111–12 * Altaner (1966) 51–52 * Bardenhewer (1908) 229–30 * Bardenhewer (1910) 201 * Bardenhewer (1913) 1:149; 2:615–16 * Goodspeed 25–26 * Jurgens 1:30–32 * Quasten 1:77–79 * Tixeront 16–17 * CATH 11:596 * CE 12:220–21 * DTC 12.2:2515–20 * EEC 2:701 * LTK 8:404–5 * ODCC 1306

xviii. On seeing the quarrel stirred up by the Jews, the centurion placed the body [of Polycarp] in the middle, as was customary, and burned it. Afterwards, we took up his bones, of more value than precious stones and finer than gold, and set them in a proper place. There, to the extent that we are able, the Lord will allow us to assemble in gladness and joy and celebrate the birthday of Polycarp's martyrdom, both in memory of those who fought the fight as well as to train and prepare those who will fight in the future.   242

---

1. See Prov 3:4; Rom 12:17; 2 Cor 8:21.
† Translated from *Lettres. Ignace d'Antioche . . .*, 3rd rev. edition, ed. and trans. Th. Camelot, SChr 10 (Paris, 1958) 232–33.

Chapter III

Second Century. West

ITALY

14. JUSTIN MARTYR

Born into a pagan Greek family living in Flavia Neapolis (Nabius) in Palestine, Justin, after exploring several pagan philosophies of the day, converted to Christianity ca. 130. He taught philosophy at Ephesus and elsewhere, eventually arriving in Rome, where he established a school of Christian philosophy—one of his pupils being Tatian the Syrian. With six of his disciples he was denounced as a Christian ca. 165. Refusing to sacrifice, Justin and his companions were scourged and then beheaded under the prefect Junius Rusticus (163–67).

Justin is one of the most important of the early Church's apologists, namely, authors writing in defense of Christianity especially during the second and third centuries. He was the first Christian author to use Aristotelian categories to establish a bridge between faith and reason, at times doing so with less than notable literary skill. Although Justin was a prolific writer, only a handful of his works have survived.

CPG 1: nos. 1073ff. * Altaner (1961) 120–27 * Altaner (1966) 65–71 * Bardenhewer (1908) 49–57 * Bardenhewer (1910) 38–46 * Bardenhewer (1913) 1:190–242 * Bardy (1929) 30–33 * Bautz 3:888–95 * Cross 48–53 * Goodspeed 101–5 * Hamell 38–42 * Jurgens 1:50–64 * Leigh-Bennett 40–54 * Quasten 1:197–219 * Steidle 26–28 * Tixeront 35–40 * Wright (1932) 249–50 * CATH 6:1325–28 * CE 8:580–86 * CHECL 38–40 * DCB 3:560–87 * DictSp 8:1640–47 * DPAC 2:1628–32 * DTC 8.2:2228–77 * EC 6:841–45 * EEC 1:462–64 * EEChr 1:647–50 * LTK 5:1112–13 * NCE 8:94–95 * NCES 8:93–95 * ODCC 915 * PEA (1894) 10.2:1332–37 * PEA (1991) 6:106–8 * RACh 19:802–47 * TRE 17:471–78

A. Harnack, *Brot und Wasser die eucharistichen Elemente bei Justin*, TU 7, 2 (Leipzig, 1891). * F.X. Funk, *Die Abendmahlselemente der Eucharistie in den ersten drei Jahrhunderten*, FLDG 3, 4 (Mainz, 1903). * P. Batiffol, *L'Eucharistie: la présence réelle et la transubstantiation*, Etudes d'histoire de théologie positive, 2nd ser. (Paris, 1906). * J. Réville, "Les origines de l'eucharistie (messe-Sainte-Cène)," RHE 56 (1907) 1–56, 141–96. * M. Goguel, *L'eucharistie des origines à Justin Martyr* (Paris, 1909). * S. Salaville, "La liturgie décrit par s. Justin et l'épiclèse," EO 12 (1909) 129–36, 222–27. * F. Wieland, *Der vorirenäische Opferbegriff* (Munich, 1909). * L. Labauche, "Lettres à un étudiant sur la sainte eucharistie," RAp 11 (1910–11) 753–61. * E. Dorsch, *Der Opfercharakter der Eucharistie einst und jetzt*, 2nd ed. (Innsbruck, 1911). * O. Casel,

"Die Eucharistielehre des hl. Justinus Martyr," Der Katholik 94 (1914) 153–76,
243–63, 331–55, 414–36. * J. Brinktrine, *Der Messopferbegriff in den ersten zwei Jahrhundert*, FThSt 21, 85–105 (Freiburg i. B., 1918). * J.B. Thibaut, *La liturgie Romaine*
(Paris, 1924) 38–56. * J.N. Greiff, "Brot, Wasser und Mischwein die Elemente der
Taufmesse," ThQ 113 (1932) 11–34. * B. Capelle, "L'histoire des rites et la participation active à la messe," QLP 18 (1933) 169–82. * J. Quasten, *Monumenta Eucharistica
et Liturgica Vetustissima* (Bonn, 1935–37) 13–21, 337–39. * J. Beran, "Quo sensu intel-
ligenda sint verba S. Justini Martyris ὅση δύναμις αὐτῷ in I Apologia, n. 67," DT
39 (1936) 46–55. * M.H. Shepherd, "The Early Apologists and Christian Worship,"
JR 18 (1938) 60–79. * O. Peler, "Logos und Eucharistie nach Justinus I Apol. c. 66,"
DT 18 (1940) 296–316. * St. Morson, "St. Justin and the Eucharist," IER 79 (1943)
323–28. * O. del N. Jesús, "Doctrina eucarística de San Justino, filósofo y mártir,"
RET 4 (1944) 3–58. * E.C. Ratcliff, "Justin Martyr and Confirmation," Theol 51
(1948) 133–39. * A.H. Couratin, "Justin Martyr and Confirmation—a Note," Theol
55 (1950) 458–60. * H.B. Porter, "The Eucharistic Piety of Justin Martyr," AThR 39
(1957) 24–33. * E. Ferguson, "The Ministry of the Word in the First Two Centuries,"
ResQ 1 (1957) 21–31. * Jungmann (1951), vol. 1, 22ff. * Jungmann (1959) 13ff. *
D. Barsotti, "L'Eucarestia come mistero d'unità e d'amore nei primi scrittori cris-
tiani," RivAM 5 (1960) 109–17. * C.I.K. Story, "Justin's Apology I, 62–64: Its Importance for the Author's Treatment of Christian Baptism," VC 16 (1962) 172–78. *
B. Neunheuser, *Baptism and Confirmation* (St. Louis, 1964) 55–56, 61–62. * W.L.
Dulière, "Un problème à résoudre: L'acceptation du sang eucharistique par les
premiers chrétiens juifs," STh 20 (1966) 62–93. * J.A. Gill, "A Liturgical Fragment
in Justin, Dialogue 29, 1," HThR 59 (1966) 98–100. * E.C. Ratcliff, "The Eucharistic
Institution Narrative of Justin Martyr's First Apology," JEH 22 (1971) 97–102. *
A. Hamman, "Valeur et signification des reseignements liturgiques de Justin," SP
13.2, 364–74; TU 116 (Berlin, 1975). * J.D.B. Hamilton, "The Church and the Language of Mystery: The First Four Centuries," ETL 53 (1977) 479–94. * M. Jourjon,
"Justin" in W. Rordorf and others, *The Eucharist of the Early Christians* (New York,
1978) 71–85. * T. Marsh, "The History of the Sacramental Concept," MilS 3 (1979)
21–56. * S. Agrelo, "El 'Logos', potencia divina que hace la Eucaristía: testimonia de
s. Justino," Ant 60 (1985) 602–63. * G.W. Lathrop, "Justin, Eucharist and 'Sacrifice':
A Case of Metaphor," Wor 64 (1990) 30–48. * G.A. Nocilli, *La catechesi battesimale ed
eucaristica di San Giustino Martire* (Bologna, 1990). * E. Ferguson, "Justin Martyr and
the Liturgy," ResQ 36 (1994) 267–78. * A.B. McGowan, "'Is There a Liturgical Text
in This Gospel?' The Institution Narratives and Their Early Interpretive Communities," JBL 118 (1999) 73–87.

14-A. Apology I[†]

Written in Rome ca. 155, this apology, sixty-eight chapters in length, was
addressed to the emperor Antoninus and his two adopted sons.

243　　LXI. I will now explain to you how we are renewed by Christ and consecrated to God. Should I fail to do this, I would be amiss in my explanation.

[†] Translated from J. Quasten, *Monumenta Eucharistica et Liturgica Vetustissima*,
vol. 1 of *Florilegium Patristicum* (Bonn, 1935) 13–21.

As many persons as are persuaded and believe that what we describe
and teach are true and are able to live accordingly, these we teach how to
pray and, while fasting, how to ask God that their past sins be forgiven;
we pray and fast. Then we bring them to a place where there is water, and
they are reborn in the same manner whereby we were reborn; they are
washed in the water in the name of the Father, the Lord of all things, and
of our Savior Jesus Christ and of the Holy Spirit,[1] for Christ said, "Unless
you are reborn, you will not enter the kingdom of heaven."[2] It is clear
to all that it is impossible for those who have been born to enter one's
mother's womb. For this reason the prophet Isaiah, as we wrote above, relates how the sins of those doing penance are remitted. He writes: "Wash.
Cleanse yourselves. Remove what is evil from your souls. Learn how to
do good. Judge the fatherless. Defend the widow. Then come, let us reason
together, says the Lord. Even though your sins be like purple, I will make
them white as wool. Though they be scarlet, I will make them as white
as snow. If you do not listen to me, the sword will devour you because
all this is what the mouth of the Lord has spoken."[3] We have received
from the apostles the reason for this [washing]. When we were first born,
we were born without our knowing it, by our parents coming together.
We were raised in bad and evil habits. So that we not remain children of
necessity or of ignorance but may become children of choice and understanding and so that we may gain the forgiveness of our past sins, the
name of the Father and Lord of all things is invoked over those who now
choose to be born again and have repented of their sins. Whoever leads
the person to be baptized to the washing calls upon God by this name
only since no one is allowed to pronounce the name of the ineffable God.
Those boldly venturing to do so are hopelessly insane. Illumination is the
name given to this washing since those being taught these things are enlightened [illuminated] in their minds. We also invoke upon these people
the name of Jesus Christ who suffered crucifixion under Pontius Pilate;
also the name of the Holy Spirit who foretold through the prophets all
things concerning Jesus.

    LXV. But after we have washed those who have believed and have joined   244
us, we bring them to where those who are called brethren have assembled.
In this way we may offer prayer in common both for ourselves and for
those who have received illumination and for people everywhere, doing
so with all our hearts so that we may be deemed worthy, now that we
have learned the truth, and by our works be found to be good citizens
and keepers of the commandments. In this way we may attain everlasting
salvation. When the prayers have concluded, we greet one another with a
kiss. Then bread and a cup containing water and wine are brought to him
who presides over the assembly. He takes these and then gives praise and

1. See Matt 28:19. 2. John 3:5. 3. Isa 1:16–20.

glory to the Father of all things through the name of his Son and of the Holy Spirit. He offers thanks at considerable length for our being counted worthy to receive these things at his hands. When the presider has concluded these prayers and the thanksgiving, all present express their consent by saying "Amen." In Hebrew this word means "so be it." And after the presider has celebrated the thanksgiving and all the people have given their consent, those whom we call deacons give to each of those present a portion of the eucharistic bread and wine and water and take the same to those who are absent.

245   LXVI. We call this food the "Eucharist." No one is permitted to partake of it except those who believe that the things we teach are true and who have been washed in the bath for the forgiveness of sins and unto rebirth and who live as Christ has directed. We do not receive these as if they were ordinary bread and ordinary drink, but just as Jesus our Savior was made of flesh through God's word and assumed flesh and blood for our salvation, so also the food over which the thanksgiving has been said becomes the flesh and blood of Jesus who was made flesh, doing so to nourish and transform our own flesh and blood. For the apostles in the memoirs they composed—these being called Gospels— handed down what they were commanded to do: Jesus took bread and gave thanks and said, "Do this in remembrance of me, this is my Body." Likewise taking the cup and giving thanks, he said, "This is my blood,"[4] and gave it to the apostles alone. [. . .]

246   LXVII. Next we continually remind one another of all this. Those capable of doing so assist the needy, and we are always together as one. And through his Son Jesus Christ and through the Holy Spirit we bless the Maker of all that nourishes us. And on the day that is called Sunday all who live in the cities or in rural areas gather together in one place, and the memoirs of the apostles and the writings of the prophets are read for as long as time allows. Then after the lector concludes, the president verbally instructs and exhorts us to imitate all these excellent things. Then all stand up together and offer prayers; as I said before, when we have concluded our prayer, bread is brought forward together with the wine and water. And the presider in like manner offers prayers and thanksgivings according to his ability. The people give their consent, saying "Amen"; there is a distribution, and all share in the Eucharist. To those who are absent a portion is brought by the deacons. And those who are well-to-do and willing give as they choose, as each one so desires. The collection is then deposited with the presider who uses it on behalf of orphans, widows, those who are needy due to sickness or any other cause, prisoners, strangers who are traveling; in short, he assists all who are in need. But Sunday is the day on which we hold our common assembly since this day is the

---

4. Luke 22:19–20; 1 Cor 11:23–25; Matt 26:26–27.

first day on which God, changing darkness and matter, created the world; it was on this very day that Jesus Christ our Savior rose from the dead.

14-B. Dialogue with Trypho the Jew[†]

The *Dialogue with Trypho the Jew* is the oldest Christian apology against Judaism that has come down to us. Preserved only in one incomplete manuscript dating from the fourteenth century, the work was written in Rome and at a time shortly after Justin's *Apology I*. It is an account of a two-day discussion, perhaps held at Ephesus, between Justin and Trypho, a historical person who is often identified with the rabbi Tarpho mentioned in the Mishnah.

XLI. The offering of the fine flour, my friends, which tradition prescribed   247
to be offered on behalf of the lepers who were cleansed of their leprosy,[1] was a type of the bread of thanksgiving [i.e., eucharistic bread] which Jesus Christ our Lord commanded us to observe in memory[2] of the suffering he endured for those who are purified from all evils. At the same time we are to thank God for having created for us the world and all that is within it; for having freed us from the sin in which we were [born]; for having totally destroyed the principalities and the powers, doing so through him who suffered in accord with his will. And so, as I said earlier, God speaks through the mouth of Malachi, who was one of the twelve [prophets] and who said the following concerning the sacrifices you offered at that time: "I will not accept sacrifices from your hands, for from the rising of the sun to its setting my name is glorified among the Gentiles but you profane it."[3] [. . .]

He goes on to speak about us, the Gentiles, who in every place offer him   248
sacrifices, namely, the eucharistic bread and the eucharistic cup, saying that "we glorify his name but you profane it."

Furthermore, the command to circumcise, requiring that children are   249
always to be circumcised on the eighth day, was a type of the true circumcision by which we are circumcised from error and iniquity through our Lord Jesus Christ, who rose from the dead on the first day after the Sabbath. This day, the day that is the first day of the week, is called the eighth day according to the cycle of all the days of the week, and yet it remains the first day.

LXX. [. . .] In this prophecy he also speaks about the "bread" of thanks-   250
giving, which Christ commanded be celebrated in memory of his being made incarnate for the sake of those who believe in him—for whom he

† Translated from the French in *Oeuvres complètes: grandes apologies. Dialogue avec le juif Tryphon, requêtes, traité de la résurrection. Justin Martyr*, intro. by J.-D. Dubois; trans. G. Archambault and others; notes by A.G. Hamman and D. Barthélemy (Paris, 1994) 161–62, 214, 278–80. (The Greek text was not available.)
1. See Lev 14:10.   2. See Luke 22:19.   3. Mal 1:10–11.

also suffered—and about the cup of thanksgiving that he handed down for us to drink in remembrance of his blood. [. . .]

251   CXVII. So it is that God anticipated all the sacrifices offered through his name, which Jesus Christ enjoined us to offer, namely, the eucharistic bread and cup, Christians celebrate these throughout the whole world. God testifies that these please him. But he completely rejects the sacrifices that you and your priests offer, saying, "I will not accept sacrifices from your hands, for from the rising of the sun to its setting my name is glorified among the Gentiles but you profane it."[4] [. . .]

252   [. . .] I also affirm that prayers and thanksgivings when offered by those who are worthy are the only sacrifices that are perfect and pleasing to God. [. . .]

253   [. . .] There is not one single group of people, whether barbarians or Greeks, or by whatever name they may be called, whether nomads or vagrants or herdsmen living in tents so that they can feed their flocks, among whom prayers and thanksgivings are not offered to the Father and Maker of the universe through the name of the crucified Jesus. [. . .]

GAUL

15. IRENAEUS OF LYONS

Irenaeus of Lyons (ca. 130–ca. 202/203), the most important theologian of the second century, was probably born in Smyrna (Izmir in modern Turkey). As a presbyter in Lyons (*Lugdunum*) he was sent in 177/178 to Rome, where he mediated the issue of Montanism. Returning to Gaul, he was ordained bishop of Lyons ca. 178, succeeding Photius, who was martyred. In 190 Irenaeus wrote to Pope Victor II (189–98) and other bishops in regard to the controversy regarding the date of Easter. Victor wished to excommunicate those bishops (Quartodecimans) who celebrated the feast on 14 Nisan and thus followed Jewish practice, rather than on the following Sunday as was the Roman tradition. This letter, found in Eusebius's *Church History* (WEC 2:2009ff.), is the last we hear of Irenaeus, who, according to some accounts, died in 202/203. Although Irenaeus is venerated as a martyr, there is no strong historical proof that he actually died in this way.

Much of Irenaeus's writing—many of his works were lost early on—focuses on defending the faith against the heterodox, especially the Gnostics, adherents of a religious movement that assumed various forms both within and without early Christianity. Often called the Father or Founder of Catholic Theology, Irenaeus frequently stressed the importance of tradition and of the authority of the church in Rome.

CPG 1: nos. 1306ff. * Altaner (1961) 150–58 * Altaner (1966) 110–17 * Bardenhewer (1908) 118–23 * Bardenhewer (1910) 96–101 * Bardenhewer (1913) 1:496–522 * Bardy

4. Ibid.

(1929) 33–36 * Bautz 2:1315–26 * Campbell 26–30 * Cross 109–15 * Goodspell 119–23 * Hamell 52–55 * Jurgens 1:84–106 * Leigh-Bennett 24–39 * Quasten 1:287–313 * Steidle 34–37 * Tixeront 77–80 * CATH 6:81–86 * CE 8:130–31 * CHECL 45–52 * DCB 3:253–82 * DHGE 25:1477–79 * DictSp 7.2:1923–69 * DPAC 2:1804–16 * DTC 7.2:2394–2533 * EC 7:192–94 * EEC 1:413–16 * EEChr 1:587–89 * LTK 5:583–85 * NCE 7:631–32 * NCES 7:570–72 * ODCC 846–47 * TRE 16:258–68

J.W.F. Höfling, *Die Lehre des Irenäus vom Opfer im christlichen Kultus* (Erlangen, 1860). * L. Hoppenmüller, "S. Irenaeus de Eucharistia," diss. (Bamberg, 1867). * J. Watterrich, *Der Konsekrationsmoment im heiligen Abendmahl und seine Geschichte* (Heidelberg, 1896) 47–60. * F.S. Renz, *Die Geschichte des Messopferbegriffs*, vol. 1 (Freising, 1901) 179–96. * S. Struckmann, *Die Gegenwart Christi in der hl. Eucharistie nach den schriftlichen Quellen der vornicänischen Zeit* (Vienna, 1905) 63–89. * J. Brinktrine, *Der Messopferbegriff in den ersten zwei Jahrhunderten* (Freiburg i. B., 1918) 127–35. * A. d'Alès, "La doctrine eucharistique de s. Irénée," RSR 13 (1923) 24–46. * V. Coucke, "Doctrina Eucharistica apud s. Irenaeum," *Collationes Brugenses* 29 (1929) 163–70. * P. Batiffol, *L'Eucharistie, la présence réelle et la transubstantiation*, 9th ed. (Paris, 1930) 167–83. * H.D. Simonin, "A propos d'un texte eucharistique de s. Irénée," RSPT 23 (1934) 281–92. * J.L. Koole, "De avondmaalsbeschouwing van den kerkvader Irenaeus," *Gereformeerd Theologisch Tijdschrift* 37 (1936) 295–303, 39 (1938) 412–17. * D. van den Eynde, "Eucharistia ex duabus rebus constans: s. Irénée, Adv. haer. IV, 18,5," Ant 15 (1940) 13–28. * F.R.M. Hitchcock, "The Doctrine of Holy Communion in Irenaeus," ChQ 129 (1939/40) 206–25. * M. Jugie, "La forme du sacrament de l'eucharistie d'après s. Irénée," in *Mémorial J. Chaine* (Lyons, 1950) 223–33. * G. Jouassard, "Témoignages peu remarqués de s. Irénée en matière sacramentaire," RSR 42 (1954) 528–39. * E. Ferguson, "The Ministry of the Word in the First Two Centuries," ResQ 1 (1957) 21–31. * E. Ferguson, "Baptism from the Second to the Fourth Century," ResQ 1 (1957) 185–97. * V. Palashkovsky, "La théologie eucharistique de s. Irénée évêque de Lyon," SP 2 (Berlin, 1957) 277–81. * P. Nautin, *Lettres et écrivans chrétiens des IIe et IIIe siècles*, Patristica 2 (Paris, 1961) 74–85, 92–104. * J. de Jong, "Der ursprungliche Sinn von Epiklese und Mischungsritus nach der Eucharistielehre des heiligen Irenaeus," ALW 9:1 (1965) 28–47. * V. Loi, "Il termine 'mysterium' nella letteratura latina cristiana prenicena," VC 20 (1966) 25–44. * P. Radopoulos, "Irenaeus on the Consecration of the Eucharistic Gifts," in *Kyriakon: Festschrift Johannes Quasten*, ed. P. Granfield (Washington, D.C., 1968) 844–46. * E.H. Pagels, "A Valentinian Interpretation of Baptism and Eucharist and its Critique of 'Orthodox' Sacramental Theology and Practice," HThR 65 (1972) 153–69. * V. Grossi, "Regula veritatis e narratio battesimale in sant'Ireneo," Aug 12 (1972) 437–63. * H.F. von Campenhausen, "Ostertermin oder Osterfasten? Zum Verständnis des Irenäusbriefs an Viktor (Euseb. Hist. Eccl. 5, 24)," VC 28 (1974) 114–38. * R. Daly, *Christian Sacrifice: The Judeo-Christian Background before Origen* (Washington, D.C., 1978) 339–59. * A. Hamman, "Irenaeus of Lyons," in W. Rordorf and others, eds., *The Eucharist of the Early Christians* (New York, 1978) 86–98. * D. Unger, "The Holy Eucharist according to Saint Irenaeus," *Laurentianum* 20 (1979) 103–64. * A. Orbe, "San Ireneo y la doctrina de la reconciliación," Greg 61 (1980) 5–50. * A. Houssiau, "Le baptême selon Irénée de Lyon," ETL 60 (1984) 45–59. * S. Agrelo, "Epiclesis y eucaristia en san Ireno," EOr 3, 1 (1986) 7–27. * M.A. Donovan, "Insights on Ministry: Irenaeus," *Toronto Journal of Theology* 2:1 (Spring 1986) 79–93. * J.M. Joncas, "Eucharist among the Marcosians: A Study of Irenaeus' Adversus

Haereses I, 13, 2," QL 71:2 (1990) 99–111. * D.N. Power, *Irenaeus of Lyons on Baptism and Eucharist: Selected Texts with Introduction, Translation, and Annotation*, Alcuin/ GROW Liturgical Study 18 (Bramcote, Nottingham, 1991). * B. Lemoine, "La controverse pascale du deuxième siècle: désaccords autour d'une date," QL 73 (1992) 223–31. * E. Lanne, "Saint Irénée de Lyon, artisan de la paix entres les églises," Ire 69 (1996) 451–76. * J.R. Kurz, "The Gifts of Creation and the Consummation of Humanity: Irenaeus of Lyon's Recapitulatory Theology of the Eucharist," Wor 83:2 (2009) 112–32.

15-A. Against (All) Heresies[†]

The *Detection and Overthrow of the Pretended but False Gnosis*, most commonly known as *Against (All) Heresies*, is Irenaeus's major opus. Although only parts of the original Greek survive, the work exists in a very literal Latin translation, dating ca. 200 according to some, and in various fragments in Syriac and Armenian. Not a homogenous book, the treatise was written over a period of time with additions and other revisions added during the years.

254   I.x.2. Having received this preaching and this faith, as we have just said, the Church, certainly dispersed throughout the whole world, has carefully guarded them as if inhabiting one house where it believes these things as if having one soul and one heart.[1] The Church harmoniously preaches them, teaches them, and passes them on as if it has only one mouth.

255   Even though languages differ throughout the world, yet the content of tradition is one and the same. The churches founded in Germany neither believe nor pass on anything else. The same is true for those in Spain, those in Celtic countries, those in the East, those in Libya, those established in the center of the world. Just as the sun,[2] being a creature of God, is one and the same throughout the whole world, so the preaching of the truth shines everywhere[3] upon all who desire to know the truth.[4] Nor will the most gifted in speech among the leaders of the churches say anything other than this—for no one is above the Master[5]—nor does one who is less gifted in words diminish this tradition; since the faith is one and the same, neither do those who preach on it at length add anything to it, nor do those who preach less remove anything from it.[6]

256   I.xiii.2. Pretending to give thanks over a cup mixed with wine and considerably prolonging the words of invocation, he [Marcus[a]] sees to it that

---

[†] Translated from *Contre les héréses. Irénée de Lyon*, ed. and trans. A. Rousseau and others, SChr 100 (Paris, 1964) 153, 211, 264, 294. David Power's *Irenaeus of Lyons on Baptism and Eucharist* has been very helpful in this section.

[a] Marcus: a Gnostic heretic whose followers, called Marcosians, relied not on the scriptural books but on apocryphal and other unauthentic writings.

1. See Acts 4:32.   2. See John 1:5.   3. See John 1:9.   4. See 1 Tim 2:4.   5. See Matt 10:24.   6. See 2 Cor 8:15; Exod 16:18.

the cup appears to be purple or red so that it was believed that Charis,[b] coming from the highest regions above, had her own blood drip into Marcus' cup in response to his invocation. Those present greatly desired to taste this drink so that the Charis invoked by this magician might come down on them also. Once again, presenting to some women a mixed cup, he ordered them to give thanks over it in his presence.[c] This done, he brought another and much larger cup than that over which the misguided woman had given thanks. Then he emptied the smaller cup into the larger one while saying, "May what is above all things, the incomprehensible and inexplicable Charis, fill up your inner self[7] and multiply her knowledge in you by sowing the mustard seed in good soil."[8] [. . .]

I.xiii.5. This same Marcus also used philters and charms with some if not all the women to dishonor their bodies. Returning to the Church of God, they often acknowledged that he had defiled their bodies and that they had experienced a violent passion for him. A certain deacon, one of our own in Asia, received him [Marcus] into his house and fell into this misfortune: the magician corrupted the deacon's beautiful wife in spirit and body, and for a long time she followed him; then, converted with great effort by the brethren, she spent the rest of her life doing penance, weeping and lamenting over the defilement she experienced on account of this magician. 257

I.xiii.7. By such words and deeds they [i.e., the disciples of Marcus] seduced a large number of women in our own district of the Rhone. With consciences branded by a hot iron,[9] some among these women did penance, doing so even in public. Others, who feared doing so, withdrew in silence, giving up on the life of God.[10] Some totally apostatized; others are in between, according to the proverb "neither without or within," and tasting this "fruit" of the seed of the sons of the "knowledge." 258

I.xxi.1. As for the tradition concerning their [the disciples of Marcus] "redemption," it happens that it is invisible and incomprehensible, for this "redemption" is itself the mother of what is incomprehensible and invisible. This is why, from the fact that the tradition is unstable, it cannot be described in a simple way and by only one formula since each of them passes it on as he or she wishes: as many teachers of this doctrine, so many "redemptions" are there. That such people were instigated by Satan 259

---

b. Charis: a name used for one of the intermediate beings in the Gnostic system.

c. David Power comments: "The exercise of such a prayer role by women used to be seen as one of the traits of heterodox bodies. Now that New Testament studies have shown the leadership of women in early house-churches and the presence of women among the prophets of early times, it is no longer clear that women were excluded from invoking liturgical blessings in ecclesial assemblies. For some, the Marcosian liturgy in this regard may simply reflect an orthodox practice, later discontinued and prohibited" (p. 13).

7. See Eph 3:16.   8. See Matt 13:31.   9. See 1 Tim 4:2.   10. See Eph 4:18.

to deny the baptism of regeneration in God and to reject all faith, we will
show in a more fitting place when we refute them.

260   I.xxi.3. Some prepare a nuptial chamber and carry out something like
a mystagogy accompanied by invocations over those who are initiated.
Thus they pretend to effect a "pneumatic" marriage resembling syzygies
from above. Others lead them to the water and, while plunging them into
it, say, "Into the name of the unknown Father of all things, in the Truth,
the Mother of all things into the name of the one who descends upon
Jesus; into the union, redemption, and communion of the Powers." Others pronounce over them Hebrew words so that those to be the initiated
are made senseless or weakened, *Basyma cacahasa eanaa irraumista diar-
bêda caèota bafobor camelanthi.* Translated, this is, "I invoke what is above
all power of the Father and is called Light, Spirit, and Life, for you have
reigned in a body." Still others proclaim "redemption" as follows: "The
Name which is hidden from the universal Deity and Domination and
Truth, which Jesus the Nazarean put on in the zones of light, Christ Jesus
who lives through the Holy Spirit for the redemption of the angels, the
name that leads to restoration: *Messia ufar magno in seenchaldia mosomeda
eaacha faronepscha Jesu Nazarene.*" Translated, this is, "I do not divide the
Spirit, the heart, and the supercelestial and merciful power of Christ. May
I take delight in your Name, Savior of the truth!" This is what those who
carry out the initiation say. The person who is initiated responds, "I am
confirmed and redeemed, and I redeem my soul from this age and from
all things that are from it, doing so in the name of Jao who has redeemed
his soul for 'redemption' in the living Christ." Finally those present make
the following acclamation, "Peace to all upon whom this Name rests!"
Then they anoint the initiated with balm. This perfume, they say, stands
for the good aroma spread over the Eons.

261   I.xxi.4. Some of them say that it is superfluous to lead [those to be initi-
ated] to the water; they mix together oil and water and, while saying formulas similar to those given above, they pour this mixture upon the head
of each person who is being initiated. This, they pretend, is "redemption."
Furthermore, they also anoint with balm. There are also others who reject
all these practices, claiming as they do that one should not carry out the
mystery of irrepressible and incorporeal realities by using sensible and
bodily things. Indeed, perfect "redemption" is the very knowledge of the
inexpressible Greatness. [. . .]

262   II.xxi.4. Being only thirty years of age when he was baptized and then
being the perfect age for a teacher, he [Jesus] came to Jerusalem so that all
could rightly acknowledge him as a teacher. [. . .] He came to save all—
all, I say, who are reborn unto God through him: the newborn, infants, the
young and the old. This is why he passed through every age: making himself an infant for infants, he sanctified the infants; making himself young,
he sanctified those of this age, and at the same time being an example of
piety, justice, and obedience. [. . .]

III.xvii.1. [. . .] It was as a dove that the Spirit of God descended upon   263
him[11]—the Spirit concerning whom Isaiah said, "And the Spirit of God
rested upon him,"[12] as we previously explained. Also, "The Spirit of the
Lord is upon me; this is why he anointed me."[13] It was this same Spirit
concerning whom the Lord said, "For it is not you who speak but the
Spirit of your Father who speaks in you."[14] And while giving his disciples the power of regeneration unto God, he said to them, "Go, teach
all nations, baptizing them in the name of the Father and of the Son and
of the Holy Spirit."[15] For God through the prophets promised that in the
end times he would pour this same Spirit "upon . . . his male and female
servants so that they might prophesy."[16] Therefore the same Spirit has
descended upon the Son of God,[17] made the Son of Man, becoming accustomed to dwelling with him in the human race, to dwelling among us, to
dwelling within God's handiwork, bringing about the Father's will in us,
and renewing us from our old state unto the newness of Christ.

III.xvii.2. This is the Spirit that David requested for the human race when   264
he said, "And strengthen me by your Spirit which governs."[18] Luke tells us
that this Spirit, after the Lord's ascension, descended upon the disciples on
Pentecost,[19] and it is the Spirit who has power over all the nations to intro-
duce them to the entrance of life and for opening the New Testament; this is
why, together in all languages,[20] they sang a hymn to God—the Spirit unify-
ing the distant tribes and offering to the Father the first fruits of all nations.

This is why the Lord promised to send the Paraclete,[21] who is to prepare   265
us for God. For just as dry wheat, without water, cannot be made into a
mass of dough or one loaf, so neither can we, being many, become one in
Christ Jesus without the water that comes from heaven. And just as dry
soil, if it does not receive water, is not fruitful, so we who were originally
dry wood,[22] could never have brought forth the fruits of life[23] without rain
graciously given from above.

By the bath [of baptism] our bodies have received the unity that ren-   266
ders them incorruptible; but our souls have received this by means of the
Spirit. For this reason both are necessary since both obtain the life of God.
Our Lord took pity on the erring Samaritan woman[24] who, not staying
with one husband, fornicated with many; he showed and promised her
"the living water" so that "she would thirst no more"[25] nor labor to obtain
the refreshing water. Henceforth she has within herself the water "flowing forth unto eternal life,"[26] the water the Lord received as a gift from
his Father and which is given to those who partake of him who sends the
Holy Spirit over all the earth.

---

11. Matt 3:16; Mark 1:10; Luke 3:22; John 1:32.   12. Isa 11:2.   13. Isa 61:1;
Luke 4:18.   14. Matt 10:20.   15. Matt 28:19.   16. Joel 3:1–2.   17. See Isa 11:2.
18. Ps 51:12.   19. See Acts 2:1ff.   20. See Acts 2:4, 11.   21. See John 15:26; 16:7.
22. See Luke 23:31.   23. See Gen 1:12; Luke 13:9.   24. See John 4:7ff.   25. John
4:14.   26. Ibid.

267   IV.xvii.1. In the fullest do the prophets indicate that it was not because
God needed their service that he prescribed the observances contained in
the Law; and, as we will show, the Lord in turn plainly taught that when
God requests an offering from us, he does so for the sake of the person
who offers.

268   When Samuel saw people neglecting justice, when they were turning
away from God's love and yet nonetheless believing they could appease
God by sacrifices and by other figurative observances, Samuel said to
them: "Does the Lord desire holocausts and sacrifices more than listening
to the voice of the Lord? Behold obedience is better than sacrifice and do-
cility better than the fat of rams."[27] David said, "You desired neither sacrifice nor oblation, but you gave me ears; you desired neither holocausts
nor sacrifices for sin."[28] By this he taught them that God prefers obedience,
which saves them, to sacrifices and holocausts, which profit them nothing for justice; at the same time he foretold the new covenant. Still more
clearly on this subject does he say in Psalm 50 [51], "If you had desired
a sacrifice, I would have offered you one; but you did not take pleasure
in holocausts; for God, sacrifice is a contrite spirit; God does not spurn a
contrite and humble heart."[29] That God lacks nothing, he affirms in the
preceding psalm: "I will not accept the calves of your house, nor the goats
of your flocks, for mine are all the animals of the forest, the beasts of the
mountains, and the oxen; I know all the birds of the sky, and the beauty
of the field is mine; if I am thirsty, I will not tell you, for mine is the world
and all that it contains. And so will I eat the flesh of bulls or drink the
blood of goats?"[30] Then, so that no one believe that it is due to anger that
God rejects all this, he adds by way of counsel, "Offer to God the sacrifice
of praise and fulfill your vows to the Most High; call upon me on the day
of distress and I will free you, and you will glorify me."[31] And so, having rejected what sinners believe can appease God, and having showed
that God has need of nothing, he exhorts and recalls those things through
which people are justified and enabled to approach God.

269   Isaiah says the same, "What are the multitude of your sacrifices to me?
says the Lord. I am filled."[32] Then, having rejected the holocausts, sacrifices, and offerings, as well as the new moons, the sabbaths, the feasts, and
all the observances connected with these, he adds, to advise what pertains
to salvation, "Wash, purify yourselves, remove what is evil from your
hearts before my eyes; cease from evil, learn how to do good, seek out
justice, save all who suffer injustice, give heed to the orphans, defend the
widow, come therefore, let us reason it out,"[33] says the Lord.

270   IV.xvii.2. He did not thereby abolish their sacrifices like an angry man,
as many dare to say, but he took pity on their blindness and taught the
true sacrifice by the offering through which he pleased God and obtained

---

27. 1 Sam 15:22.   28. Ps 40:6.   29. Ps 51:16–17.   30. Ps 50:9–13.   31. Ps 50:14–15.
32. Isa 1:11.   33. Isa 1:16–18.

life from him. As he said in another place, "For God, sacrifice is a contrite heart; for God, the odor of sweetness is a heart that glorifies him who formed it."[34]

If it were out of anger that God rejected their sacrifices as being unworthy to obtain divine mercy, he would not have advised them in regard to their salvation. God, being merciful, did not deprive them of such good counsel. Through Jeremiah he said to them, "Why do you bring me incense from Saba and cinnamon from a distant land? Your holocausts and sacrifices are not pleasing to me."[35] He adds: "Hear the word of the Lord, all you of Judah. This is what the Lord God of Israel says: Direct your ways and your customs, and I will have you dwell in this place. Be not proud of the lies which will be of no profit to you, namely, 'This is the temple of the Lord. This is the temple of the Lord.'"[36] — 271

IV.xvii.3. Again, indicating to them that he did not lead them out of Egypt in order that they might offer him sacrifice but so that they, forgetting the idolatry of the Egyptians, might hear the voice of God, who was their salvation and glory, he said through Jeremiah: "This is what the Lord said, Gather together your holocausts with your sacrifices and eat flesh; for I did not speak to your fathers nor did I command anything in regard to holocausts and sacrifices on the day when I had them depart Egypt. Here is what I commanded: Hear my voice and I will be your God, and you will be my people; walk in all my ways whichever I will command you so that it may go well with you. But they have not listened nor paid attention; they have walked according to the thoughts of their evil heart and have turned back rather than moving ahead."[37] And again through the same person, "Let whoever glories, glory in this, namely, to understand and know that I am the Lord who brings about mercy, justice, and judgment upon the earth." He adds, "For it is in this that I take pleasure, says the Lord,"[38] and not in sacrifices, holocausts, and oblations. [. . .] — 272

IV.xvii.4. Consequently God did not seek sacrifices and holocausts from them but rather faith, obedience, and justice unto their salvation. As God said through the prophet Hosea when teaching them his will, "I desire mercy rather than sacrifice, and knowledge of God more than holocausts."[39] Our Lord also warned them of the same, saying, "If you would have known what this means, 'I desire mercy and not sacrifice,' never would you have condemned the innocent."[40] In this way he bore witness that the prophets were preaching the truth, and he accused them [those listening] of being foolish due to their own fault. — 273

IV.xvii.5. He directed his disciples to offer God the first fruits of his creation, not as if God needed them but so they themselves would not be unfruitful or ungrateful. He took the bread, which is created, and gave thanks, saying, "This is my Body."[41] Likewise for the cup, which is part of — 274

34. See Ps 50 (?).   35. Jer 6:20.   36. Jer 7:2–4.   37. Jer 7:21–24.   38. Jer 9:23.
39. Hos 6:6.   40. Matt 12:7.   41. Matt 26:26.

the creation to which we belong, and he revealed it to be his Blood, and he taught that it was the new offering of the new covenant.[42] It is this very same offering which the Church has received from the apostles and which throughout the world it offers to God who feeds us with the first fruits of his gifts in the new covenant.

275   Among the twelve prophets it was Malachi who spoke of this beforehand: "I do not find pleasure in you, says the omnipotent Lord, and I will accept no sacrifice from your hands; for from the rising to the setting of the sun my name is glorified among the nations, and in every place incense as well as a pure sacrifice are offered to my name; for my name is great among the nations, says the omnipotent Lord."[43] In this way he very clearly indicates that the former people will cease offering to God, although in every place a sacrifice—one that is pure—will be offered to him, and that his name will be glorified among the nations. [. . .]

276   IV.xviii.1. And so the Church's offering, which the Lord taught is to be offered throughout the entire world, is a pure sacrifice in God's sight and pleases him. God has no need of our sacrifice, but those who offer are glorified if their gifts are accepted. By this gift are shown the honor and affection we give to the King. It is this gift which the Lord desires us to offer in all simplicity and innocence, for he said, "When you offer your gift at the altar and there recall that your brother has something against you, leave your gift before the altar, and first go and be reconciled with your brother; then, when you return, offer your gift."[44] So it is necessary to offer God the first fruits of his creation, as Moses says, "Do not appear before the Lord with empty hands,"[45] so that we, by expressing our thanks to him through the very things that please us, may receive the honor that comes from God.

277   IV.xviii.2. Offerings as such have not been condemned: offerings were there [among the Jews] and they are also found here; sacrifices existed among the [Jewish] people, and they exist in the Church. Its species alone has changed; no more is the offering made by slaves but by those who are free. There is only one and the same Lord, but there is a character proper to the offering of slaves and to that of those who are free so that through the oblation itself is shown the distinctive sign of freedom, since with God nothing is indifferent, meaningless, or lacking in design. This is why they [the Jews] had tithes of their goods consecrated to him, whereas those who have been freed dedicate all their possessions to the Lord's use; joyfully and freely giving not the least of their goods, they hope for greater things, as was true of the poor widow who placed her whole livelihood in God's treasury.[46]

278   IV.xviii.3. From the beginning God looked favorably upon the gifts of Abel because Abel offered them with sincerity and righteousness. Yet God did not do the same concerning Cain's gifts since Cain's heart was

---

42. See Matt 26:28.   43. Mal 1:10–11.   44. Matt 5:23–24.   45. Deut 16:16.
46. See Luke 21:4.

full of jealousy and malice in regard to his brother. Therefore God, exposing Cain's hidden feelings, said, "Have you not sinned if you brought it rightly but did not divide it rightly? Be still"[47] because God is not pleased by sacrifice. Should some dare to offer a sacrifice that is outwardly clean, correct, and lawful, yet if in their hearts they do not share correct communion with their neighbor and do not fear God, they do not deceive God by offering this sacrifice with an appearance of propriety while sinning internally; what profits such a person is not offering sacrifice but rather eliminating the evil that has been born within. Lacking this, the sin by a counterfeit action makes the person his or her own murderer. Therefore the Lord also said, "Woe to you, scribes and Pharisees, hypocrites, because you are like whitened sepulchers. Outside, the sepulcher appears beautiful, but within it is full of the bones of the dead and of all types of filth; so you also on the outside appear just to others, yet inside, you are full of evil and hypocrisy."[48] Although they were thought to offer correctly according to outward appearances, within they had a jealousy akin to that of Cain: and so they, like Cain, killed the Just One, disregarding the counsel of the Word.[49] For [God] said to him, "Be still."[50] But he did not assent. Now what else is to "be still" than to cease from the intended violence? And he said similar things to them, "You blind Pharisee, first clean the outside of the cup so that what is outside be clean."[51] But they did not listen. For behold, says Jeremiah, "neither your eyes nor your heart are good, but in your covetousness you have turned them toward shedding innocent blood, and for practicing injustice and murder."[52] And again Isaiah says, "You have taken counsel, but not through me; you have made covenants, but not through my Spirit."[53] And so that their inmost desires and thoughts, brought to life, may show that God is without blame—for God reveals what is secret but does no evil—when Cain was not at rest, God said to him, "It [i.e., sin] seeks you out, but you must master it."[54] Likewise he said to Pilate, "You would have no power over me unless it had been given you from above."[55] God has always delivered the just so that they, having patiently endured sufferings, may be tested and approved, and that evildoers, according to their bad deeds, may be condemned and cast outside. Consequently we are not sanctified by sacrifices since God does not need them; but it is the dispositions of those who offer which make holy the sacrifice, provided these be pure; they move God to accept the offering as if from a friend. "As to the sinner, he says, whoever sacrifices a calf, it is as if one killed a dog."[56]

IV.xviii.4. Since the Church offers with sincerity, rightly is its gift considered a pure sacrifice in God's sight, as Paul said to the Philippians, "I am full, having received from Epaphroditus the things you sent, a

279

---

47. Gen 4:7, LXX.   48. Matt 23:27–28.   49. See Jas 5:6.   50. Gen 4:7, LXX.
51. Matt 23:26.   52. Jer 22:17.   53. Isa 30:1, LXX.   54. Gen 4:7.   55. John 19:11.
56. Isa 66:3, LXX.

fragrant offering, a sacrifice acceptable and pleasing to God."[57] For we are to present an offering to God, and in all things we are to be grateful to the Creator, doing so with a pure mind, in faith, without hypocrisy, with firm hope, in fervent love, being the first fruits of his own creation. The Church alone offers this pure oblation to the Creator, offering it with a thanksgiving that comes from his creation. The Jews, however, do not offer, their hands being full of blood;[58] they have not received the Word through whom offering is made to God, nor do all the assemblies of the heretics. Some, in fact, say that there is a Father other than the Creator, but, in offering him gifts taken from our own created world, they show that he desires the property of others and desires what is not his own. Others say that our world comes from failure, ignorance, and passion; and offering the fruits of ignorance, passion, and failure, they sin against their Father, insulting rather than thanking him.

280   Again, how will they be certain that the bread over which they give thanks is the Body of their Lord, and that the cup is his Blood if they do not say that he is the Son of the Creator of the world, namely, God's Word through whom the wood is fruitful, the fountains flow, and "the earth gives first the blade, then the ear, and then the full corn in the ear."[59]

281   IV.xviii.5. Again, how can they say that the flesh, nourished by the Lord's Body and Blood, can be corruptible and not partake of life? Therefore they should either change their thinking or cease offering the things we have just mentioned. Our thinking agrees with the Eucharist, and the Eucharist in turn confirms our thinking. For we offer to him what is his, harmoniously proclaiming the communion and unity of the flesh and the Spirit; for just as the bread which comes from the earth, having received the invocation of God, no longer is common bread but the Eucharist and consists of two parts, one of earth, the other of heaven—so our bodies, participating in the Eucharist, are no longer subject to corruption since they have hope in the resurrection.

282   IV.xviii.6. Indeed we offer to God not because God is in need but to give him thanks with the help of his gifts and to sanctify creation. For just as God does not need things that come from us, so we need to offer something to God as Solomon said, "Whoever has pity on the poor lends to God."[60] God, who needs nothing, accepts our good actions so that we can give his good things in return.[61] As our Lord said, "Come, blessed of my Father, receive the kingdom prepared for you: for I was hungry, and you gave me to eat; I was thirsty, and you gave me to drink; I was a stranger, and you welcomed me; nude, and you clothed me; sick, and you visited me; in prison, and you came to me."[62] God, therefore, having no need for these things, nonetheless desires that we do them for our own benefit. In this way we will not lack fruit, just as the Word commanded the people to

---

57. Phil 4:18.   58. See Isa 1:15.   59. Mark 4:28.   60. Prov 19:17.   61. See ibid. 62. Matt 25:34–36.

make offerings, even though he had no need of them, so that they might learn how to serve God. And so the Word desires that we also frequently and continuously offer our gift at the altar.

There is, then, a heavenly altar toward which our prayers and offerings   283
are directed. There is also a temple, as John in the Book of Revelation says, "And God's temple was opened."[63] As to the tabernacle he says, "Behold God's tabernacle in which he will dwell among mortals."[64]

V.II.2. Vain in every respect are those who despise the entire dispensa-   284
tion of God, denying, as they do, the salvation of the flesh and rejecting its rebirth since they say that the flesh is incapable of becoming incorrupt- ible. If there is no salvation for the flesh, then the Lord did not redeem us with his blood,[65] nor is the eucharistic cup a sharing in his Blood.[66] Blood can only come forth from veins, from flesh, and from the rest of what makes us human. Made human, the Word of God has redeemed us by his own blood, as the apostle says, "In whom we have redemption by his blood, the forgiveness of our sins."[67] Since we are his members[68] and are nourished through creation—creation which he gives us as he makes the sun rise and the rain fall as he wishes[69]—the cup, taken from creation, he has declared to be his own blood.[70] Through his blood our own blood is strengthened. Bread, taken from creation, he has declared to be his own Body[71] through which our bodies are strengthened.

V.II.3. When the mixed cup and the baked bread receive the word of God   285
and become the Eucharist, namely, the Blood and Body of Christ, and when the substance of our flesh is thereby strengthened, how can such people pre- tend that the flesh is incapable of receiving God's gift, which is eternal life— the flesh nourished by Christ's Body and Blood, and which is his member, as the blessed apostle says in his Letter to the Ephesians, "We are members of his Body,"[72] formed of his flesh and bones? He [Paul] did not say this of any spiritual and invisible person—"for the spirit has neither bone nor flesh,"[73] but he speaks of the arrangement whereby Christ became a human being with flesh, nerves, and bone. It is this very organism that is nourished by the cup which is Christ's Blood and that is strengthened by the bread that is his Body. Just as a cutting of wood from the vine when planted in the soil produces fruit in its season, and just as a grain of wheat, after fall- ing to the ground[74] and decomposing there, springs up in manifold increase through the Spirit of God who supports all things[75]—and subsequently through the wisdom [of God] serves human use and then, receiving the word of God, becomes the Eucharist, namely, Christ's Body and Blood—so our bodies, nourished by this same Eucharist and after having been placed in the earth and decomposing there, will rise at their appointed time. [. . .]

---

63. Rev 11:19.   64. Rev 21:3.   65. See Col 1:14.   66. See 1 Cor 10:16.   67. Col 1:14.   68. See 1 Cor 6:15; Eph 5:30.   69. See Matt 5:45.   70. See Luke 22:20; 1 Cor 11:25.   71. See Luke 22:19; 1 Cor 11:24.   72. Eph 5:30.   73. Luke 24:39.   74. See John 12:24.   75. See Wis 1:7.

15-B. Demonstration of the Apostolic Teaching[†]

For a long time, only the title of this work was known, but in 1904 an Armenian translation was discovered; it was published in 1907. The work, not polemical, is a compendium, as it were, of Christian doctrine.

286   3. [. . .] This is what the rule of faith obtains for us as has been handed down to us by the presbyters [elders?], the disciples of the apostles. First, it persuades us to remember that we have been baptized for the forgiveness of sins in the name of God the Father, in the name of Jesus Christ, the incarnate Son of God who died and rose, and in the Holy Spirit of God. It teaches us that baptism is the seal of eternal life and is rebirth in God so that, no longer children of mortals, we are children of the eternal and everlasting God. [. . .]

287   42. And so do believers keep themselves [with bodies unstained and souls incorruptible] if the Holy Spirit constantly remains in them, the Holy Spirit who, given by God at baptism, is retained by the one who has received it. [. . .]

[†] Translated from *Démonstration de la prédication apostolique. Irénée Lyon*, ed. and trans. L.M. Froidevaux, SChr 62 (Paris, 1959) 88–89, 140–41.

Chapter IV

Second Century. East

ASIA MINOR

16. PLINY THE YOUNGER AND TRAJAN THE EMPEROR

Pliny the Younger (*Gaius Plinius Caecilius Secundus*) was born ca. 61 A.D. He was the nephew and adopted son of Pliny the Elder. As a Roman senator he was sent in 111 to be governor of Bithynia and Pontus in Asia Minor, seemingly to bring much needed reforms to that area's local government. Presumably it was here that he died ca. 113.

Noted as a letter writer, it was at Rome that Pliny initially published nine books of letters covering the years 97 to 109. A tenth book, which appeared after his death, contains his most famous letter (X.xcvi), that to the emperor Trajan (52 or 53–117), requesting assistance as to how Pliny should deal with the Christians who were considered as members of a secret sect. The emperor's reply (X.xcvii) is also contained in the same book.

Bautz 7:745–49 * CATH 11:516–18 * CHECL 59 * EC 9:1627–28 * EEC 2:699 * EEChr 2:928 * LTK 8:357–58 * NCE 11:442–43 * NCES 11:420–21 * ODCC 1301 * PEA (1894) 21.1:439–56 * PEA (1991) 9:1141–44

J. Variot, "Les lettres de Pline le Jeune: correspondance avec Trajan relativement aux chrétiens de Pont et de Bithynie," RQH 24 (1878) 80–153. * E.-Ch. Babut, "Remarques sur les deux lettres de Pline et de Trajan relatives aux chrétiens de Bithynie," RHL, n.s., 1 (1910) 289–305. * A. Kurfess, "Plinius und der urchristliche Gottesdienst," ZNeW 35 (1936) 295ff. * R.M. Grant, "Pliny and the Christians," HTR 41 (1948) 273–74. * W. Schmid, "Ein Verkannter Ausdruck der Opfersprache in Plinius' Christenbrief," VC 7 (1953) 75–78. * L. Herrmann, "Les interpolations de la lettre de Pline sur les chrétiens," Latomus 13 (1954) 343–55. * F. Fourrier, "La lettre de Pline à Trajan sur les chrétiens (X, 97)," RTAM 31 (1964) 161–74. * F. Smuts, "Waarvan is die Christene voor Plinius aangekla?" *Acta Classica* 8 (1965) 71–85. * D.H. Tripp, "Pliny and the Liturgy—Yet Again," SP 15.1 (1984) 581–85. * F. Manns, "'Ante lucem' dans la lettre de Pline le Jeune à Trojan (Ep. X, 96)," Ant 62 (1987) 338–43. * F.J. van Beeck, "The Worship of Christians in Pliny's Letter," StudLit 18:3–4 (1988–89) 121–31. * D.H. Tripp, "The Letter of Pliny," in StLit, 80–81. * M. Testard, "'. . . carmenque Christo quasi Deo dicere . . . ,'" RELA 72 (1994) 138–58.

16-A. Letter from Pliny the Younger to Trajan the Emperor (X.xcvi)[†]

288   It is my custom, O lord, to refer all questionable issues to you. Who can better resolve my doubts and instruct my ignorance?

289   Never have I been present when Christians have been questioned in court. And so I do not know what offense is to be punished or investigated and to what extent. Nor am I certain whether any distinction should be made among Christians on the basis of age, whether the young should be treated differently than adults, whether pardon should be granted to those renouncing their beliefs, whether someone who once was a Christian gains nothing by ceasing to be a Christian, and whether the name itself without the offense is to be punished or whether only offenses consistent with the name are to be punished.

290   Meanwhile, this is the procedure I followed in regard to all who were brought before me on the charge of being Christians. I asked them if they were Christians. If they answered affirmatively, I asked them a second and third time, threatening them with punishment. If they persisted, I ordered their execution. Whatever the nature of their admission, I believed that their stubbornness and firm obstinacy were not to go unpunished. There were others of similar insanity, but since they were citizens of Rome, I ordered that they were to be sent to that city.

291   Before long and as is often true, the charges increased in variety as they became more widespread. There exists an anonymous writing containing the names of many accused persons. From among these I considered dismissing those who denied that they were or ever had been Christians if they repeated after me an invocation of the gods, if they offered wine and incense to your image which I ordered to be brought into court for this purpose along with the images of the gods, and if they cursed the name of Christ, which, as I understand it, no true Christian can be forced to do. Others, whose names an informer gave me, first admitted the charge and then denied it; they said that they had ceased to be Christians two or more years previously and some of them even twenty years previously. All venerated your image and the images of the gods and cursed the name of Christ.

292   They also declared that the substance of their guilt or error amounted to no more than this: they customarily gathered before dawn on a fixed day to sing in alternation a hymn to Christ as if to a god, and they bound themselves by an oath, not in a criminal conspiracy, but to refrain from robbery, theft, or adultery, from breaking their word, from reneging on a deposit. After this they usually dispersed, reassembling later on in order to take food of a common and harmless kind. And so I believed that it was all the more necessary to seek the truth from two female slaves, who are

---

[†] Translated from *Epistolarum Libri Decem*, ed. R.A.B. Mynors, Scriptorum Classicorum Biblotheca Oxoniensis (Oxford, 1963) 338–40.

called "ministers,"[a] doing so by means of torture. I found nothing except a degenerate, excessive superstition.

I have, therefore, postponed any further consideration while awaiting   293
your counsel. The matter seems worthy of your consideration, especially in light of the number of persons to be tried. For numerous persons of every age and every class, of each gender, are being brought to trial, something that is likely to continue. Not only the towns but villages and the countryside are being defiled through contact with this evil superstition. It seems possible for this to be checked and cured since the people have indeed begun to frequent the temples, which had been almost entirely abandoned for a long time. And the sacred rites, having been abandoned, are again being performed; the flesh of sacrificial meat is on sale everywhere though till recently it was hard to find anyone buying it. It is easy to believe from this that a large number of people could be corrected if they were given an opportunity to make a retraction.

16-B. Letter from Trajan to Pliny the Younger (X.xcvii)[†]

You acted correctly, my dear Pliny, in investigating the cases of those de-   294
nounced to you as being Christians. It is impossible to formulate a general principle that can be applied as a fixed norm. These people are not to be sought out; if they are brought before you and found guilty, they must be punished. Yet if anyone denies being a Christian and proves this by offering supplications to our gods, this person shall be pardoned as being repentant however suspect this person's former conduct may have been. Anonymous accusations, however, shall not be introduced into the proceedings. They set a very bad example and are foreign to the spirit of our age.

17. EPISTLE OF THE APOSTLES[††]

This document, also called the *Testament of Our Lord in Galilee*—not to be confused with the *Testamentum Domini* (WEC 3:**142**)—is perhaps the most widely known of the apocryphal epistles of the apostles. The work presents itself as a series of revelations given by the risen Lord to the eleven apostles. Redacted in Egypt or Asia Minor, the document, originally written in Greek (now lost), exists in Ethiopic, Coptic (incomplete), and Latin (one leaf). Some date it as early as 130; others as late as 160.

Altaner (1961) 82–83 * Altaner (1966) 124–25 * Cross 85 * Goodspeed 22–24 * Quasten 1:150–53 * Steidle 282 * Tixeront 72 * CATH 1:703 * DTC 1.2:1602 * EEChr 1:382 * LTK 3:732 * NCE 2:412 * ODCC 1592

---

a. Some translate the Latin *ministrae* as "deaconesses."

[†] Translated from *Epistolarum Libri Decem*, 340.

[††] Translation (adapted) from M.R. James, *The Apocryphal New Testament* (Oxford, 1926) 487ff.

B. Poschmann, *Paenitentia Secunda* (Bonn, 1930) 104ff. * J. Hoh, *Die kirchliche Busse im zeiten Jahrhundert* (Breslau, 1932) 64–72.

295   5. [. . .] When we had no bread but only five loaves and two fishes, he commanded the people to sit down, their number being five thousand not including the children and the women. We set pieces of bread before them, and they ate and were filled, and from what remained over we filled twelve baskets full of the fragments, asking one another and saying, "What mean these five loaves?" They are the symbol of our faith in the Lord of the Christians (in the great Christendom), even in the Father, the Lord Almighty, and in Jesus Christ our Redeemer, in the Holy Spirit the Comforter, in the holy Church, and in the remission of sins.

296   15. But you commemorate my death. Now when the Pasch comes, one of you will be cast into prison for my Name's sake; and he will be in grief and sorrow because you keep the Pasch while he is in prison and separated from you. [. . .] And I will send my power in the form of my angel Gabriel, and the doors of the prison shall be opened. And he shall come forth and come unto you and keep the night watch with you until the cock crows. And when you have accomplished the memorial which is made of me, and the agape, he shall again be cast into prison, for a testimony, until he shall come out of there and preach what I have delivered to you. And we said to him: "Lord, is it then needful that we should again take the cup and drink?" He said to us: "Yes, it is needful until the day when I come again with them that have been put to death for my sake."

297   27. For unto that end I went down to the place of Lazarus and preached to the righteous and the prophets, that they might come out of the rest which is below and come up into that which is above; and I poured out upon them with my right hand the water of the life and forgiveness and salvation from all evil as I have done to you and to them that believe in me. But if anyone believes in me and does not obey my commandments, although having confessed my name, he or she has no profit from this but runs a vain race; for such will find themselves in perdition and destruction because they have despised my commandments.

18. ACTS OF JOHN[†]

The apocryphal *Acts of John*, written no later than the early third century, purports to be an account of Saint John's missionary travels in Asia Minor. Perhaps originating from the area of Ephesus, the work, originally in Greek and evidencing certain Docetist tendencies, has come down to us in various incomplete manuscripts.

[†] Translated from R.A. Lipsius and M. Bonnet, *Acta Apostolorum Apocrypha*, vol. 2.1 (Hildesheim, 1990) 192ff.

Altaner (1961) 76–77 * Altaner (1966) 137–38 * Bardenhewer (1913) 1:437–42 *
Bardenhewer (1908) 105–6 * Bardenhewer (1910) 84–85 * Cross 79–80 * Goodspeed
70–73 * Quasten 1:135–37 * Steidle 280 * Tixeront 70–71 * CATH 6:411 * DCB 1:29 *
DTC 1.1:354–57 * EEChr 1:12 * NCE 2:411 * ODCC 881

H. Lietzmann, *Messe und Herrenmahl* (Bonn, 1926) 240–43. * E. Freistedt, *Altchristliche Totengedächtnistage und ihre Beziehungen zum Jenseitsglauben und Totenkultus der Antike*, LQF 24 (Münster, 1928). * P. Batiffol, "L'Eucharistie" in *La présence réelle et la transubstantiation*, 9th ed. (Paris, 1930) 189–203. * J. Quasten, *Monumenta Eucharistica et Liturgica Vetustissima* (Bonn, 1935) 339–41. * A.C. Rush, *Death and Burial in Christian Antiquity*, SCA 1 (Washington, D.C., 1941) 262–64.

72. The next day John, accompanied by Andronicus and the brethren, came to the sepulcher at dawn—it now being the third day after Drusiana's death—that we might break bread there. [. . .]   298

85. Having said this, John prayed, took bread, and carried it into the sepulcher to break. He said: "We give glory to your name which converts us from error and from cruel deceit. We give glory to you revealed to us what we have seen. We bear witness to your loving kindness which appears in various ways. We praise your good name, Lord, who pointed out those refuted by you. We give thanks to you, Lord Jesus Christ, because we believe that your grace is unchanging. We give thanks to you who had need of our nature that should be saved. We give thanks to you who has given us this sure faith, for you alone are God, both now and ever. We your servants give you thanks, O Holy One, for we have assembled according to your command and are gathered out of the world."   299

86. Having thus prayed and having glorified God, he went out of the sepulcher after imparting to all the brethren the Eucharist of the Lord. [. . .]   300

94. Before he was taken by the lawless Jews, who also were governed by the lawless serpent, he gathered all of us together and said: "Before I am handed over to them, let us sing a hymn to the Father, and so may we go forth to what lies before us." He told us, therefore, to form as it were a ring, holding one another's hands; he stood in the midst of them and said, "Answer Amen to me." He began, then, to sing a hymn and to say: 301

Glory be to you, Father.
And we, going about in a ring, answered him: Amen.
Glory be to you, Word. Glory be to you, Grace. Amen.
Glory be to you, Spirit. Glory be to you, Holy One.
Glory be to your glory. Amen.
We praise you, O Father, we give thanks to you, O Light,
wherein darkness does not dwell. Amen. [. . .]

109. And he [John] asked for bread and gave thanks as follows: "What praise or what offering or what thanksgiving shall we, breaking this bread, name other than you only, Lord Jesus? We glorify your name which was spoken by the Father; we glorify your name which was spoken   302

through the Son; we glorify you entering through the Door. We glorify the
Resurrection which you showed us. We glorify your way, we glorify your
seed, your word, your grace, your faithfulness, your salt, your unspeakable treasure, your plough, your net, your greatness, your diadem; for
us you were called the Son of Man, who gave us truth, rest, knowledge,
power, the commandments, confidence, hope, love, liberty, refuge in you.
You, Lord, are alone the root of immortality, the font of eternity, and the
seat of the ages. Called by all these names for our sake who now call upon
you by them, may we make known your greatness which now is invisible
to us but can be seen only by the pure, being portrayed in your manhood
only."

303   110. He broke the bread and gave it to all of us, praying over each of the
brethren that he might be worthy of the grace of the Lord and of the most
holy Eucharist. He himself likewise partook and said, "May I also share a
portion with you," and "Peace be with you, my beloved."

19. ACTS OF PAUL[†]

In his *On Baptism* (WEC 1:26-E) Tertullian speaks unfavorably about a presbyter in Asia Minor who was deposed from his office for writing a certain
Acts of Paul, which relates the story of a woman named Thecla, a disciple of
Paul, who baptized herself. And so the *Acts of Paul*, certainly a piece of romantic fiction, originates before the year 190. The content and extent of the
Acts only became known in 1904 when a fragment of a Coptic translation
in the library of the University of Heidelberg was published.

The work contains three independent treatises: (1) The Acts of Paul and
Thecla (from which the passages given below are taken), (2) The Correspondence of Paul with the Corinthians, and (3) the Martyrdom of Paul.

Altaner (1961) 73–74 * Altaner (1966) 136–37 * Bardenhewer (1908) 100–101 *
Bardenhewer (1910) 80–81 * Bardenhewer (1913) 1:418–24 * Goodspeed 65–70 *
Quasten 1:130–33 * Tixeront 72–73 * CATH 1:702 * DCB 1:29 * DTC 1.1:361–62 *
EEChr 1:12–13 * LTK 7:1510–11 * NCE 2:410 * ODCC 1238

304   [. . .] Then they sent in many beasts, while Thecla stood and stretched
out her hands and prayed. When she had finished her prayer, she turned
and saw a great pit full of water, and said, "Now is the time for me to
wash." And she threw herself in, saying, "In the name of Jesus Christ I
baptize myself on the last day." [. . .]

305   [. . .] But as Paul went in, the guards, being asleep, he broke bread and
brought water, gave her to drink of the word and dismissed her to her
husband Hieronymus. But he himself prayed.

[†] Translation from *New Testament Apocrypha*, vol. 2, rev. ed., ed. W. Schneemelcher,
English translation ed. R. McL.Wilson (Louisville, 1992) 245, 252–53, 258, 264.

[. . .] And immediately, when the Spirit that was in Myrta was at peace, each one took of the bread and feasted according to custom [. . .] amid the singing of psalms of David and of hymns. And Paul too enjoyed himself. [. . .] 306

But Paul could not be sorrowful because of Pentecost, this being a kind of festival for those who believe in Christ, both catechumens as well as believers; there was great joy and abundance of love, with psalms and praises to Christ, to the confirmation of those who heard. [. . .] 307

20. ACTS OF PETER[†]

This apocryphal work, originally in Greek, was written toward the end of the second century, probably in Asia Minor.

Altaner (1961) 74–75 * Altaner (1966) 134 * Bardenhewer (1908) 98–100 * Bardenhewer (1910) 79–80 * Bardenhewer (1913) 1:414–18 * Cross 81 * Goodspeed 73–78 * Steidle 279 * Tixeront 69 * CATH 4:702 * DCB 1:29 * DTC 1.1:360–61 * EEChr 1:13 * LTK 8:99 * NCE 2:410 * ODCC 1261

II. They brought Paul bread and water for the sacrifice so that he might pray and distribute it to every one. Among those present was a lady named Rufina who also desired to receive the Eucharist from Paul. As she approached Paul, who was filled with the spirit of God, he said, "Rising from the side of one who is not your husband but an adulterer, you, attempting to receive the Eucharist of God, do not worthily approach the altar of God." [. . .] 308

21. MELITO OF SARDIS

Very little is known of the life of Melito, bishop of Sardis in Lydia. Writing ca. 190 to Pope Victor (189–99), Polycrates of Ephesus refers to Melito as a "eunuch who lived entirely in the Holy Spirit, who lies in Sardis, waiting for the visitation from heaven when he will rise from the dead" (Eusebius, *Church History*, V.xxiv.5). Furthermore, according to Polycrates, Melito ranks among the "great luminaries" of Asia.

A list of Melito's writings has come down to us through Eusebius (WEC 2:**81**), yet the vast majority of these works exist only in fragments or have been entirely lost. But a fourth-century papyrus text of a Homily on the Passion, or the Pasch, was discovered and published in 1936 by Campbell Bonner; other manuscripts containing the text have since been located.

CPG 1: nos. 1092ff. * Altaner (1961) 133–35 * Altaner (1966) 88–89 * Bardenhewer (1908) 62–63 * Bardenhewer (1910) 105–6 * Bardenhewer (1913) 1:547–57 * Bautz

---

[†] Translated from *Acta Apostolorum Apocrypha*, vol. 1, ed. R.A. Lipsius and M. Bonnet (New York, 1990) 36.

5:1219–23 * Cross 103–9 * Goodspeed 112–15 * Hamell 42 * Jurgens 1:81 * Quasten 1:242–48 * Steidle 32 * Tixeront 82 * CATH 8:1126–29 * CE 10:166–67 * DCB 3:894–900 * DictSp 10:979–90 * DPAC 2:2207–9 * DTC 10.1:540–47 * EC 8:645–46 * EEC 1:551 * EEChr 2:745–46 * LTK 7:86–87 * NCE 9:631–32 * NCES 9:477–78 * ODCC 1068 * PEA (1894) 15.1:553–54 * PEA (1991) 7:1192–93 * TRE 22:424–28

C. Bonner, "The Homily on the Passion by Melito Bishop of Sardis," *Annuaire de l'Institut de philologie et d'histoire orientales et slaves* 4 (1936) 108–19. * C. Bonner, "The Homily on the Passion by Melito, Bishop of Sardis," in *Mélanges F. Cumont*, vol. 1 (Brussels, 1936) 107–19. * C. Bonner, "The New Homily of Melito and Its Place in Christian Literature," *Actes du Ve Congrès international de papyrologie* (Oxford, 1937) 94–97. * C. Bonner, "Two Problems in Melito's Homily on the Passion," HThR 31 (1938) 175–90. * G. Zuntz, "On the Opening Sentence of Melito's Paschal Homily," HThR 36 (1943) 290–315. * E.J. Wellesz, "Melito's Homily on the Passion: An Investigation into the Sources of Byzantine Hymnography," JThSt 44 (1943) 41–52. * H.H. Straton, "Melito of Sardis, Preacher Extraordinary," AThR 29 (1947) 167–70. * A. Wifstrand, "The Homily of Melito on the Passion," VC 2 (1948) 201–23. * C. Bonner, "The Text of Melito's Homily," VC 3 (1949) 184–85. * P. Nautin, "L'homélie de 'Méliton' sur la Passion," RHE 44 (1949) 429–38. * R.M. Grant, "Melito of Sardis on Baptism," VC 4 (1950) 33–36. * P. Nautin, *Le dossier d'Hippolyte et de Méliton dans les florilèges dogmatiques et chez les historiens modernes*, Patristica 1 (Paris, 1953). * O. Perler, *Ein Hymnus zur Ostervigil von Méliton? (Papyrus Bodmer XII)*, Paradosis 15 (Fribourg i. S., 1960). * S.G. Hall, "Melito in the Light of the Passover Haggadah," JThSt, n.s., 22 (1971) 29–46. * G.F. Hawthorne, "Christian Baptism and the Contribution of Melito of Sardis," in D.E. Aune, ed., *Studies in the New Testament and Early Christian Literature: Essays in Honor of Allen P. Wikgren* (Leiden, 1972) 241–51. * S.G. Hall, ed., *Melito of Sardis: On Pascha and Fragments* (Oxford, 1979). * A. Hansen, *The "Sitz in Leben" of the Paschal Homily of Melito of Sardis with Special Reference to the Paschal Festival in Early Christianity*, diss. (Ann Arbor, 1981). * F. Trisoglio, "Dalla Pasqua ebraica a quella cristiana in Melitone di Sardi," Aug 28 (1988) 151–85. * L. Cohick, "Melito of Sardis' 'Peri Pascha' and Its 'Israel,'" HThR 91 (1998) 351–72. * A. Stewart-Sykes, *The Lamb's High Feast: Melito, Peri Pascha, and the Quartodeciman Paschal Liturgy at Sardis*, Supplements to *Vigiliae Christianae* 42 (Boston, 1998). * L. Cohick, *The Peri Pascha Attributed to Melito of Sardis: Setting, Purpose, and Sources*, Brown Judaic Studies 327 (Providence, RI, 2000).

21-A. Homily on the Passion[†]

Melito—being a Quartodeciman, namely, one of those Asiatic Christians who observed the Christian Pasch on the same day as the Jews observed the Passover—no doubt preached the following homily on this day. There is no explicit mention of baptism. Melito, comparing the two Testaments, presents the Exodus and the paschal meal as types or figures of Christ's redemptive work.

[†] Translated from *Sur la Pâque*, trans. and ed. O. Perler, SChr 123 (Paris, 1966). Subheads are adapted from those given in the French translation of the text.

Mystery of the Pasch

1. The text of Scripture on the Hebrew Exodus[1] has been read, and the words of the mystery have just been explained: how the sheep was sacrificed and how the people were saved.[2] 309

2. Understand, then, dearly beloved, that the mystery of the Pasch is both new and old,[3] eternal and temporary,[4] corruptible and incorruptible,[5] mortal and immortal. 310

3. According to the Law it is old,[6] but according to the Logos it is new; in its figure it is temporary, in its grace, eternal;[7] corruptible in the sacrifice of the lamb, incorruptible in the life of the Lord;[8] mortal by burial in the earth, immortal is his resurrection from among the dead. 311

4. Old is the Law, but new is the Logos; the type is temporary, grace is eternal; corruptible is the lamb, incorruptible is the Lord; sacrificed as a lamb, resurrected as God. For "like a sheep he was led away to slaughter,"[9] yet he was not a sheep; like a lamb without a voice;[10] yet he was not a lamb. The figure has passed away, and the truth has been found. 312

5. Replacing the lamb is God who has come,[11] replacing the sheep is a man, and the man is Christ who contains all things.[12] 313

6. Certainly the sacrifice of the sheep, the observance of the Pasch, and the writing of the Law have been fulfilled in Christ Jesus,[13] in view of all that occurred in the old Law and even more in the new order.[14] 314

7. For the Law has become the Logos,[15] the old becomes new[16]—both coming from Sion and Jerusalem[17]—the commandment is grace, the type is truth,[18] the lamb is the Son,[19] the sheep is a man, and the man is God.[20] 315

8. Born as a Son,[21] led forth as a lamb, sacrificed as a sheep,[22] and buried as a man,[23] like God he rose again from among the dead, by nature being God and man. 316

9. He is all things:[24] the law in that he judges, the Logos in that he teaches,[25] grace in that he saves,[26] father in that he begets, Son in that he is begotten,[27] sheep in that he suffers,[28] man in that he is buried, God in that he rises. 317

10. This is Jesus Christ: "to him be glory forever and ever."[29] 318

11. This is the mystery of the Pasch as described in the Law, as just read. 319

---

1. See Exod 12:1–32. 2. See Exod 12:21, 27; Deut 16:2; Isa 53:7; 1 Cor 5:7; 1 Pet 1:18ff.; Titus 2:14; Jude 5. 3. See Matt 13:52. 4. See 2 Cor 4:18. 5. See 1 Cor 15:53ff. 6. See John 1:17; 2 Cor 3:1–16. 7. See John 1:16ff. 8. See Eph 6:24. 9. Isa 53:7; Acts 8:32. 10. See Isa 53:7; Acts 8:32. 11. See John 1:14, 29, 36. 12. See Wis 1:7; Eph 4:10; 1 Cor 8:6; Gal 3:28; Col 1:15–18; Heb 1:3. 13. See Rom 10:4; Matt 5:17. 14. See Heb 2:10. 15. See John 1:14. 16. See 2 Cor 5:17. 17. See Isa 2:3; Mic 4:2. 18. See John 1:14, 17; Rom 6:14. 19. See John 1:29, 36; 1 Cor 5:7; Rev 5:6, 12. 20. See John 1:12–14. 21. See Matt 1:21–25; Luke 1:31; 2:7. 22. See Isa 53:7. 23. See 1 Cor 15:4. 24. See 1 Cor 15:28; Col 1:19; 3:11; Eph 1:23. 25. See John 1:9. 26. See John 1:14, 16ff.; Eph 2:5, 8. 27. See John 1:18; Heb 1:5; 5:5; Acts 13:33 (Ps 2:7). 28. See 1 Cor 5:7. 29. 2 Tim 4:18; Gal 1:5; see 2 Pet 3:18.

I. Typological Explanation of the Jewish Pasch

The Exodus account

320   I wish to explain in detail the words of Scripture:[30] how God gave orders to Moses in Egypt when he, on the one hand, wanted to subject the Pharaoh to slavery, and when, on the other hand, he wanted to deliver Israel from slavery through the hand of Moses.

321   12."Behold, he says, you will take a lamb without flaw or blemish, and toward evening you will sacrifice it" with the children of Israel,[31] and at night you will eat in haste[32] and you will not break any of its bones.[33]

322   13. You will do this, as is written:[34] in one and the same night you will eat it, by families and tribes,[35] your loins gird, your staff in hand.[36] This is the Pasch of the Lord,[37] an eternal memorial for the children of Israel.[38]

323   14. Take some blood from the sheep, and then anoint the doorposts of your houses, by placing on them the sign of blood in order to ward off the angel.[39] For behold I will strike Egypt and in a single night Egypt will be left without offspring, both human and of animals.[40]

324   15. Then Moses, having slaughtered the sheep[41] and with the children of Israel having accomplished at night the mystery, marked the doors of the houses to protect the people and to ward off the angel.

Egypt's misfortune

325   16. Once the sheep was slaughtered[42] and the Pasch was eaten,[43] once the mystery was accomplished and the people had rejoiced, and once Israel was marked, then the angel began to strike Egypt,[44] a country not initiated into the mystery, not participating in the Pasch, not marked with blood, not protected by the Spirit; it was the enemy, the unbeliever.

326   17. In a single night the angel smote Egypt and left it childless. For the angel, having bypassed Israel and seeing it marked with the blood of the sheep, went against Egypt and overcame the stubborn Pharaoh with grief, clothing him not with mourning garb or a tattered cloak but with all of Egypt in distress, mourning its firstborn.

327   18. For all Egypt, plunged into pain and calamity, into tears and beating the breast, went to the Pharaoh; it was completely in mourning not only in its appearance but also in its soul; rending not only outward garb but also its nursing breasts.

328   19. It was a strange sight: on one side were those beating their breasts, on the other side those crying out in sorrow. In the middle sat the grieving Pharaoh on sackcloth and ashes,[45] clothed in a deep darkness as in a funeral garment, girded by all of Egypt as by a tunic of grief.

---

30. See Exod 13:3–32.   31. See Exod 12:3, 5ff.; 1 Pet 1:18ff.   32. See Exod 12:9, 11.
33. Exod 12:46; Num 9:12; see John 19:36.   34. See Exod 12:11.   35. See Exod 12:8;
Num 9:11.   36. See Exod 12:11.   37. See Exod 12:11, 27.   38. See Exod 12:14, 17, 24.
39. See Exod 12:7, 13, 22.   40. See Exod 12:12, 29; Ps 135:8.   41. See Exod 12:28.
42. See ibid.   43. See Exod 12:46.   44. See Exod 12:29.   45. See Jonah 3:6.

20. For Egypt clothed the Pharaoh like a garment of lamentation. This was 329 the tunic weaved for the body of the tyrant; this was the garment with which the Angel of Justice clothed the merciless Pharaoh: bitter grief, impenetrable darkness,[46] and the loss of the children. The angel continued to dominate the firstborn, for swift and insatiable was the death that struck them.

21. A strange trophy could be seen over the dead who had fallen at a 330 single blow.[47] And the route of those who fell became the nourishment of Death.

22. If you listen, you will be astonished at this unbelievable misfortune. 331 This is what befell the Egyptians: a long night and an impenetrable darkness,[48] a groping death, a destroying angel,[49] and a hell consuming[50] their firstborn.

23. But who was more unheard of and terrible you still have to learn. 332 In deep darkness insatiable Death was hiding; and the unfortunate Egyptians were groping in this darkness. But on the order of the angel, death, ever watchful, seized the firstborn of the Egyptians.

24. If anyone, then, was groping the darkness, he was led away to 333 Death. If a firstborn griped with his hands a dark body, he uttered from his frightened soul a mournful and terrible cry:[51] "Whom does my hand touch? Whom does my soul fear? What darkness surrounds my entire body? If my father, help me! If my mother, help me! If my mother, have pity on me! If my brother, speak to me! If my friend, be kind to me! If my enemy, depart from me! For I am a firstborn."

25. But before the firstborn could be silenced, the great Silence grasped 334 him and said: "You are my firstborn. It is I, the Silence of death, who are meant for you."

26. Another firstborn, noticing the seizure of others who were firstborn, 335 denied his own identity to avoid dying a cruel death. "I am not a firstborn. I am the third offspring." But death, incapable of being deceived, seized the firstborn who, head forward, fell silently. In one blow the firstborn of the Egyptians perished.[52] The first to be begotten, the first to be born, the one who was desired, the one who was cherished, was struck down: not only the firstborn of humans but also those of dumb animals.

27. Heard throughout the plains of the country was the bellowing of 336 animals grieving over those they nourished: the heifer for its calf, the mare for its colt, and the other beasts who brought forth; bitterly and pitifully they grieved over their firstborn.

28. There was lamentation and the striking of the breast at the destruc- 337 tion, at the death, of the firstborn. All Egypt gave off the odor of unburied corpses.[53]

29. The sight was terrible: Egyptian mothers with dishevelled hair, dis- 338 traught fathers screaming in Egyptian, "How wretched are we! At a single

---

46. See Exod 10:21.   47. See Wis 18:12.   48. See Wis 17:2; Exod 10:21.   49. Ps 35:5.   50. See Prov 1:12.   51. See Wis 18:10.   52. See Wis 18:12.   53. Ibid.

blow we have been deprived of our firstborn infants."[54] Striking their breasts, they clapped their hands to the dance of death.

339   30. This was the unhappiness that afflicted Egypt, a land instantly deprived of its infants.

Israel protected by the blood of the lamb:
a prefigure of the blood of the Lord

340   Israel, however, was protected by the slaying of the sheep[55] and was given light by the blood that was shed;[56] the death of the sheep was like a rampart for the people.

341   31. O strange and inexplicable mystery! The slaying of the sheep was the salvation of Israel, the death of the sheep became the life of the people; and the blood warded off the angel.

342   32. Tell me, O angel, what held you off? The slaying of the sheep or the life of the Lord? The death of the sheep or the figure of the Lord? The blood of the sheep or the Spirit of the Lord?

343   33. Clearly you were kept away because you saw the mystery of the Lord being realized in the sheep, the life of the Lord in the slaying of the sheep, the figure of the Lord in the death of the sheep. This is why you refrained from striking Israel, but only Egypt did you deprive of its infants.

344   34. What is this unexpected mystery? Egypt stricken for its loss? Israel protected for its salvation?[57] Listen to the meaning of the mystery.

Figure and model

345   35. Dearly beloved, what has been said and what has happened is nothing if it is separated from the symbolic meaning and from the plan that has been sketched beforehand. Everything done and everything said participate in the symbol—words in their symbolic meaning, the event in the prefiguring—so that just as the event is made known by its figure so also words are clarified by their symbol.

346   36. If something is to be built, there must be a model by which we can see what will be built. For this reason we construct a model out of wax, clay, or wood: namely, that what will be constructed—taller in height, stronger in resistance, beautiful in form, and rich in construction—may be seen through a small and perishable sketch.

347   37. But when is realized that to which the figure was destined, then is destroyed what formerly bore the image of the future. Now it is useless because it ceded its image to what exists in truth. What was formerly precious becomes worthless when what is truly precious appears.

348   38. Everything has its proper time:[58] the model has its proper time, the material has its proper time. You construct the model of the work. You desire this because in it you see the image of what will come.[59] You furnish

---

54. Ibid.   55. See Exod 12:13, 23; Wis 18:6–9.   56. See Eph 5:14; Heb 6:4; 10:32.
57. See Wis 19:6.   58. See Eccl 3:1–8.   59. See Col 2:17; Heb 8:5; 10:1.

materials for the model. You desire this because of what will arise because of it. You complete the work; that alone you desire, that alone you love, for in it alone you see the model and the material and the reality.

Figures of the Old Testament fulfilled in the New Testament

39. What is true for corruptible things is surely true for incorruptible things. What is true for earthly things, is surely true for heavenly things.[60] The salvation given by the Lord and truth have been prefigured in the people of Israel; the prescriptions of the Gospel have been proclaimed beforehand by the Law.   349

40. The people, then, were like the sketch of a plan, and the Law like the drawing of a parable; the Gospel is the explanation and fulfillment of the Law,[61] and the Church is the reservoir of reality.   350

41. The model, then, was precious before the reality, and the parable was wonderful before its interpretation. In other words, the people were honored before the Church was built, and the Law was admirable before the Gospel was revealed.[62]   351

42. But once the Church was established and before the Gospel was preached, the model became useless, yielding its power to the reality; and the Law came to an end, transferring its power to the Gospel.[63] Just as the figure became useless when it transferred its image to what truly exists, and just as the parable became useless when it was clarified by its interpretation,   352

43. So also was the Law fulfilled when the Gospel was revealed,[64] and the people of Israel lost their identity when the Church was established, and the model was abolished when the Lord was revealed.[65] And today what formerly was precious has become worthless after what is precious by nature was revealed.   353

44. Formerly the slaying of a sheep was precious; now it is worthless because of the life of the Lord. The death of a sheep was precious; now it is worthless because of the salvation of the Lord. The blood of a sheep was precious; now it is worthless because of the Spirit of the Lord. The silent lamb was precious;[66] now it is worthless because of the blameless Son.[67] The temple here below was precious; now it is worthless because of Christ on high.[68]   354

45. Jerusalem here below was precious; now it is worthless because of Jerusalem on high.[69] The small inheritance was precious;[70] now it is worthless because of abundant grace.[71] For it is not in one place nor in a small area[72] that God's glory has been established, but divine grace has been

---

60. See John 3:12.   61. See John 1:16–18; Matt 5:17; Luke 4:21; Rom 10:4. 62. See John 1:17; Rom 3:31; 7:12, 14, 16; 1 Tim 1:8.   63. See Rom 8:4; Gal 4:4; Eph 1:10.   64. See 2 Cor 4:4–6.   65. See 1 Tim 3:16.   66. See Isa 53:7.   67. See 1 Pet 1:19; Heb 9:14.   68. See Rev 21:22.   69. See Gal 4:24–26; Heb 12:22; Rev 3:12; 21:2.   70. See Num 34:2; 36:2.   71. See Ps 2:8.   72. See Deut 16:5ff.

poured out to the ends of the earth,[73] and there the omnipotent God has pitched his tent[74] through Jesus Christ "to whom be glory forever and ever. Amen."[75]

The structure of salvation

356   46. You have heard the explanation of the figure and what corresponds to it. Listen also to the structure of the mystery. What is the Pasch? The name comes from what happened: from *pathein* [to suffer] comes *paschein* [to suffer or: to celebrate the Passion = Pascha]. Learn, then, who it is who suffers and who shares in the pain of the one who suffers,[76] and why the

357   47. Lord came to earth: so that, clothing himself with the suffering one,[77] he carries this person off to the highest heavens.

The sin of humankind

358   It was through the Word[78] that "God in the beginning created heaven and earth"[79] and all that is in them. He made humankind from the earth and breathed life into them.[80] Then he placed humankind in Paradise, toward the east, in Eden,[81] in order to live there in happiness. As a law, God commanded, "From every tree of Paradise you may eat for nourishment, but from the tree of the knowledge of good and evil you may not eat; on the day you do you will die."[82]

359   48. But just as humankind, like a lump of earth capable of receiving two kinds of seeds,[83] was by nature disposed to receive good and evil, so hostile and greedy advice was received; touching the tree, he broke the commandment, disobeyed God, and was then thrown into this world as if into a prison of the condemned.[84]

360   49. He multiplied, lived a long time,[85] returned to the dirt for having eaten from the tree,[86] leaving an inheritance to his children. As an inheritance he bequeathed his children not chastity but unchasteness,[87] not incorruptibility but corruptibility,[88] not honor but dishonor, not freedom but slavery, not royalty but tyranny, not life but death,[89] not salvation but perdition.

361   50. Extraordinary and terrible was the destruction of mortals upon the earth.[90] This is what happened to them: they were carried off by tyrannical Sin and led to the waters of passions where they were swamped by insatiable pleasures: by adultery,[91] by fornication, by immodesty,[92] by evil thoughts, by love of money,[93] by murder,[94] by the spilling of blood,[95] by the tyranny of wickedness, by the tyranny of lawlessness.

---

73. See Mal 1:10–12; Acts 2:17 (Joel 3:1); Titus 3:6.   74. See Zech 2:14ff.; Rev 21:3.
75. 2 Tim 4:18; Gal 1:5; see 2 Pet 3:18.   76. See Heb 4:15.   77. See Phil 2:5–11.
78. See Wis 9:1; Ps 33:6; John 1:3.   79. Gen 1:1; see 2:4.   80. See Gen 2:7.   81. Gen 2:8.   82. Gen 2:16–17.   83. See Matt 13:24–30.   84. See Gen 3.   85. See Gen 3:16, 20; 4:1, etc.; 6:3.   86. See Gen 2:17; 3:19.   87. See Gen 2:25; 3:7.   88. See Wis 2:23.
89. See Gen 3:4, 19; Rom 5:12.   90. See Rom 1:24–32.   91. See Matt 15:19.   92. See 1 Pet 4:3.   93. See 1 Tim 6:10.   94. See Matt 15:19; Rom 1:29.   95. See Rom 3:15 (Prov 1:16; Isa 59:7).

51. For the father drew the sword against his son, and the son raised his hand against his father and impiously struck the breasts that fed him; a brother killed brother,[96] and the host was unjust to the guest, and friend killed friend, and man slew man, by the right hand of the tyrant.

52. All on earth became guilty of murder, fratricide, patricide, infanticide.[97] But something more frightful and strange was found: a mother touched the flesh that she brought into the world; she also touched those being nourished at her breasts; and she killed in her womb the fruit of her womb; and the unhappy mother became a dreadful tomb, having devoured the infant she carried within her.[98]

53. Enough! However, one will still find other strange things, things that are more frightful and more shameless: a father coveting the bed of his daughter, a son that of his mother, a brother that of his sister, a man that of another man,[99] "each covets his neighbor's wife."[100]

54. Sin rejoiced at this. Being the collaborator of Death, it first penetrated the souls of mortals and prepared for it like fodder the bodies of the dead.[101] Upon every soul sin placed its mark, and those it marked have begun to end their days.[102]

55. All flesh, then, fell under the domination of sin,[103] and every body under the power of death,[104] and every soul was expelled from the house of flesh.[105] What had been taken from the earth was reduced to earth,[106] and what had been given from God[107] was imprisoned in Hades. There was the dissolution of beautiful harmony and the disintegration of a beautiful body.

56. Humankind, divided by Death, was encircled by unhappiness and a strange captivity—like a captive[108] having been dragged along under the shadow of Death.[109] The image of the Father[110] lay abandoned, alone. This is why the mystery of the Pasch was fulfilled in the body of the Lord.

The passion of the Lord, prefigured and announced

57. But the Lord had already preordained his own sufferings in the patriarchs, the prophets, and in all the people, having sealed them through the Law and the prophets.[111] If something is to be new and wonderful, it must be prepared in advance; in this way, once it comes into being, it is believable because it has been prefigured for a long time.

58. The same is true for the mystery of the Lord—long prefigured and today made visible. This is believable because it has come to pass, even though deemed extraordinary by mortals. Old and new is the mystery of

362

363

364

365

366

367

368

369

---

96. See Gen 4:8; 1 John 3:12.   97. See John 8:44; 1 John 3:12.   98. See Deut 28:53–57.   99. See Rom 1:27.   100. Jer 5:8.   101. See Rom 5:12–21.   102. See Prov 1:12.   103. See Rom 7:14, 17.   104. See Rom 7:24.   105. See 2 Cor 5:1. 106. See Gen 3:19.   107. See Gen 2:7; Eccl 12:7.   108. See Eph 4:8 (Ps 68:18). 109. Matt 4:16; Luke 1:79 (Isa 9:1); Job 3:5; 12:22, etc.   110. See Gen 1:26ff.; Sir 17:3; Wis 2:23.   111. See Luke 24:25–27, 44ff.; Acts 3:18; 8:32–35; 17:2ff.

the Lord: old according to its figure, new according to grace. But if you look at this figure, you will see the truth through the figure's fulfillment.

370   59. If you desire that the mystery of the Lord be seen, look at Abel who was likewise slain,[112] at Isaac who was also bound,[113] at Joseph who was also sold,[114] at Moses who was also exposed,[115] at David who was also persecuted,[116] at the prophets who also suffered because of Christ.[117]

371   60. Look also at the sheep that was slain in Egypt, at him who struck Egypt and who through blood saved Israel.[118]

372   61. Furthermore, it is always through the voice of the prophets that the mystery of the Lord is announced. Moses said to the prophets, "And you see your life suspended before you, night and day, and you will certainly not believe in your Life."[119]

373   62. And David, "Why do the nations rage? Why do the people plot in vain? The kings of the earth take their stand, and the princes gather against the Lord and against his Anointed."[120]

374   63. And Jeremiah, "I am like an innocent lamb led to slaughter. They devised schemes against me, saying: 'Come, let us cast wood on his bread and cut him off from the land of the living, and certainly his name will be remembered no longer.'"[121]

375   64. And Isaiah: "Like a sheep he was led to slaughter and like a lamb that is silent before its shearers, he did not open his mouth. Who will tell his generation?"[122]

376   65. Numerous other things were announced by many of the prophets about the mystery of the Pasch which is Christ: "to whom be glory forever and ever. Amen."[123]

The figure fulfilled

377   66. He is coming out of heaven[124] to earth in order to suffer; he clothed himself with this by the womb of a virgin[125] from whom he came forth as a man. With a body capable of suffering he took upon himself the suffering of one who suffered;[126] he destroyed the sufferings of the flesh and by his own spirit killed the death that destroys life.

378   67. He was led like a lamb and slaughtered like a sheep.[127] He freed us from slavery to the world[128] as he freed us from the land of Egypt. He delivered us from the bonds of slavery to the devil[129] as he delivered us from the hand of the Pharaoh. He sealed our souls with his own Spirit[130] and the members of our body with his own blood.

---

112. See Gen 4:8.   113. See Gen 22:9.   114. See Gen 37:28.   115. See Exod 2:3.
116. See 1 Sam 18:6–11.   117. See Matt 5:12; 23:31; Acts 7:52; Jas 5:10.   118. See Exod 12:3ff.   119. Deut 28:66.   120. Ps 2:1ff.; Acts 4:25–26.   121. Jer 11:19.
122. Isa 53:7–8.   123. 2 Tim 4:18; Gal 1:5; see 2 Pet 3:18.   124. See John 6:33, 41–42, 51.   125. See Luke 1:26–38; Phil 2:6ff.   126. See Isa 53:4; Matt 8:17; 1 Pet 2:21–25.   127. See Jer 11:19; see Isa 53:7; Acts 8:32; Rev 5:12.   128. See 1 Pet 1:18; Titus 2:14.   129. See Heb 2:14ff.   130. See Eph 1:13; 4:30; 2 Cor 1:22.

68. He covered death with shame and sent the devil into mourning as 379
Moses did to the Pharaoh. He smote iniquity[131] and deprived the children
of injustice, as Moses did to Egypt. He delivered us from slavery into
freedom,[132] from darkness into light,[133] from death into life,[134] from tyranny
into an eternal kingdom.[135] He made us a new priesthood and a chosen
people forever.[136]

69. He is the Pasch that is our salvation.[137] He suffered much in many 380
[who came before him]. He was killed in Abel,[138] bound in Isaac,[139] exiled
in Jacob,[140] sold in Joseph,[141] exposed in Moses,[142] sacrificed in the lamb,[143]
persecuted in David,[144] dishonored in the prophets.[145]

70. He became incarnate in a virgin,[146] hung on a cross,[147] buried in 381
the earth,[148] raised from the dead,[149] and lifted up toward the highest
heavens.[150]

71. He is the silent lamb,[151] the lamb that was slaughtered,[152] the lamb 382
born of Mary,[153] the fair ewe; he was taken from the flock,[154] dragged off
to be slaughtered,[155] slain during the evening[156] and buried at night. No
bone of his was broken;[157] his body in the earth knew no corruption;[158]
he rose from the dead[159] and raised up humankind from the depths of
the tomb.[160]

II. The Ungrateful Refusal of Israel

72. He was put to death. And where? In the middle of Jerusalem. Why? 383
Because he cured its lame, cleansed its lepers, restored sight to its blind,
and raised up its dead.[161] This is why he suffered. It is written somewhere
in the Law and in the prophets: "They have returned evil for good, and
my soul is forlorn.[162] They plot evil against me, saying, 'Let us bind the
Just One, for he confounds us.'"[163]

Reproaches addressed to Israel: the unspeakable crime

73. O Israel, why have you committed this new crime? You dishonored 384
him who honored you. You despised him who valued you.[164] You denied

---

131. See Titus 2:14.   132. See Rom 8:21; Gal 5:1.   133. See 1 Pet 2:9; Col 1:12–13;
Eph 5:8, 12–14; John 3:19; Acts 26:18; 2 Cor 4:6.   134. See 1 John 3:14.   135. See
2 Pet 1:11.   136. See Exod 19:6; 1 Pet 2:5–9; Rev 1:6; 5:10; Titus 2:14.   137. See
1 Cor 5:7.   138. See Gen 4:8.   139. See Gen 22:9.   140. See Gen 28:1ff.   141. See
Gen 37:28.   142. See Exod 2:3.   143. See Exod 12:1–28.   144. See 1 Sam 18:6–11.
145. See Matt 5:12; 23:29–35; Acts 7:52.   146. See Matt 1:23 (Isa 7:14); Luke 1:26ff.
147. See Gal 3:13 (Deut 21:22ff.); Acts 5:30; 10:39.   148. See 1 Cor 15:4.   149. See
Rom 8:34.   150. See Mark 16:19; Acts 1:11; 1 Tim 3:16.   151. See Jer 11:19; Rev
5:12.   152. See Isa 53:7; Acts 8:32.   153. See Matt 1:21, 23 (Isa 7:14), 25; Luke 1:31.
154. See Exod 12:3, 5, 21.   155. See Isa 53:7.   156. See Exod 12:6.   157. See Exod
12:46; Num 9:12; Ps 34:20; John 19:33, 36.   158. See Acts 2:27, 31 (Ps 16:10).
159. See Rom 8:34.   160. See 1 Cor 15:1–58; Eph 4:8 (Ps 68:18).   161. See Matt
11:5; Luke 7:22.   162. Ps 35:12; see Gen 44:4; Ps 38:20; 1 Sam 25:21.   163. Isa 3:10,
LXX.   164. See Isa 52:14.

him who confessed you. You repudiated him who proclaimed you.[165] You killed him who gave you life.[166] What have you done, O Israel?

385   74. Has it not been written for you, "You will not shed innocent blood lest you die miserably"?[167] "I have," says Israel, "killed the Savior." Why? "Because he had to suffer."[168] You are in error, O Israel, in such quibbling in regard to the murder of the Lord.

386   75. He had to suffer, but not by you. He had to be dishonored, but not by you.[169] He had to be judged, but not by you. He had to be hung on a cross, but not by your right hand.

387   76. These, O Israel, are the words that you should have uttered to God: "O Master, if your Son had to suffer and if this was your will, may he suffer but not by me;[170] may he suffer by people of another race, may he be judged by the uncircumcised, may he be nailed [to the cross] by a tyrannical hand,[171] but no, not by me."

388   77. But you, O Israel, you did not utter these words to God. You have not purified yourself before your Master; you have not

389   78. been intimidated by his works; neither by the withered hand restored healthy to the body;[172] nor by the eyes of the blind opened by his hand;[173] nor by the paralyzed bodies made sound by his voice;[174] nor by the most wonderful miracle of a man already dead for four days and raised from the tomb.[175] You, on the contrary, have scorned all this. At the time of the Lord's immolation, toward evening, you prepared for him

390   79. sharp nails[176] and false witnesses, ropes and whips, vinegar and gall, the sword and afflictions, as for a bloody brigand.[177] Lashing lashed his body[178] and placing thorns on his head,[179] you even bound his good hands[180] which formed you from the earth,[181] and you gave him gall to drink, he who nourished you with life;[182] and you put to death the Savior on the day of the Great Feast.

391   80. And you were enjoying yourself;[183] he, on the other hand, was hungry; you were drinking wine and eating bread, he had vinegar and gall;[184] your face was radiant, his was somber; you were rejoicing, he was afflicted; you were singing psalms, he was condemned; you were beating time, he was being nailed;[185] you were dancing, he was being buried; you were reclining on a soft couch,[186] he was in a tomb and coffin.

---

165. See Acts 3:14; Matt 23:37.   166. See Acts 3:15; 5:30; 1 Thess 2:15.   167. Jer 7:6; 22:3.   168. See Matt 16:21; Mark 8:31; Luke 9:22; 24:26; Acts 3:18; 17:3.   169. See Isa 53:3.   170. See Matt 26:42; Mark 14:36; Luke 22:42.   171. See John 18:31; 19:6ff.   172. See Matt 12:9–13; Mark 3:1–5; Luke 6:6–10.   173. See Matt 9:27–31; 11:5; Luke 7:22.   174. See Luke 5:18–26; Matt 9:2–8; Mark 2:3–12.   175. See John 11:1–44.   176. See John 20:25.   177. See Matt 26:59–62; Mark 14:55–59; Luke 22:66–71.   178. See John 19:1; Matt 27:26.   179. See Matt 27:29; Mark 15:17; John 19:5; John 19:2.   180. See Matt 27:2; John 18:12, 24; Mark 15:1.   181. See Gen 2:7.   182. See Matt 27:34 (Ps 69:21), 48.   183. See Amos 6:4–6.   184. See Matt 27:34, 48; Ps 69:21.   185. See John 20:25; Luke 24:40.   186. See Amos 6:4.

Israel's injustices and ingratitude

81. O criminal Israel, why have you committed this unspeakable injustice[187] of hastening your Savior into unmentionable sufferings, your Master, who formed you, who created you, who honored you, who named you "Israel"?[188]   392

82. But you have not been found to be "Israel," for you have not seen God;[189] you have not recognized the Lord; you have not known, O Israel, that it is he, the Firstborn of God,[190] who was begotten before the morning star,[191] who made light to rise, who made the day to shine, who separated the darkness,[192] who established the first boundary, who suspended the earth,[193] who dried up the abyss,[194] who spread out the firmament,[195] who brought order to the world,[196]   393

83. who arranged the stars in the heaven, who had the luminaries shine,[197] who created the angels in heaven, who placed there the thrones,[198] who made for himself mortals on earth.[199] It was he who chose you,[200] who guided you from Adam to Noah, from Noah to Abraham, from Abraham to Isaac and Jacob and to the twelve patriarchs.[201]   394

84. He led you to Egypt[202] and protected you; with great care he nourished you.[203] He gave you light by a column of fire and covered you with a cloud.[204] He divided the Red Sea[205] and led you through it[206] and scattered your enemy.[207]   395

85. He gave you manna from heaven;[208] he gave you drink from the rock;[209] he gave you the Law on Horeb;[210] he gave your descendants the Promised Land;[211] he sent you the prophets,[212] who raised up your kings.[213]   396

86. He came to you, he who cured your suffering ones and who raised up those among you who were dead. It is against him that you act sacrilegiously, against him that you commit injustice. It is he whom you sent to death. It is he whom you sold for a piece of silver[214] after having put a price of two drachmas on his head.[215]   397

Against ungrateful Israel

87. O ungrateful Israel, come, be judged before me for your ingratitude. What value have you placed on being guided by him? On the election   398

---

187. See Mic 6:3–4.   188. See Gen 32:29; 35:10.   189. See Gen 32:31.   190. See Heb 1:6.   191. See Ps 110:3.   192. See Gen 1:3–5; Ps 136:7–9.   193. See Gen 1:6–9.   194. See Gen 1:2.   195. See Gen 1:6–8; Ps 136:6.   196. See Sir 16:25.   197. See Gen 1:14–18; Ps 136:7–9.   198. See Col 1:16.   199. See Gen 2:7.   200. See Isa 44:1ff.; Ps 33:12; 47:5; Acts 13:17.   201. See Acts 7:8.   202. See Jer 2:6.   203. See Gen 37–50; Exod 1–12.   204. See Exod 13:21, etc.; Ps 78:14; 105:39.   205. See Exod 14–15; Ps 136:13.   206. See Ps 136:14; 106:9; Wis 10:18.   207. See Ps 136:15; 106:11; Wis 10:19.   208. See Exod 16:4–35; Ps 78:24; 105:40; 1 Cor 10:3.   209. See Exod 17:4–7; Ps 136:16; 1 Cor 10:4, etc.   210. See Exod 19–31.   211. See Josh 11:23ff.; Ps 78:55; 136:21ff.   212. See Matt 23:34.   213. See 1 Sam 8:5, etc.; Acts 13:21ff.   214. See Matt 26:14–15; Mark 14:10–11; Luke 22:3–5.   215. See Matt 17:24–27.

of your fathers?[216] On the descent into Egypt? And on being fed there by good Joseph?[217]

399   88. What value did you place on the ten plagues?[218] On the column of fire during the night? On the cloud during the day?[219] On the passage through the Red Sea?[220] What value did you place on the gift of manna from heaven?[221] On the distribution of water from the rock?[222] On the giving of the Law on Horeb?[223] On the inheritance which is the Promised Land?[224] On the blessings you have received?

400   89. What value have you placed on those who suffer? On those whom he cured when he was present? Value for me, then, the withered hand, which he restored to the body![225]

401   90. Value those born blind to whom he gave light by his word![226] Value, then, the dead who were buried,[227] whom he raised from the tomb after three, four days! Priceless are the gifts he gave you. And you, far from honoring him, have only shown him ingratitude in return; you have given him evil for good,[228] suffering for joy, and death for life,

402   91. him for whom you should die.

The pagans treated him better

Should a pagan king be taken captive by his enemies, war is waged on his behalf, a rampart is scaled, a city is destroyed, ransoms are sent, messengers are dispatched, so that he be recovered, that his life be restored, or that he, if dead, receive a burial.

403   92. You, on the other hand, have voted against your Savior.[229] In fact, he, before whom the nations bowed,[230] whom the uncircumcised admired, whom foreigners glorified,[231] for whom even Pilate washed his hands,[232] it is he whom you sent to death during the Great Festival.

The bitter herbs: a figure of Israel's punishment

404   93. This is why the Feast of the Unleavened Bread is bitter for you, as has been written for you, "You will eat unleavened bread with bitter herbs."[233] Bitter for you the nails you sharpened,[234] the tongue you whetted,[235] the false witnesses you presented,[236] the bonds you prepared,[237] the whips you wove,[238] Judas whom you paid.[239] Herod whom you obeyed,[240] Caiaphas whom you trusted,[241] the gall you prepared,[242] the vinegar you

---

216. See Gen 12:1ff.   217. See Gen 37–48.   218. See Exod 7:14–12:36.   219. See Exod 13:21.   220. See Exod 14–15.   221. See Exod 16:4–35.   222. See Exod 17:4–7. 223. See Exod 19–31.   224. See Josh 11:23, etc.; Ps 78:55; 136:21ff.   225. See Matt 12:13.   226. See Matt 9:27ff.; 11:5; 15:30; John 9:1ff.; 11:37.   227. See Matt 11:5; John 11:1ff.   228. See Gen 44:4; Ps 35:12; Jer 18:20.   229. See Matt 26:59–66.   230. See Matt 2:2, 11; 15:25.   231. See Matt 8:5–13; John 12:20ff.   232. See Matt 27:24. 233. Exod 12:8.   234. See John 20:25.   235. See Matt 27:6–23.   236. See Matt 26:59–61.   237. See Matt 27:2; John 18:12, 24.   238. See Matt 27:26; John 19:1. 239. See Matt 26:14ff.   240. See Luke 23:7–15; Acts 4:27.   241. See Matt 27:20. 242. See Matt 27:34; Ps 69:22.

cultivated,[243] the thorns you gathered,[244] the hand you made bloody. You sent your Savior to death in the middle of Jerusalem.

Invitation to the pagans

94. Listen, all families of the nations,[245] and see: an unspeakable murder   405
has taken place in the middle of Jerusalem, in the city of the Law, in the city of the Hebrews, in the city of the prophets, in the city believed to be just. And who has been slain? I blush to say this, and yet I have to speak. If the murder had occurred during the night, or if it had taken place in an uninhabited area, it would be easy to remain silent; but now in the middle of the street or the city,[246] yes, in the middle of the city—with all looking on—the unjust murder of the Just One was committed.[247]

95. And so he was raised upon a cross, and an inscription was added,[248]   406
indicating him who was slain.[249] Who is this person? It is hard to say; yet not to say is still more dreadful. But listen while trembling before him on whose account the earth trembled.[250]

96. He who suspended the earth is himself suspended,[251] he who fixed   407
the heavens is himself fixed [upon the cross];[252] he who strengthened everything is held upon the cross; he who is the Master is insulted;[253] he who is the king of Israel is removed[254] by the hand of Israel.

97. O unheard-of murder! O unheard-of injustice! The appearance of   408
the Master has been changed, his body stripped naked;[255] he was not even considered worthy of a garment so that he not be seen.[256] This is why the luminaries turned away, and with them the day became dark[257] so as to conceal the naked one upon the cross, thus obscuring not the Lord's body but human eyes.

98. And when the people were not trembling, the earth trembled;[258]   409
when the people were not seized with fright, the heavens were frightened; when the people did not tear apart their garments, the angel did so;[259] when the people were not lamenting, it was the "Lord who thundered from heaven and the Most High who spoke."[260]

The destruction of Israel

99. O Israel, this is why you did not tremble in the presence of the Lord,   410
you were not seized with fear in the presence of the Lord, you did not lament in the presence of the Lord, you did not utter cries of sorrow for your firstborn; you did not tear your garments when the Lord was hung, so you tore them for those of your own who were slain. You abandoned

243. See Matt 27:48; Ps 69:22.   244. See Matt 27:29.   245. See Ps 22:28; 96:7. 246. See Wis 2:10–20; Isa 52:13–53:2.   247. See Acts 3:14.   248. See John 3:14; 8:28; 12:32, 34.   249. See John 19:19ff.; Mark 15:26.   250. See Matt 27:51.   251. See Acts 5:30; 10:39 (Deut 21:22).   252. See Acts 2:23.   253. See Matt 27:39–43.   254. See Matt 27:42; Mark 15:32; John 1:49; 12:13.   255. See Matt 27:35; John 19:23ff. 256. See Matt 27:35; John 19:23ff.   257. See Matt 27:45; Mark 15:33; Luke 23:44–45. 258. See Matt 27:51.   259. See Matt 27:51.   260. Ps 18:13; see John 12:28.

the Lord; you were not found by him.[261] You crushed the Lord; you were crushed down by the earth. You lie dead;

411   100. He rose from among the dead[262] and ascended into heaven above.[263]

Epilogue

The triumph of Christ

412   Being Lord, he assumed human nature, he suffered for those who suffer,[264] he was bound for those in bonds, he was judged for the guilty,[265] he was buried for those who are entombed.

413   101. He rose from among the dead and cries out to you,[a] "Who will judge me?[266] Let him face me! I freed the condemned; I gave life to the dead;[267] I raised up him who was buried.[268]

414   102. "Who speaks in opposition to me?" "I," he says, "am the Christ,[269] I who have destroyed death,[270] triumphed over the enemy,[271] trampled hell underfoot,[272] bound the strong,[273] and carried off mortals to the heights of heaven." "It is I," he says, "the Christ."[274]

Call to receive the forgiveness of sins

415   103. "Come, then, all families of men[275] steeped with sins, and receive the forgiveness of sins.[276] For I am your forgiveness;[277] I am the Pasch of salvation;[278] I am the lamb that was immolated for you;[279] I am your ransom;[280] I am your life;[281] I am your resurrection;[282] I am your light;[283] I am your salvation;[284] I am your king;[285] I lead you to the heights of heaven;[286] I will raise you up;[287] I will show you the eternal Father;[288] I will raise you up with my right hand."

Final apotheosis

416   104. This is he who made heaven and earth,[289] who in the beginning formed the human race,[290] who was announced by the Law and the

---

a. Some suggest that nos. 101 and 102 may have been parts of a preexisting liturgical hymn.

261. See Rom 10:20ff. (Isa 65:1ff.).   262. See Rom 8:34.   263. See Mark 16:19; Acts 1:2, 11, 22; 1 Tim 3:16.   264. 1 Pet 2:21.   265. See 1 Pet 2:23.   266. Isa 50:8ff.; see Mic 6:1ff.   267. See Rom 4:17; 8:11; 1 Cor 15:22.   268. See John 6:39–40, 44, 54.   269. See Mark 14:61ff.   270. See 1 Cor 15:26; 2 Tim 1:10.   271. See Col 2:15.   272. See Acts 2:27 (Ps 16:10).   273. See Matt 12:29; Mark 3:27.   274. See Eph 4:8–10 (Ps 68:19).   275. See Ps 22:28; 96:7.   276. Acts 10:43; 26:18; 2:38.   277. See Eph 1:7; Col 1:14.   278. See 1 Cor 5:7.   279. See John 1:36; Rev 5:12.   280. See Matt 20:28; Mark 10:45; 1 Tim 2:6; 1 Cor 1:30; Eph 1:7; Col 1:14; Rom 3:24; Heb 9:15.   281. See John 1:4; 6:33, 35, 48; 11:25; 14:6; Col 3:3ff.; 2 Tim 1:10; 1 John 1:2; 5:11ff.   282. See John 11:25.   283. See John 1:4, 9; 3:19; 8:12; 9:5; 12:46; 1 John 1:5; Luke 2:32; Acts 13:47 (Isa 49:6); 1 Pet 2:9.   284. See Acts 4:12; 13:47 (Isa 49:6); 2 Tim 2:10; Heb 2:10; 5:9; 1 Pet 2:2.   285. See Matt 21:5 (Zech 9:9); John 12:15; John 1:49; 18:33, 37; Rev 15:3; 17:14; 19:16.   286. See Eph 4:8–10 (Ps 68:19).   287. See John 5:21; 6:40.   288. See John 14:8ff.   289. See Gen 1:1.   290. Gen 2:7.

prophets,[291] who was incarnate in a virgin,[292] who hung upon a cross,[293] who was buried in the earth,[294] who was raised from among the dead,[295] who ascended to the highest heavens,[296] who is seated at the right hand of the Father,[297] who has the power to judge and to save all;[298] through him the Father created everything[299] from the beginning and for the ages.

105. He is the "alpha and omega";[300] he is the "beginning and the end,"[301]—the inexplicable beginning and the incomprehensible end—, "he is the Christ";[302] he is the King;[303] he is Jesus;[304] he is the Strategus;[b] he is the Lord;[305] he was raised from among the dead;[306] he is seated at the right hand of the Father.[307] He bears the Father and is borne by the Father;[308] "to him be glory and power forever. Amen."[309]   417

Melito: On the Pasch[c]
    Peace to the writer and to the reader and to those who love the Lord with simplicity of heart.[310]   418

GREECE

22. ARISTIDES OF ATHENS. *APOLOGY*[†]

Little is known of the life of Aristides. But in 1878 an Armenian fragment of an *Apology* attributed to him was published at Venice. Then in 1889 a Syriac manuscript of the whole work was discovered on Mount Sinai. This in turn led to the discovery of the work's original Greek found in the religious novel *Lives of Barlaam and Josaphat,* which appear among the writings of John of Damascus (ca. 655–ca. 750). The treatise has two sections: the first (chapters i–xiv) treats the false teaching of the Barbarians, Greeks, and Jews; the second (chapters xv–xvii) gives the true teaching of the Christians, the standard by which all other religious doctrines are to be judged. In many ways the work resembles the Letter to Diognetus (WEC 1:**34**).

CPG 1: nos. 1062–67 * Altaner (1961) 118–19 * Altaner (1966) 64–65 * Bardenhewer (1913) 1:171–86 * Bardenhewer (1908) 46–48 * Bardenhewer (1910) 36–38 * Bautz

---

b. Strategus: a Greek official having broad military, political, and civil powers.
    c. This subhead appears in the manuscript tradition.
    291. See Luke 24:25–27.   292. See Matt 1:23 (Isa 7:14); Luke 1:26ff.   293. See Acts 5:30 (Deut 21:22); 10:39, etc.   294. See 1 Cor 15:4.   295. See Rom 8:34.   296. See Mark 16:19; Acts 1:2, 11, 22; 1 Tim 3:16.   297. See Ps 110:1; Matt 26:64; Mark 16:19; Rom 8:34; Col 3:1; Eph 1:20; 1 Pet 3:22.   298. See John 5:22, 27–29.   299. See John 1:3; Col 1:16ff.   300. Rev 1:8; 21:6; 22:13.   301. Rev 21:6; 22:13.   302. John 7:26, 41; Acts 9:22; see Matt 16:16; 26:63ff.   303. See Matt 21:5 (Zech 9:9); John 12:15; John 1:49; 18:33, 37; Rev 15:3; 17:14; 19:16; Matt 27:11, 37, 42; Mark 15:2, 32; Luke 23:3, 38; John 18:37.   304. See Matt 1:21; Acts 4:10–12.   305. See Acts 2:36; Phil 2:11.
306. See Rom 8:34.   307. See Mark 16:19; Acts 1:2; 11:22; 1 Tim 3:16.   308. See John 10:30, 38; 14:9, 11, 20; 16:15, 32; 17:21.   309. Rev 1:6.   310. See Acts 2:46.
    † Translation (modified) from ANF 10 (i.e., vol. 9) 277–78.

1:212–13 * Cross 45–47 * Goodspeed 97–99 * Hamell 37 * Jurgens 1:48–49 * Quasten 1:191–95 * Tixeront 34–35 * CATH 1:822 * CE 1:712–13 * CHECL 37–38 * DCB 1:160 * DHGE 4:187–91 * DPAC 1:346–47 * DTC 1.2:1864–67 * EC 1:1907–8 * EEC 1:72–73 * EEChr 1:111–12 * LTK 1:973 * NCE 1:798 * NCES 1:666–67 * ODCC 101 * PEA (1991) 1:1100 * RACh 1:652–54

G.C. O'Ceallaigh, "Marcianus Aristides, on the Worship of God," HThR 51 (1958) 227–54.

419   xv. Christians [. . .] give thanks to God every hour, doing so for all meat and drink and other blessings. [. . .] If there are any among them who are poor and needy, and if they have no spare food, they fast two or three days in order to supply to the needy their lack of food. They observe the precepts of their Messiah with much care, living justly and soberly as the Lord their God commanded them. Every morning and every hour they give thanks and praise to God for his loving kindness toward them; and for their food and their drink they offer thanksgiving to him. And if any righteous person among them passes from the world, they rejoice and offer thanks to God, and they escort the body as if the deceased were setting out from one place to another near-by. And when a child has been born to one of them, they give thanks to God.[a] And if moreover it happens to die in childhood, they give thanks to God the more, as for one who has passed through the world without sin. And further if they see any one of them dies in ungodliness or in one's sins, for such they grieve bitterly and sorrow as for one who goes to meet his or her doom.

SYRIA

23. THEOPHILUS OF ANTIOCH

Converted to Christianity as an adult, Theophilus was, according to Eusebius (*Church History*, IV.xx), the sixth bishop of Antioch and is considered among the early Christian apologists. Few details are known of his life. He died between 185 and 191.

CPG 1: nos. 1107ff. * Altaner (1961) 131–33 * Altaner (1966) 75–77 * Bardenhewer (1908) 65–67 * Bardenhewer (1910) 52–54 * Bardenhewer (1913) 1:278–90 * Bardy (1929) 60–61 * Goodspeed 117–18 * Hamell 43 * Jurgens 1:73–77 * Quasten 1:236–42 * Steidle 32–33 * Tixeront 45–47 * CATH 14:1113–18 * CE 14:625–26 * DCB 4:993–99 * DictSp 15:530–42 * DPAC 2:3405–6 * DTC 15.1:530–36 * EC 11:1952–53 * EEC 2:831–32 * EEChr 2:1122 * LTK 9:1472 * NCE 14:72 * NCES 13:932–33 * ODCC 1606 * PEA (1894) 5.2 (n.s.) 2149

W. Hartke, "Ueber Jahrespunkte und Feste, insbesondere das Weihnachtsfest," *Akademie der Wissenschaft. Sektion für Altertumswissenschaft* 6 (Berlin, 1956) 13–17.

---

a. Give thanks: some understand this as a hidden reference to baptism.

23-A. Discourse to Autolychus[†]

This defense of Christianity, written to answer the objections of a certain Autolychus, a heathen friend of Theophilus, is the only writing of Theophilus to have come down to us. In three books the author shows the superiority of the Christian religion over that of the pagans.

I.12. As to your laughing at me and calling me "Christian," you do not know what you are saying. First, because what is anointed is sweet and useful; it is not to be laughed at. Can any ship be serviceable and seaworthy unless it has first been caulked? What tower or house is beautiful and useful unless it has been anointed? And what person upon entering this life or a gymnasium is not anointed with oil? And what work has either decoration or beauty unless it is anointed and burnished? Also, the air and all that is under heaven is in a certain way anointed by light and spirit. Are you unwilling to be anointed with the oil of God? And so we are called Christians because we are anointed with the oil of God.

420

EGYPT

24. *LETTER OF BARNABAS*[††]

The *Letter of Barnabas* is neither a letter nor the product of Barnabas, the good friend of Paul. More a theological discourse, it has two sections: chapters I–XVII focusing on the Old Testament; chapters XVIII–XXI being of a moral nature and describing, as does the *Didache* I–VI (WEC 1:178–86), the ways of light and darkness.

The work, originally written in Greek, states nothing about its author nor does it claim apostolic authority. Nonetheless, Clement of Alexandria (WEC 1:44) and Origen (WEC 1:43) both say that the "letter" comes from the hand of Barnabas. Yet the fact that the author has a distinct and evident bias against Judaism and even views the Old Testament as the work of the devil militates against the letter being written by a disciple of Paul, who saw the Old Testament as a cherished and divine institution.

Once commonly believed to have originated from the area of Alexandria, the manuscript's homeland might be Syria or Asia Minor.

There is great variety as to the document's date, anywhere from 70–150, with the years 117–32 perhaps being more probable.

CPG 1: no. 1050 * Altaner (1961) 80–82 * Altaner (1966) 53–55 * Bardenhewer (1908) 22–25 * Bardenhewer (1910) 20–23 * Bardenhewer (1913) 1:86–98 * Bardy (1929) 67–68 * Goodspeed 20–22 * Hamell 25–26 * Jurgens 1:13–16 * Quasten 1:85–92 * Steidle 281 * Tixeront 18–19 * CATH 1:1256 * CE 2:299–300 * DCB 1:260–65 * DHGE

[†] Translated from PG 6:1041–42.
[††] Translated from *Epître de Barnabé*, trans. and ed. P. Prigent, SChr 172 (Paris, 1971) 160–67, 182–89.

6:848 * DictSp 1:1245–47 * DPAC 1:481–84 * DTC 2.1:416–22 * EC 2.865 * EEC
1:111–12 * EEChr 1:167–68 * LTK 2:18 * NCE 2:103 * NCES 2:102 * ODCC 159 * PEA
(1894) 3.1:25 * PEA (1991) 2:453 * RACh 1:1207–17 * TRE 5:238–41

K. Thieme, *Kirche und Synagoge: die ersten nachbiblischen Zeugnisse ihres Gegensatzes
im Offenbarungsverständnis: der Barnabasbrief und der Dialog Justins des Märtyrers*, neu
bearbeitet und erläutert, Kreuzritterbücherei 3 (Olten, 1945). * E. Ferguson, "Baptism
from the Second to the Fourth Century," ResQ 1 (1957) 185–97. * L.W. Barnard,
"The Epistle of Barnabas—A Paschal Homily?" VC 15 (1961) 8–22. * B. Neunheuser,
Baptism and Confirmatio (St. Louis, 1964) 60–61. * L.W. Barnard, "The Day of the Resurrection and Ascension of Christ in the Epistle of Barnabas," RB 78 (1968) 106–7.
* G. Saber, "Le baptême dans l'Epitre de Barnabé," Mel 4, no. 2 (1968) 194–214
[Arabic, French summary]. * K. Wengst, *Tradition und Theologie des Barnabasbriefes*,
Arbeiten zur Kirchengeschichte 42 (Berlin and New York, 1971). * F.S. Barcellona,
ed., *Epistola di Barnaba = Barnabae Epistula: introduzione, testo critico, traduzione, com-
mento, glossario e indici*, Corona Patrum 1 (Turin, 1975). * J.-L. Vesco, "La lecture du
psautier selon l'Epître de Barnabé," RBibl 93 (1986) 5–37. * J.C. Paget, "The Epistle
of Barnabas: Outlook and Background," Wissenschaftliche Untersuchungen zum
Neuen Testament 2, series 64, diss. (Tübingen, 1994). * R. Hvalvik, "The Struggle
for Scripture and Covenant: The Purpose of the Epistle of Barnabas and Jewish-
Christian Competition in the Second Century," Wissenschaftliche Untersuchungen
zum Neuen Testament 2, series 82, diss. (Tübingen, 1996).

421   XI.1. Let us now see whether the Lord has taken care to reveal in advance anything concerning the water [of baptism] and the cross.

422   XI.2. As to the water, Scripture when speaking about Israel says that
they did not know how to receive the baptism that brings the pardon of
sins but that they should obtain another for themselves.

423   XI.3. The prophet, in fact, says: "O heaven, be astounded and let the
earth tremble the more at this since this people have done two evil things:
they have forsaken me, the living source of water, and they have dug out
for themselves a cistern of death. Is Sinai, my holy mountain, a rock in
the desert? For you will be like young birds, flying away when they are
ejected from the nest."[1]

424   XI.4. And the prophet also says: "I will walk before you and level the
mountain and I will break the gates of brass, and I will shatter the iron
bars, and to you I will bestow secret, hidden, invisible treasures. In this
way they may indeed know that I am the Lord God."

425   XI.5. And "you will dwell in the lofty cave of a strong rock where water
is never lacking. You will see the king in his glory, and your soul will meditate on the fear of the Lord."[2]

426   XI.6. By another prophet he says: "Whoever acts thus will be like this
tree which, planted by streams of water, will produce fruit in due time. Its
leaves will not fall; all that they do will prosper. It is not the same for the
impious, no, not at all. Rather, they are like the dust that the wind chases

---

1. Jer 2:12–13; Isa 16:1–2.   2. Isa 45:1–3; 33:16–18.

from the face of the earth. This is why the impious shall not be raised in judgment, nor will sinners stand in the counsel of the just. For the Lord knows the way of the just, but that of the ungodly will perish."[3]

xI.7. Notice that he describes at the same time the water and the cross.   427

xI.8. This is what he means to say: Happy are those who have planted   428
their hope in the cross and have gone down into the water. For, he says, their reward will be given "in due season." At that time, he says, I will repay. But now, when he says "its leaves will not fall," he means that every word of faith and love coming from your mouth will be for many the reason for their conversion and hope.

xI.9. Yet another prophet says, "And the land of Jesse will be celebrated   429
more than any other."[4] This means that he glorifies the vessel of his Spirit.

xI.10. What does he then say? "There was a river flowing from the right   430
and wonderful trees growing out of it. Whoever eats from it will live forever."[5] The meaning here is that when we go down into the water, we are full of sins and blemishes, but when we ascend out of the water we bear fruit in our hearts, having in spirit fear and hope in Jesus.

xI.11. "Whoever eats of these will live forever."[6] This means, he says,   431
that whoever hears these words and believes will live forever.

xv.1. Furthermore, as to the Sabbath, this is what is written in the Deca-   432
logue which God personally gave to Moses on Mount Sinai: "With a pure hand and a pure heart keep holy also the Sabbath of the Lord."[7]

xv.2. Elsewhere he says, "If my children observe the Sabbath, then I will   433
be merciful to them."[8]

xv.3. As to the Sabbath, he mentions it at the beginning of creation: 434
"And in six days God made the work of his hands. He completed it on the seventh day, a day on which he rested and which he made holy."[9]

xv.4. Pay attention, my children, to the meaning of the phrase "He com-   435
pleted it in six days." This means that the Lord will lead the universe to its completion in six thousand years. He himself is my witness when he says, "Behold, one day of the Lord will be like a thousand years."[10] And so, my children, it is "in six days," in six thousand years, that the universe will end.

xv.5. "And on the seventh day he rested."[11] This means that when his   436
Son will have come to put an end to the time of the lawless one, to judge the lawless, and to change the sun, the moon, and the stars, he shall then rest on the seventh day.

xv.6. Furthermore, he says, "You shall keep it holy with pure hands and   437
a pure heart."[12] If, then, anyone can now by having a pure heart sanctify this day which God has made holy, then we are totally deceived.

xv.7. To be sure, when we enjoy true rest, when we shall be able to do   438
so because we have been made righteous ourselves and have received

---

3. Ps 1:3–6.   4. Unidentifiable citation.   5. Unidentifiable citation but cf. Ezek 47:1–12.   6. Ezek 47:9.   7. Exod 20:8. Cf. Ps 24:4.   8. Jer 17:24.   9. Gen 2:2–3.   10. Ps 90:40.   11. Gen 2:2.   12. Exod 20:8.

the promise, when there is no more sin but when all things have been renewed by the Lord, then we shall indeed keep it holy because we ourselves have first been made holy.

439   xv.8. Finally he said to them: "Your new moons and your Sabbaths I do not endure."[13] Notice how he expresses himself: your present Sabbaths are not acceptable to me; only the Sabbath I have made, and on which, after having given rest to all things, I will make a beginning on the eighth day, namely, the beginning of another world.

440   xv.9. So it is that we celebrate as a joyful feast the eighth day on which Jesus rose from the dead and after manifesting himself ascended into heaven.

---

13. Isa 1:13.

Chapter V

Third Century. West

AFRICA

25. MINUCIUS FELIX

Little is known of Minucius Felix. He was active in the last part of the second century or in the first part of the third century. A convert, most probably an African, a lawyer, and according to some the first Christian author to write in Latin, he is known for only one work that has come down to us, namely, the *Octavius*.

CPL nos. 37ff. * Altaner (1961) 162–66 * Altaner (1966) 146–48 * Bardenhewer (1908) 70–72 * Bardenhewer (1913) 1:303–15 * Bardenhewer (1910) 55–58 * Bardy (1930) 37–39 * Bautz 5:1564–67 * Cross 146–48 * Goodspeed 166–67 * Hamell 44–45 * Jurgens 1:109–11 * Labriolle (1947) 1:163–92 * Labriolle (1968) 109–30 * Quasten 2:155–63 * Steidle 71 * Tixeront 49–51 * CATH 9:249–50 * CE 10:336–37 * DACL 11.2:1388–1412 * DCB 3:920–24 * DictSp 10:1268–72 * DPAC 2:2259–62 * DTC 10.2:1793–98 * EC 8:1057–58 * EEC 1:562–63 * EEChr 2:753 * LTK 7:275–76 * NCE 9:883 * NCES 9:658 * ODCC 1091 * PEA (1991) 8:241 * TRE 23:1–3

25-A. The Octavius[†]

This defense of Christianity against the accusations of the pagans assumes the literary form of a conversation that took place in Rome between Minucius, his friend Octavius, and the pagan Caecilius. Its forty chapters focus not on doctrinal matters but on moral conduct and are directed toward those who have little, if any, understanding of Christianity. Unlike apologies directed toward the Jews, this work contains no citations from Scripture.

Greatly disputed is the question of the work's relationship to Tertullian's *Apology* (WEC 1:**26-B**), written ca. 197. Does Tertullian depend on Minucius or vice versa? Today the common, though not universal, opinion is that Minucius knew of and relied upon Tertullian's work, thus most probably dating the author of the *Octavius* in the third century.

29. [. . .] You believe that our religion worships a criminal and his cross. Doing so you stray far from the truth, believing as you do that

441

[†] Translated from *M. Minucii Felicis Octavius Julii Firmici Materni Liber de errore profanarum religionum*, ed. C. Halm, CSEL 2 (Vienna, 1867) 42–43, 45–46.

a criminal deserved to be considered divine or that an earthly being
was able to be considered as such. [. . .] We neither worship nor desire
crosses. But you, who consecrate gods made out of wood, adore wooden
crosses, perhaps as part of your gods. Your standards together with your
banners and camp flags are nothing else, are they, than gilded and decorated crosses? Your trophies of victory not only imitate the appearance
of a simple cross but also that of a man affixed to it. Surely we naturally
see the sign of the cross in a ship moving along under its swelling sails,
when it glides by with expanded oars. When the military yoke is raised
on high, it is the sign of the cross; also when someone adores God with
a pure mind, with hands that are outstretched. So it is that the sign of
the cross is supported either by natural reason, or your own religion is
formed in regard to it.

442   32. Do you think that we are concealing what we worship since we have
neither temples nor altars? [. . .] Am I to offer to God the victims and sacrifices he has brought forth for me so that I might throw back to him his
own gift? It is ungrateful when the victim suitable for sacrifice is a good
disposition, a pure mind, a sincere conscience. So it is that whoever cultivates innocence petitions God; whoever cultivates righteousness offers to
God; whoever refrains from deceit makes propitiation to God, whoever
snatches someone from danger slaughters the richest victim. These are
our sacrifices, these are God's rites. And so whoever among us is the most
righteous is also the most religious. [. . .]

26. TERTULLIAN

Tertullian (*Quintus Septimus Florens Tertullianus*) was born between ca. 155
and 160 of pagan parents in Carthage. Converted shortly before 193, he
was a prolific writer whose works, some of which have been lost, cover a
variety of areas, for example, morality, apologetics, church discipline. It is
not certain whether he was ordained a priest. By 207 his rigorism led him
to Montanism, which condemned other Christians as being too lax.

Called the "Father of Latin Theology," Tertullian wrote in a Latin that is
elegant, terse, and at times obscure, his writing being especially important
for the history of baptism, penance, and Christian prayer. The year of his
death is unknown.

CPL nos. 1ff. * Altaner (1961) 166–82 * Altaner (1966) 148–63 * Bardenhewer (1908)
179–90 * Bardenhewer (1910) 157–67 * Bardenhewer (1913) 2:332–94 * Bardy (1930)
28–36 * Bautz 11:695–720 * Cross 135–45 * Goodspeed 159–66 * Hamell 70–73 * Jurgens 1:111–61 * Labriolle (1947) 1:84–159 * Labriolle (1968) 56–102 * Leigh-Bennett
55–76 * Quasten 2:246–340 * Steidle 63–70 * Tixeront 109–19 * Wright (1928) 21–93 *
CATH 14:931–36 * CE 14:520–25 * CHECL 133–39, 206–11 * DCB 4:818–64 * DictSp
15:271–95 * DPAC 2:3413–24 * DTC 15.1:130–71 * EC 11:2025–33 * EEC 2:818–20
* EEChr 2:1107–9 * LTK 9:1344–48 * NCE 13:1019–22 * NCES 13:834–38 * ODCC
1591–92 * PEA (1894) 5.1 (n.s.) 822–45

SACRAMENTUM

E. de Backer, *Sacramentum, le mot et l'idée représentée par lui dans les oeuvres de Tertullien* (Louvain, 1911). * D. Michaélidès, *"Sacramentum" chez Tertullien* (Paris, 1970). * T. Marsh, "The History of the Sacramental Concept," MilS 3 (1979) 21–56.

BAPTISM

A. d'Alès, "'Pompa Diaboli,'" RSR 1 (1910) 571–90. * E. Fruetsaerrt, "De baptismo," RSR (1911) 462–66. * E. Amann, "L'ange du baptême dans Tertullien," RSR (1921) 208–21. * K. Köhler, "Das Agraphon bei Tertullian De bapt. 20," ThStKr (1922) 169ff. * S. Eitrem, "Tertullian De bapt. 5 'sanctified by drowning,'" CR (1924) 69. * A. d'Alès, "Tertullien De baptismo 5," RSR (1924) 292. * B. Capelle, "Le symbole romain au second siècle," RB 39 (1927) 33–45. * A.D. Nock, "Pagan Baptisms in Tertullien," JThSt 28 (1927) 289–90. * F.J. Dölger, "Die Apollinarischen Spiele und das Fest Pelusia: zu Tertullian De baptismo 5," AC 1 (1929) 150–55. * F.J. Dölger, "Die Taufe an den Apollinarischen und den Pelusischen Spielen," AC 1 (1929) 156–59. * F.J. Dölger, "Tertullian kein Zeuge für eine Taufe in den Mysterien von Eleusis," AC 1 (1929) 143–49. * F.J. Dölger, "Esietus: Der Ertrunkene oder der zum Osiris Gewordene: ein sprachgeschichtliche Beitrag zu Tertullian De baptismo 5," AC 1 (1929) 174–83. * F.J. Dölger, "Der erste Gebet der Täuflinge in der Gemeinschaft der Brüder," AC 2 (1930) 142–55. * F.J. Dölger, "Die Sünder in Blindheit und Unwissenheit: ein Beitrag zu Tertullian De baptismo 1," AC 2 (1930) 222–26. * F.J. Dölger, "Tertullian über die Bluttaufe," AC 2 (1930) 117–41. * J.W. Ph. Borleffs, "Zu Tertullian De baptismo," PhW 51 (1931) 251–55. * F.J. Dölger, "Zwei neue Textheilungsversuche zu Tertullian De baptismo 16, 2," AC 3 (1932) 216–19. * B. Leeming, "A Note on a Reading in Tertullian's De baptismo 'Credo quia non credunt,'" Greg 3 (1933) 423–31. * F.J. Dölger, "Die Eingliederung des Taufsymbols in den Taufvollzug nach den Schriften Tertullians: zu Tertullian De baptismo 2, 1," AC 4 (1934) 138–46. * J.M. Restrepo-Jaramillo, "Tertuliano y la doble fórmula en el símbolo apostólico," Greg 15 (1934) 3–58. * F.J. Dölger, "Religiöse Waschung als Sühne für Meineid (De baptismo 5)," AC 6 (1940) 73. * E.C. Ratcliff, "The Relation of Confirmation to Baptism in the Early Roman and Byzantine Liturgies," Theol 49 (1946) 258–65, 290–95. * P.-H. Menoud, "La baptême des enfants dans l'Eglise ancienne," VerC 2 (1948) 15–26. * P. Schepens, "De baptismo 5," RSR (1948) 112–13. * Chr. Mohrmann, "Tertullien, De baptismo 2, 2," VC 5 (1951) 49. * W. Bedard, "The Symbolism of the Baptismal Font in Early Christian Thought," diss. (Washington, D.C., 1951). * F.X. Lukman, "Das Anblasen des Teufels beim Taufgelöbnis," in *Festschrift für R. Egger*, vol. 1 (Klagenfurt, 1952) 343–46. * E. Ferguson, "Baptism from the Second to the Fourth Century," ResQ 1 (1957) 185–97. * P.S. Horgan, *Tertullian's Teaching on Christian Baptism* (Washington, D.C., 1966). * C. Vona, "Consonanze ed echi del 'De Baptismo' di Tertulliano nella letteratura dell'evo patristico," Div 11 (1967) 117–79. * A. Houssiau, "L'engagement baptismal," RTL 9 (1978) 138–65. * K. McDonnell, "Communion Ecclesiology and Baptism in the Spirit: Tertullian and the Early Church," TS 49:4 (December 1988) 671–93. * M.E. Johnson, "Tertullian's *Diem baptismo sollemniorem* Revisited: A Tentative Hypothesis on Baptism at Pentecost," in *Studia Liturgica Diversa: Essays in Honor of Paul F. Bradshaw*, ed. M.E. Johnson and L.E. Phillips (Portland, 2004) 31–43.

EUCHARIST

F.X. Dieringer, "Die Abendmahlslehre Tertullians," *Katholik* 44:1 (1864) I 277–318. * C. Leimbach, *Beiträge zur Abendmahlslehre Tertullians* (Gotha, 1874). * P. Scharsch,

"Eine schwierige Stelle über die Eucharistie bei Tertullian (Adv. Marcionem 4, 40)," *Katholik* 89 (1909) 21–33. * B. Stakemeier, "La dottrina di Tertulliano sul sacramento dell' Eucarestia," *Rivista storico-critica delle scienze teologiche* (1909) 199ff., 265ff. * P. Batiffol, *L'Eucharistie: la présence réélle et la transubstantiation*, 9th ed. (Paris, 1930) 204–6. * E. Janot, "L'Eucharistie à Carthage," VS 23 (1930) 269–82. * J.M. Frochisse, "A propos des origines du jeûne eucharistique," RHE 28 (1932) 594–609. * F.J. Dölger, "Sacramentum Infanticidii," AC 4 (1934) 188–228. * F.J. Dölger, "Zu Dominica Sollemnia bei Tertullianus," AC 6 (1940) 108–17. * F.R.M. Hitchcock, "Tertullian's Views on the Sacrament of the Lord's Supper," ChQ 134 (1942) 21–36. * E. Dekkers, *Tertullianus en de geschiedenis der liturgie* (Brussels and Amsterdam, 1947) 49–67. * J. Beran, "De ordine missae secundum Tertulliani 'Apologeticum,'" in *Miscellanea Liturgica in Honorem L. Cuniberti Mohlberg*, vol. 2 (Rome, 1949) 7–32. * F.X. Dieringer, "Die Abendmahlslehre Tertullians," *Der Katholik* 44:1 (1964) 277–318. * P.T. Camelot, "Un texte de Tertullien sur l'amen de la communion," LMD, no. 79 (1964) 108–13. * W.L. Dulière, "Un problème à résoudre: l'acceptation du sang eucharistique par les premiers chrétiens juifs," STh 20 (1966) 62–93. * V. Saxer, "Tertullian," in W. Rordorf and others, *The Eucharist of the Early Christians* (New York, 1978) 132–55. * J.D. Laurance, "'Sacerdos vice Christi': A Study in the Theology of Eucharistic Leadership according to Cyprian of Carthage," diss. (Notre Dame, 1983). * G. Bavaud, "Le laïc peut-il célébrer l'Eucharistie? (Tertullien: 'De exhortatione castitatis' VII, 3)," REAug 43 (1996) 213–21.

AGAPE

F.X. Funk, "L'Agape," RHE 4 (1903) 5–23. * P. Batiffol, "La controverse sur l'Agape," BLE, 3rd ser., 6 (1904) 185–206. * F.X. Funk, "Tertullien et l'Agape," RHE 5 (1904) 5–15. * F.X. Funk, "La question de l'Agape: un dernier mot," RHE 7 (1906) 5–15.

PENANCE, SIN, FORGIVENESS OF SINS

S. Harent, "La discipline pénitentielle dans l'Eglise primitive: réponse à M. l'abbé Vacandard," Et 81 (1900) 577–607. * G. Esser, *Die Bullschriften Tertullians De paenitentia und De pudicitia und das Indulgenzedikt des Papstes Kallistus* (Bonn, 1905). * S. Charrier, "Tertullien et les martyrs-pénitenciers," RevAug 10 (1907) 582–84. * P. de Labriolle, "Vestiges d'apocryphes dans le De paenitentia de Tertullien 12, 9," BALAC 1 (1911) 127–28. * A. Vanbeck, "La pénitence dans Tertullien," RHL (1912) 350–69. * A. d'Alès, *L'Edit de Calliste* (Paris, 1914) 136–71. * F.H. Hallock, "Third Century Teaching on Sin and Penance," AThR 4 (1921/22) 128–42. * S.W.J. Teeuwen, "De Voce 'Paenitentia' apud Tertullianum," Mnem 55 (1927) 410–19. * E. Fruetsaert, "La réconciliation ecclésiastique vers l'an 200," NRTh (1930) 379–91. * J. Hoh, "Die Busse bei Tertullian," ThGl 23 (1931) 625–38. * C. Chartier, "L'excommunication ecclésiastique d'après les écrits de Tertullien," Ant (1935) 301–44, 499–536. * K. Rahner, "Sünde als Gnadenverlust in der frühchristlichen Literatur, IV, Tertullian," ZkTh 60 (1936) 471–510. * B. Poschmann, *Paenitentia Secunda* (Bonn, 1940) 270–348. * G.H. Joyce, "Private Penance in the Early Church," JThSt 42 (1941) 18–42. * C.B. Daly, "The Sacrament of Penance in Tertullian," IER 69 (1947) 693–707, 815–21; 70 (1948) 731–46, 832–48; 73 (1950) 156–69. * C.B. Daly, "Novatian and Tertullian," ITQ 19 (1952) 33–43. * K. Rahner, "Zur Theologie der Busse bei Tertullian," in *Abhandlungen über Theologie und Kirche: Festschrift für K. Adam* (Düsseldorf, 1952) 139–67. * G. Teichtweier, *Die Sündenlehre des Origenes*, Studien zur Geschichte der kath. Moraltheologie 7 (Regensburg, 1958). * B. Poschmann, *Penance* *and the Anointing of the Sick* (St. Louis, 1964) 38–49. * J.-C. Fredouille, "Du 'De paeni-tentia' de Tertullien au 'De paenitentiae institutione' de Pacian," REAug 44 (1998) 13–23. * C. Munier, "La discipline pénitentielle d'après Tertullien," *Connaissance des pères de l'Eglise,* no. 71 (1998) 37–50.

MARRIAGE

H. Crouzel, "Deux textes de Tertullien concernant la procédure et les rites du mar-iage chrétien," BLE 74 (1973) 3–13. * R. Uglione, "Il matrimonio in Tertulliano: tra esaltazione e disprezzo," EphL 93 (1979) 479–94. * B. du Plessis, "La célébration du mariage dans les premiers siècles chrétiens," *Résurrection,* no. 16 (1988) 3.

ORDERS, PRIESTHOOD

G. Bardy, "Le sacerdoce chrétien d'après Tertullien," VS 58 (1939) 109–24. * G. Otranto, "'Nonne et laici sacerdotes sumus?' (Exh. cast. 7, 3)," VetChr 8 (1971) 27–47. * D. Powell, "Ordo Presbyteri," JThSt, n.s., 26 (1975) 290–328. * P. Mattei, "'Habere ius sacerdotis': sacerdoce et laïcat au témoignage de Tertullien 'De exhor-tatione castitatis' et 'De monogamia,'" RevSR 59 (1985) 200–201. * G. Bavaud, "Le laïc peut-il célébrer l'eucharistie? (Tertullien: "De exhortatione castitatis" VII, 3)," REAug 43 (1996) 213–21.

PRAYER

W. Haller, "Das Herrengebet bei Tertullian," *Zeitschrft für praktische Theologie* 12 (1890) 327–54. * E.v.D. Goltz, *Das Gebet in her ältesten Christenheit* (Leipzig, 1901) 279–82. * G. Loeschke, *Die Vaterunsererklärung des Theophilus von Antiochien: Eine Quellenuntersuchung zu den Vaterunsererklärungen des Tertullian, Cyprian, Chromatius und Hieronymus* (Berlin, 1908). * J. Moffat, "Tertullian on the Lord's Prayer," ExpT 18 (1919) 24–41. * E. Boisvert, "La prière chrétienne d'après Tertullien," *Les cahiers franciscains* 3 (1933) 185–98. * F.J. Dölger, "Das Niedersitzen nach dem Gebet: ein Kommentar zu Tertullian, De oratione 16," AC 5 (1936) 116–37. * B. Simovic, "Le pater chez quelques pères latins," *France franciscaine* 21 (1938) 193–222, 245–64. * O. Schäfer, "Das Vaterunser, das Gebet des Christen: eine aszetische Studie nach Tertullian De oratione," ThGl 35 (1943) 1–6. * A.J.B. Higgins, "'Lead us not into temptation': Some Latin Variants," JThSt 46 (1945) 179–83. * E. Dekkers, *Tertullianus en de geschiedenis der liturgie* (Brussels/Amsterdam, 1947) 117–26. * H. Pétré, "Les leçons du 'Panem nostrum quotidianum,'" RSR 38 (1951) 63–79. * D.Y. Hadidian, "The Background and Origin of the Christian Hours of Prayer," TS 25 (1964) 59–69. * V. Saxer, "'Il étendit les mains à l'heure de sa Passion': le thème de l'orant-te dans la littérature chrétienne des IIe et IIIe siècles," Aug 20 (1980) 335–65. * D.R. Stuck-wisch, "Principles of Christian Prayer from the Third Century: A Brief Look at Ori-gen, Tertullian and Cyprian with Some Comments on Their Meaning for Today," Wor 71:1 (January 1997) 2–19.

OTHER TOPICS

P. de Labriolle, "'Mulieres in ecclesia taceant': un aspect de la lutte antimon-taniste," BALAC 1 (1911) 3–24, 103–22. * J. Schümmer, *Die altchristliche Fastenpraxis mit besonderer Berücksichtigung der Schriften Tertullians,* LQF 27 (Münster i. W., 1933). * M.M. Baney, *Some Reflections of Life in North Africa in the Writings of Tertullian* (Washington, D.C., 1948). * C.B. Daly, "Liturgical Worship in Tertullian's Africa," IER, 5th ser., 95 (1960) 136–46. * T.P. O'Malley, *Tertullian and the Bible: Language, Im-agery, Exegesis,* Latinitas Christianorum Primaeva 21 (Nigmegen, 1967). * D.E. Groh, "Christian Community in the Writings of Tertullian: An Inquiry into the Nature and Problems of Community in North African Christianity," diss. (Ann Arbor, 1970). * V. Saxer, *Morts, martyrs, reliques en Afrique aux premiers siècles: les témoignages de Tertullien, Cyprien et Augustin à la lumière de l'archéologie africaine*, Theologie historique 55 (Paris, 1980). * P. Erny, "Le signe de la croix chez Tertullien," *Présence orthodoxe* no. 79 (1988) 19–28. * C. Munier, *Autorité épiscopale et sollicitude pastorale, IIe-VIe siècles* (Aldershot, England, and Brookfield, VT, 1991). * W. Bähnk, *Von der Notwendigkeit des Leidens: die Theologie des Martyriums bei Tertullian*, Forschungen zur Kirchen-und Dogmengeschichte 78 (Göttingen, 2001).

26-A. To the Gentiles[†]

Divided into two books, this defense of the Christian religion was written in 197.

443   I.XIII. Others, certainly in a more courteous fashion, believe that the sun is a Christian god since, as is known, we pray facing the east and make Sunday a day of joy. Do you do less? Do not many of you, at times striving to adore the heavenly bodies, move your lips as you face the sunrise? Certainly it is you who have received the sun into the week, and you have chosen this day from among all the days as the day on which to refrain from bathing or postpone doing so till evening, or as a day for resting or for participating in banquets. Doing such, you deviate from your own religious observances and go to those of foreigners: the Sabbath and "the Purification" are Jewish holydays; also Jewish are the ceremonies of the lamps, fasting with unleavened bread, and propitiatory prayers, all of these certainly being foreign to your gods. So that I may digress no longer, you, reproaching us with the sun and its day, should acknowledge how close you are to us; we are not all that distant from Saturn and your days of rest.

26-B. Apology[††]

This treatise, written in 197, was one of the most widely circulated of Tertullian's works in ancient times.

444   II. [. . .] Pliny the Younger, while governing a province and after condemning a number of Christians to death and driving others from their positions, was still disturbed by their large numbers. So he consulted with Trajan the emperor as to what should be done with the rest. All Pliny discovered was that, except for stubbornly refusing to offer sacrifice, they assembled early in the morning to sing to Christ as to a god and to strengthen their way of life, prohibiting murder, adultery, dishonesty, falsehood, and other crimes. Trajan then wrote back, saying that the Christians were not to be sought out, but those brought forward were to be punished.[a]

[†] Translated from *Opera*, CCL 1 (Turnhout, 1953) 32.
[††] Translated from CCL 1:88ff.
a. See WEC 1:**16-A** and **16-B**.

xvi. Certainly there are others who more reasonably and with more plau-   445
sibility believe that the sun is our god. [. . .] This suspicion arises from the
fact that we pray while facing the east. Yet many of you, at times attempting
to worship the heavenly bodies, move your lips while facing the direction
of the sunrise. Likewise, if we rejoice on Sunday, although doing so for a
far different reason than to worship the sun, we take second place to those
who set aside the day of Saturn [Saturday] as a day for leisure and feasting,
although they are far from Jewish custom, which is unknown to them.

xxx. We pray for the safety of our rulers to the eternal God, to the true and   446
living God, whose favor beyond that of all others they should prefer. [. . .]
Unceasingly do we pray for all our rulers. We pray that they may have a
long life, that the empire be secure, that the imperial household be safe, that
armies be brave, that the senate be faithful, that the people be righteous, that
the world be at peace, and for whatever the people and Caesar desire.

xxxix. We gather as one body and congregation so that we might   447
wrestle with God in our prayers, a violence pleasing to him. We also pray
for our rulers, for their ministers and for those in power, for the state of
the world, for peace, and for the end to be delayed. We gather to read the
sacred writings, should present circumstances require either a warning
or an examination; with the holy words we nourish our faith, enliven our
hope, strengthen our trust, and no less by teaching God's precepts we
strengthen our way of life. Also exhortations, reprimands, and holy cen-
sures take place there. With great seriousness do we carry out the work
of judging, for among those who feel that they are in God's sight it is the
greatest example of the judgment yet to come; if a person has so failed,
he or she is dismissed from sharing in prayer together, from joining the
assembly, and from participating in all holy activity. Presiding over us
are the elders who have been proven, an honor not purchased but result-
ing from testimony since nothing of God can be purchased. There is also
a treasury which does not result from huge contributions as if things of
religion could be purchased. [. . .] These are not used for feasting, drinking, and unwelcome gluttony; rather, they are for feeding and burying
the poor, for the orphaned and the needy, for the elderly who are house-
bound, and also for those who have undergone shipwreck, for those exiled in the mines, on islands, or in prison. [. . .]

26-C. On the Shows†

Addressed to the catechumens, this treatise dates from about 198–200 and
condemns all public performances as being the work of the devil.

iv. [. . .] Upon entering the water, we openly declare the Christian faith   448
as we use the words prescribed by law; we testify aloud that we have renounced the devil, his pomp, and his angels. Is it not especially in regard

---

† Translated from CCL 1:231ff.

to idolatry that we think of the devil, his pomp, and his angels? To speak
briefly, it is from here that we have every unclean and worthless spirit. If,
therefore, the whole apparatus of the shows is based on idolatry, surely
we may presume that our baptismal renunciation refers to the shows
which have been handed over to the devil, his pomp, and his angels by
means of idolatry. [. . .]

449   xxv. How terrible it is to go from God's Church to that of the devil, from
heaven—as they say—to faith! From uplifting your hands to God and then
to wearying them by applauding an actor! From saying aloud the "Amen"
to what is holy and then to cheering on a gladiator! To cry "forever" to
anyone other than God and Christ!

26-D. The Prescription of Heretics[†]

Writing ca. 200, Tertullian argues against heretics in general, saying that
since the Scriptures belong to the Church alone, dissidents have no right
to employ the holy books in their argumentation.

450   xxxvi. [. . .] How happy is that Church upon which the apostles poured
forth their whole teaching with the shedding of their blood, where Peter
suffered a passion like the Lord's. [. . .] Let us see what it has learned,
what it has taught, what communion it has enjoyed even with our
churches in Africa. It acknowledges the one Lord God, who is the Creator
of the universe, and Jesus Christ born of the Virgin Mary and the Son of
God the Creator, the resurrection of the body; it brings together the Law
and the prophets, the Gospels and the letters of the apostles, from which it
absorbs its faith; this faith it seals with water, clothes with the Holy Spirit,
nourishes with the Eucharist, exhorts to martyrdom, and so receives no
one who stands against such a custom.

451   xli. I will not omit describing the conduct of heretics, how useless it
is, how dried up, how human, lacking seriousness, authority, order, as
behooves what they believe. To begin with, it is not certain who is a catechumen or who is a member of the faithful; both approach, both listen,
both pray, even the pagans should they perhaps be present among them.
[. . .] Their catechumens are seen as perfect before they are instructed.
How shameless are these heretical women who dare to teach, to argue, to
perform exorcisms, to promise cures, and perhaps even to baptize. Their
ordinations are thoughtless, insignificant, capricious. Now they install
neophytes, now those bound by worldly duties, now those who have
fallen away from us by apostasy, so that they bind them by means of vanity since they are unable to do so through truth. Nowhere is it easier to
be promoted than in the camp of the rebels where the very fact of being
present makes one qualified. And so it happens that today one man is

---

[†] Translated from CCL 1:216ff.

their bishop, tomorrow another; today's deacon is tomorrow's reader; today's presbyter is tomorrow's layman, since even on laymen do they impose the tasks of the priesthood.

26-E. On Baptism[†]

Tertullian's treatise on this sacrament dates either from the very end of the second century or the very beginning of the third. It was occasioned by the attacks on baptism made at Carthage by a woman named Quintilla.

I. Our purpose is to treat the sacrament of water, the water that washed away sins contracted at the time of our former blindness, the water that freed us unto eternal life. Such a treatise will not be useless, instructing both those who are being formed in the faith as well as those who, being content to believe without searching out the grounds of our traditions, only possess—by reason of their ignorance—a faith subject to temptations. Not long ago there arrived among us a most deadly viper from the Cainite heresy[a] whose doctrine led astray a large number of people. Quite naturally it focused on baptism. Vipers, asps, and basilisks ordinarily seek out dry and waterless places. But as little fishes who take our name from *ichthus*,[b] Jesus Christ, we are born in water, and it is only by remaining in the water that we are saved. This is why this monstrous woman, who normally did not even have the right to teach,[1] discovered that the best way to kill these little fishes was to remove them from the water.

II. In fact, how great is a heresy's power either for corrupting the faith or for completely hindering a person from adhering to it so that the heresy attacks the very foundations of faith. Nothing so assails the human mind as the contrast between the apparent simplicity of divine work and the greatness of the effects promised. This is true. Everything happens with the greatest simplicity, without splendor, without extraordinary preparation. In short, without any cost a person goes down into the water and is washed while certain words are said. The person emerges from the water not much or not at all [bodily] cleaner. This is why some do not believe that eternity is gained in this way. It's true. The solemnities in honor of the idols base their authority and the faith one puts in them upon external display, pomp, and expense. O miserable incredulity which refuses God what is properly his: simplicity and power. What then? Is it not wonderful that both can wash away sin? But are we not to believe this just because it is wonderful! On the contrary, this is why we are to believe even more. Is

452

453

[†] Translated from *Traité du baptême*, ed. R.F. Refoulé, trans. in cooperation with M. Drouzy, SChr 35 (Paris, 1952).

a. Cainite heresy: teaching followed by certain second-century Gnostics.

b. The first letters in Greek for "Jesus Christ, son of God, savior" are from the word "fish," that is, *ichthus*.

1. See 1 Tim 2:11–12; 1 Cor 14:34–35.

it not fitting for the divine to surpass all admiration? We also admire, but we believe. For the rest, if incredulity stands in wonder, it is because incredulity lacks belief; incredulity stands in wonder because what it judges as worthless is simple; what is magnificent it judges, as it were, impossible. But that it be exactly as you think, God's word has given you beforehand a sufficient denial. It says, "God chose what is foolish in the world to shame the wise."[2] And also, "What is difficult for mortals is easy for God."[3] For if God is both wise and powerful—something even those who disregard the divine do not deny—he has taken for the material of his divine work the very opposite of wisdom and power, namely, that which is foolish and impossible since every power springs forth from whatever challenges it.[4]

454   III. Mindful of this statement as a conclusive rule, we ask if it is so foolish and impossible to be created again by means of water. Since water has merited to be the dispenser of such great grace, I think we must examine the importance of this liquid, which from the beginning has existed in abundance. Water is one of those elements which before the ordering of the world and in the original chaos reposed in God's hands. "In the beginning," it is written, "God created the heavens and the earth. But the earth was invisible and unorganized, and darkness covered the deep, and the spirit of God was carried over the waters."[5] We must honor this age of the waters, the antiquity of this substance. But we also venerate its privilege since water was the abode of the divine Spirit who preferred it to the other elements. The darkness was formless, lacking the adornment of the stars; the abyss was forbidding; the earth was unprepared; and the sky was but a rough mass. Only water, a perfect material from the beginning and being fecund and simple, offered itself as pure, as a throne worthy of its God. Must we also recall the ordering of the world, an ordering which consists in a type of regulating the waters by God? In order to suspend the heavenly firmament, God divided the waters in half.[6] To make the earth dry, God separated the waters. Then once the world was divided into its various elements so that it could be given inhabitants, we have the first waters, these being ordered to bring forth living creatures.[7] These first waters gave birth to what is alive, and so there is no reason to be surprised that the waters of baptism still produce life. As to the work of creating the human race,[8] did not water play a part here also? If the material for this creation were taken from the earth, then the earth could not have been used for this purpose without water or dampness. The earth was completely impregnated by these waters, separated since the fourth day into their places, but which still imbued the soil. I could exhaust this subject or recall at length the importance of water—its power or agreeableness, its qualities, its benefits, its usefulness to the world—but I fear that I would appear to be collecting various reasons for praising water rather than the

—————————

2. 1 Cor 1:27.   3. Luke 18:27.   4. 2 Cor 12:9.   5. Gen 1:1–2.   6. See Gen 1:6ff.
7. See Gen 1:20ff.   8. See Gen 2:7.

reasons for baptism. Yet doing so, I would teach in a much richer way in order to show that there can be no doubt: if God makes use of water in all that he does, God also makes it fecund when it concerns the sacraments; if water governs life here on earth, water also obtains life for heaven.

ɪᴠ. To this end, it is enough to mention briefly what happened at the beginning, the things that have us recognize a foundation of baptism: the Spirit which from the beginning hovered over the waters and remained there to give them life. A Spirit of holiness was carried over the holy water,[9] or, rather, the water borrowed its holiness from the Spirit it bore. For whatever is placed beneath another necessarily seizes its quality from what is above. This is especially true when the corporeal comes into contact with the spiritual: because of its subtile material, the spiritual easily penetrates and remains. And so it is by this Spirit of sanctity that water is sanctified in its nature and itself sanctifies. But one might ask whether we are baptized in the waters that existed in the beginning? Surely they are not the same, unless in the sense that they belong to the same genus albeit to a different species. Yet what is attributed to the genus overflows into the species. There is no difference between being washed in the sea or in a stream, in a river or in a font, in a lake or in the pool of a house. Likewise, there is no difference between those whom John baptized in the Jordan[10] and those whom Peter baptized in the Tiber. Likewise, the eunuch, whom Philip baptized with some water found by chance on the road,[11] derived from this neither more nor less in regard to salvation. All waters, by reason of the ancient claim that marked them in the beginning, participate in the mystery of our sanctification once we have invoked God over them. As soon as God is invoked, the Spirit comes from heaven, hovers over the waters which it sanctifies with its presence, and the waters, thus sanctified, are in turn granted the power to sanctify. Surely baptism may be compared to a simple action: sins foul as if they were dirt; water cleanses us from them. Nonetheless, sins do not physically appear on the body since people do not carry on their skin the stains of idolatry, the stains of debauchery, or the stains of fraud. But it is the spirit, however, which soils, the spirit which is the author of sin. For the spirit commands; the body is at its service. Both share in the sin: the spirit because it commands and the flesh because it carries out the command. Therefore, since the intervention of an angel[12] has bestowed upon the water a certain power of healing, the spirit is washed in the water by means of the body, whereas the flesh is purified in the water by means of the spirit.

ᴠ. Even the pagans, who are strangers to spiritual things, attribute an analogous power to their idols, but they delude themselves since their waters are empty. Thus by a bath they are initiated into certain mysteries, like those of Isis or Mithras. They also carry the gods with them to the baths. For purposes of purification they sprinkle lustral water upon their

455

456

---

9. See Gen 1:2. 10. See Matt 3:6. 11. See Acts 8:36. 12. See John 5:4.

country estates, homes, temples, and whole cities. At the time of the Apollonian and Pelusian games they are washed, believing that by doing so they obtain regeneration and the pardon of their sins. Likewise, whoever among the ancients was guilty of murder had to atone through a water of purification. If by nature the waters have the property of attracting spirits and thereby charming the idol who inspires these purifications, then how much more real power will these waters have from the authority of the God who gives these waters their whole nature. If they believe that a religious practice can make water capable of healing, then can any religious practice be superior to the one that proclaims the living God? Here again we see that the devil is at work trying to imitate the divine work when he also practices baptism among his own. But is there any true resemblance? The impure one purifies; the traitor sets free; the condemned one absolves. The devil will destroy his own work if he washes away the sins that he himself inspires. Truly this witnesses against those who reject the faith when they do not believe in the divine works so that they might believe in the claims of God's rival. Is it not true that, apart from every sacred rite, the impure spirits dwell upon the waters, trying to take command of the divine Spirit which was made to brood upon them at the world's beginning? The dark springs and the remote brooks know something of this, and these bathing pools and aqueducts, these reservoirs and wells which in houses are said to spirit away—all do so precisely through the power of an evil spirit. They are called "esietics,"[c] or "lymphatics," or "hydrophobics," those whom the waters have killed or stricken with insanity or terror. Why have we reported all this? We have done so that there be less of a problem in believing in the presence of God's holy angel over the waters for the purpose of our salvation, whereas the evil angel employs water in order to destroy us. If the appearance of the angel over the waters seems to be something new, it was prefigured. At the pool of Bethesda an angel intervened, stirring up the water.[13] Those complaining of ill-health awaited its coming, for the first person to go down into the water and wash therein ceased to complain. This bodily remedy was a figure announcing the spiritual remedy; it accorded with the rule that bodily realities always prefigure spiritual realities. This is why, God's grace assisting in all things, the waters and the angel received a greater power. Alleviating evils of the body, they now heal the soul. Bringing about temporal salvation; they now restore eternal life. They set free one person once each year; now they save all people, destroying death through the forgiveness of sins; once the sin is forgiven, the penalty is also forgiven. In this way we are returned to God according to God's image,[14] we who were once conformed to God's image—*imago* refers to the natural image, *similitudo* refers

---

c. "Esietics": perhaps from the Egyptian *Hasie* and meaning the "blessed immortal." Death by drowning had, for the Egyptians, a religious character.

13. See John 5:2ff.   14. See Gen 1:26.

to what is eternal—for we find this spirit of God which we had received from the wind but afterward lost through sin.[15]

VI. This does not mean that it is in the water that we receive the Holy Spirit. But purified in the water, we are prepared by the angel to receive the Spirit.[16] Once again the figure has preceded the reality. Just as John was the forerunner of the Lord and prepared his way,[17] so the angel who presides at baptism makes straight the path for the coming of the Holy Spirit by removing sins through a faith sealed in the [name of the] Father, the Son, and the Holy Spirit. For if all God's word is based on three witnesses,[18] how much more God's gift! By virtue of the baptismal blessing we have as witnesses of the faith the very ones who guarantee salvation. This same number of divine names also suffices to establish our hope. And since the witness of the faith and the promise of salvation are pledged under the three names, so mention of the Church is necessarily added. For where the Three—Father, Son, and Holy Spirit—are found, there also is found the Church[19] which is the body of the Three.

VII. Coming up from the bath, we are thoroughly anointed with blessed oil in conformity with ancient practice whereby a person was customarily raised to the priesthood by being anointed with oil from a horn;[20] in this way Aaron was anointed by Moses.[21] The name "Christ" has its origin here, from the "chrism" which signifies the anointing and which also gives its name to the Lord. For it is this anointing, made spiritual, which in the Spirit Christ received from God the Father, as we read in Acts, "They gathered together in this city against your holy Son whom you anointed."[22] For us also the anointing flows over the body, but it profits us spiritually: just as the baptismal rite is a physical action since we are immersed into water, so its effect is spiritual because it frees us from our sins.

VIII. Then hands were laid upon us while a blessing invoked and invited the Holy Spirit to come. If human ingenuity can make a stream of air descend upon the water, and if the hands of an artist can animate these two associated elements with another stream of such beauty, then why cannot God modulate with holy hands the sublime melody of the Spirit upon the human person?[d] But this rite [of the laying on of hands] comes from the old ceremony in which Jacob blessed his grandsons Ephrem and Manasses, sons of Joseph.[23] He placed his crossed hands upon their heads in the form of a cross with the intent that, by forming the image of Christ upon them, they would henceforth portend the blessing that would come to us through Christ. So it is that this most Holy Spirit comes from the Father and willingly descends upon these purified and blessed bodies. The Spirit reposes upon these waters[24] of baptism

---

d. The reference is to a hydraulic organ.

15. See Gen 2:7.   16. See Matt 3:3; 11:10.   17. See John 3:28.   18. See Deut 19:15; 2 Cor 13:1.   19. See Matt 18:20.   20. See Exod 30:30.   21. See Lev 8:12.   22. Acts 4:27.   23. See Gen 48:14.   24. See Gen 1:2.

as if recognizing its ancient throne, the Spirit which under the form of a dove descended upon the Lord.[25] In this way the Holy Spirit manifested its nature, for the dove which even in its body lacks bitterness is altogether simple and innocent. This is why we are told to "be as simple as doves,"[26] something that does not lack a connection with the figure that preceded it: after the waters of the Deluge had purified the old filth, after the baptism of the world, if I can put it this way, it was the dove, sent forth from the ark and returning with an olive branch—a symbol of peace even for the pagans[27]—which came as a messenger announcing to the world that the heavenly anger was appeased. And so according to a similar order but one whose effect is completely spiritual, the dove, which is the Holy Spirit, flies toward the earth, that is, toward our body which comes out of the bath and is washed of its former sins. The Spirit brings God's peace as a messenger from heaven where the Church is the figure of the ark. Yet the world returned to its sin, and so the parallel between baptism and the flood is not a happy one. Yes, this is why the world is destined to burn[28] just as every person who returns to sin after baptism is destined to burn. But this should also be understood as a sign, as a warning to us.[29]

460   IX. How many are the favors of nature, privileges of grace, ritual solemnities, as well as figures, preparations, and prayers, all arranged on behalf of the cult of water! First, these are the people who were set free in Egypt and passing through water escaped the power of the Egyptian king; the water killed the king and his army.[30] Is there a more evident figure of the sacrament of baptism? Here the pagans are released from the world by means of water; they leave behind the devil, their old tyrant, crushed down under the water. Another symbol: the piece of wood that Moses threw into the water cured the water of its bitterness and rendered it fit to drink.[31] This wood was Christ himself curing the waters which previously were full of poison and bitterness; Christ changed them into a very healthy water, that of baptism. Water flowed from the rock[32] for the people, and it accompanied them. For if this rock was Christ,[33] there can be no doubt that baptism receives its consecration from this water flowing from Christ.[e] To strengthen the meaning of baptism, how privileged was water with God and with Christ! Christ never appeared without water. He was baptized in water.[34] And when he was invited to the wedding feast, water initiated the beginning of his power.[35] Announcing the word, he invites those who are thirsty to drink of his eternal water.[36] Speaking of love, he declares that the cup of water given to one's neighbor is an act

---

e. Literally the Latin reads: "We see that baptism is consecrated by the water in Christ."

25. See John 1:32.   26. Matt 10:16.   27. See Gen 8:11.   28. See 2 Pet 3:7.   29. See 1 Cor 10:11.   30. See Exod 14.   31. Exod 15:25.   32. See Exod 17:6.   33. See 1 Cor 10:4.   34. See Matt 3:13.   35. See John 2:7.   36. See John 4:14.

of love.[37] It is next to a well that Christ regains his strength.[38] He walks on the water,[39] taking delight in crossing over it;[40] with water he washes the feet of his disciples.[41] Witnesses in regard to baptism continue on to the Passion: when he was condemned to the cross, water again is involved, used for the hands of Pilate.[42] And water flows forth when Christ's side is pierced by the soldier's lance.[43]

x. Thus far our instruction, according to our limited means, has focused on all that lies at the basis of the baptismal observance. I will now continue by treating, always as best I can, some secondary problems pertaining to the subject. The baptism already announced by John gave rise to the question Christ asked of the Pharisees: Is John's baptism from heaven or from the earth?[44] The Pharisees were unable to give a firm reply since they did not understand that they no longer believed.[45] But we, having so little understanding, can to the extent of our little faith answer that this baptism was certainly divine. But only by its institution, not by its effects. John, as we read, was sent by the Lord for this precise task;[46] after all, he remained a man. He conferred nothing of heaven; he was at the service of heavenly gifts; he was charged with exhorting to penance[47] and penance depends on the human will. This is why the doctors of the Law and the Pharisees, refusing to believe, were unwilling to repent. But if penance is a human work, John's baptism necessarily depended on the same order of things. If his baptism were from heaven, it would have bestowed the Holy Spirit and remitted sins. But it is God alone who forgives sins and grants the Spirit.[48] Yet the Lord himself affirmed that the Spirit would not descend before he had ascended to the Father.[49] The servant cannot give what the Lord has not yet granted. So true is this that further on in the Acts of the Apostles we find that those who were baptized by John had not received the Holy Spirit; in fact, they didn't even know the Spirit's name.[50] What was unable to obtain heavenly gifts was therefore not from heaven. We see it well. What was heavenly in John, his spirit of prophecy, was no longer present once the Spirit completely passed upon the Lord, so that John sent forth [his disciples] to ask whether the Lord, whom he had preached and whose coming he had pointed out, was indeed the one who was to come.[51] Thus the baptism of penance was given as a disposition for the pardon and sanctification which Christ was to bring. We read, in fact, that "John proclaimed a baptism of repentance for the forgiveness of sins":[52] this was said in regard to the forgiveness yet to come since penance precedes and forgiveness comes afterwards.[53] This is how John "prepared the way." But the one who prepares is not the one who accomplishes. The person who prepares

461

---

37. See Matt 10:42. 38. See John 4:6. 39. See John 6:19. 40. See Matt 14:34. 41. See John 13:5. 42. See Matt 27:24. 43. See John 19:34. 44. See Matt 21:25. 45. See Isa 7:9. 46. See Luke 3:3. 47. See Acts 19:4; Mark 1:4. 48. See Mark 2:7. 49. See John 16:7. 50. See Acts 19:2. 51. See Matt 11:3. 52. Mark 1:4. 53. See Matt 11:10.

disposes so that another may accomplish. John himself recognized that he gave nothing of heaven when he said in regard to Christ, "The one who is of the earth speaks of the things of heaven; but the one who comes from heaven is above all."[54] He likewise declares that he baptizes only with the baptism of penance and that soon will come he who will baptize "with the Spirit and fire."[55] True and solid faith is baptized in water unto salvation, but a faith that is simulated and weak is baptized in fire unto judgment.

462   XI. But it can be objected that the Lord came and yet did not baptize. In fact, we read, "Although it was not Jesus himself but his disciples who baptized,"[56] as if John had preached that Jesus would baptize with his own hands. Certainly the passage is not to be understood in this way, but simply according to the common way of speaking, as when someone says, "The emperor has promulgated a decree" or "The prefect has condemned him to be beaten." Is it the emperor himself who promulgates? Is it the prefect himself who administers the beating? We always speak of the person who has something done as the one who actually does it. And so we must understand "He will baptize you"[57] as follows, "You will be baptized at his command or in his name." Let no one be surprised not to see Christ baptizing. With what baptism would he have done so? With the baptism of penance? What, then, was the purpose of his Precursor? For the forgiveness of sins? He could have remitted them with a single word.[58] With a baptism in his own name? Out of humility he was concealing himself. In the name of the Holy Spirit? But Christ had not yet ascended to his Father. In the name of the Church? He still had not established the Church upon his apostles. This is why his disciples baptized as ministers, as did John the Precursor and with the same baptism as John's so that one not think that it was a question of another baptism, for there is no other baptism except that which Christ instituted afterwards. But at this moment the apostle could still not bestow it since the Savior was not yet glorified,[59] nor had he as yet established the efficacy of baptism by his passion and resurrection. Our death could not be destroyed without the Lord's passion, nor can life be restored without his resurrection.

463   XII. But since it is prescribed that no one can be saved without baptism, especially since the Lord said that "no one can see life without being born of water,"[60] there arise scrupulous, yes thoughtless, objections. According to this precept, how are the apostles saved since we do not see them, other than Paul,[61] receiving the Lord's baptism? Since Paul is the only one among them to have received Christ's baptism, then either—to save the precept—we must prejudge the danger of the others who did not receive the water of Christ or, if their salvation has been assured without their being baptized, we must hold that the precept is nonapplicable. God knows that I have heard remarks of such kind. And I say this in order that

---

54. John 3:31.   55. Matt 3:11.   56. John 4:2.   57. Matt 3:11.   58. See Matt 9:2.   59. See John 7:39.   60. See John 3:5.   61. See Acts 9:18.

no one believe me so reckless as to imagine, in my passion to write, things that inspire doubt in others. Now I will respond as best I can to those who deny that the apostles were baptized. Indeed, if they had received John's baptism, why did they desire the Lord's baptism since the Lord himself gave the rule of only one baptism when he spoke to Peter who requested to be washed, "Whoever has bathed one time has no need to do so again."[62] Christ certainly would not have said this if Peter had not already been baptized. This is a remarkable argument against those who, desiring to destroy the sacrament of water, take away from the apostles even the baptism of John. How improbable it would be if John's baptism had not prepared the way of the Lord among the very ones who were destined to prepare the Lord's way in the whole world. The Lord himself, who did not have to do penance, was himself baptized. Was baptism not necessary for sinners? And if others were not baptized, it is because they were not yet companions of Christ but rivals in faith, being doctors of the Law and Pharisees. The fact that Christ's adversaries did not desire baptism shows us, on the one hand, that the followers of Christ were baptized and did not react like his rivals, especially when the Lord to whom they were attached had praised John when he said, "Among those born of women no one is greater than John the Baptist."[63] Others—and their argument is rather forced—contend that the apostles received a substitute for baptism on the day when, in the boat, they were covered with waves,[64] and when Peter began to sink in the sea upon which he was walking.[65] But, in my mind, to be washed away or swallowed up by a violent sea is quite different from being baptized as a religious observance. Furthermore, the ship prefigures the Church which, on the sea of the world, is disturbed by the waves of persecutions and temptations, while the Lord in his patience seems to be asleep till the last moment when, awakened by the prayers of the saints,[66] he restrains the world and grants peace to his own. Now, either the apostles received baptism in some way or else they remained unbaptized, and in the latter case the Lord's words to Peter regarding one baptism [67] apply to us alone. In both instances it is quite rash to make quick judgments regarding the salvation of the apostles since for them the privilege of being the first to be called and then to live in personal familiarity with Christ could well have substituted for baptism. For it seems to me that the person they followed was the very person who promised salvation to those who believe in him. "Your faith has saved you"[68] . . . "your sins are forgiven":[69] this is what Christ said to someone who believed but had not yet been baptized. If the apostles lacked faith, I do not know anyone whose faith is safe. At a single word from the Lord one left his tax booth;[70] another left his father and his boat;[71] another gave up his livelihood; and

---

62. John 13:10.   63. Matt 11:11.   64. See Matt 8:24.   65. See Matt 14:30.   66. See Matt 8:25.   67. See John 13:10.   68. Matt 9:22.   69. Matt 9:2.   70. See Matt 9:9.
71. See Matt 4:22.

another did not worry about burying his father;[72] even before hearing it, he carried out this essential precept of the Lord, "Whoever loves father or mother more than me is not worthy of me."[73]

464   xiii. This is where these impious ones bring up objections. They go so far as to say that baptism is not necessary for those for whom faith suffices: Abraham found grace before God not by reason of the sacrament of water but by reason of the sacrament of faith.[74] But in every order of things what happens subsequently is definitive; what follows surpasses in value all that precedes. Formerly, before the Lord's passion and resurrection, salvation was obtained by faith alone; but since Christ's nativity, passion, and resurrection have become objects of faith for believers, the sacrament itself is enlarged: the seal of baptism was added, a type of garment for the faith which previously was nude and which now has no more power without the faith to which it is joined. Thus was the law of baptism established and its formula prescribed, "Go, teach all the nations, baptizing them in the name of the Father and of the Son and of the Holy Spirit."[75] The following prescription was added to this law, "No one can enter the kingdom of heaven without being reborn of water and the Spirit."[76] This binds faith to the necessity of baptism. Henceforth all who believe are baptized. And Paul himself, as soon as he believed, was baptized.[77] This is what the Lord commanded when Paul fell blind, "Get up," he said, "and go to Damascus; there you will be told everything that you are to do,"[78] namely, to receive baptism, the only thing he lacked. For the rest, he had been sufficiently instructed and believed that the Nazarene was the Lord, the Son of God.[79]

465   xiv. But those who object call attention to the apostle himself who says, "Christ did not send me to baptize."[80] As if this argument would do away with baptism! Why, then, did Paul baptize Gaius, Crispus, and the household of Stephanas?[81] Furthermore, even if Christ had not sent Paul to baptize, Christ commanded the other apostles to do so. These lines were addressed to the Corinthians in light of the conditions of the time: divisions and discords broke out among them[82] since one claimed to belong to Paul, another to Apollos.[83] This is why the apostle, out of love for peace and so as not to seem to claim all ministries for himself, declares that he has been sent not to baptize but to preach. Preaching comes first. Baptism follows. Yet, as I believe, whoever can rightfully preach can also rightfully baptize.

466   xv. I do not know whether other questions are bantered about in regard to the baptismal controversy. And so I will explain what I omitted above, doing so to avoid giving the impression of interrupting the flow of my discourse. Certainly there is only one baptism, and this according to the

---

72. See Matt 8:22.   73. Matt 10:37.   74. See Gen 15:6.   75. Matt 28:19.   76. John 3:5.   77. See Acts 9:18.   78. Acts 22:10.   79. See Acts 22:8.   80. 1 Cor 1:17.   81. See 1 Cor 1:14, 16.   82. See 1 Cor 11:18.   83. See 1 Cor 3:4.

Lord's Gospel and according to the letters of Paul. The reason is that there is only one God and only one Church above.[84] What should be done in regard to the heretics can be considered by those who are more competent than I. My writing here is addressed only to us; heretics, however, do not share in our rites; they are outsiders because they are not in communion with us. I am not bound to recognize in them what is imposed on me. We do not share the same God with them nor do we have the one and the same Christ. Nor do we share the same baptism because it is not the same baptism. Since they do not have a baptism as properly required—no doubt about it—it is not baptism which they possess; and since they do not possess baptism, they cannot have it counted. And since they do not have it, they cannot receive it. As to the rest, we have already treated this at length in a work written in Greek.[f] Only one time, then, do we enter the baptismal bath, and only one time are our sins there washed away because they are never to be repeated. Israel, on the other hand, washes each day because it dirties itself each day. So that this custom may not be observed by us also, the precept of one baptism was established. Happy this water with which we wash and which sinners cannot mock! It is not contaminated by the continual presence of dirt. It stains those who wash in it a second time.[g]

XVI. We have, certainly, a second bath, which itself is also one. It is the baptism of blood concerning which the Lord said that he had to be baptized[85] even though he was already baptized. As John has written, he came "by water and by blood,"[86] by water that he might be baptized, by blood that he might be glorified. Accordingly, he called us by water; he chose us by blood. These two baptisms flow together from the wound in his pierced side[87] since those who believe in his blood are still to be washed in water, and those who have been washed in water still have to shed their blood. This second baptism replaces the water bath when it has not been received, and restores it when it has been lost.

XVII. To conclude this instruction, it remains for us to recall the rules for giving and receiving baptism. As to conferring it, the high priest—who is the bishop—has the primary right when he is present. After him, it belongs to the priest and the deacon, but never without the bishop's permission out of respect due to the Church since peace is preserved when this respect is preserved. Furthermore, the laity can also baptize. What all receive in the same degree, all can give in the same degree (the Lord's disciples were already called bishops, priests, and deacons!). Baptism is akin to the word of the Lord which no one can rightfully hide. Baptism also comes from God; all can confer it. But what reserve and modesty

467

468

---

f. This treatise no longer exists.

g. SChr has the following note: "The meaning of this passage is unclear. Surely Tertullian means that receiving a second baptism would constitute a sin of heresy" (p. 88).

84. See Eph 4:5.   85. See Luke 12:50.   86. 1 John 5:6.   87. See John 19:34.

are required for the laity, more even than for clerics who themselves are
to prove that they do not encroach upon the bishop's ministry. Jealousy
in regard to the episcopacy is the mother of all divisions. The most holy
apostle has said, "All things are lawful, but not all things are opportune."[88]
Follow this rule when necessary according to circumstances of place, time,
or persons. In such a case the boldness of the one who brings assistance
is justified by the urgency of the danger. To refuse the help that one can
freely give is to be guilty of the loss of another. But will the impudence
of the woman who has already usurped the right of teaching go so far as
to arrogate for herself the right of baptizing?[89] No! . . . least there rise up
some new beasts similar to the first. One pretended to suppress baptism;
another will desire to confer it herself. And if these women invoke the
Acts which incorrectly bear the name of Paul, and claim the example of
Thecla in defense of their right to teach and to baptize, they should know
that a priest in Asia forged this work, covering his own authority with
that of Paul. Convicted of fraud, he stated that he so acted out of love for
Paul, and he was then deposed. In fact, is it likely that the apostle gives a
woman the power of teaching and of baptizing, he who restricted a wife's
permission to teach? "Let women be silent," he says, "and let them question their husbands at home."[90]

469   XVIII. Those whose function it is to baptize should understand that baptism is not to be given lightly. "Give to everyone who asks of you"[91] has
its own particular meaning, one that refers to almsgiving. It is much better
for us to reflect on another saying, namely, "Do not give what is holy to
the dogs; and do not throw your pearls before swine."[92] Or also this, "Do
not impose hands hastily and do not participate in the sins of another."[93]
If Philip so quickly baptized the eunuch, we should remember that the
Lord had testified his favor toward him in an explicit and manifest way; it
was the Spirit who commanded Philip to take this route.[94] For his part, the
eunuch was not idle; there was no sudden desire urging him on to request
baptism, but he had gone to the temple to pray and he worked hard at
reading the Holy Scriptures.[95] So it was fitting for the apostle, gratuitously
sent by God, to discover him. Then, once again, the Spirit commanded
Philip to join the eunuch by the latter's chariot.[96] At that moment a text,
relative to the faith itself, was presented; the exhortation was received;
the Lord was proclaimed; faith was not delayed; water was immediately
found; and then the apostle, his mission completed, was snatched away.[97]
Paul also was immediately baptized.[98] Simon, his host,[h] had recognized in
him a subject of election; in advance God's favor gave signs of the divine

h. Actually it was at Jude's house that Ananias laid hands on Saul, after which
Saul was baptized.
88. 1 Cor 6:12; 10:23.   89. See 1 Cor 14:34.   90. 1 Cor 14:34-35.   91. Luke
6:30.   92. Matt 7:6.   93. 1 Tim 5:22.   94. See Acts 8:26.   95. See Acts 8:28.   96. See
Acts 8:29.   97. See Acts 8:36, 39.   98. See Acts 9:18.

choice.[99] Every candidate for baptism can deceive and be deceived. This is why according to each person's condition, disposition, and even age, it is preferable to defer baptism, especially when it concerns very young children. Other than in absolute necessity, are sponsors to risk failing in their promises because they die or because they are disappointed by the growth of an evil disposition in the one who has been baptized? Certainly the Lord said, "Let the little children come to me."[100] Yes, let them come, but when they are older, when they can be taught, when they can be instructed about the person to whom they come. Let them become Christians when they are capable of knowing Christ. Why is this innocent age hastening to the remission of sins? We act with more foresight in secular affairs! Are we to confide divine gifts to those to whom we do not confide earthly goods? May they at least be capable of requesting salvation so that you may take care that salvation is given only to the one who requests it. For no less serious a reason, it is necessary to defer the baptism of the unmarried since temptation awaits them; the same is true for virgins because of their immaturity; likewise for widows because of their instability.[101] Delay baptism till they marry or grow stronger in the practice of continence. If one understands what baptism imposes, its reception rather than its delay would be feared the more: a faith that is whole is assured of salvation.

xix. The Pasch stands out as the more solemn day for baptism since the Lord's passion in which we are baptized is therein completed. It will not be inconsistent to interpret as a figure this passage where the Lord, about to celebrate the Passover for the last time, sent his disciple to prepare for it, as he said to them, "You will find a man carrying some water."[102] It was through the sign of water that he indicated the place where he would celebrate the Passover. In addition, the time of Pentecost is a most propitious time for celebrating baptism. During these days the Risen Lord frequently showed himself to his disciples.[103] This was when the grace of the Holy Spirit was given to them,[104] and which allowed them to hope in the Lord's coming.[105] It was at this time, after his ascension into heaven, that the angels told the apostles that the Lord would return, just as he ascended into heaven, precisely at Pentecost. Also Jeremiah who says, "I will gather them from the ends of the earth for a day of feasting,"[106] designates by this the time of Pentecost, the time which, properly speaking, is a "day of feasting." And yet every day belongs to the Lord. Every hour, every time is suitable for baptism. Even though the ceremony might be different, grace is in no way affected.

xx. Those preparing for baptism should invoke God through fervent prayers, fasting, genuflections, and vigils. They should also prepare themselves by confessing all their past sins, doing so in memory of the baptism

470

471

---

99. See Acts 9:15.   100. Matt 19:14.   101. See 1 Tim 5:13.   102. Mark 14:13.
103. See Acts 1:3.   104. See Acts 2:4.   105. See Acts 1:11.   106. Jer 31:8.

of John of which it is said that people received it while "confessing their sins."[107] We can rejoice that we do not publicly confess our sins and evil deeds. By afflicting the flesh and the spirit, we make satisfaction for sin and also fortify ourselves in advance against future temptations. "Watch and pray," says the Lord, "that you may not enter into temptation."[108] The reason the apostles were tempted at the time of the Lord's arrest was, I believe, that they were asleep, and so they abandoned him.[109] The one who remained close by the Lord and defended him with the sword,[110] even went so far as to deny him three times,[111] for it was predicted that no one can enter the heavenly kingdom without experiencing temptation. And immediately after his baptism the Lord himself, observing a fast of forty days, was assailed by temptations. And so someone might ask whether we too are to fast after our baptism. Nothing hinders us from doing so unless it be the necessity for rejoicing and for giving joyful thanks for salvation. But as far as I understand, the Lord wished to symbolically return against Israel the reproach he recently incurred. The people, after passing through the sea and entering the desert, spent forty years there, being nourished by the divine abundance.[112] In spite of this, the people were more mindful of their belly and gullet than of God.[113] This is why the Lord, after his baptism, went off into the desert where, during a fast of forty days, he showed that those who are of God do not live by bread alone but by God's word,[114] and that temptations coming from a full and unrestrained stomach are conquered by abstinence. Therefore, blessed ones, God's grace awaits you. You will ascend from the most holy bath of new birth.[115] For the first time you will extend your hands with your brethren in the house of your mother. You will ask the Father, ask the Lord for the abundance of his charisms as a special gift of divine grace.[116] *Ask and you will receive,*[117] he says. You have asked, and you have found. You have knocked, and it has been opened to you. I request only one more thing: that you remember in your prayers Tertullian the sinner.

26-F. On Prayer†

This treatise, dating between 198 and 206 and addressed to the catechumens, is the earliest exposition of the Lord's Prayer.

472   VI. How skillfully has divine Wisdom arranged the order of this prayer so that after mentioning heavenly things, namely, God's name, will, and kingdom, it goes on to request earthly necessities. "For the Lord said, 'Seek first the kingdom and then these things will also be given you.'"[1] Yet

---

107. Matt 3:6.   108. Matt 26:41.   109. See Matt 26:56.   110. See Matt 26:51.
111. See Matt 26:75.   112. See Exod 16:13.   113. See Num 11:5.   114. See Matt 4:2, 4.
115. See Titus 3:5.   116. See 1 Cor 12:4.   117. Matt 7:7.
    † Translated from *Opera*, CCL 1 (Turnhout, 1953) 26off.
    1. Matt 6:33; Luke 12:31.

it is in a spiritual sense that we should understand, "Give us this day our daily bread."[2] Christ is "our bread" because Christ is life and bread is life ("I am," he says, "the bread of life" and somewhat later, "the bread is the word of the living God which descends from heaven"[3]), then because his Body is believed to be in the bread, "this is my Body."[4] Thus by requesting daily bread, we are requesting life everlasting in Christ and inseparable union with the Body of Christ.

XVI. As to the custom observed by some of sitting down once their prayer has ended, I see no reason for this unless they wish to imitate children. What do I mean here? If Hermas, whose writings almost always bear the title "The Shepherd," had not sat down on his bed at the conclusion of his prayer but did something else, would we also claim as our own this practice? Surely not! The phrase "when I had prayed and sat upon my bed"[a] is simply narrative and is not the equivalent of something we must do. Otherwise if no bed were present, we could not pray. And to sit in a chair or on a bench would violate what he had written. Furthermore, since the pagans sit before the gods they adore, so we reprove what is done before idols. This is why it is considered a sin of irreverence, even among the pagans should they be able to understand this. If it is disrespectful to sit down before a person whom you most highly revere and honor, how much more irreligious is it to do so before the living God with the angel of prayer standing nearby. Unless we are reproaching God because prayer has exhausted us! 473

XVIII. Another custom has developed, namely, that at the end of the prayer those who are fasting refrain from the kiss of peace, which is the seal of prayer. Yet at what time is it more appropriate to give the peace to the brethren than when our prayer, more praiseworthy because of our devotion, ascends to heaven. In this way they participate in our charity, they who have contributed to it by passing on their peace to their brethren. Is any prayer complete when separated from the holy kiss? Does the peace hinder any work done for the Lord? From what type of sacrifice does one leave without exchanging the peace? Whatever be the reason, it will not be stronger than the observance of the precept commanding us to hide our fasting.[5] We are recognized to be fasting when we refrain from the kiss. But even if there is a reason, still that you may not be guilty of breaking this rule, you may if you so desire, forgo extending the peace at home since it is there that you are among those from whom you cannot totally conceal your fasting. Wherever else you can hide your acts of piety, you should be mindful of this precept; in such a way you will satisfy the discipline in public and follow custom when at home. So on Good Friday, a day on which fasting is a general and somewhat public obligation, rightly 474

---

a. *The "Shepherd" of Hermas*, Vision v.1 (not in WEC).

2. Matt 6:11; see Luke 11:3. 3. See John 6:31ff. 4. Matt 26:26; Mark 14:22; Luke 22:19. 5. See Matt 6:16ff.

do we forgo giving the peace, not concerned about hiding what we do with everyone else.

475   XIX. Likewise in regard to the stational days, many do not believe that they should attend the sacrificial prayers because receiving the Lord's Body would break their fast. Does the Eucharist, therefore, free us from a service devoted to God or does it bind us more closely to God? Will your station not be even more solemn if you also stand at the altar of God? Each remains intact if you receive the Lord's Body and reserve it:[b] participation in the sacrifice and the fulfillment of a duty. If the word "station" comes from military usage (for we are indeed God's army), certainly neither joy nor sadness occurring in the camp releases the soldiers from assuming guard duty. Those who are joyful follow the commands that are given more freely; those who are sad do so more attentively.

476   XXIII. As to kneeling, prayer allows different customs in that there are some, a very few, who do not kneel on the Sabbath, this being a dissenting practice now strongly defended in the churches. The Lord will give his grace so that its proponents will either yield or, without scandalizing others, will follow their own opinion. According to our traditions, only on the day of the Lord's resurrection should we refrain not only from kneeling but from every expression and act of worry, postponing any business dealing so as not to make way for the devil.[6] The same holds true for the time of Pentecost which is characterized by the same joyous celebration. In other respects, who would hesitate to prostrate before God every day for at least the first prayer at daybreak? During the times when we observe the fasts and the stations there is to be no prayer except when kneeling and with humility. For we not only pray but beseech and offer satisfaction to God our Lord.

477   XXIV. Nothing is prescribed as to the times of prayer except that we are to pray at all times and places. But since we are not to pray in public, how can we pray in every place? "In every place," he said,[7] that favoring circumstances or necessity offer. The apostles did not act contrary to the precept when, in prison and with the guards listening, they prayed and sang to God[8] or when Paul on a ship and in the presence of all gave thanks.[9]

478   XXV. As to the time for prayer, it will not be useless to observe certain hours outwardly, namely, the times of common prayer that mark off the divisions of the day, namely, Terce, Sext, and None, whose observance is found in the Scriptures. It was at the third hour when the Holy Spirit was first sent upon the disciples who had gathered together.[10] It was at the sixth hour when Peter, on the day he experienced a vision of all creation in a large sheet, went up higher so that he could pray.[11] Likewise, it was at the ninth hour when John entered the temple where he cured the

b. Perhaps by taking it home.

6. See Eph 4:27.   7. See Luke 18:1; Eph 6:18; 1 Thess 5:17; 1 Tim 2:8.   8. See Acts 16:25.   9. See Acts 27:35.   10. See Acts 2:1ff.   11. See Acts 10:9ff.

paralytic.[12] Although all these took place without any precept, it would, however, be good to establish some presupposition that would make binding the admonition to pray and would be like a law that from time to time wrestles us from our daily affairs to such a task. This, we read, was done by Daniel according to the teaching of Israel.[13] In such a way we adore, at least no less than three times a day, as being in debt to the Three: Father, Son, and Holy Spirit. Certainly we are not including the rightful prayers which without any urging, are to be said at dawn and at dusk. But it is appropriate for the faithful not to take food or go to the bath before having prayed, for refreshment and nourishment of the spirit are to be preferred to those of the flesh because heavenly things come before those of earth.

xxvi. You are not to let one of the brethren who has entered your house   479
depart without a prayer ("You have seen," he said, "one of the brethren, you have seen the Lord."[c]); this should especially be observed in the case of strangers lest perhaps he or she be an angel.[14] But once this individual has been received by the brethren, attend first to heavenly rather than earthly refreshment. For in this way your faith will immediately be declared openly. Or how can you say "Peace be to this house"[15] unless you exchange the peace with those who are in the house?

xxvii. Those more careful in prayer are accustomed to add the Alleluia   480
to their prayers and to psalms that allow all to respond at the end. Surely this practice is very good; by acclaiming and honoring God the prayer, being filled out, can be directed like a rich victim to him.

xxviii. It is to God's altar, together with a display of good works and   481
amid the singing of psalms and hymns, that we are to bring this prayer wholeheartedly devoted to him, supported by faith, cared for by truth, pure in its innocence, clean because of our chastity, and crowned by our love for each other. It will obtain for us whatever we request from God.

26-G. To My Wife[†]

Writing early in the third century, Tertullian counsels his wife on how she should live after his death. If she remarries, she certainly is not to marry a pagan.

II.iv. May she see how she values her duties to her husband. Certainly   482
she cannot satisfy the Lord according to what is required if she has at her side the servant of the devil, a man who will act as an agent of his master in obstructing the duties and devotions of the faithful. If a station is to be

---

c. Some see this as a possible corruption of a scriptural passage; see Matt 25:40; Gen 18:3; 19:2; Heb 13:2.

12. See Acts 3:1ff.   13. See Dan 6:6ff.   14. See Heb 13:2.   15. Luke 10:5–6; see John 20:19.

† Translated from CCL 1:388ff.

observed at daybreak, the husband arranges to meet her at the baths; if
fasts are to be observed, on the same day the husband is engaged in ban-
queting; if necessity requires that she go out to perform a task of Christian
charity, something needs to be done at home. [. . .] Who will allow her to
be taken from his side so that she, if need be, can attend nocturnal gatherings? Moreover, who will unconcernedly allow her to pass the night at
the paschal solemnities? Who will without any suspicion let her go to the
Lord's Supper, which they defame? Who will allow her to steal into prison
to kiss the wounds of the martyrs? [. . .]

483   II.v. "Yet some husbands endure and are not disturbed by what we
do." It is precisely here, then, that sin is found: namely, that the heathens
know the things that we do, that the unjust are aware of our activities, and
that we are allowed to do something only by reason of their goodness.
Whoever "endures" something cannot be ignorant of it, or, if something
is concealed because the husband does not endure it, he is feared. Since
Scripture commands that we work for the Lord, both without another
knowing and without pressure on ourselves, it does not matter in which
area you fail, whether in what your husband may know if he is tolerant
or in the difficulties you yourself may have in avoiding his intolerance.
"Do not," he says, "throw your pearls before swine lest they trample them
and turn about to destroy you also."[1] Your pearls are also the distinguish-
ing marks of your daily conduct. The greater the care you take to conceal
them, so much the more do you make them suspect and more scrutinized
by the curiosity of the Gentiles. Do you conceal yourself when you sign
your bed, your body? When with your breath you blow away something
impure? Also when you rise during the night so that you might pray?
Will you not be seen as if you are engaging in some type of magic? Will
your husband not know what you are tasting in secret before you take any
food? And if he knows it to be bread, will he not believe it to be the bread
that we say it is? [. . .]

484   II.viii. What type of marriage bond exists between two believers who
share in one hope, one promise, one discipline, one and the same obedience! Both are brethren; both serve together; there is no difference of spirit
or of body, and truly two are in one flesh.[2] Where the body is one, the
spirit is also one: together they pray, together they instruct one another,
together they fast, teaching each other, exhorting one another, supporting one another. Both are equally in the Church of God, equally at God's
banquet, equally sharing times of distress, persecutions, consolations. Neither conceals, neither avoids the other, neither is harsh toward the other.
With generosity the sick are visited; the needy are fed. Alms are freely
bestowed, the sacrifice is attended without difficulty, daily devotions are
carried out without impediments; there is no furtive signing, no anxious
congratulations, no silent blessings. Psalms and hymns resound between

---

1. Matt 7:6.   2. See Gen 2:24; Matt 19:6; 1 Cor 6:16.

the two, and they mutually challenge each other as to who sings best to
the Lord. Christ rejoices when he hears and sees all this. To these he sends
his peace. Where two are, there he himself is.[3] Where he is, there the evil
one is not. [. . .]

26-H. On Penance[†]

Writing in 203, Tertullian in chapters IV to VI treats the penance that is to
precede baptism, whereas the second half of the book is an exposition on
the "second" penance, which, for psychological reasons, is granted only
once.

IV. And so for all sins, whether of the flesh or of the spirit, whether in
deed or in desire, he who has decreed that punishment take place after
judgment has also promised to give pardon when he said to the people,
"Repent and I will save you."[1] Also, "I am the living God, says the Lord,
and I prefer penance to death."[2] Penance, therefore, is life since it is preferable to death. And so you, a sinner like myself[3] and even less a sinner than
I since I acknowledge my superiority in sin, should throw yourself upon
penance and embrace it as a shipwrecked[4] person embraces the plank of
salvation. You have been submerged under the waves of sin; penance will
support you and lead you to the port of divine mercy. Seize this blessed
and unanticipated opportunity so that you, once nothing before the Lord
other than a drop in the bucket,[5] a grain of dust driven through the air,[6]
a potter's vessel,[7] will one day become a tree, a tree planted by the water
which always retains its leaves and gives fruit in due time,[8] and which
will see neither fire nor the axe.[9]

VI. Nor do I deny that the divine favor, namely, the forgiveness of sins,
is granted to those who will enter the water; but to be fortunate enough to
arrive at such a point, effort is required. [. . .] Let those who are classified
among the hearers not flatter themselves that they are still allowed to sin.
From the time you know the Lord, you should fear him; from the time you
look toward him, you should revere him. For the rest, what good is it to
know the Lord if you remain attached to the same things as formerly, before you knew him? What, then, differentiates you from a perfect servant
of God? Or is there one Christ for the baptized and another Christ for the
hearers? Is there a different hope, or reward, a different fear of judgment,
a different necessity for doing penance? The baptismal bath is the seal of
faith, but the faith of baptism begins with and is commended by the faith
of penance. We have not been washed in baptism in order that we may

485

486

---

3. See Matt 18:20.
† Translated from CCL 1:326ff.
1. Ezek 18:32.　2. Ezek 33:11.　3. See 1 Tim 1:15.　4. See 1 Tim 1:19.　5. See Isa
40:15.　6. See Ps 1:4; Dan 2:35; Hos 13:3.　7. See Jer 19:11; Rom 9:21.　8. See Ps
1:3.　9. See Matt 3:10.

cease sinning; rather, we have ceased sinning since we have been washed
within. Such, in fact, is the first baptism of the hearer whose fear is perfect
since the Lord has already been experienced, whose faith is healthy since
the hearer's conscience has already embraced penance once and for all.

487   VII. Lord, Christ, may your servants speak of the discipline of penance
or hear it spoken of only when, as hearers, they have the duty of avoiding sin. Afterwards, may they, not needing it, know nothing of penance.
It bothers me to add mention of a second hope or one which is already
the final one. My fear is that by referring to the means which it offers of
still performing penance, I appear to indicate that we still have time for
sinning. May no one so understand my words as if the road of sin were
still open because the road for penance is still open; may no one transform
God's superabundant mercy[10] into a desire for human rashness. May no
one be worse, sinning as often as pardon is given, because the Lord is better. For the rest, those who have not put an end to their sins will surely
discover that an end has been assigned to their immunity. We have escaped once; let us not place ourselves in danger even if we seem to escape
a second time. Many people who have survived a shipwreck henceforth
put some distance between themselves and ships and the sea; they honor
God's gift, namely, the fact that they were saved, by recalling the danger. I
praise their fear; I love the respect they show; they do not desire to burden
the divine mercy; they fear that they will be seen as trampling underfoot
what they have received; certainly with good care they avoid experiment-
ing a second time with what they have learned to fear. Thus by checking
their presumption they give proof of their fear. Human fear honors God.[11]
The most stubborn enemy never relaxes his evil; in fact, he rages most
when he feels that someone has been completely freed; he burns most
when someone tries to quench him. He has to grieve and moan when sins
are forgiven, when so many deadly works are destroyed in us,[12] when
so many titles of his ancient authority are removed. He grieves that sinners, servants of Christ, will judge him and his angels.[13] This is why the
devil spies on them,[14] attacks them, besieges them, with the hope that he
can either strike their eyes with the concupiscence of the flesh, or ensnare
their souls in unlawful worldly delights, or destroy their faith by a fear
of civil authorities, or through perverse instructions lead them from the
right path. Never does the devil lack scandals or temptations. Foreseeing these poisons, God has permitted the gate of forgiveness to remain
a little open, even though it had been closed and locked by the washing.
In the vestibule God has placed a second penance which is available to
those who knock,[15] but one time only since it is already the second time;
yet never again since the previous time had been useless. Is not this one
time enough? You have what you did not merit; you have lost what you

---

10. See Luke 1:78; Rom 5:17.   11. See Sir 1:11.   12. See Wis 1:12; Rom 6:2.
13. See 1 Cor 6:3.   14. See 1 Pet 5:8.   15. See Matt 7:7.

received. If the Lord's kindness gives you what is required to recover what you have lost, be grateful for the benefit that he repeats or increases. For to restore is greater than to give since it is worse to have lost than it is not to have received at all. Yet if someone should carry out a second penance, his or her spirit should not on this account be cut down and destroyed. Surely be ashamed to sin again but not to do penance again; be ashamed to be placed again in danger but not to be freed from it; when a person falls again, the remedy is repeated. You will prove your thankfulness to the Lord if you do not refuse what he again offers you. You have offended him, but you can still reconcile yourself to him: you are dealing with one to whom you can make amends and who certainly desires it.

ix. Insofar as this second and one penance is stringent, it must be seri-   488
ously tested: it is not enough to produce it within one's conscience but it must be manifested by doing something. This action is more commonly designated by the Greek word *exomologesis*; by this we confess our sins to the Lord, certainly not as if he did not know them but so that satisfaction is prepared for by confession; confession gives birth to penance; by penance God is appeased. Exomologesis, then, is a discipline enjoining us to prostrate and humble ourselves. It imposes on us, even in regard to what we eat and wear, a manner of living that draws down God's mercy. It orders us to lie down upon sackcloth and ashes,[16] to cover the body with filth, to afflict the soul with sorrow, to punish severely all that has caused us to sin. Furthermore, it requires that we take only very plain food and drink for the good not only of the stomach but assuredly that of the soul, that we nourish prayer mostly by fasting, that we sigh, cry, and groan day and night to the Lord our God, that we throw ourselves at the feet of the presbyters, that we kneel before the altar of God, that we request all the brethren to intercede on our behalf. Exomologesis does all this to encourage repentance, in order to honor the Lord through fear of peril, so that by pronouncing judgment on the sinner it might ward off God's wrath and by punishment here on earth it will cancel—I do not say prevent—eternal suffering. This is why when it prostrates someone, it raises up that person; when it soils, it cleanses; when it accuses, it excuses, when it condemns, it forgives. To the extent that you showed no mercy toward yourself, so, believe me, God will be merciful to you.

x. There are very many who flee from this task because it makes public   489
what they have done, or they postpone it from day to day, thinking more about their shame, I believe, than about their salvation, as do those who, having contacted some sickness in the private parts of the body, avoid making this known to the doctors, and so they perish along with their modesty. Evidently shame finds it intolerable to offer satisfaction to the Lord who has been offended, to regain possession of the salvation that has been lost. Truly you are indeed a brave person when you lift your

---

16. See Dan 9:3; Jonah 3:5–6.

head while sinning but lower it when requesting forgiveness. I have no place for shame when I profit at its expense and when in a certain way it exhorts, "Don't worry about me. It is better that I die rather than you." [. . .] Why do you flee as if from scoffers, from those who share your misfortunes? The body cannot rejoice when one of its members suffers;[17] it is necessary that the whole body suffer together and collaborate toward a remedy. Where we find one or another of the faithful, there we find the Church;[18] the Church indeed is Christ.[19] So when you extend your hands toward the knees of the brethren, you touch Christ, you exhort Christ. Likewise, when the brethren shed tears over you, it is Christ who is suffering, it is Christ who entreats the Father. What the child requests is always readily granted.[20] Truly, to hide sin promises great profit to modesty. To be sure, when we conceal something from the knowledge of others, do we not also conceal it from the Lord? Is this the extent to which we compare human opinion and God's judgment? Or is it better to be condemned in secret than to be forgiven in public? But it pains to undertake exomologesis in this way. I prefer to say that we suffer pain because we have sinned, but when penance is to be undertaken, suffering disappears since salvation occurs. It hurts to be cut, to be cauterized, to be tortured by the sting of certain medicinal powders; nonetheless, disagreeable remedies justify the pain by the cure they effect; present evil is accepted because of future advantage.

490 　　xii. Since, therefore, you know that against hell there exists, after the first line of defense constituted by the Lord's baptism, a second help in exomologesis, why do you desert your salvation? Why do you delay undertaking what you know will cure you? [. . .]

26-I. On the Dress of Women[†]

Here Tertullian, writing after 206, warns Christian women to shun pagan customs of dress.

491 　　II.xi. [. . .] Only for grave reasons are you to appear in public: when you go to visit a sick member of the community, when the sacrifice is offered, or when God's word is celebrated. Each of these is a serious and holy activity, requiring no extraordinary clothing. [. . .]

26-J. Against Marcion[††]

This, the longest of Tertullian's writings and composed of five books, was written between 207 and 212. It is the best source of information regarding

---

17. See 1 Cor 12:26.　18. See Matt 18:20.　19. See Col 1:24.　20. See Luke 11:11–13.

　[†] Translated from CCL 1:366.

　[††] Translated from CCL 1:455ff.

Marcion, a well-known heretic who rejected not only the complete Old Testament but also many books from the Christian Scriptures.

I.xiv. Indeed till now the Lord has not condemned the water of the Creator by which he washes his own, nor the oil by which he anoints them, nor the union of milk and honey whereby he nourishes them like small children, nor the bread by which he makes present his own Body. [. . .]   492

26-K. On the Resurrection of the Dead[†]

Writing ca. 210–12, Tertullian argues against all who deny the resurrection of the body.

VIII. The body is washed that the soul might be cleansed; the body is anointed so that the soul might be hallowed; the body is signed so that the soul may be strengthened; the body is covered by the imposition of hands so that the soul may be enlightened by the Spirit; the body feeds on Christ's Body and Blood so that the soul may be fattened on God. [. . .]   493

26-L. On the Soul[††]

Written early in the third century and most probably after Tertullian had become a Montanist, this is the second largest of Tertullian's writings. It well demonstrates the author's familiarity with the Greek philosophers.

IX. At present we have among us a sister who has been allotted various gifts of revelation. These she experiences in the Spirit during the Sunday solemnities in church. She has dealings with the angels and at times also with the Lord; she sees and hears hidden mysteries, some hearts she reads, and she takes remedies to those who need them. Whether it be during the reading of the Scriptures, during the chanting of the psalms, while sermons are being given, or while petitions are being made, all these are occasions when she experiences visions. [. . .] Once the ceremonies are over and the people have been dismissed, she ordinarily reports to us what she has seen. [. . .]   494

26-M. On the Crown[†††]

Written in 211, the *De corona* treats the participation of Christians in the army.

III. [. . .] Let us ask whether tradition, without being written down, should be accepted. Surely we will say that it should not be received unless we have other unwritten practices that we maintain and lay claim to   495

[†] Translated from *Opera*, CCL 2 (Turnhout, 1954) 931.
[††] Translated from CCL 2:792.
[†††] Translated from CCL 2:1042–43.

by custom alone. To be brief, let me begin with baptism. Shortly before we
enter the water, namely, in the church and under the bishop's hand, we
solemnly renounce the devil, his pomp, and his angels. Next, we are immersed three times, responding somewhat more at length than the Lord
determined in the Gospel.[1] Then, when received as children, we taste a
mixture of milk and honey, and from that day on throughout the whole
week we do not bathe daily. We receive the sacrament of the Eucharist,
which the Lord commanded[2] to be taken by all at the time when we eat,
receiving it also during predawn meetings and only from the hands of
those presiding. Each year, on the day of their birthdays [into heaven], we
make offerings for the deceased. On Sundays it is forbidden to fast and
also to kneel when at worship. From Easter to Pentecost we rejoice in the
same exemption. We are greatly distressed should any of the bread or anything from the cup, even what is our own, fall to the ground. We trace the
sign on our forehead at every step forward and at every movement, each
time we arrive and depart, when we put on our clothing and footwear,
when we bathe, when at table, when lighting the lamps, when reclining,
when sitting, and when performing the ordinary actions of daily life.

26-N. On Idolatry[†]

Dating from about 211, this treatise discusses the Christian's relationship
with paganism.

496   xiv. [. . .] O better the fidelity of the pagans to their own sect, which
claims no Christian solemnity for itself! Neither the Lord's Day nor Pentecost, even if they had known them, would they have shared with us;
their fear would be that of appearing as Christians. We do not fear being
publicly known as heathens. [. . .] Among the heathens each festival day
occurs only once each year; but you have such a day every eight days.
Separate the individual heathen festivals and put them in a row; they will
not equal a Pentecost.

26-O. On Fasting[††]

Dating from Tertullian's Montanist period, this work defends the rigorist Montanist practice in regard to fasting and attacks what is done by
Catholics.

497   xiv. Observing, therefore, the times and days and months and years,[1] do
we Galaticize? Clearly we do if we observe the Jewish ceremonies, the legal
solemnities; in this regard the apostle teaches just the opposite, curbing the

---

1. See Matt 28:19.   2. See 1 Cor 11:23–25; Matt 26:27; Mark 14:23.
[†] Translated from CCL 2:1115.
[††] Translated from CCL 2:1272–73.
1. See Gal 4:10.

continued existence of the Old Testament, which is now buried in Christ, and establishing the existence of the New. Yet if there is a new creation in Christ,[2] our solemnities should also be new: if the apostle has erased all devotion to times and days and months and years, why do we celebrate the Pasch each year during the first month? Why do we rejoice for fifty days? Why do we set apart the fourth and the sixth days for the stations, and the Preparation Day for fasting? Although at times you prolong your fast over the Sabbath, never is this day to be observed as one of fasting except at the Pasch, according to a reason given elsewhere. Certainly, for us every day by reason of its general consecration is a feastday. [. . .]

26-P. On Flight in Persecution[†]

Departing from his previous opinion (*To My Wife* 1.3), the author holds that fleeing in times of persecution contradicts God's will.

xiv. "But how," you ask, "shall we gather to celebrate the solemnities of   498
the Lord?" Certainly just as the apostles did. They were protected by faith, not by money, and if faith can move a mountain,[1] so all the more can it remove a soldier. Let wisdom, not bribery, be your protection. Even if you bribe the military, you will not be immediately safe from the people. [. . .] Lastly, if you are unable to gather during the day, you have the night, with the light of Christ shining bright against the darkness. [. . .]

26-Q. Against Praxeas[††]

Written after Tertullian had become a Montanist and thus probably in 213 or shortly thereafter, this treatise is directed against Praxeas, a heretic who so strove to maintain the unity of the Trinity that he completely and erroneously identified the Father with the Son.

xxvi. [. . .] After his resurrection the Lord says he will send to his dis-   499
ciples the promise of his Father.[1] Lastly he commands them to baptize into the Father, and the Son, and the Holy Spirit,[2] not into one. For we are washed not once but three times, at the mention of each Person's name.

26-R. On Modesty[†††]

Written during his Montanist period and probably against a bishop in Carthage, this treatise contradicts what Tertullian wrote in his work on penance. Introducing a distinction between "forgivable" sins and

---

2. See 2 Cor 5:17.
[†] Translated from CCL 2:1155.
1. See 1 Cor 13:2.
[††] Translated from CCL 2:1198.
1. See Luke 24:49.   2. See Matt 28:19.
[†††] Translated from CCL 2:1286ff.

"unforgivable" ones, serious sins are forgiven only by Christ in heaven, not by a public act, not through the visible Church and its ministers.

500　III. [. . .] "For if," they say, "penance lacks pardon, you are not to do penance. For nothing is to be done in vain. Furthermore, penance is done in vain if it lacks pardon. Yet all penance is to be practiced. Therefore all pardon follows so that penance is not done in vain. Furthermore, penance is done in vain if it lacks pardon." Therefore rightly do they oppose us in that they have usurped to themselves also the fruit of penance, namely, pardon. As to those who seek to obtain peace here on earth, penance is done in vain. As for us who remember that it is only the Lord who forgives sins and certainly mortal sins, penance is not done in vain. [. . .]

501　V. [. . .] There stands the idolater, there stands the murderer, and in their midst is the adulterer. Together they sit doing the work of penance. Together they shudder in sackcloth and ashes; they groan together; they say the same prayers, they petition on the same knees, they invoke the same mother. Now what will you do, most kind and gentle discipline? Either you must act the same toward all of them—for "blessed are the peacemakers"[1]—or if not the same to all of them, then you must become one of us. Once and for all you condemn the idolater and the murderer, and yet you excuse the adulterer from their midst? [. . .]

502　XVIII. So God's mercy, which prefers that sinners do penance rather than die,[2] looks at those who are still ignorant and still unbelieving; it is for these that Christ came to set free; not for those who already know God and have learned the mystery of faith. If God's kindness extends to those who are still ignorant and to unbelievers, then penance will be an invitation to clemency, except for the penance that follows faith. Here penance can obtain from the bishop pardon for lesser offenses; from God alone for those that are greater and irremissible.

503　XIX. [. . .] Nor are we to overlook the distinction among sins, which was the starting point of our digression. John approved this, namely, that there are certain daily offenses from which no one is immune. For who will not be unfairly angry and remain so after sunset,[3] or raise the hand, or carelessly speak evil, or swear rashly, or break a solemn promise, or lie out of human respect or necessity? How tempted we are when doing business, when carrying out official duties, when occupied with daily affairs, when eating or seeing or hearing! Now if there were no pardon for these sins, then no one would be saved. Sins like these will be forgiven through Christ who successfully pleads with the Father.[4] In contrast to these sins we have the graver and deadly ones, those not receiving pardon: homicide, idolatry, fraud, denial, blasphemy, certainly adultery and fornication, and whatever else violates God's temple. [. . .]

---

1. Matt 5:9.　2. See Ezek 33:11.　3. See Matt 1:22; Eph 4:26.　4. See 1 John 2:1; Rom 8:34.

XXI. "The Church," you say, "has the power to forgive sins." This is true.   504
And I acknowledge it even more than you do since I have the Paraclete
himself speaking through the new prophets, "The Church can forgive sin,
but I will not lest they commit others also." [. . .] I now ask you about
your claim: from where do you usurp this right for the Church? Is it because the Lord said to Peter, "On this rock I will build my Church; I have
given you the keys of the kingdom of heaven," or "Whatever you bind on
earth will be bound in heaven; whatever you loose on earth will be loosed
in heaven,"[5] that you believe you have been given the power to bind and
to loosen, namely, to every Church akin [*propinquam*] to Peter? What kind
of person are you when you overthrow and change the Lord's obvious
intention of granting this to Peter personally? "On you," he says, "I will
build my Church," and "I will give to you the keys," not to the Church;
and "whatever you will bind and loose," not what they shall loose or
bind. [. . .] The power of binding and loosening given to Peter has nothing to do with the capital sins of the faithful. [. . .] Therefore the Church
will indeed pardon sins, but it is the Church through a spiritual man and
not through a number of bishops. For authority and judgment belong to
the Lord, not to the servant; to God, not to the priest.

XXII. But you even pour out this power on the martyrs. No sooner has   505
anyone, and this by common agreement, been placed in bonds—less
stringent ones in the recent and nominal imprisonments—than adulterers immediately approach, fornicators immediately approach, prayers
immediately resound, the tears of each of the defiled immediately form
pools; and none are more eager to buy their way into prison than those
who have lost [the fellowship of] the Church. [. . .] Paul at Ephesus had
already been condemned to fight with the beasts when he decreed that
the incestuous person was to be destroyed. It is enough that the martyrs
purge their own sins. It is a sign of ingratitude or pride to bestow on others what was gained at great expense. Who except the Son of God alone
has redeemed another by dying? [. . .]

27. CYPRIAN OF CARTHAGE

Cyprian (*Thascius Caecilius Cyprianus*) was born of wealthy parents, probably in Carthage and sometime between 200 and 210. Well known as a
rhetorician, he converted to Christianity about 246 through the influence
of the priest Caecilius, whose name he apparently adopted. Ordained
shortly thereafter, he was elected and ordained a bishop in 248/249.
When the Decian persecution made life miserable for the Christian community, Cyprian fled to the hills surrounding Carthage, an action that
subjected him to no little criticism. Nonetheless, the bishop continued to
guide his flock by means of letters. Returning to the city in 251, Cyprian

---

5. Matt 16:19.

was beheaded in 258, a time when the Valerian persecution was in its initial stages.

A great admirer of Tertullian (WEC 1:**26**), yet not a speculative or theoretical thinker, Cyprian wrote on a relatively large number of pastoral subjects, among which were the question of reconciling the lapsed and that of whether to recognize as valid baptisms celebrated by heretical and schismatic groups. The lapsed were Christians who in some way acknowledged the pagan gods, for example, by burning incense before the idols or even by obtaining certificates stating that they had indeed done so. Cyprian, espousing a position between rigorism and excessive leniency, allowed the lapsed to be reconciled provided they did penance for a period of time appropriate to the sin; reconciliation was also permitted at the time of death even if the appointed period for penance had not yet been completed. As to the issue of—as it were—rebaptizing heretics, Cyprian vigorously opposed Pope Stephen (254–56), who advocated the Roman tradition of recognizing such baptisms. Cyprian, on the other hand, supported by several African synods, defended the African practice of again baptizing such persons since in his mind there could be no true sacraments outside the Church.

Although a Christian for only twelve years and despite his profound disagreement with Pope Stephen, Cyprian was a true "man of the Church," a staunch opponent of heresy and schism. "Whoever wishes to have God as a Father must first have the Church as a Mother" (Letter 74, VII in WEC 1:589).

CPL nos. 38ff. * Altaner (1961) 193–99 * Altaner (1966) 172–81 * Bardenhewer (1908) 190–98 * Bardenhewer (1910) 167–76 * Bardenhewer (1913) 2:394–464 * Bardy (1930) 40–46 * Bautz 1:1178–83 * Cross 148–54 * Goodspeed 170–78 * Hamell 73–77 * Jurgens 1:216–39 * Labriolle (1947) 1:193–247 * Labriolle (1968) 131–68 * Leigh-Bennett 114–34 * Quasten 2:340–83 * Steidle 72–76 * Tixeront 120–23 * Wright (1928) 95–137 * CATH 3:397–401 * CE 4:583–89 * CHECL 152–57 * DACL 3.2:3214–15 * DCB 1:739–55 * DHGE 13:1149–60 * DictSp 2.2:2661–69 * DPAC 1:678–83 * DTC 3.2:2459–70 * EC 3:1685–91 * EEC 1:211–12 * EEChr 1:306–8 * LTK 2:1364–66 * NCE 4:564–66 * NCES 4:457–60 * ODCC 441 * PEA (1894) 4.2:1938–41 * PEA (1991) 3:253–54 * RACh 3:463–66 * TRE 8:246–54

BAPTISM

J. Ernst, *Die Ketzertaufangelegenheit in der altchristlichen Kirche nach Cyprian* (Mainz, 1901). * J. Ernst, *Stephan und der Ketzertaufstreit* (Mainz, 1905). * A. d'Alès, "'Pompa Diaboli,'" RSR 1 (1910) 571–90. * J. Ernst, "Untersuchungen über Cyprian und den Ketzertaufstreit," ThQ (1911) 230–81, 364–403. * P. Galtier, "La consignation à Carthage et à Rome," RSR 2 (1911) 350–83. * J.B. Bord, "L'autorité de s. Cyprien dans la controverse baptismale jugée d'après s. Augustin," RHE 18 (1922) 445–68. * F.J. Dölger, "Der Kuss im Tauf- und Firmungsritual nach Cyprian von Karthage und Hippolt von Rom," AC 1 (1929) 186–96. * N. Zernov, "Saint Stephen and the Roman Community at the Time of the Baptismal Controversy," ChQ 117 (1934) 304–36. * H. Koch, *Gelasius im kirchenpolitischen Dienste seine Vorgänger, der Päpste Simplicius* *und Felix III: Ein Beitrag zur Sprache des Papstes Gelasius I und früherer Papstbriefe* (Munich, 1935) 79–82. * H. Kayser, "Zur marcionitischen Taufformel (nach Cyprian)," ThStKr 108 (1937–38) 370–86. * H.J. Carpenter, "'Symbolum' as a Title of the Creed," JThSt 43 (1942) 1–11. * E.L. Hummel, *The Concept of Martyrdom according to St. Cyprian of Carthage*, SCA 9 (Washington, D.C., 1946) 108–66. * A. Stenzel, "Cyprian und die 'Taufe im Namen Jesu,'" *Scholastik* 30 (1955) 373–87. * E. Ferguson, "Baptism from the Second to the Fourth Century," ResQ 1 (1957) 185–97. * B. Neunheuser, *Baptism and Confirmation* (St. Louis, 1964) 100–102. * J.-Ch. Didier, "Le baptême des enfants: considérations théologiques III: la tradition de l'Eglise du IIe siècle à la mort de s. Augustin (430)," *L'ami du clergé* 76 (1966) 326–33. * L. Campeau, "L'origine de la querelle baptismale," ScE 21 (1969) 329–56; 22 (1970) 19–47. * P. Gaudette, "Baptême et vie chrétienne chez s. Cyprien de Carthage," LThPh 27 (1971) 160–90, 251–79. * G.W. Clarke, "Cyprian's Epistle 64 and the Kissing of Feet in Baptism," HThR 66 (1973) 147–52. * K. Duchatelez, "Le principe de l'économie baptismale dans l'antiquité chrétienne," Ist 18 (1973) 327–58. * J. Patout Burns, "On Rebaptism: Social Organization in the Third Century Church," JECS 1 (1993) 367–403. * M. Labrousse, "La baptême des hérétiques d'après Cyprien, Optat et Augustin: influences et divergences," REAug 42 (1996) 223–42. * P. Mattei, "Baptême hérétique, ecclésiologie et Siracide 34, 25: note sur l'influence de Cyprien dans un text de Pacien de Barcelone," RTL 30 (1999) 180–94.

EUCHARIST

A. Harnack, *Brot und Wasser die eucharistichen Elemente bei Justin*, TU 7, 2 (Leipzig, 1891) 120–24. * A. Scheiwiler, *Die Elemente der Eucharistie in den ersten drei Jahrhunderten* (Mainz, 1903) 105–19. * S. Struckmann, *Die Gegenwart Christi in der hl. Eucharistie nach den schriftlichen Quellen der vornizänischen Zeit* (Vienna, 1905) 306–21. * P. Batiffol, *L'Eucharistie*, 9th ed. (Paris, 1930) 226–47. * A. Pons, "La communion d'après les deux grands docteurs Cyprien et Augustin et d'après la pratique de l'ancienne église d'Afrique," in *XXXe Congrès Eucharistique International* (Carthage, 1930; Tunis, 1931) 149–70. * E. Janot, "L'Eucharistie à Carthage," VS 23 (1930) 269–82. * S. Salaville, "L'épiclèse africaine (d'après s. Cyprien)," EO 39 (1941–42) 268–82. * M. Pallegrino, "Eucaristia e martirio in San Cipriano," in *Convivium Dominicum* (Cantania, Sicily, 1959) 135–50. * M. Todde, *Lettera sull'Eucaristia: testo di San. Cipriano / Tradotto e presentato da Mauro Todde* (Bergamo, 1965). * B. Renaud, "Eucharistie et culte eucharistique selon saint Cyprien," diss. (Louvain, 1967). * R. Johanny, "Cyprian of Carthage," in W. Rordorf and others, *The Eucharist of the Early Christians* (New York, 1978) 156–82. * D. Romos-Lissón, "Tipologias sacrificiales-eucáristicas del Antiquo Testamento en la epístola 63 de san Cipriano," Aug 22 (1982) 187–97. * G.G. Willis, "St. Cyprian and the Mixed Cup," DR 100 (April 1982) 110–15. * J.D. Laurance, "Eucharistic Leader according to Cyprian of Carthage: A New Study," StudLit 15:2 (1982–83) 66–75. * J.D. Laurance, "Le président de l'eucharistie selon Cyprien de Carthage: un nouvel examine," LMD, no. 154 (1983) 151–65. * B. de Margerie, "Saint Cyprien donnait-il l'eucharistie aux divorcés-remariés?" RTAM 60 (1993) 273–75. * J.D. Laurance, *"Priest" as Type of Christ: The Leader of the Eucharist in Salvation History according to Cyprian of Carthage*, American University Series 7, Theology and Religion 5 (New York, 1984).

RECONCILIATION

J. Stufler, "Die Behandlung der Gefallenen zur Zeit der decischen Verfolgung," ZkTh 31 (1907) 577–618. * J. Stufler, "Einige Bemerkungen zur Busslehre Cyprians,"

ZkTh 33 (1909) 232–47. * A. d'Alès, "La réconciliation des 'lapsi' au temps de
Dèce," RQH 91 (1912) 337–83. * B. Poschmann, "Zur Bussfrage in der cyprianis-
chen Zeit," ZkTh 37 (1913) 25–54, 244–65. * A. Vanbeck, "La pénitence dans s.
Cyprien," RHL 18 (1913) 422–42. * H. Koch, *Cyprianische Untersuchungen* (Bonn,
1926) 79–82, 211–85. * B. Capelle, "L'absolution sacerdotale chez Cyprien," RTAM
7 (1935) 221–34. * M.C. Chartier, "La discipline pénitentielle d'après les écrits de s.
Cyprien," Ant 14 (1939) 17–42, 135–56. * B. Poschmann, *Paenitentia Secunda* (Bonn,
1940) 368–424. * G.H. Joyce, "Private Penance in the Early Church," JThSt 42 (1941)
18–42. * J.H. Taylor, "St. Cyprian and the Reconciliation of Apostates," TS 3 (1942)
27–46. * K. Rahner, "Die Busslehre des hl. Cyprian von Karthage," ZkTh 74 (1952)
252–76. * M. Bévenot, "The Sacrament of Penance and St. Cyprian's 'De lapsis,'"
TS 16 (1955) 175–213. * B. Poschmann, *Penance and the Anointing of the Sick* (St.
Louis, 1964) 52–62. * L.C. Landini, "The Penitential Discipline in the Epistles of St.
Cyprian of Carthage," diss. (Notre Dame, 1970). * M.-F. Berrouard, "La pénitence
publique durant les six premiers siècles (histoire et sociologie)," LMD 118 (1974)
92–130. * H. Gützow, *Cyprian und Novatian: der Briefwechsel zwischen die Gemeinden
in Rom und Karthago z. Zeit d. Verfolgung d. Kaisers Decius* (Tübingen, 1975). * G.
Picenardi and V. Fattorini, "La riconciliazione in Cipriano di Cartagine ('Ep. 55') e
Ambrogio di Milano ('De paenitentia')," Aug 27 (1987) 377–406.

Prayer

J. Schindler, "Der hl. Cyprian über das Gebet des Herrn," *Theolische.–praktische.
Quartalschrift* 40 (1887) 285–89, 535–45, 809–12. * E.v.D. Goltz, *Das Gebet in der ältesten Christenheit* (Leipzig, 1901) 279–87. * G. Loeschke, *Die Vaterunsererklärung
des Theophilus von Antiochien: eine Quellenuntersuchung zu den Vaterunsererekl. des
Tertullian, Cyprian, Chromatius und Hieronymus* (Berlin, 1908). * J. Moffat, "Cyprian
on the Lord's Prayer," *Expositor* 18 (1919) 176–89. * H. Koch, *Cyprianische Untersuchungen* (Bonn, 1926) 136–39. * B. Simovic, "Le Pater chez quelques pères latins II:
s. Cyprian," *La France franciscaine* 21 (1938) 245–64. * A.J.B. Higgins, "Lead us not
into temptation: Some Latin Variants," JThSt (1945) 179–83. * H. Blakeney, "Matthew VI, 3 (De dominica oratione. 7)," ExpT 57 (1945–46) 279. * C. Dumont, "Lectio
divina: la lecture de la Parole de Dieu d'après s. Cyprien," BVC 22 (1958) 23–33. *
D.R. Stuckwisch, "Principles of Christian Prayer from the Third Century: A Brief
Look at Origen, Tertullian and Cyprian with Some Comments on Their Meaning
for Today," Wor 71:1 (January, 1997) 2–19.

Other Topics

J.B. Poukens, "Sacramentum dans les oeuvres de s. Cyprien: étude lexicographique,"
BALAC 2 (1912) 275–89. * A. d'Alès, "'Nihil innovetur nisi quod traditum est': deux-
ième note," RSR 6 (1916) 302–6. * J.C. Navickas, *The Doctrine of St. Cyprian on the Sacraments* (Wurzburg, 1924). * G. Bardy, "Le sacerdoce chrétienne d'après s. Cyprien,"
VS 60 (1939) 87–119. * R. Fluck, "La vie de la communauté chrétienne au IIIe siècle
à travers la correspondence de s. Cyprien," *Jeunesse de l'Eglise* 4 (1945) 89–124. * E.
Ferguson, "Ordination in the Ancient Church," ResQ 5 (1961) 17–32, 67–82, 130–46. *
V. Saxer, *Vie liturgique et quotidienne à Carthage vers le milieu du IIIe siècle*, Studi di anti-
chità cristiana 29 (Rome, 1969). * W. Renaud, "L'Eglise comme assemblée liturgique
selon s. Cyprien," RTAM 38 (1971) 5–68. * M. Bévenot, "'Sacerdos' as Understood by
Cyprian," JThSt, n.s., 30 (1979) 413–29. * V. Saxer, *Morts, martyrs, reliques en Afrique
aux premiers siècles: les témoignages de Tertullien, Cyprien et Augustin à la lumière de
l'archéologie africaine*, Théologie historique 55 (Paris, 1980).

27-A. To Donatus[†]

Drafted about 246, this letter to Donatus, a friend of Cyprian, describes the journey of Cyprian's conversion.

16. Most beloved Donatus, [. . .] now as the sun is already descending toward evening, may we spend in joy whatever remains of the day. May the hour when we eat not lack heavenly grace. May the temperate meal resound with psalms. Since your memory is strong and your voice is melodious, may you undertake this task as you customarily do.

506

27-B. On the Lapsed[††]

Written after Cyprian's return (spring of 251) to Carthage following the Decian persecution, the treatise explains what to do with those who compromised their faith during the previous time of stress.

15. [. . .] Likewise the apostle testifies and says, "You cannot drink the cup of the Lord and the cup of the devil, you cannot partake of the Lord's table and that of the devil."[1] And again he threatens and denounces the obstinate and the stubborn, saying, "Whoever eats the bread or drinks the cup of the Lord unworthily will be guilty of the Lord's Body and Blood."[2]

507

16. All these admonitions being disdained and scorned, violence is inflicted on his Body and Blood. Even more than when they denied him, they with their hands and their mouth commit a crime against the Lord. Even before their sins have been atoned, before they have confessed their crime, before their conscience has been purified through sacrifice and the hand of the priest, before the offense against the offended and threatening Lord has been appeased, they believe that peace consists of what some would sell with deceitful words. This is not peace but war, nor is a person who is separated from the Gospel joined to the Church. Why do they say that an injury is a benefit? Why do they call an impiety a piety? Why do they block the weeping of penance on the part of those who should continuously weep and entreat their Lord? Why do they pretend to receive them in communion? This is to the lapsed as hail is to the harvest, as wild stars are to the trees, as a destructive wilderness is to cattle, as a violent storm is to ships. Such people take away the solace of hope, overturn a tree from its roots, creep to a deadly infection by unwholesome speech, dash the ship on the rocks so that it does not enter the harbor. This facility does not grant peace but removes it, does not grant communion but hinders in regard to salvation. This is another persecution and another

508

[†] Translated from *Sancti Cypriani Episcopi Opera*, vol. 2, ed. M. Simonetti, CCL 3 A (Turnhout, 1976) 13.

[††] Translated from *Sancti Cypriani Episcopi Opera*, vol. 1, ed. R. Weber, CCL 3 (Turnhout, 1972) 229ff.

1. 1 Cor 10:20.   2. 1 Cor 11:27.

temptation through which the punctilious enemy continues to proceed against the lapsed by a hidden plundering so that their weeping might be stilled, their sorrow might be silenced, the memory of their sin might disappear, that the groaning of their hearts be restrained, that the weeping of their eyes be halted; nor is a lengthy and full penance to be sought from the grievously offended Lord, even though it is written, "Remember from where you have fallen and do penance."[3]

509   17. None are to deceive themselves, none are to be misled. Only the Lord can be merciful. He alone, who bore our sins, who suffered for us, whom God handed over for our sins, can forgive sins committed against him. We cannot be greater than God. A servant cannot forgive what has been a greater crime committed against the Lord so that this also be added to the sin of those who have lapsed, they being ignorant of what was declared, "Cursed are those who place their hope in mortals."[4] We are to pray to the Lord for he is pleased by our amends, the Lord who said that he will deny whoever denies him, the Lord who alone has received all judgment from the Father. We indeed believe that the merits of the martyrs and the works of the just avail much with the judge, but this will occur when the day of judgment comes, when the present age and the world end, when God's people will stand before the judgment seat of Christ.

510   18. For the rest, if they are in extreme haste, if they rashly believe that they can forgive the sins of all or dare to abrogate the Lord's commands, not only does this not profit the lapsed but is prejudicial to them. [. . .]

511   25. Learn what happened when I myself was present and what I witnessed. There were some parents who, as it happened, were taking flight. Because of their fear they acted imprudently and left their young daughter in the care of a nurse, who handed the child over to the magistrates. In the presence of an idol to which the people flocked the magistrates gave the child bread mixed with wine since the child, because of its age was still unable to eat meat. This was what remained from the sacrifice of those who perish. The mother, afterwards, recovered her daughter, but the child was no more able to speak or indicate the evil deed that took place than she was earlier able to comprehend or prevent it. Therefore through ignorance the mother brought the daughter with her when we were offering sacrifice. But the child, mingling with the saints [the members of the assembly], became impatient with our prayer and supplications. At one moment she was trembling with tears, at another moment she was tossed about by emotional excitement. As if by the coercion of a torturer the soul of such a young child confessed a consciousness of what had taken place, doing so with such signs as she could. Once the solemnities were completed, the deacon began to present the cup to all who were present. As the others received it, the little girl in turn approached. At the prompting

---

3. Rev 2:5.   4. Jer 17:5.

of the divine majesty she turned away, firmly tightened her mouth with obdurate lips, and refused the cup. Nonetheless, the deacon persisted and poured out for the resisting girl some of the sacrament of the cup. What followed was gasping and vomiting: the Eucharist could not remain in a profaned body and mouth; the drink sanctified in the Lord's blood burst forth from the polluted stomach. So great is the Lord's power, so great the Lord's majesty! What is hidden in the darkness is disclosed under his light; nor did hidden sins deceive God's priest.

26. [. . .] There was a woman who with unworthy hands tried to open a chest in which reposed the holy [Body] of the Lord; she was deterred from touching it by fire rising up from the box. And there was a man, himself defiled, who dared to join the others in receiving, secretly, a part of the sacrifice celebrated by a priest. He could neither touch nor eat the holy [Body] of the Lord since he discovered, upon opening his hands, that he held a cinder. [. . .]   512

28. Furthermore, how much greater is the faith and how deeper is the fear of those who—though not bound by the sin of sacrificing [to idols] or of obtaining a certificate—nonetheless thought about doing so and now with sorrow and simplicity confess this to God's priests, make an open avowal of conscience, put aside the burden of their soul, and seek out the saving cure even for little and moderate wounds, knowing that it is written, "God is not mocked."[5] God cannot be mocked, deceived, or tricked by any deceptive ploy. Truly they sin the more who, thinking that God is like humans, believe they escape the punishment of their sins even if they have not openly confessed these sins. In his precepts Christ says, "The Son of Man will be ashamed of those who are ashamed of me."[6] Can people consider themselves to be Christian if they are embarrassed by or fearful of being Christians? How can a person who either blushes at or fears belonging to Christ actually be with Christ? Clearly such will sin less by not seeing the idols, by not profaning the sanctity of the faith as people stand around and hurl insults, by not polluting their hands by deadly sacrifices, by not defiling the mouth with profaned food. The advantage here is that the sin is less, not that the conscience is blameless. Pardon for sin is more easily obtained, not that there is immunity from sin. May penance continue to be practiced, may the Lord's mercy be sought lest what appears to be less in the nature of the sin be increased by neglecting reparation.   513

29. Brethren, I ask that each of you confess your own sin while you remain in the world, while your confession is possible, while satisfaction and the forgiveness given through the priests is pleasing to God. May we turn to the Lord with all our hearts, and expressing penance for our sin with true sorrow, let us beg for God's mercy. May our soul bow down before him, may our sorrow make amends to his majesty, may all our hope rely on him, who tells us how we ought to ask, "Return," he says,   514

---

5. Gal 6:7.   6. Mark 8:38; Luke 9:26.

"to me with all your heart and together with fasting, with weeping, and
with mourning. Rend your hearts and not your clothing."[7] May we return
to the Lord with all our heart. Let us appease his wrath and displeasure
through fasting, tears, and lamentation, as he himself admonishes.

27-C. On the Lord's Prayer[†]

To a degree this treatise, written in 251 or 252, is based upon Tertullian's
opus on the same subject, but Cyprian's thought is more developed.

515   4. [. . .] When we gather as one with the brethren and celebrate the
divine sacrifices with God's priest, we are to be mindful of moderation
and proper order. We are not to bandy about our prayers with disordered
voices nor to beseech God with a confused wordiness when we should do
so with modesty since God hears the heart, not the voice.

516   8. Before all else the teacher of peace and the master of unity did not
desire that we pray individually and privately, with each person praying
only for himself or herself. We do not say, "My father, who are in heaven"
or "give me this day my bread."[1] Nor does each one request that only his
or her debt be forgiven or that he or she alone not be kept from temptation
and delivered from evil. Our prayer is public and communal. When we
pray we do so not for one person only, but we entreat for all the people
because we, all the people, are one. The God of peace and the master of
harmony, who taught unity, wished that one person pray for all people
just as he bore all in one. [. . .]

517   12. Then we say, "Hallowed be your name," not that we wish God to be
sanctified by our prayers, but we ask God that his name be sanctified in
us. Furthermore, by whom is God sanctified, the God who himself sanctifies? But because he said, "Be holy because I am holy,"[2] we seek and ask
that we, made holy in baptism, might persevere in what we began to be.
Each day we pray for this because we need daily sanctification since we
who daily fail may purge away our sins by constant sanctification. [. . .]

518   18. As the prayer continues, we ask and say, "Give us this day our daily
bread," which can be understood both spiritually and literally because
each interpretation is divinely advantageous for salvation. For Christ is
the bread of life, and this bread does not belong to all but is ours. And to
the degree that we say "Our Father," because he is the father of those who
understand and believe, so we speak of "our bread" since Christ is the
bread of those who touch his body. We request that this bread be given to
us daily so that we, who are in Christ and daily receive his Eucharist as the
food of salvation, may not by the interposition of some more serious sin

---

7. Joel 2:12–13.
    [†] Translated from *Sancti Cypriani Episcopi Opera*, vol. 2, ed. M. Simonetti, CCL 3 A
(Turnhout, 1976) 91ff.
    1. See Matt 6:11.   2. Lev 19:2.

be prohibited, as abstaining and not communicating, from receiving the heavenly bread and thus be separated from the Body of Christ who himself instructs and says, "I am the bread of life who comes down from heaven. Whoever eats this bread will live forever. The bread that I will give is my flesh for the life of the world."[3] When, therefore, he says that whoever will eat his bread shall live forever—as it is evident that those who share his Body and receive the Eucharist by right of Communion are living—so we must pray and fear lest anyone, abstaining, is separated from Christ's Body as Christ himself threatens, saying, "Unless you eat the flesh of the Son of Man and drink his blood, you will not have life in you."[4] Therefore we ask that our bread, namely, Christ, be given to us daily so that we who abide and live in Christ may not draw back from his sanctification and body.

31. Beloved, when we stand for prayer, we ought to be watchful and diligent in praying with all our being. May every bodily and worldly thought depart; may the soul, when you are at prayer, think only of the object of your prayer. This is why the priest before the prayer prepares the minds of the brethren by a preface as he says, "Lift up your hearts" so that when the people respond, "We lift them up to the Lord," they might be reminded that they should think of nothing other than the Lord. [. . .]   519

34. Speaking of prayer, we find that the three children with Daniel, children strong in faith and victorious in captivity, observed the third, sixth, and ninth hours,[5] namely, as a sacrament of the Trinity which is to be revealed in the last times. The first hour as it progresses to the third hour shows the perfect number of the Trinity; the fourth hour progressing to the sixth hour declares another Trinity; and when the ninth hour is completed from the seventh the perfect Trinity is enumerated every three hours. In the past God's worshipers, having spiritually determined the spaces of the hours, were subject to them for the established and proper times for prayer. Later, it was made evident that formerly the sacraments existed because the just once prayed in this way. For at the third hour the Holy Spirit, who fulfilled the grace of the Lord's promise, descended upon the disciples.[6] Likewise, it was at the sixth hour that Peter, ascending to the roof, was instructed both by God's sign and word advising him to admit all to the grace of salvation since previously he had doubts about baptizing the Gentiles.[7] And from the sixth hour to the ninth the crucified Lord washed away our sins by his blood and, in order to redeem us and give us life, he then perfected his victory by his passion.   520

35. But for us, dearest brethren, in addition to the hours of prayer observed in ancient times, now the times and sacraments have grown in number. We are to pray in the morning so that the Lord's resurrection be observed with prayers since this is what the Holy Spirit indicated in the Psalms, "My King and my God because I will pray to you, O Lord, in the morning and you will hear my voice; in the morning I will be near you   521

---

3. John 6:51.   4. John 6:53.   5. See Dan 3:24ff.   6. See Acts 2:15.   7. See Acts 10:9.

and contemplate you."[8] The Lord also speaks through the prophet, "Early in the morning they will watch for me, saying: Let us go and return to the Lord our God."[9] Once the sun has set and the day has ended, we must again pray. Since Christ is the true sun and the true day, it is when the sun and the worldly day depart that we pray and request that the light return to us; we pray for the coming of Christ which will provide us with the grace of eternal life. It is in the Psalms that the Holy Spirit declares that Christ is called the day. "The stone," he says, "that the builders rejected has become the cornerstone. This was done by the Lord and is wonderful in our eyes. This is the day that the Lord has made; let us exult and rejoice in it."[10] Also, Malachi the prophet testifies that Christ is called the sun, "For you who fear the Lord's name the sun of justice will arise, and healing is in its wings."[11] Although the holy Scriptures say that Christ is the true sun and the true day, Christians are exempt from no hour when God should be frequently and always adored. In this way we, who are in Christ—namely, in the true sun and in the true day—are to devote ourselves throughout the whole day to entreaties and prayers; and when according to the law of the world the night comes and goes in revolutions, the nocturnal darkness cannot harm those who pray because the children of the light experience the day even during the night. If there is light in the heart, can one be without light? Or if a person has Christ as the sun and the day, does not this individual have the sun and the day?

522   36. Always being in Christ, who is the light, let us not cease praying during the night. So it was that Anna the widow unceasingly prayed and watched, pleasing God, as written in the Gospel, "Never leaving the temple, she served there day and night in prayer and fasting."[12] May the Gentiles, who remain unenlightened, take heed of this. Also the Jews who, abandoning the light, remain in darkness. May we, dearly beloved, who are always in the Lord's light, who remember and retain—by the grace received—what we have begun to be, reckon night for day. We are to believe that we are always walking in the light; may not be obstructed by the darkness we have escaped; may prayer never cease during the nocturnal hours; may times for prayer never be lost due to idleness or laziness. Spiritually made new and reborn through God's kindness, may we be what we are to become. In the kingdom there will be only light without any night; so may we keep vigil during the night as if it were during the day. Since we are not to cease praying and giving thanks, we on earth are always to pray and offer thanks.

27-D. On Works and Almsgiving[†]

Written in 252, this is an exhortation to Christian charity at a time when Carthage was being devastated by a terrible plague.

---

8. Ps 5:3b–4.   9. Hos 6:1.   10. Ps 118:22–24.   11. Mal 4:2a.   12. Luke 2:37b.
[†] Translated from CCL 3 A, 55ff.

2. [. . .] Just as the fire of hell is extinguished by the flow of the saving   523
water, so the flame is extinguished by almsgiving and works of justice.
Baptism forgives sin once and for all; good works, like baptism, again
grant God's mercy [. . .].

15. [. . .] Your eyes, covered with blackness and unable to see because   524
of the night, fail to see the indigent and the poor. Being rich and prosperous, you come to the Lord's Supper without any offering; yet you believe
that you celebrate this Supper when you receive part of the offering presented by a person who is poor.

27-E. Letters

The corpus of Cyprian's writings contains eighty-one letters, sixty-five
from Cyprian himself and sixteen to Cyprian or to the clergy of Carthage.
Some twenty-seven letters were written during the Decian persecution;
six during the Valerian persecution. Unfortunately some of these epistles
have been lost. Nonetheless, those that do exist show Cyprian's pastoral
and practical concern for all the members of the Church.

27-E-1. LETTER 1. TO THE PRESBYTERS AND PEOPLE OF FURNI[†]

II. Carefully considering and wisely providing for this, the bishops who   525
preceded us decided that no brother departing [this life] should name a
cleric as his executor or administrator. Should anyone do so, then no offering is to be made for him, nor is the sacrifice to be celebrated for his
repose. Neither does anyone who desires to call presbyters and ministers
away from the altar deserve to be named in the priestly prayer at the altar.
This is why you are not to make any offering for the repose of Victor who,
contrary to the recent provision enacted by presbyters in a council, dared
to appoint the presbyter Germinius Faustinus to be his executor. Nor are
you allowed to pray in the church in his name so that the decree of the
presbyters, conscientiously made out of necessity, may be observed by us;
at the same time the rest of the brethren are to be given an example that
no one is to call away to worldly concerns the presbyters and ministers of
God's altar and Church. [. . .]

27-E-2. LETTER 5. TO THE PRESBYTERS AND DEACONS[††a]

II. I also request that your ingenuity and care not be wanting for restor-   526
ing the peace. Even if the brethren, motivated by love, desire to come
together and visit the good confessors whom divine honor has already
made well-known in their glorious beginnings, nonetheless I believe that

---

[†] Translated from *Sancti Cypriani Episcopi Opera*, vol. 3, ed. G.F. Diercks, CCL 3 B
(Turnhout, 1994) 3–4.

[††] Translated from CCL 3 B, 27–28.

a. Written while Cyprian was hiding from the civil authorities who were perse-
cuting Christians.

this should be done cautiously, not in crowds, and not with many people gathering all at once. In this way enmity will not be aroused, permission to enter [the prison] will not be refused, and we, being insatiable and desiring much, will not lose everything. Therefore take care and see to it that this be done in a safe manner and with moderation so that the presbyters among the confessors may offer [the sacrifice] one by one, taking turns, each with a deacon, since a change of persons and of those gathering lessens ill-will. [. . .]

27-E-3. LETTER 12. TO THE PRESBYTERS AND DEACONS[†]

527　11. Lastly, also note the days when they [those in prison] pass from this life so that we can commemorate them among the memory of the martyrs; as a matter of fact, Tertullian [. . .] has written and is writing and indicating to me the days on which our blessed brethren in prison pass to immortality by means of a glorious death, and here we celebrate offerings and sacrifices to commemorate them. These, with the Lord's protection, we will soon celebrate with you. [. . .]

27-E-4. LETTER 15. TO THE MARTYRS AND CONFESSORS[††]

528　1. [. . .] You sent me a letter asking that your desires be considered, namely, that peace be granted to some of the lapsed once the persecution has ended and we begin to come together as one and meet with the clergy. Yet contrary to the law of the Gospel, contrary also to your respectful petition, and before the most serious and the most extreme sin has been confessed, before the bishop or cleric has imposed the hand for penance, some presbyters dare to offer and give them the Eucharist. In this way they dare to profane the holy Body of the Lord although it is written, "Whoever shall eat the bread and drink the cup of the Lord unworthily will be guilty of the Lord's Body and Blood."[1]

529　11. Certainly pardon can be given to the lapsed in this regard. Would not a dead person hasten to receive life? Who would not run quickly to be saved? But those in authority are to observe the precept and instruct those who are hurrying too quickly or are ignorant, so that those watching over the sheep may not become their butchers. For to grant destructive things is to deceive. The person who has lapsed is not in this way raised up but, due to an offense against God, is driven toward destruction. Let them learn from you what they should have taught. Let them reserve your requests and desires for the bishop; let them await a time that is ripe and peaceful for granting the peace you request. Before all else, the mother should first receive peace from the Lord; then according to your wishes, the peace of her children should be considered.

[†] Translated from CCL 3 B, 69–70.
[††] Translated from CCL 3 B, 86–87, 89.
1. 1 Cor 11:27.

iv. I have written both to the clergy and to the people about this and   530
have ordered that these letters be read by you. But you ought to diligently
amend what you do so that you designate by name those to whom you
wish the peace to be given. I hear that some receive certificates saying,
"May such a person along with friends be allowed to receive Communion," something never done by the martyrs since such an ambiguous
and blind petition would soon heap ill-will upon us. The door is opened
wide when it says, "Such a person along with friends" and presented
to us are twenty, thirty, and more, all said to be neighbors and relatives,
freedmen and domestics of the individual who received the certificate.
Therefore I request that you designate in the certificate only those whom
you see, those whom you know, those whose penance you perceive to be
almost completed, and so send us letters in conformity with the faith and
discipline.

27-E-5. LETTER 16. TO THE PRESBYTERS AND DEACONS[†]

ii. [. . .] For lesser offenses sinners may do penance for a designated   531
time, and according to established practice come to confession, and by the
imposition of the hand by the bishop and clergy be rightfully received into
communion. But now they are admitted to communion and their name
is given when their time [of penance] is still unfinished, while persecution still continues, while the peace of the Church itself has not yet been
reestablished. Even though the penance has not yet been carried out, the
confession has not yet been made, and the hand of the bishop and clergy
has not yet been imposed, the Eucharist is given to them although it is
written, "Whoever shall eat the bread and drink the cup of the Lord unworthily will be guilty of the Lord's Body and Blood."[1]

27-E-6. LETTER 17. TO THE BRETHREN[††]

ii. I hear that some of the presbyters, neither mindful of the Gospel, nor   532
considering what the martyrs have written to me, nor reserving to the
bishop the honor of his priesthood and his [episcopal] chair, have already
begun to associate with the lapsed, to offer for them, and to give them the
Eucharist when all this should have taken place in due time. If in the case
of lesser sins, which are not committed against God, penance is done for
a designated time and confession takes place with an examination of the
penitent's life, and no one can come to Communion till the bishop or cleric
has first imposed hands, is it not all the more fitting that in regard to the
most serious and extreme sins we observe caution and restraint according
to what the Lord has established? [. . .]

[†] Translated from CCL 3 B, 92–93.

1. 1 Cor 11:27.

[††] Translated from CCL 3 B, 97.

27-E-7. LETTER 18. TO THE PRESBYTERS AND DEACONS[†]

533   1.2. In that I see no opportunity for going to you and since summer has already begun, a season infested with continuous and serious sickness, I believe that we must deal with those of our brethren who have received certificates from the martyrs and who can be aided by their [the martyrs'] privileged position before God. If those with certificates should be seized by some misfortune or the danger of illness and my return is not anticipated, then before any presbyter who is present—if a presbyter cannot be found and death is imminent, then even in the presence of a deacon—they may confess their sin. The hand being imposed on them for penance, they may come to the Lord by the peace that the martyrs by their letters to us have desired be granted to them.

27-E-8. LETTER 20. TO THE PRESBYTERS AND DEACONS AT ROME[††]

534   III. Afterwards some of the lapsed, either of their own accord or instigated by another, rushed forward with an audacious demand, hoping they might rely on such a violent effort in order to extort the peace promised them by the martyrs and confessors. In this regard twice did I write to the clergy and commanded that my two letters be read to them. My intent was to alleviate if possible such violence for the time being. If any departing this life had received a certificate from the martyrs and, having confessed, had hands imposed on them for repentance, they were to be sent to the Lord with the peace promised them by the martyrs. In this I did not enact a ruling or rashly make myself its author. But when it seemed appropriate that the martyrs be honored and that the force of those desiring to upset everything be held in check, and furthermore when I had read the letter that you recently sent to our clergy through Crementius the subdeacon stating that help should be given to those who, having lapsed, become ill and penitently desire communion, I decided to abide by your judgment. In this way what we do—and we should be united and agree in all things—may not differ in any way. As to the situations of the others, even though they have received certificates from the martyrs, I have ordered that these cases be deferred and held over till I can be present so that, once peace has been granted us by the Lord and a number of bishops have begun to gather, we, also profiting from your counsel, may be able to organize and reform everything. [. . .]

27-E-9. LETTER 29. TO THE PRESBYTERS AND DEACONS[†††]

535   2. Know then that I made Saturus a reader and Optatus the confessor a deacon, men whom by general advice I had already placed close to the

---

[†] Translated from CCL 3 B, 100–101.
[††] Translated from CCL 3 B, 108–10.
[†††] Translated from CCL 3 B, 138.

clergy: as to Saturus, when we once or twice had entrusted him with the reading at Easter; and as for Optatus, when we made him one of those who were instructing the hearers [the catechumens]. Doing so we were ascertaining whether the qualities required of those preparing for the clerical state were present in them. [. . .]

27-E-10. LETTER 30. THE ROMAN CLERGY TO CYPRIAN[†]

VIII. Long desiring to act moderately in these matters, we thought that   536
nothing new should be done before the appointment of a new bishop. Although our number was larger, we acted together with certain neighboring bishops and with others whom the violent persecution drove out of other provinces and are now at some distance. We believe that the lapsed should be handled in somewhat a restrained manner. And so in the meantime, while a bishop is not granted us by God, the cases of those who can bear the delays of postponement should be left undecided. But for those whose case cannot be deferred because death is imminent—provided they have done penance, have frequently confessed their misdeeds, and with tears, groaning, and weeping have given proof of a sorrowing and truly penitential heart, and provided as far as one can tell that there is no hope of their surviving—then let them be cautiously and carefully assisted. God himself knows what he will do with these and how he will judge them. For our part we should anxiously take care that the ungodly not praise our leniency nor that the truly penitent accuse us of being too severe and harsh. [. . .]

27-E-11. LETTER 55. TO ANTONIAN[††a]

XVII. In them [sinners] there exists what can be revived unto faith by   537
subsequent penance. By penance strength is armed with virtue. There can be no arms if one becomes weak through despair; if, unpleasantly and cruelly separated from the Church, one should turn to the Gentiles or to worldly works; if a person rejected by the Church passes over to the heretics and schismatics where later on he or she is killed because of [Christ's] name. Such cannot be crowned in his or her death. Therefore, dearest brother, once the cases of all individuals were examined, it was decided that those who had received certificates should in the meanwhile be admitted, and that those who offered sacrifice should be assisted at death because confession does not exist among the deceased, nor can we compel anyone to penance if the fruit of penance is withdrawn. Should the battle come first, one will be strengthened by us and found prepared for it; but if infirmity should afflict before the battle, a person will depart with the consolation of peace and of being in communion.

[†] Translated from CCL 3 B, 149–50.
[††] Translated from CCL 3 B, 275ff.
a. Antonian: a bishop in Numidia.

538   xviii. Nor do we predict when the Lord will judge. Yet if he finds the penance complete and correct, he will then approve what we have determined. Should anyone deceive us under the pretense of doing penance, God, who is not mocked and who looks into the human heart, will judge what we have imperfectly discerned; the Lord will correct the decision of his servants. Nonetheless, my dearest brother, we should remember what is written, "A brother helped by a brother will be exalted."[1] Also, the apostle said, "Take care that you yourselves are not tempted. Be not tempted; bear one another's burdens, and you will fulfill the law of Christ."[2] Also, rebuking the proud and shattering their arrogance, he said, "Those who believe that they stand should take care lest they fall."[3] Elsewhere he says, "Who are you to judge another's servants. They stand or fall before their own lord. They will stand, for God is able to make them stand."[4] John also proves that Jesus Christ the Lord is our advocate and the intercessor for our sins: "My little children, I write these things to you so that you do not sin; and if any sin, we have an Advocate with the Father, Jesus Christ the righteous, and he atones for our sins."[5] And Paul the apostle said, "While we were still sinners Christ died for us. Much more therefore, now justified by his blood, we will be saved through him from [God's] wrath."[6]

539   xix. Thinking of his love and mercy, we should not be so bitter nor harsh nor inhuman in supporting our brethren. Rather, let us mourn with those who mourn, weep with those who weep, and, as far as possible, raise them up with the help and comfort of our love. We should be neither too harsh and stubborn in repelling their penance nor overly lax and easy in recklessly granting communion. Behold, a wounded comrade lies injured by the enemy in battle. It is there that the devil tries to kill the wounded; it is here that Christ exhorts so that those he has redeemed may not completely perish. Which of the two do we assist? Where do we stand? Do we favor the devil that he might kill? Or do we pass by our prostrate half-living comrade as did the priest and Levite in the Gospel? Or do we, as priests of God and Christ, imitate what Christ did and taught? Do we snatch the injured from the enemy's jaws so that we might keep them alive and cured for God who judges?

540   xx. Dearest brother, do not think that the strength of the brethren will be lessened or that martyrdoms will decrease because penance is extended to the lapsed and that hope of peace is offered to the penitent. The strength of those who truly believe remains. As to those who fear and love God with their whole heart, their moral uprightness continues steady and strong. We even grant adulterers a time for penance, after which peace is given. Yet for all that, virginity is not lacking in the Church nor does the glorious objective of sexual restraint decrease through the sins of others.

---

1. Prov 18:19, LXX.   2. Gal 6:1–2.   3. 1 Cor 10:12.   4. Rom 14:4.   5. 1 John 2:1–2.
6. Rom 5:8–9.

The Church, crowned with so many virgins, flourishes; chastity and modesty continue on in glory. The vigor of continence is not broken because penance and pardon are extended to the adulterer. To support pardon is one thing; to arrive at glory is something completely different. For those thrown into a prison, it is one thing not to leave the prison till the last farthing has been paid; it is another thing to receive the wages of faith and virtue. When a person is tortured by a prolonged sorrow for sins, it is one thing to be cleansed and purged at length by fire; it is something completely different to have washed away all sins through suffering. It is one thing to await God's sentence on the day of judgment; another to be immediately crowned by the Lord.

xxi. Certainly among our predecessors there were some bishops here   541
in our own province who believed that peace was not to be granted to adulterers and in this matter did not allow any opportunity for penance. Nonetheless, these bishops did not withdraw from the college of their fellow bishops. Nor did they rupture the unity of the Catholic Church by their obstinate harshness or control so that those who did not grant peace to adulterers, even though others did, were not separated from the Church. The bond of harmony remaining and the indivisible sacrament of the Catholic Church enduring, each bishop arranges and directs his own actions and will have to give an account of his actions to the Lord.

xxiii. In the Gospel the Lord, revealing the love of God the Father, said: 542
"Is there anyone among you who, if your son requests bread, will give him a stone? Or if he requests a fish, will give him a serpent? If therefore you, being evil, know how to give good things to your children, how much the more will your Father in heaven give good things to those who request them?"[7] Here the Lord compares a human father who has been offended by a sinful and evil son to the eternal and generous love of God the Father. The human father sees that this son has reformed, has cast aside his sins, and has returned to a restrained and good way of life, to the path of innocence by the sorrow of penance. This being true, how much more does our one and true Father, who is good, merciful, and faithful—yes, goodness, mercy, and faithfulness itself—rejoice when one of his children repents, not threatening punishment to those who are now doing penance or mourning or lamenting, but rather promising pardon and leniency. Wherefore in the Gospel the Lord calls those who mourn blessed since the person who mourns arouses mercy. Those who are obstinate and proud heap up wrath against themselves and the punishment of the future judgment. Therefore, dearest brother, we have decided that those who fail to repent, who fail to show wholehearted sorrow for their sins with evidence of their sorrow, are to be absolutely kept from the hope of communion and peace if they begin to ask for these while they are sick or in danger; the motivation here is not penance for sin but the warning of an imminent

---

7. Matt 7:9–11.

death. Those who fail to reflect on the fact that they will die are not worthy to receive consolation at the time of death.

543   xxiv. As to Novatian[b] of whom you, dearest brother, desired that I write you concerning the heresy he introduced, know first of all that we should not even inquire what he teaches since he teaches outside [the Church]. Whoever or whatever one may be, a person who is not within the Church of Christ is not a Christian. Although Novatian may brag about himself and use lofty words to proclaim his own philosophy or eloquence, yet those who have not retained fraternal love or ecclesiastical unity have lost what they formerly were. Unless he seems to you to be a bishop who, after being ordained in the Church by sixteen fellow bishops, strives through ambition to be made a false and extraneous bishop by deserters! Yet since there is one Church apportioned by Christ into many members, so there is one episcopate, diffused in a harmonious number of many bishops, he, despite what God has handed down, despite the mutual and universal compact unity of the Catholic Church, is attempting to form a human Church and is sending his new apostles through numerous cities so that he might establish some new foundations of his own organization. Although throughout all the provinces and in each city there are ordained bishops, advanced in years, sound in faith, proven in adversity, outlawed during times of persecution, he dared to create above them other and pseudo-bishops. He did this as if he could either wander over the whole world, obstinate in his novel undertaking, or destroy the structure of the ecclesiastical body by sowing discord, not knowing that schismatics, always initially fervent, are unable to increase what they illicitly begin and immediately fade away with their jealousy. But Novatian was incapable of holding the episcopal position, even though he was previously made a bishop, since he withdrew from the body of his fellow bishops and from the unity of the Church. The apostle admonished that we should bear with one another[8] so as not to withdraw from the unity established by God. He also said, "Bear with one another in love, making every effort to preserve the unity of the Spirit in the bond of peace."[9] Therefore, those who fail to attend to the unity of the Spirit or to the bond of peace and thus separate themselves from the bond of the Church and from the college of bishops have neither episcopal power nor dignity since they desire to maintain neither the peace nor the unity of the episcopate.

544   xxix. This is to close and remove the path of sorrow and penance. In the Scriptures the Lord God speaks well of those who return to him and repent; yet repentance itself is taken away by our harshness and cruelty. When the fruit of penance is done away with, then repentance itself is

---

b. Novatian: a Roman presbyter (d. 257/258) disappointed by the election of Cornelius as bishop of Rome in 251; he joined a highly rigorist yet orthodox faction and became a rival to Cornelius.

8. See Eph 4:2.   9. Eph 4:2–3.

eliminated. If we find that no one should be hindered from doing penance, then peace may be given according to the mercy of the Lord, who is kind and loving; then the groaning of those who mourn is to be considered; then the fruit of penance is not to be denied to those who grieve. Among the dead there is no confession, there can be no penance there; and so those who have wholeheartedly done and requested penance should meanwhile be received into the Church and kept in it since when the Lord comes to his Church, he will certainly judge those he finds within it. Those are apostates and deserters, antagonists and enemies, as well as those who scatter Christ's Church—even if they have been martyred for his name outside the Church—cannot, as the apostle says, be admitted to the peace of the Church because they have not kept the unity of the Spirit or that of the Church.[10]

27-E-12. LETTER 57. TO CORNELIUS[†a]

I. My dearest brother, some time ago and after consulting with each   545
other we decided that those who as the result of persecution had been led astray by the adversary and had lapsed and stained themselves with unlawful sacrifices were to undergo a long and thorough penance; and if the sickness proves to be very grave, they may receive peace should death be at hand. It is not permissible nor does the Father's love nor does divine mercy permit that the Church be closed to those who knock[1] or that the help of salvation be refused to those who mourn and beseech; otherwise, departing this world they would be sent to the Lord without communion and peace. For the Lord himself, who decreed that what was bound on earth was also bound in heaven, also decreed that what is first loosed in the Church is also loosed in heaven.[2] Now we see that a day of further and new battle is imminent, and we are warned by numerous and continuous indications to prepare and arm ourselves for the battle announced to us by the adversary. And so by our exhortations we should also prepare the people committed to us by divine benevolence; we should gather into the Lord's camp all Christ's soldiers who desire arms and request to do battle. In light of this necessity we have decided that peace should be extended to those who have not disassociated themselves from the Lord's Church, who from the first day of their lapse have not ceased to do penance, lament, and invoke the Lord. We have decided that these should be armed and equipped for the imminent battle.

II. We must comply with well-grounded indications and warnings so   546
that the shepherds not desert the sheep who are in danger but that the whole flock be gathered together and that the Lord's army be armed for

---

10. See Eph 4:2–3.
† Translated from CCL 3 B, 301–4.
a. Cornelius: bishop of Rome 251–53.
1. See Matt 7:7.   2. See Matt 16:19; 18:18.

the battle of the heavenly campaign. It was fitting that the penance of those in mourning be rightfully extended for a longer time—help being provided to the sick only at the time of death—so long as peace and tranquility were present. This allowed the tears of those doing penance to be prolonged for a long time and for assistance to be given at a late hour to the sick who were at the point of death. But now peace is necessary not for the sick but for the strong, nor are we to grant communion to the dying but to the living so that we may not leave unarmed and exposed those whom we have aroused and exhorted to battle. Rather, let us fortify them with the protection of Christ's Body and Blood. Since the Eucharist has been instituted to protect those receiving it, we are to arm with the Lord's abundant protection those whom we desire to be safe from the enemy. For how do we teach or urge them to shed their blood in confessing the Lord's name if we refuse Christ's Blood to those about to do battle? Or how do we make them fit for the cup of martyrdom if we do not first allow them to drink the cup of the Lord in the Church by right of communion?

547   III. [. . .] It is our episcopate's great honor to have extended peace to the martyrs so that as priests, who daily celebrate God's sacrifices, we may prepare victims and sacrifices for God. [. . .]

27-E-13. LETTER 63. TO CECIL[ta]

548   I. Dearest brother, I know that many bishops, set over the Lord's churches throughout the world, hold fast to the exercise of evangelical truth and the Lord's traditions. By no human and novel custom do they depart from what Christ taught and did. Some, however, either out of ignorance or naiveté in blessing and ministering the Lord's cup to the people do not do what Jesus Christ, our Lord and our God, the founder and teacher of this sacrifice, did and taught.[b] I have likewise believed it to be religious and necessary to write you this letter so that if anyone still be held in this error, such a person by the light of truth may return to the root and origin of the Lord's tradition. Do not think, dearest brother, that what I write is my own teaching or is a human teaching, or that I do this on my own initiative. No, my ability is limited. I write with humble and restrained moderation. But when God's inspiration and command enjoin anything, the faithful servant must comply with the Lord. Servants should be acquitted of arrogantly appropriating anything to themselves since unless they do what is commanded, they are forced to fear offending the Lord.

549   II. As you well know, I have been admonished that the tradition of the Lord is to be followed when the cup is offered, and that we are to

---

† Translated from *Sancti Cypriani Episcopi Opera*, vol. 4, ed. G.F. Diercks, CCL 3 C (Turnhout, 1960) 339–416.

a. Cecil: bishop of Biltha in Africa.

b. This letter is directed against the Aquarians, also called the *Hydroparastatae*, a sect or sects using only water in their celebration of the Eucharist.

do nothing other than what the Lord was the first to do. And so it is for this reason that the cup offered in his memory is mixed with wine.[1] Since Christ said, "I am the true vine,"[2] certainly Christ's blood is wine; it is not water. Nor can his blood—his blood by which we are redeemed and receive new life—be present within the cup if the cup itself does not contain wine by which the blood of Christ is revealed, as is commanded by the sacrament and by the testimony of all the Scriptures.

III. Also in Genesis we find, as to the sacrament, that Noah anticipated the same and projected the figure of the Lord's passion in that he drank wine, that he was inebriated, that he was naked in his house, that he was reclining with naked and uncovered thighs, that his second son saw his nudity and made it public, that he was covered up by the oldest and youngest son.[3] We need not pursue other details. All we have to understand is that Noah, showing himself to be a type of future truth, drank wine, not water, thus being an image of the Lord's passion.[4]

550

IV. We also see the sacrament of the Lord's sacrifice prefigured in the priest Melchizedek since, according to the testimony of the divine Scriptures, "Melchizedek the king of Salem brought forth bread and wine. He was a priest of the most high God, and he blessed Abraham."[5] Melchizedek was a type of Christ as the Holy Spirit indicates in the Psalms, where the Father says to the Son, "Before the daystar I begot you. You are a priest forever according to the order of Melchizedek."[6] This order certainly comes and descends from that sacrifice. Melchizedek was a priest of the most high God; he brought out bread and wine; he blessed Abraham.[7] For who is more of a priest of the most high God than our Lord Jesus Christ who offered a sacrifice to God the Father and he offered what Melchizedek offered, namely, bread and wine,[8] namely, his Body and Blood. As to Abraham, his blessing, which preceded,[9] extends down to our own people.[10] For if Abraham believed in God and it was imputed to him for righteousness,[11] so it is that those who believe in God and live by faith are found to be righteous and are already blessed and justified in faithful Abraham,[12] for as Paul the Apostle says: "Abraham believed in God and it was reckoned to him as righteousness. You know, then, that those who believe are children of Abraham. Foreseeing that God would justify the Gentiles by faith, Abraham predicted that all nations would be blessed in him. Therefore those who believe are blessed with faithful Abraham."[13] Therefore in the Gospel we find that Abraham's children have been raised up from the stones, namely, gathered from the nations.[14] And when he praised Zacchaeus, the Lord said, "Today salvation has come to this house because this one is a son of Abraham."[15] So that in Genesis Abraham's

551

1. See 1 Cor 11:22–25. 2. John 15:1. 3. See Gen 9:20–21. 4. See Gen 9:21.
5. Gen 14:18–19. 6. Ps 110:3–4. 7. See Gen 14:18–19. 8. See Matt 26:26–28.
9. See Gen 14:18. 10. See Gen 12:2–3. 11. See Gen 15:6; Gal 3:6. 12. See Gal 3:8–9. 13. Gal 3:6–9. 14. See Matt 3:9. 15. Luke 19:9.

blessing of the priest Melchizedek might be correctly celebrated, the image of Christ's sacrifice precedes, namely, as constituted in the bread and wine.[16] The Lord, carrying out and perfecting, offered bread and the cup mixed with wine,[17] and he who is the fullness of truth fulfilled the truth of the prefigured image.

552   v. Furthermore, through Solomon the Holy Spirit predicts the type of the Lord's sacrifice when mentioning the victim that has been offered, the bread and the wine, the altar, and the apostles, "Wisdom has built her house, she has placed under it her seven columns, she has slaughtered her victims, she has mixed her wine in the cup and spread her table." "She has sent out her servants inviting with lofty words to the cup, saying, 'Let the simple turn to me.' And to the unwise she said, 'Come, eat of my bread and drink the wine I have mixed for you.'"[18] The Spirit declares the wine to be mixed, namely, prophetically announcing that the Lord's cup was mixed with water and wine, so that it is evident that what took place during the Lord's passion was foretold.[19]

553   vi. The blessing of Judah also shows a figure of Christ when it says that he [Christ] should be praised and honored by his brothers; that he should press down the neck of his enemies who are departing and fleeing, doing so with hands that carried the cross and conquered death; that he himself is the lion from the tribe of Judah; that he reclines while sleeping in his passion and arises and is himself the hope of the Gentiles.[20] To these the divine Scriptures add, "He will wash his garment in wine and his clothing in the blood of the grape."[21] As to the blood of the grape, what else is meant other than the cup of the Lord's blood?

554   vii. In Isaiah the Holy Spirit says the same in regard to the Lord's passion, "Why are your garments red and your clothing as from treading the wine press full and well-trodden?"[22] Can water turn garments red? Or is it water in the wine press that is stepped on and pressed out? Surely, therefore, wine is mentioned so that by wine the Lord's blood may be understood and that what was later on manifested in the Lord's cup might earlier be foretold by the prophets. This reading and pressing of the wine press are also spoken of since, just as we cannot drink wine unless a bunch of grapes has been trampled upon and pressed, so we cannot drink Christ's blood unless Christ was first trampled upon and pressed and had earlier partaken from the cup he gave to believers.

555   viii. When the holy Scriptures mention only water, baptism is foretold, as we find in Isaiah: "Do not remember what happened formerly and do not consider the things of old. Behold, I will do new things which will now spring forth, and you will know it. I will make a path in the desert and rivers in the dry place to give drink to my chosen people, the people I have acquired so that they might proclaim my praise."[23] It was there that

---

16. See Gen 14:18–19.   17. See Matt 26:26–28.   18. Prov 9:1–5.   19. See John 19:34.   20. See Gen 49:8–10.   21. Gen 49:11.   22. Isa 63:2.   23. Isa 43:18–21.

God foretold through the prophets that among the nations, in places that were formerly dry, abundant rivers would soon flow and would provide water for God's chosen people, namely, for those made children of God through the regeneration of baptism.[24] Again it is foretold and stated beforehand that if the Jews thirst and search for Christ, they will drink with us, namely, they will acquire the grace of baptism. "If they thirst, he will lead them through the deserts; he will provide water for them from the rock; he will split the rock and my people shall drink."[25] This was fulfilled in the Gospel when Christ, who is the rock, was struck by a lance during his passion.[26] Recalling what was foretold by the prophet, he declared: "Let anyone who is thirsty come to me and drink. As the Scripture says, rivers of living waters will flow out of his stomach."[27] So that it be even more evident that the Lord is here speaking not about the cup but about baptism, the Scripture adds, "He said this about the Spirit whom those who believe in him were to receive."[28] For it is through baptism that the Holy Spirit is received, and so those who have been baptized and have received the Holy Spirit are able to drink from the Lord's cup. Let it disturb no one that when the divine Scripture speaks of baptism it says that we thirst and drink since the Lord also says in the Gospel, "Blessed are those who hunger and thirst after justice"[29] because what is received with an eager and thirsty longing is taken in more fully and more abundantly. So it is that the Lord says to the Samaritan woman, "Everyone who drinks of this water will thirst once again. But whoever drinks from the water that I will give will never thirst again."[30] This signifies the baptism of the saving water which, when once received, cannot be repeated. The cup of the Lord is always thirsted for and drunk from in the Church.

ix. We do not need many arguments, my dearest brother, to prove that the word "water" always stands for baptism, and so we must understand it in this way. When the Lord came, he showed the truth of baptism and the cup by commanding that the lasting water, the water of eternal life, be given to believers in baptism; yet he taught by his own authoritative example that the cup be mixed, that is, containing a mixture of wine and water. On the eve of his passion he took the cup, blessed it, and gave it to his disciples, saying:[31] "Drink, all of you, from this, for this is the blood of the covenant which will be shed for many unto the forgiveness of sins. I tell you, I will not drink from the fruit of the vine until the day when I shall drink new wine with you in my Father's kingdom."[32] Here we find that the cup offered by the Lord was mixed, and it was wine that he called his Blood. So it is evident that Christ's Blood is not offered if there is no wine in the cup, nor is the Lord's sacrifice celebrated with a legitimate sanctification unless the offering and our sacrifice accord with his passion. But how are we to drink the new wine from the fruit of the vine in

556

---

24. See Isa 43:19–20.   25. Isa 48:21.   26. See 1 Cor 10:4.   27. John 7:37–38.
28. John 7:39.   29. Matt 5:6.   30. John 4:13.   31. See Matt 26:27.   32. Matt 26:27–29.

the kingdom of the Father[33] if we, in the sacrifice of God the Father and of Christ, do not offer wine or, not following a tradition from the Lord, fail to mix the Lord's cup?

557　x. The blessed apostle Paul, chosen and sent by the Lord and appointed to teach the truth of the Gospel, said in his Epistle: "On the night he was betrayed Jesus took bread, gave thanks, broke it, and said, 'This is my Body which is given for you. Do this in memory of me.' Likewise after the meal he took the cup, saying: 'This cup is the new covenant in my blood: Do this, as often as you drink it, in memory of me. For as often as you eat this bread and drink the cup, you proclaim the death of the Lord until he comes.'"[34] But if the Lord has commanded, and if the apostle has confirmed and handed down the same, namely, that as often as we drink in memory of the Lord, we do what the Lord has done,[35] then we find that we are not observing the Lord's command unless we also do what he has done. Likewise, by mixing the cup we do not deviate from the Lord's teaching. In no way are we to digress from the evangelical precepts; disciples are to observe and do what the teacher taught and did. Elsewhere the apostle more steadfastly and firmly says: "I am amazed that you are so quickly departing from him who called you to grace, going to another gospel, not that there is another gospel except that there are those who disturb you and wish to alter the Gospel of Christ. But if we or an angel from heaven preach to you anything other than what we have proclaimed to you, may such be accursed. As we have said before and now repeat: should anyone proclaim to you anything other than what you have received, let such a person be damned."[36]

558　xi. Since neither the apostle nor the heavenly angel can proclaim or teach anything different from what Christ once taught and from what his apostles announced,[37] I greatly wonder as to the origin of the custom whereby, contrary to the practice of the Gospel and the Apostles, in certain places only water is offered in the Lord's cup; water alone cannot express Christ's blood. The Holy Spirit is not silent on this in the Psalms where mention is made of the Lord's cup, "Your cup cheers me like the best [wine]."[38] Also, the cup that cheers certainly is mixed with wine since water alone cannot cheer anyone. So it is that the Lord's cup inebriates just as in Genesis Noah, drinking wine, was inebriated.[39] But the inebriation of the Lord's cup and blood is unlike that of worldly wine since in the psalm the Spirit says, "Your cup gives cheer, there is added: like the best."[40] This means that the Lord's cup so inebriates those drinking that it makes them sober; it leads their minds back to spiritual wisdom with the result that each person abandons a worldly taste for an understanding of God. Just as common wine moderates one's outlook, relaxes the soul, and banishes all sorrow, so when the Lord's Blood and the cup of salvation have been

---

33. See Matt 26:29.　34. 1 Cor 11:23–26.　35. See 1 Cor 11:25.　36. Gal 1:6–9. 37. See Gal 1:8.　38. Ps 23:5, LXX.　39. See Gen 9:21.　40. Ps 23:5, LXX.

drunk, the memory of the old man is cast aside, previous worldly dealings are forgotten,[41] and the sad and sorrowful breast, previously oppressed by tormenting sins, is soothed by the joy of the divine goodness. Only a person who drinks within the Lord's Church can rejoice if what is drunk clings to the Lord's truth.

xii. How distorted and contrary it is that although the Lord at the wedding feast changed water into wine,[42] we would change wine into water, even though the sacramental reality warns and teaches us that we are to offer wine when celebrating the Lord's sacrifice. Because spiritual grace was in short supply among the Jews, so also was wine, "for the vineyard of the Lord of hosts was the house of Israel."[43] Christ, however, teaching and showing that the Gentiles come after the Jews and that by their meritorious faith would later on gain the place lost by the Jews, changed water into wine.[44] And so at the wedding feast of Christ and the Church, with the Jews being absent, he showed that the Gentiles would come in abundance and meet. Water, says the Apocalypse, signifies the people, "The waters you saw, upon which the prostitute is seated, are peoples and multitudes, the nations of the peoples and tongues."[45] We see this also contained in the sacrament of the cup.

xiii. Since Christ bore all of us when he bore our sins,[46] we see that the water stands for the people whereas the wine stands for the Blood of Christ. When water is united with the wine in the cup, the people are made one with Christ; the believing people are joined and united with him in whom they believe. The water and the wine, joined and united, are so mixed together in the Lord's cup that this mixture cannot be dissolved. As a result, nothing can separate the Church—namely, the people established in the Church who faithfully and steadfastly cling to what they believe—from Christ so as to prevent their indivisible love from enduring and remaining. In blessing the Lord's cup neither wine alone nor water alone is to be offered. If only wine, then Christ's Blood would be without us; if only water, then we would be without Christ. But when both are mixed together and closely joined, then we have the spiritual and heavenly sacrament. The Lord's cup, therefore, is neither wine only nor water only; each is to be mingled with the other. Nor can the Lord's Body be flour only or water only; both are to be mixed together, joined, and formed into one loaf. In this very sacrament our people are shown to be one, and just as many grains, when they are gathered and ground down and mixed together, form one loaf, so we know that we are one body in Christ who is the living bread to whom all of us are joined and united.[47]

xiv. Therefore, dearest brother, no one should believe that we are to follow the custom of those who maintain that water alone should be offered in the Lord's cup. The question is whom are they following. For if it is

559

560

561

---

41. See Eph 4:22–23.　42. See John 2:1–11.　43. Isa 5:7.　44. See John 2:9.
45. Rev 17:5.　46. See 1 Pet 2:24.　47. See John 6:50–51, 59.

only Christ who is to be followed in the sacrifice that he offered, certainly we are to obey Christ, imitate him, and do what he commanded when, according to the Gospel, he said, "No longer do I call you servants but friends if you do what I command you."[48] That we are to listen to Christ alone, the heavenly Father bears witness, "This is my beloved Son in whom I am well-pleased; listen to him."[49] If it is only Christ who is to be heard,[50] we should pay no attention to what anyone before us believed was to be done but to what Christ, who is before all, did first. We should not follow human custom but that of God since God speaks through the prophet Isaiah, "Teaching the human commandments and doctrines, in vain do they worship me."[51] The Lord also repeats this in the Gospel, "You reject God's commandment that you might follow your own tradition."[52] Elsewhere he says, "Whoever breaks one of the least of these commandments and teaches others to do so, will be called least in the kingdom of heaven."[53] If it is not allowed to break the least of these commandments,[54] how much the more is it not permitted to break those that are so great, so important, so relevant to the sacrament of the Lord's passion and our redemption. Or can human tradition change what has been divinely instituted? If Jesus Christ, our Lord and God, is himself the high priest of God the Father, and was the first to offer himself as a sacrifice to the Father, and commanded that this be done in his own memory,[55] certainly the office of Christ is carried out by the priest who imitates what Christ did and who in the Church offers a true and full sacrifice to God the Father when he offers it according to what he understands Christ to have offered.

562   xv. The discipline of all religion and of truth is defeated if what is spiritually enjoined is not faithfully observed. There are some who fear that at the morning sacrifice, if they taste the wine, they may exhale the fragrance of Christ's Blood.[56] And so when the community in its offerings is ashamed of Christ's blood and its shedding, then during times of persecution it begins to separate itself from Christ's suffering. Yet the Lord says in the Gospel, "The Son of Man will be ashamed of those who are ashamed of him."[57] And the apostle, "Should I please others, I should not be Christ's servant."[58] How can we shed our blood for Christ if we are ashamed to drink Christ's Blood?

563   xvi. Are there any who delude themselves with the idea that although in the morning water alone appears to be offered, yet when we come for supper, we offer a mixed cup? But when we eat, we cannot summon the people to our meal so that we might celebrate the truth of the sacrament with the whole community being present. But the Lord offered the mixed cup not in the morning but after supper.[59] Therefore should we celebrate the Lord's sacrifice after the evening meal so that by frequent repetition

---

48. John 15:14–15.   49. Matt 17:5.   50. See Matt 17:5.   51. Isa 29:13.   52. Mark 7:9.   53. Matt 5:19.   54. See ibid.   55. See 1 Cor 11:25.   56. See Acts 2:15. 57. Mark 8:38.   58. Gal 1:10.   59. See Matt 26:20; 1 Cor 11:25.

we might offer the mixed cup? It was fitting for Christ to offer the sacrifice in the evening so that the hour of sacrifice might show the setting and evening of the world, as is written in Exodus, "And the whole assembled congregation of the children of Israel shall kill it [the lamb] in the evening."[60] Also in the Psalms, "The lifting up of my hands as an evening sacrifice."[61] We, however, celebrate the Lord's resurrection in the morning.

XVII. And because we mention his passion in all our sacrifices—the sacrifice we offer being the Lord's passion—we are to do only what he did since, according to Scripture, as often as we offer the cup in memory of the Lord and his passion,[62] we do what corresponds with what the Lord has done. Dearest brother, if any of our predecessors either out of ignorance or naiveté have not observed and complied with what the Lord taught us by his example and instruction, may the Lord's kindness pardon such a person's simplicity. But we cannot be forgiven, we who have been admonished and taught by the Lord to offer his cup mixed with wine just as was offered by the Lord; we are to write our colleagues about this so that the evangelical law and the Lord's tradition may be everywhere observed and that there be no divergence from what Christ taught and did. 564

XVIII. To disregard these things, to continue on in former error, is nothing other than to be reprimanded by the Lord who in the Psalms reproaches: "Why do you declare my ordinances and take up my covenant into your mouth since you hated my instruction and cast my words behind you? If you saw a thief, you ran along with him and cast your lot with adulterers."[63] If we set forth the Lord's righteousness and covenant and not do what he did, is this anything other than to disregard his words and despise his teachings, to commit not earthly but spiritual thefts and adulteries?[64] To steal the Lord's words and actions away from evangelical truth is to corrupt and pervert the divine precepts. As is written in Jeremiah, "What has straw in common with wheat? Therefore, says the Lord, I am against the prophets who steal my words from one another, and lead my people astray by their lies and errors."[65] The same prophet in another place says, "And she committed adultery with stone and tree, and yet in all this she did not return to me."[66] We should carefully, fearfully, and religiously take care that we not be found guilty of theft and adultery. For if we are priests of God and Christ, I do not know whom we should follow more than God and Christ. It is Christ who says in the Gospel, "I am the light of the world. Whoever follows me will not walk in the darkness but will have the light of life."[67] So that we do not walk in the darkness,[68] we are to follow Christ and observe his precepts because as we find elsewhere when he sent his apostles, he said, "All power in heaven and on earth is given to me. Go, therefore, and teach all nations, baptizing them in the name of the Father and of the Son and of the Holy Spirit, teaching them to 565

---

60. Exod 12:6.   61. Ps 141:2.   62. See 1 Cor 11:26.   63. Ps 50:16–18, LXX.   64. See Ps 50:17, LXX.   65. Jer 23:28, 30, 32.   66. Jer 3:9–10.   67. John 8:12.   68. See ibid.

observe all I have commanded you."[69] So if we wish to walk in the light of Christ,[70] we are not to forgo his precepts and warnings. We give thanks that while he instructs us as to what we should do in the future, he overlooks what we, erring due to our inexperience, have done in the past. And since his second coming is approaching, more and more does his kind and abundant love illumine our hearts with the light of his truth. [. . .]

27-E-14. LETTER 64. TO FIDUS[ta]

566   II. You say that infants should not be baptized within the second or third day of birth and that the ancient law of circumcision should be considered. In your opinion the newly born should not be baptized and sanctified till the eighth day.[1] Our council thought altogether differently. No one agreed with your thinking in this matter, but all of us decided that God's mercy and grace should not be denied to any human being. As the Lord said in his Gospel, "The Son of Man did not come to destroy the lives of human beings but to save them."[2] As far as possible, no soul is to be lost. For what is lacking to those whom God's hands have formed in the womb? For as we see, as time moves on so those who are born are seen to develop. Whatever has been made by God is perfected by the majesty and work of God the Maker.

567   III. Belief in the divine Scriptures tells us that the divine gift exists equally among all, whether infants or adults. Elisha, entreating God, so laid himself upon the widow's infant son who was lying dead that Elisha's head was upon the child's head and his face was upon the child's face, his feet upon the child's feet, and his limbs upon the child's limbs.[3] If we think about this according to our physical nature, an infant cannot be equated with an adult or with someone advanced in years, nor are an infant's small limbs able to fully match and substitute for those of an older person. But there [in the incident of Elisha and the child] is expressed the divine and spiritual equality that all are alike and equal since all were once created by God. Depending on age there may be physical differences among bodies, but God sees no difference except that the grace given to the baptized is granted in a larger or smaller degree according to the age of those receiving it, whereas the Holy Spirit is not bestowed with measure[4] but with the Father's love and kindness to all. For just as God does not discriminate against particular persons, so he does not discriminate on the basis of age. As to the granting of heavenly grace, he shows himself as a father equally to all.

568   V. [. . .] If anything could hinder us from obtaining grace, then sins that are more grave can more impede those who are adults and elderly

---

69. Matt 28:18–20.   70. See John 8:12.
† Translated from CCL 3 C, 419–20, 422.
a. Fidus: an African bishop.
1. See Luke 1:59; 2:21.   2. Luke 9:56.   3. 2 Kgs 4:32–37.   4. See John 3:34.

and older. Since sins are forgiven even to the most serious sinners once these sinners have come to believe—no matter how greatly they formerly sinned against God—and since baptism and grace are forbidden to no one, all the more they should not be forbidden to an infant who as a newborn has not sinned other than, having been bodily born after Adam, has contracted by its first birth the contagion of the ancient death. That it is not one's own sins but those of another that are forgiven makes it easier to receive the forgiveness of sins.

27-E-15. LETTER 67. TO FELIX, AELIUS, AND THEIR PEOPLE[†a]

IV. [. . .] The priest is to be chosen in the presence of the people and under the eyes of all. By public judgment and testimony he is to be approved as the Lord commanded Moses in the Book of Numbers, "Take Aaron your brother and his son Eleazar up to the mountain and impose hands on them before the whole assembly; strip Aaron of his clothes and put them on his son Eleazar, and let Aaron die there."[1] God commands that a priest be appointed before all the people, namely, God instructs and shows that priestly ordinations are not to occur without the knowledge of those present so that the sins of evildoers may be disclosed before the people and the merits of the good may be made known; also that the ordination, subject to the approval and judgment of all, may be just and legitimate. Later on this was followed when, in accord with divine teaching, Peter in the Acts of the Apostles spoke to the people regarding the ordination of a bishop [i.e., an apostle] to replace Judas, "Peter stood up amidst the disciples, and the crowd was in one place."[2] We see that the apostles observed this not only for the ordination of bishops and priests but also for that of deacons. In the same Acts it is written, "And the Twelve called together the whole group of disciples and said to them."[3] This gathering of all the people was done with attention and care so that no unworthy person might steal into the ministry of the altar or the priestly office. It happens that unworthy individuals are at times ordained, not according to God's will but because of human presumption. What does not come from a legitimate and proper ordination displeases God as God himself makes known through Hosea the prophet, "They make a king but not through me."[4]

569

V. This is why you are to follow and retain the practice received from divine tradition and apostolic usage, a practice observed among us also and throughout almost all the provinces, namely, that for correctly celebrating ordinations the neighboring bishops within the same province should gather with the people for whom the candidate is ordained. And the bishop is to be selected in the presence of the people who are fully

570

---

† Translated from CCL 3 C, 452–54.

a. Felix: a priest; Aelius: a deacon. In Emerita or Merida, Spain.

1. Num 20:25–26. 2. Acts 1:15. 3. Acts 6:2. 4. Hos 8:4.

knowledgeable as to the life of each [candidate] and who have investigated each one's conduct. We see that you did this in ordaining our colleague Sabinus so that, by a vote of the whole community and by the judgment of the bishops who had gathered with you and had written you concerning him, hands were imposed on him. [. . .]

27-E-16. LETTER 69. TO MAGNUS[ta]

571   v. [. . .] The Lord's sacrifices declare a Christian unity, a unity that is firm and inseparable. For when the Lord said that the bread was his Body, bread brought together by mixing many grains, and when he said that the wine was his Blood, wine pressed from many grapes and clusters, he also had in mind the one flock which is joined together by the mingling of many persons into one. [. . .]

572   xiv. Indeed the Holy Spirit is not given piecemeal but is totally poured out upon the believer. For if the daytime is born for all equally and if the sun's light is diffused upon all alike,[1] how much more does Christ, the true sun and the true day, give with similar equality the light of life eternal in his Church! In Exodus we see the mystery celebrated with equality: the manna flowed down from heaven and by prefiguring what was to come showed forth the sustenance of the heavenly bread and the food of the Christ who was to come. For there an omer was equally collected by each person without distinction as to sex or age.[2] So it appeared that Christ's kindness and heavenly grace, which were to follow, were equally divided among all; without sexual differences, without distinction of age, without partiality toward persons, the gift of spiritual grace being poured upon all.[3] To be sure, the same spiritual grace received by believers in baptism is either diminished or increased according to one's behavior and subsequent actions, just as in the Gospel the Lord's seed is sowed all over; yet according to the type of soil some seed is destroyed and some increases in a variety of ways, bringing forth fruit thirty, sixty, or a hundredfold.[4] Besides, when each was called to receive a denarius, did human understanding lessen what God distributed equally?[5]

573   xv. Should any be concerned that some of the sick who were baptized while ill are still tempted by unclean spirits, they should know that the devil's stubborn evil perdures up to the saving water; yet in baptism the devil loses all the poison of his wickedness. An example of this is Pharaoh the king who struggled for a long time and was delayed by his lack of faith. He was able to resist and prevail till he came to the water; when he did so, he was conquered and vanquished.[6] As the blessed apostle Paul says, "For I do not want you to be unaware, my brothers and sisters, that

---

[t] Translated from CCL 3 C, 493–95.

a. Magnus: an African Christian who consulted Cyprian about baptism.

1. See Matt 5:45.   2. See Exod 16:15–18.   3. See Rom 2:11.   4. See Matt 13:3–8; Mark 4:3–20; Luke 8:5–15.   5. See Matt 20:9–10.   6. See Exod 14:21–31.

all our ancestors were under the cloud and all crossed through the sea and all were baptized into Moses in the cloud and in the sea."[7] He adds, "All these were examples for us."[8] The same occurs today when exorcists, by the human voice and divine power, scourge, burn, and torment the devil. Although he often claims to be departing and leaving those who are of God,[9] the devil's very words deceive, and he practices what was formerly done by the Pharaoh and with the same stubborn and fraudulent deceit.[10] When, however, a person comes to the saving water and to the sanctification of baptism, we should know and believe that it was here that the devil was defeated and that a person dedicated to God is set free through divine kindness. For when scorpions and serpents, who thrive on dry ground, are thrown into the water, they cannot prevail or retain their poison. The same is true of evil spirits, who are called scorpions and serpents and are trampled on by the power granted by the Lord.[11] No longer can they abide in the body of a baptized and sanctified person in whom the Holy Spirit begins to dwell.

xvi. Finally, it is our experience that the sick who were baptized out of necessity and who obtained grace are now free from the unclean spirit which previously excited them, and they live in the Church as they lead laudable and credible lives and each day progress in increasing heavenly grace by growing in their faith. On the other hand, there are those who were baptized in good health and who, afterwards beginning to sin, are made to retreat by the unclean spirit's return. Thus it is evident that in baptism the devil is expelled by the believer's faith and returns if this faith afterwards fails. [. . .]

574

27-E-17. LETTER 70. TO JANUARIUS AND THE OTHER NUMEDIAN BISHOPS[†]

I. Beloved brothers, when we were together in council we read the letter you sent us about those who appear to have been baptized by heretics and schismatics. You asked whether these are to be baptized when they come to the one Church. Although you follow the truth and certainty of Catholic discipline in this matter, you thought we should be consulted due to our mutual love. We gave our opinion—not a new one—but we join you in equally agreeing with a long-standing opinion decreed by our predecessors and followed by us: we judge and hold it as certain that no one can be baptized outside the Church since only one baptism is established in the holy Church. As the Lord wrote, "They have forsaken me, the fountain of the living waters, and dug for themselves broken cisterns, which can hold no water."[1] Holy Scripture also admonished, "Stay away from strange

575

---

7. 1 Cor 10:1–2.   8. 1 Cor 10:6.   9. See Matt 12:43–44; Luke 11:24–25.   10. See Exod 7:13.   11. See Luke 10:19.

[†] Translated from CCL 3 C, 502–11.

1. Jer 2:13.

water and do not drink from a strange fountain."[2] The priest, then, is to cleanse and sanctify the water so that through baptism it may wash away the sins of the person who is baptized since the Lord said through the prophet Ezekiel: "And I will sprinkle clean water upon you, and you will be cleansed from all your impurities and from all your idols. And I will cleanse you and give you a new heart and a new spirit."[3] How can anyone who is impure, in whom the Holy Spirit is not found, cleanse and sanctify the water since in Numbers the Lord says, "Whatever an unclean person touches will be unclean"?[4] Or how can those who are outside the Church and thus unable to take away their own sins forgive the sins of others?

576   II. Moreover, the very question asked in baptism testifies to the truth. For when we say, "Do you believe in eternal life and in the forgiveness of sins through the Holy Church?", we understand that sins can only be remitted in the Church; sins cannot be forgiven among the heretics where the Church does not exist. Accordingly, those who claim that heretics are able to baptize should either change the question or vindicate the truth unless they concede that a Church exists among those who, they claim, have baptism. The baptized are also to be anointed so that, having received the chrism, namely, the anointing, they can be God's anointed ones and possess the grace of Christ. Further, it is by the Eucharist that the oil used to anoint the baptized is sanctified on the altar. However, a person having neither Church nor oil cannot sanctify that creature of oil. And so there can be no spiritual anointing among the heretics since it is evident that in no way can the oil be sanctified or the Eucharist celebrated among them. We ought to know and remember what is written, "Let not the oil of the wicked anoint my head."[5] This is what the Holy Spirit foretold in the Psalms lest anyone wandering and straying from the path of truth be anointed by the heretics and enemies of Christ. But what prayer can a sacrilegious and sinful priest say for a baptized person? It is written, "God does not hear the sinner; but God does hear whoever worships God and does his will."[6] Can anyone give what he or she does not have? Can a person who has lost the Holy Spirit do spiritual things? Therefore the simple folk who come to the Church must be baptized and renewed so that within the Church they may be sanctified by the holy ones as is written, "Be holy because I am holy, says the Lord"[7] so that one who has been enticed into error and baptized outside [the Church] may put this aside also in a true and ecclesiastical baptism since a person coming to God while seeking a priest [bishop?] comes by the deceit of error upon an impious one.

577   III. Approving the baptism of heretics and schismatics means assenting to their baptism. One part cannot be empty and the other useful. If one can baptize, one can give the Holy Spirit. But if a person cannot bestow the Holy Spirit since whoever is appointed outside [the Church] does not

---

2. Prov 9:18, LXX.   3. Ezra 36:25–26.   4. Num 19:22.   5. Ps 141:5.   6. John 9:31.
7. Lev 19:2.

have the Holy Spirit, such a person cannot baptize those who come. There is one baptism; the Holy Spirit is one; and the one Church,[8] founded by Christ our Lord upon Peter, has its origin and foundation in unity.[9] [. . .]

27-E-18. LETTER 71. TO QUINTUS[†a]

I. [. . .] I do not know by what presumption some of my fellow bishops   578
are led to believe that when those who have been washed by the heretics come to us, they should not be baptized since, as they say, there is only one baptism.[1] To be sure, there is one baptism in the Catholic Church because the Church is one, and there can be no baptism outside the Church. Since there cannot be two baptisms, if the heretics truly baptize, they have baptism. And those who on their own authority grant this power to them acquiesce and consent that Christ's enemy and adversary seems to have the power of washing, purifying, and sanctifying someone. We, however, say that those coming from outside the Church are not rebaptized by us but are baptized. Nor do they receive anything outside the Church since nothing exists there, but they come to us where they find and receive grace and truth because grace and truth are one.[2] Furthermore, some of our fellow bishops would prefer to honor heretics than to agree with us; asserting that there is only one baptism, they do not want us to baptize those who come to us. And so they either make two baptisms, saying that baptism exists among the heretics. Or, and certainly this is more serious, they attempt to rate more highly and prefer the washing of the heretics to the true and recognized baptism of the Catholic Church. They give no consideration to what is written, "If one is washed by a dead person, of what profit is the washing?"[3] It is evident that those not in Christ's Church are to be considered as among the dead. Nor can a person receive life from a dead person when there is one Church which, having obtained eternal life, both lives forever and gives life to God's people.

II. In this regard they claim they are following the old custom when   579
among the ancients there existed heresy and the first beginnings of schism; those involved departed from the Church within which they had been baptized, and so it was not necessary to baptize them when they returned to the Church and did penance. This is what we observe today. It suffices to impose hands for penance upon those whom we know were baptized in the Church and have left us for the heretics if afterwards, recognizing their sin and separating themselves from error, they return to the truth and to their parent. They were sheep, driven apart and wandering, whom the shepherd may receive into his fold.[4] If someone who was not

---

8. See Eph 4:4–5.   9. See Matt 16:18.

† Translated from CCL 3 C, 516–19.

a. Quintus: a bishop in Mauretania.

1. See Eph 4:5.   2. See John 1:14, 17.   3. Sir 34:30, 25, LXX.   4. See Matt 18:12–13; Luke 15:4–5.

previously baptized comes, as a common stranger he or she must be baptized to become a sheep since in the holy Church there is one water that makes sheep. [. . .]

27-E-19. LETTER 72. TO STEPHEN[†a]

580   I. [. . .] The primary reason we wrote you and consulted with your authority and wisdom pertains more to the priestly authority and to the unity of the universal Church as well as to the dignity coming from the ordering of the divine disposition. It concerns those who have been washed outside the Church and have been soiled by the stain of profane water among the heretics and schismatics. When they come to us and to the one Church, they should be baptized since imposing hands on them for receiving the Holy Spirit is not enough; they are also to receive the Church's baptism. For only then can they be fully sanctified and be children of God,[1] being born from the mystery as is written, "No one can enter God's kingdom without first being born of water and the Spirit."[2] Also, in the Acts of the Apostles we find that the apostles observed this and preserved the truth of the saving faith. In the house of Cornelius the centurion, after the Holy Spirit came down upon the Gentiles who were present, they—glowing with the warmth of their faith, wholeheartedly believing in the Lord, and filled with the Holy Spirit—blessed God in various tongues. Despite this, the blessed apostle Peter, mindful of the divine precept and of the Gospel, commanded that those who had already been filled with the Holy Spirit be baptized so that nothing seem to be neglected in regard to what the apostles taught concerning the divine law and the Gospel. Heretics are unable to use baptism; the enemies of Christ cannot profit from the grace of Christ. [. . .]

581   II. Beloved brother, we go on to add—and this by common consent and authority—that any presbyter or deacon who has been previously ordained in the universal Church and subsequently became a traitor by rebelling against this Church is, upon his return, to be received. The same is true for those heretics who have been advanced by a sacrilegious ordination at the hands of false bishops and antichrists and, contrary to what Christ has called for and in opposition to the one and divine altar, have attempted to offer false and impious sacrifices. These also should be received upon their return. The only condition is that they function as members of the laity; it is enough that those who showed themselves to be enemies of peace should not, upon their return, possess the arms of ordination and dignity which they used to rebel against us. It is proper that the priests and ministers who devote themselves to the altar and its sacrifice remain untouched and unstained since the Lord God says in Leviticus,

---

† Translated from CCL 3 C, 524–27.
a. Stephen: bishop of Rome 254–57.
1. See Rom 8:14; Gal 4:4–6.   2. John 3:5.

"No person having a stain or a blemish will come forth to offer gifts to God."[3] The same is also found in Exodus, "And may the priests who approach the Lord God be sanctified lest the Lord depart from them."[4] Also, "When they come to serve at the altar of the holy place, they shall not bring guilt upon themselves should they die."[5] Is there any greater sin or more unsightly stain than to oppose Christ, than to have shattered the Church which was purchased and established with his blood, than—being forgetful of evangelical peace and love—to have fought with the anger of hostile discord against the unified and harmonious people of God? Even after such men return to the Church, they cannot reinstate or bring back with them the deceased whom they seduced, who thus perished outside the Church and without communion and peace; on judgment day the authors and leaders of their destruction will have to answer for what they did to the souls of those who died. When these leaders return, it is enough that pardon be given; faithlessness is not to be rewarded in the household of faith.[6] If we honor those who withdrew from us and opposed the Church, then what do we have for those who are good and innocent?

27-E-20. LETTER 73. TO JUBAIANUS[†a]

VI. Jeremiah the prophet accurately rebukes profane and illicit baptism   582
when he says, "Why do those who afflict me prevail? My wound is incurable; how will I be cured? It has become for me as a deceitful water lacking faith."[1] Through the prophet the Holy Spirit here speaks of a water that deceives and lacks faith. What is this deceitful and faithless water? Surely water that conceals any resemblance to baptism and by an unreal pretense frustrates the grace of faith. But if due to bad faith a person can be baptized outside the Church and obtain the forgiveness of sins, according to the same faith such a person could obtain the Holy Spirit, and it would not be necessary to impose hands on those who come so that they might receive the Holy Spirit and be sealed. Either both can be obtained without the Church through faith, or neither can be received outside the Church.

VII. It is, moreover, evident where and through whom sins can be for-   583
given; namely, through baptism. The Lord first gave this power to Peter, upon whom he built his Church and whom he appointed and showed to be the source of unity: whatever Peter loosed on earth would also be loosed in heaven.[2] Also, after the resurrection the Lord said to his apostles: "'As the Father has sent me, so I send you.' When he said this, he breathed upon them and said to them, 'Receive the Holy Spirit. Whose sins you will forgive, they will be forgiven. Whose sins you will retain, they will be retained.'"[3] From this we know that only those placed in charge of the

---

3. Lev 21:17, 21.   4. Exod 19:22.   5. Exod 28:43, LXX; see 30:20–21.   6. See Gal 6:10.
† Translated from CCL 3 C, 536–39.
a. Jubaianus: a bishop in Mauretania.
1. Jer 15:18.   2. See Matt 16:18–19.   3. John 20:21–23.

Church and who base themselves on the law of the Gospel and on what the Lord determined are permitted to baptize and forgive sins; outside, however, nothing can be bound or loosed, since without no one can bind or loose.

584   ix. In regard to those who were baptized in Samaria, some hold that when the Apostles Peter and John went there, hands only were imposed on these people so that they might receive the Holy Spirit, and that they were not again baptized.[4] Yet, dearest brother, in no way does this pertain to the case at hand. The believers in Samaria believed with a true faith and did so within the one Church, which alone is allowed to baptize and forgive sins. They were baptized by the deacon Philip[5] whom the same apostles had sent. And since they were licitly baptized according to the Church, they were not to be baptized again. Peter and John did only what was lacking, namely, after praying for them and imposing hands upon them, they invoked the Holy Spirit to be poured forth upon them.[6] This also occurs among us: those who are baptized in the Church are brought to the Church's leaders so that by means of our prayer and the imposition of hands they might obtain the Holy Spirit and be perfected by the Lord's seal.

27-E-21. LETTER 74. TO POMPEY[†a]

585   i. [. . .] Since you wished to know what our brother Stephen[b] replied to my letter, I have sent you a copy of his answer. Reading it, you will increasingly notice his error as he attempts to align himself with the heretics who stand against Christians and against God's Church. For among other matters, whether they be arrogant or irrelevant or self-contradictory and which he ignorantly and impulsively wrote, he added, "Should anyone come to you from any heresy whatsoever, do nothing except what has been handed down, so that hands are imposed on them unto penance since heretics themselves characteristically do not baptize those who come to them but only admit them to communion."

586   ii. He has forbidden those coming from any heresy whatsoever to be baptized in the Church, namely, he considered the baptism conferred by heretics as valid and legitimate. And whereas individual heresies have their own individual baptisms and diverse sins, he, being in communion with the baptism of all, has heaped up within himself the sins of all. He taught that nothing other than what has been handed down is to be done. It is as if the innovator would be the person who holds fast to unity and claims one baptism[1] for the one Church. To be sure, the innovator is the person who is forgetful of unity, who adopts the lies and infections of

---

4. See Acts 8:14–17.   5. See Acts 8:5–6, 16.   6. See Acts 8:17.
† Translated from CCL 3 C, 564–65, 571–72.
a. Pompey: an African bishop.
b. Stephen: bishop of Rome 254–57.
1. See Eph 4:5.

their profane washing. May there be no innovations, he says, beyond what has been handed down. Yet what is the origin of what has been handed down? Does it come to us from the authority of the Lord and the Gospel? Or does it flow from the directives and letters of the apostles? What is written down must be done as God testifies and admonishes Joshua the son of Nun, "This book of the Law shall not depart out of your mouth; day and night you shall meditate on it so that you may do all that is written in it."[2] Likewise, the Lord, sending forth his disciples, commanded that they baptize and teach the nations to observe everything he commanded them.[3] Should the Gospel prescribe or should the epistles or Acts of the Apostles say that those coming from any heresy whatsoever are not to be baptized but that hands only should be imposed on them, then let this holy and divine tradition be followed. [. . .]

v. If heretics attribute the effect of baptism to the power of the divine name so that those who have been baptized, no matter where or how, are considered to be renewed and sanctified, then why do they not lay hands upon the baptized so that they may receive the Holy Spirit? Does not the same power of the divine name prevail in the laying on of hands as, so they contend, prevailed in the sanctification of baptism? If someone born outside the Church can become God's temple,[4] then why cannot the Holy Spirit be poured out upon this temple? The sanctified—those whose sins have been cast away through baptism and who have been spiritually remade into new persons[5]—have certainly been rendered fit to receive the Holy Spirit since the apostle says, "As many of you as were baptized into Christ have put on Christ."[6] A person baptized among the heretics, who is able to put on Christ, is much more capable of receiving the Holy Spirit, the Spirit sent by Christ. Otherwise, for it to be possible that a person baptized outside the Church might put on Christ and yet be unable to receive the Holy Spirit, the one who is sent would be greater than the one who sends. It is as if a person could put on Christ without the Spirit, thereby separating the Spirit from Christ.[7] Furthermore, it is foolish to say that, although the second birth by which we are born in Christ through the bath of regeneration is spiritual, a person can be spiritually born among heretics who deny the very existence of the Spirit.[8] Water alone is unable to wash away sins and sanctify people unless these people possess the Holy Spirit. Therefore it is necessary for them to concede that the Spirit is present where they say baptism exists, or that there is no baptism where the Spirit is not found because baptism cannot exist without the Spirit.

vi. But what does it mean to assert and contend that those who have not been born in the Church can be children of God? The blessed apostle clearly shows and proves that it is in baptism that the old self dies and the new self is born.[9] He says, "He saved us through the washing of

587

588

2. Josh 1:8.   3. See Matt 28:19.   4. See 1 Cor 3:16; 2 Cor 6:16.   5. See Eph 4:23–24.   6. Gal 3:27.   7. See ibid.   8. See Titus 3:5.   9. See Eph 4:22–24.

regeneration."[10] If regeneration is in the baptismal washing, how can heresy, which is not a spouse of Christ, bring forth children to God through Christ? The Church alone, which is joined and spiritually united to Christ, can bring forth children as the same apostle again says, "Christ loved the Church and gave himself up for her in order to sanctify her, cleansing her by the washing of water."[11] If the Church, then, is the beloved and the spouse who alone is sanctified by Christ and is cleansed by his washing, it is evident that those in heresy, not being Christ's spouse and not being cleansed or sanctified by his washing, cannot bring forth children to God.

589   VII. To continue, it is not through the imposition of hands that those who are born receive the Holy Spirit but in baptism so that they, already born, may receive the Spirit, as happened to the first man.[12] God first formed him and then breathed into his nostrils the breath of life. The Spirit cannot be received unless there exists someone who has already received the Spirit. Since Christians are born in baptism—the baptismal generation and sanctification belonging exclusively to Christ's spouse which can give spiritual birth and generate children to God—then where and from whom and to whom is one born who is not a child of the Church? Whoever wishes to have God as a Father must first have the Church as a Mother. [. . .]

27-E-22. LETTER 75. FIRMILIAN[a] TO CYPRIAN[†]

590   VII. [. . .] Other heretics also, if they have separated themselves from God's Church, have no power or grace since power and grace are rooted in the Church where preside the presbyters [bishops?] who have the power to baptize, to lay on hands, and to ordain. For just as a heretic may not lawfully ordain or impose hands, so neither may a heretic baptize. [. . .]

591   X. [. . .] Suddenly there arose a woman who in a state of ecstasy passed herself off as a prophet and acted as though she were full of the Holy Spirit. [. . .] Earlier the devil's deceptions and deceits moved this woman to undertake many things to mislead the faithful; among others by which she deceived many she frequently dared to pretend to sanctify the bread and celebrate the Eucharist and to offer a sacrifice to the Lord without the rite of the customary words; she also baptized many while using the customary and appropriate words of questioning so that nothing might seem to be different from the pattern observed by the Church.

592   XI. What, then, are we to say about such a baptism in which the most evil devil baptized by means of a woman? Do Stephen[b] and those agreeing with him really approve of this, especially since neither the trinitarian symbol nor the proper and ecclesiastical questioning were lacking? Can anyone believe that sins were pardoned or that the regeneration of the

---

10. Titus 3:5.   11. Eph 5:25–26.   12. See Gen 2:7.
† Translated from CCL 3 C, 588ff.
a. Firmilian: bishop of Caesarea in Cappadocia.
b. Stephen: bishop of Rome 254–57.

saving washing was properly accomplished where everything, being but an image of the truth, was done through the devil? Unless, perhaps, that those defending heretical baptism confidently assert that it was also the devil who gave the grace of baptism in the name of the Father, and of the Son, and of the Holy Spirit. [. . .]

xi. What are we to understand when Stephen says that Christ's presence   593
and holiness can be found among those baptized by the heretics? According to the apostle, "Whoever is washed in Christ has put on Christ."[1] Since the apostle does not lie, whoever has been baptized has put on Christ. But if they have put on Christ, then they could have received the Holy Spirit who had been sent by Christ. It would be useless to impose hands on whoever comes in order to receive the Spirit unless they divide the Spirit from Christ so that Christ can surely be found among the heretics but not the Holy Spirit.

xxi. What is to be said about those who come from heresy and are ad-   594
mitted without the Church's baptism? Should they have died, they are considered as catechumens who die before baptism; having abandoned their error and yet prevented by death from being baptized, they attain no small advantage of truth and faith even though they have not yet gained the fullness of grace. Those who are still alive are to be baptized with the Church's baptism so that their sins may be forgiven. [. . .]

28. PSEUDO-CYPRIAN. *TO NOVATIAN*[†]

Found among the works of Cyprian, this treatise by an unknown contemporary of the African bishop is directed against Novatian, a Roman priest, an antipope, and a martyr. As can be seen from this work, Novatian had modified his thinking regarding the lapsed, eventually adopting a very rigorist position.

CPL no. 76 * Altaner (1961) 199 * Altaner (1966) 177 * Bardenhewer (1908) 199 * Bardenhewer (1910) 174 * Bardenhewer (1913) 2:444–46 * CE 4:588–89

2. [. . .] Two birds were sent forth from the ark, one a raven, the other   595
a dove.[1] The raven bore the image of the unclean, the image of those who would live in perpetual darkness throughout the whole world, the image of future apostates who, feeding on impure things, would no longer be able to return to the Church. We read that the raven, sent out, did not return. Therefore those similar to this bird, namely, similar to the impure spirit, will no longer be able to return to the Church even though they

---

1. Gal 3:27.

[†] Translated from *S. Thasci Caecili Cypriani Opera Omnia*, vol. 3, ed. G. Hartel, CSEL 3.3 (Vienna, 1871) 55ff.

1. See Gen 8:6–12.

desire to do so. This the Lord forbade when he ordered Moses to "expel from the camp all that is leprous and unclean."[2] The dove that was sent forth and then came back is signified by those who do not tarry, since this bird had no place whereupon to rest its feet. Noah allowed it back into the ark. But on the seventh day when the dove was again sent out, Noah received it back, the dove bearing an olive leaf in its mouth.

596   3. Beloved brothers, I do not reflect upon these matters casually nor in a way that disagrees with human wisdom, but rather in a manner that the heavenly Lord has graciously allowed us to express. And so I say that the dove itself presents us with a two-fold image. The first and principal image, one that existed in the past from the beginning of divine activity, is that of the Spirit. Through its mouth the dove prefigured the sacrament of baptism, which is given for the salvation of the human race and by divine design celebrated only in the Church. Sent forth three times from the ark and flying over the water, the dove already signified the sacraments of our Church. Whence Christ the Lord commanded Peter and his other disciples, saying, "Go, therefore, and make disciples of all nations, baptizing them in the name of the Father and of the Son and of the Holy Spirit,"[3] namely, that the Trinity which was figuratively at work through the dove at Noah's time is presently at work in the Church through us.

597   13. [. . .] What led this Novatian to become so wicked, so profligate, so mad with the rage of dissension, I cannot discover. When he belonged to the one household, namely, to the Church of Christ, he always lamented over the sins of his neighbors as if these sins were his own; he bore the burdens of his brethren as the apostle urges.[4] With words of heavenly comfort he strengthened those uncertain in the faith. But now since beginning to practice that heresy of Cain which revels only in killing, he does not even refrain from harming himself. Moreover, if he had read that "the righteousness of the just will not free them on the day they sinned, nor will the evil of the impious harm them from the day of their conversion,"[5] then for a long time now he would be doing penance in ashes, he who is always opposed to the penitents, he who more easily labors to destroy what is standing than to build up what lies in ruins, he who has again made many of our brethren most miserable heathens, frightened as they are by what he falsely says against them, namely, that the repentance of the lapsed is useless and can profit them nothing toward salvation; and yet Scripture says, "Remember from where you have fallen and do penance; so that I will not come to you unless you do penance."[6] Indeed, writing to the seven churches and having them face up to their crimes and sins, Scripture says that they are to repent. To whom was this said? Surely to those redeemed at the great price of his blood.

598   14. Novatian, you impious and wicked heretic! After so many and such great sins which you knew some had willingly committed in the Church,

---

2. Num 5:2.   3. Matt 28:19.   4. See Gal 6:2.   5. Ezek 33:12.   6. Rev 2:5.

and before you yourself became an apostate from God's household, you taught that these sins could be erased from memory provided they were followed by a good life, as Scripture confirms, "If those who are evil turn away from their evil deeds and follow righteousness, they will live in eternal life and not die in their evil."[7] Through their good deeds the sins they committed will be destroyed. Today you draw back as to whether the wounds of the lapsed are to be cured, the lapsed who have fallen, stripped by the devil, and laid low by "the torrent of water which the serpent spewed out of his mouth after the woman."[8] The apostle says, "But what am I to say? In this I do not praise you because when you come together it is not for the better but for the worse."[9] For where rivalry and dissension exist among you, are you not carnal and do you not walk according to the world? Nor should we be astonished that Novatian now dares to carry out such abominable and oppressive measures against the lapsed since we have other instances of such mismanagement. Saul, once a good man in addition to other things, was later brought down by envy and strove to do whatever would be against David, whatever would harm him. [. . .]

29. PSEUDO-CYPRIAN. *ON REBAPTISM*[†]

Written in Africa and probably before Cyprian's death, this treatise defends the validity of baptism celebrated by heretics, a position directly opposite that of Cyprian. The author, an anonymous bishop, distinguishes between spiritual baptism (namely, that of the Holy Spirit and given by the imposition of the bishop's hand) and water baptism (namely, that associated with invoking the name of Jesus).

CPL no. 59 * Altaner (1961) 200 * Altaner (1966) 177 * Bardenhewer (1908) 199–200 * Bardenhewer (1910) 174 * Bardenhewer (1913) 2:448–50 * Jurgens 1:242 * Tixeront 125 * DTC 3.2:2465 * EC 4:1449 * PEA (1894) 4.2:1940

H. Koch, *Die Tauflehre des Liber de rebaptismate* (Braunsberg, 1907). * J. Ernst, "Die Tauflehre des Liber de rebaptismate," ZkTh 31 (1907) 648–99. * G. Rauschen, "Die pseudo-cyprianische Schrift de rebaptismate," ZkTh 41 (1917) 83–110.

1. I hear that some of the brethren inquired about the procedure to be followed regarding those who, having been baptized in heresy and yet baptized in the name of our God Jesus Christ, leave behind their heresy and hasten as supplicants to the Church of God. Here they wholeheartedly do penance and, finally understanding that their error has been condemned, petition the Church for the help of salvation. The question is whether, conforming to the most ancient practice and ecclesiastical tradition, it suffices that since they were baptized outside the Church but in the 599

---

7. Ezek 18:21.   8. Rev 12:15.   9. 1 Cor 11:22, 17.

[†] Translated from *S. Thasci Caecili Cypriani Opera Omnia*, vol. 3, CSEL 3.3 (Vienna, 1871) 69ff.

name of Jesus Christ our Lord only the hand of the bishop be imposed on them for receiving the Holy Spirit, this imposition giving them a second and perfected seal of the faith. Or must they be baptized again since, lacking this, they receive nothing just as if they had never been baptized in the name of Jesus Christ?

600   Consequently there was a discussion on what people asserted or replied concerning this new question. Each side was most zealous in refuting what the other side wrote. It seems to me that in this type of dispute no controversy or debate would have emerged if each party had been satisfied with the venerable authority of all the churches and, being humble enough, desired to innovate nothing, thus allowing no opportunity for contradiction. Surely to be condemned is whatever is uncertain and ambiguous, whatever prudent and dependable people disagree on, if this be judged contrary to the ancient, memorable, and most solemn observance of all who are deserving, holy, and faithful. Once something has been arranged and settled, whatever is contrary to the peace and tranquility of the churches results only in discord, rivalry, and division. [. . .]

601   2. To those undertaking a discussion of the saving and new—namely, spiritual and evangelical—baptism, first of all there is the celebrated proclamation, known to all and initiated by John the Baptist, who diverged somewhat from the law, namely, from the most ancient baptism of Moses, and who prepared the way for a new and true grace. By announcing a future spiritual baptism, John gained the attention of the Jews, preceding this by a baptism of water and repentance which he meanwhile practiced. He exhorted them, "the one who comes after me is stronger than I. I am not worthy to loosen his sandals." He will baptize you in the "Holy Spirit and with fire."[1] Consequently our discussion should begin here. In the Acts of the Apostles our Lord, after his resurrection, confirmed what John said when the Lord commanded that "they not leave Jerusalem but await that promise of the Father which you have heard from me; for John indeed baptized with water, but in a few days you will be baptized with the Holy Spirit."[2] Peter likewise repeated these words of the Lord when he was explaining himself to the apostles: "When I began speaking, the Holy Spirit came down upon them as it did upon us in the beginning; and I recalled what the Lord said, 'John indeed baptized with water, but in a few days you will be baptized with the Holy Spirit.' If, therefore, he gave them the same gift he gave to us who believe in the Lord Jesus Christ, who was I that I could hinder the Lord?"[3] And again: "My brothers, you know how from early days God made his choice among us so that the Gentiles through my mouth should hear the word of the Gospel and believe. And God, who knows hearts, gave witness, giving them the Holy Spirit, just as he did for us."[4] For this reason we should consider the strength and power of what John said. For the Lord

---

1. Matt 3:11; Mark 1:7; Luke 3:16; John 1:27.   2. Acts 1:4–5.   3. Acts 11:15–17.
4. Acts 15:7–8.

told those who would afterwards be baptized that they should believe, that
they should be baptized not by him in water for repentance but in the Holy
Spirit. Since none of us can doubt this statement, it is obvious why people
are baptized in the Holy Spirit, for it was especially in the Holy Spirit alone
that those who believed were baptized because John distinguished, saying
that he baptized in water but the one to come would baptize in the Holy
Spirit, doing so by God's grace and power. [. . .]

3. [. . .] Just as at the imposition of the bishop's hand the Holy Spirit   602
is given to each believer, so after Philip's baptism the apostles laid hands
on the Samaritans, thereby conferring the Holy Spirit on them.[5] For this to
take place, they prayed for the Samaritans since the Spirit had not yet descended upon any of them, this happening only after they were baptized
in the name of the Lord Jesus. Also, it was after our Lord's resurrection,
when he breathed upon his apostles and said to them, "Receive the Holy
Spirit,"[6] that at last the Holy Spirit was given them.

4. Since this is so, what do you think, my brother? Suppose someone is   603
not baptized by a bishop and consequently does not immediately receive
the laying-on of the hand, and suppose that this same person should die
before receiving the Holy Spirit, do you believe that this individual has or
has not received the Holy Spirit? Indeed the apostles themselves and the
disciples, who also baptized and themselves were baptized by the Lord,
did not immediately receive the Holy Spirit since the Spirit had not yet
been given because Jesus had not yet been glorified. But the conferral of
the Spirit occurred shortly after his resurrection just as the Samaritans,
baptized by Philip, did not receive the Spirit till the apostles, invited to
go from Jerusalem to Samaria in order to lay hands upon them, conferred
the Holy Spirit through the imposition of the hand. The reason for doing
so was that within such a short period of time any person who had not
received the Holy Spirit could have died, thus being cheated of the grace
of the Holy Spirit. No one can doubt that at present it customarily and
frequently happens that many of the baptized die without the imposition
of the bishop's hand, and yet these are considered perfect believers. This
is like the case of the Ethiopian eunuch who, returning from Jerusalem
and reading the prophet Isaiah, had doubts and at the Spirit's prompting
heard the truth from Philip the deacon. The eunuch believed and was baptized. When the eunuch came up out of the water, the Spirit of the Lord
snatched away Philip, and the eunuch saw him no longer.[7] Rejoicing, the
eunuch continued on although, as you notice, no bishop imposed a hand
upon him so that he might receive the Holy Spirit.

Now if you admit that this is true and believe that such a baptism   604
brings salvation and do not oppose the opinion of all the faithful, then
you must admit that just as this principle is more widely discussed, so
the other can more widely be established, namely, that only through the

5. See Acts 8:14–17.   6. John 20:22.   7. See Acts 8:27–39.

imposition of the bishop's hand, because baptism in the name of Jesus Christ our Lord preceded, can the Spirit also be given to another person who does penance and believes. According to Holy Scripture, those believing in Christ are to be baptized in the Spirit so that these also may not appear to have less than those who are perfect Christians. Nor should it be necessary to ask what type of baptism was it in which they attained the name of Jesus Christ. Except, perhaps, in that earlier discussion concerning those who were baptized only in the name of Christ Jesus, you should decide that these can be saved without the Holy Spirit; or that the Holy Spirit is not given in this way but only through the imposition of the bishop's hand; or that it is not only the bishop who can bestow the Holy Spirit.

605   5. [. . .] Furthermore, as you are not ignorant, the Holy Spirit is found to have been given by the Lord to believers who have not been baptized with water, as we read in the Acts of the Apostles: "While Peter was still speaking these words, the Holy Spirit came down upon all who heard the word. The circumcised believers accompanying Peter were amazed because the gift of the Holy Spirit was also poured out on the Gentiles for they could hear them speaking in tongues and giving praise to God. Then Peter responded: 'Can anyone withhold the water so that these, who have received the Holy Spirit just as we have, may not be baptized?' He commanded them to be baptized in the name of Jesus."[8] Later on Peter taught us most fully about the same Gentiles, "And he placed no difference between them and us, their hearts being purified through faith."[9] There will be no doubt that people can be baptized in the Holy Spirit without water; as you notice, these were baptized before being baptized with water so that what John and our Lord proclaimed might be fulfilled, since they received the grace of the promise both without the imposition of the apostles' hands and without the washing which later on they received. With purified hearts they were at the same time and because of their faith forgiven their sins. And so the baptism that followed conferred on them one thing only, namely, that they received also the invocation of the name of Jesus Christ so that they seem to be lacking nothing in regard to the wholeness of their service and faith.

606   6. Looking at it from the opposite side of the discussion, here is what was obtained by our Lord's disciples upon whom, being already baptized, the Holy Spirit descended on Pentecost. Coming down from heaven by God's will—not of the Spirit's own design but sent forth for this very task—the Spirit rested upon each of them.[10] The disciples were already righteous; as we have said, they had been baptized with the Lord's baptism, as were the apostles themselves who on the night the Lord was taken prisoner deserted him, each and every one. Even Peter, who bragged that he would remain steadfast in his faith and who most obstinately protested what the Lord foretold, in the end denied him. In this way it was shown to us that whatever sins the apostles had meanwhile committed in any way

---

8. Acts 10:44–48.   9. Acts 15:9.   10. See Acts 2:1–4.

were by their subsequent sincere faith certainly remitted through baptism of the Holy Spirit. Nor, as I believe, was there any other reason why the apostles advised those whom they addressed in the Holy Spirit to be baptized in the name of Christ Jesus except that the power of the name of Jesus, when invoked upon any person whomsoever, was able to offer that individual no little benefit toward obtaining salvation, as Peter relates in the Acts of the Apostles, "for there is no other name under heaven given to the human race in which we are to be saved."[11] The apostle Paul reveals this, showing that God exalted our Lord Jesus and "gave him a name that is to be above every name, that at the name of Jesus every knee should bend, in heaven, on earth, and under the earth, and that every tongue should confess that Jesus is Lord in the glory of the Father."[12] When the name of Jesus is invoked over someone who is to be baptized, even though the baptism takes place [among those] in error, at some future time this person might understand the truth, correct the error, come to the Church and the bishop, and sincerely proclaim our Jesus before all. Then when the bishop's hand is imposed, the Holy Spirit could also be received nor would the earlier invocation of the name of Jesus be lost. No one can find fault with this. Yet if this invocation takes place [among those] in error, it stands by itself and profits nothing toward salvation. Otherwise, even the Gentiles and the heretics, abusing the name of Jesus, could attain salvation without the true and complete procedure. [. . .]

10. Additionally, what will you say about those who, often enough, are baptized by bishops whose conduct is most evil and who at last—God willing—are convicted of their wickedness and are deprived of their office and from all association with the community? Or what do you decide concerning those who were baptized by bishops with perverse ideas, bishops who are ignorant? Or by bishops who did not speak clearly or honestly, or who spoke in a way different from what befits our traditional belief regarding the sacrament? Or by bishops who have asked anything or, asking, hear from those replying what least should be asked about or given an answer? This, however, does not greatly harm our true faith, even though such more simple men may hand down the mystery of faith in a way that is not as rich and as well-ordered as yours. With your singular carefulness you will surely say that these also should be baptized again since they lack baptism and for this reason are unable to receive intact the divine and pure mystery of faith. 607

Nonetheless, O best of men, let us grant and concede to the heavenly powers their strength, to the dignity of the divine majesty its proper workings. Understanding how beneficial it is, may we willingly find comfort therein. Since our salvation is established upon baptism of the Spirit, which for the most part is linked to baptism of water, then whenever we baptize, let us do so integrally and solemnly, with all that is assigned in writing and without separating anything. But should necessity have 608

---

11. Acts 4:12.   12. Phil 2:9–11.

required that a lesser cleric [one who is not a bishop] baptize, then let us wait for its conclusion so that it either be added by us [the bishops] or be held back to be supplied by the Lord. If, however, it was conferred by those unknown to us, let the matter be corrected as is possible and is permitted. Since there is no Holy Spirit outside the Church, there can be no sound faith not only among the heretics but also among those in schism. Therefore those who do penance and are reformed through the teaching of truth and through their own faith, a faith that has later been improved by a purified heart, should be aided only by a spiritual baptism, that is, by the imposition of the bishop's hand and by supplying the Holy Spirit. The complete seal of faith has rightly been given in this way and for this reason in the Church so that invoking the name of Jesus, which cannot be done away with, may not seem to be held in contempt by us. Such is not fitting even though this invocation, if none of what we have mentioned follows, may avail nothing in terms of salvation. [. . .]

30. COMMODIAN

Little is known of the life of this poet. Some say he was born in Gaza in Palestine and perhaps became a bishop toward the end of his life. Athens, Africa (the more common opinion), Rome, Syria, as well as Arles are mentioned as possible places where he spent his life. As to the chronological period of his writing activity, the third century is, on the basis of internal evidence, frequently mentioned by many who thus consider Commodian to be the first Christian Latin poet; others place him as late as the fifth century.

Knowledgeable in the Scriptures yet at times given to heterodox understandings, Commodian often wrote in an obscure fashion and with a general disregard for the rules of Latin grammar. His two works are the *Instructions against the Gods of the Pagans* and the *Apologetic Hymn against the Jews and the Pagans*, the latter being a reworking of the book of Revelation.

CPL nos. 1470ff. * Altaner (1961) 485–87 * Altaner (1966) 181–82 * Bardenhewer (1908) 225–27 * Bardenhewer (1910) 197–98 * Bardenhewer (1913) 2:584–93 * Bardy (1930) 50–52 * Bautz 1:1114–15 * Cross 187–88 * Hamell 85 * Labriolle (1947) 1:257–73 * Labriolle (1968) 175–87 * Quasten 4:259–64 * Steidle 79 * Tixeront 123–24 * CATH 2:1355–56 * CE 4:165–66 * DCB 1:610–11 * DHGE 13:402–5 * DPAC 1:743–45 * DTC 3.1:412–19 * EC 4:63–65 * EEC 1:187–88 * EEChr 1:271 * LTK 2:1275–76 * ODCC 383 * PEA (1894) 4.1:773–74 * PEA (1991) 3:102–3 * RACh 3:248–52

30-A. Instructions against the Gods of the Pagans[†]

The second book of this collection of eighty poems (of unequal length and all except two being acrostic) is a series of exhortations to the various

---

[†] Translated from *Commodiani Carmina*, ed. J. Martin and P.F. Hoving, CCL 128 (Turnhout, 1960) 66ff.

classes of Christians, e.g., catechumens, readers, ministers, clerics, etc. The author, writing in hexameter and using the Latin word accent rather than the length of the Latin syllable, urges them to avoid sin and fulfill their duties.

II.ɪ. (v.) To Catechumens   609
    As a believer in Christ you have abandoned idols.
Using few words, I warn all of you for the sake of your salvation.
If, early on, you lived in error,
now vowed to Christ you henceforth will leave all things behind.
Since you acknowledge God, be a good and approved recruit.
May virginal modesty reside in you as in a lamb.
May your mind await what is good; take care that you do not sin as formerly;
baptism removes only the original stain.
Any catechumen who sins is struck with punishment;
marked with punishment, you will live in Christ but not without harm.
Above all, always avoid grave sin.

II.ɪv. (vɪɪɪ.) To Penitents   610
    You have become a penitent; pray both day and night.
Do not stray far from your mother, the Church,
and the Almighty will be merciful to you.
And so the confession of your sin will not be in vain.
Prostrate yourself in your sin and cry out before all.
If your wound is grave, seek a physician;
and even in your punishment you will be able to ease your suffering.
Certainly I acknowledge that I also was one of you,
and I likewise once experienced the terror of ruin.
Furthermore, I warn those who have been wounded to walk with prudence;
may they soil beard and hair with the dust of the earth;
may they wear sackcloth and supplicate the Almighty King.
He will assist you so that you do not disappear from among his people.

II.xxɪɪ. (xxvɪ.) To Readers   611
    I warn certain readers to learn
to give the world an example of a good life,
to flee quarrels and avoid all strife,
to restrain and lay aside all pride.
Also respect, as is right, the elders.
Beloved children, become like Christ your Master;
may your goodness make you like the lilies in the field.
Become happy by obeying God's precepts.
You are flowers among the people;
you are the lamps of Christ.
Remain as you are, and you will be able to recall it.

612   II.xxiii. (xxvii.) To Ministers
      Deacons, chastely carry out the ministry of Christ.
   Be servants of your Master's orders.
      Do not desire to flee the person of the righteous judge.
   If you are wise, do all that is entrusted to you.
   Look on high; always be devoted to God's orders.
   Without wavering carry out your holy ministry to God.
   In all circumstances be ready and give a good example;
   show reverence to the pastors,
   and Christ will thereby approve you.

613   II.xxx. (xxxiv.) To Clerics
      They will gather together at Easter, which is our most happy day.
   May they who request daily nourishment rejoice.
   May they be given what suffices, wine and food.
   Do you perhaps look back when these things are recalled for you?
   In a moderate meal there is nothing to give to Christ.
   If you yourselves fail to do this,
   then how will you be able to teach the people
   justice and the Law, even once a year?
   Also, you will be rightfully reproached.

ITALY

31. HIPPOLYTUS OF ROME

Little is known of the personal life of Hippolytus, whose dates are often
given as ca. 170–ca. 236. Eusebius (ca. 260–ca. 340) knew of him, and in his
Church History (VI.20, 22) called him a bishop, although not knowing his see.
A short list of treastises ascribed to Hippolytus are included in Eusebius's
book. Later evidence speaks of a presbyter called Hippolytus being banished
to the island of Sardinia in the year 235. And if we are to believe a burial
inscription composed by Pope Damasus (WEC 2:52) , Hippolytus was a fol-
lower of the Novatian schism, yet eventually being reconciled to the Church.
The Roman Martyrology (1584), placing his feast on August 13, gives the
following notice: "At Rome the blessed Hippolytus, martyr, who gloriously
confessed the faith, under Emperor Valerian. After enduring other torments,
he was tied by the feet to the necks of wild horses and, being cruelly dragged
through briars and brambles, and having all his body lacerated, he yielded
up his spirit. On the same day blessed Concordia, his nurse, suffered. Being
scourged in this presence with leaded whips, she went to our Lord together
with nineteen others of his household, who were beheaded beyond the
Tiburtine Gate and who were buried with him in the Agro Verano."
    Historians speculate upon various details of Hippolytus's life, for ex-
ample, his nationality. Some propose the Greek East since Hippolytus
shows an intimate knowledge of Greek philosophy and thought; he also

wrote in Greek, being the last well-known Christian author in Rome to do so. Other topics for historical discussion include Hippolytus's relationship to the popes as well as to the followers of Novatian.

The relatively large number of books listed in the Hippolytan corpus presents its own problems. Scholars point out that many works attributed to Hippolytus—works whose titles we know—no longer exist. They are simply lost, perhaps due to the fact that Greek was no longer used in Rome. Complicating matters is that Christian antiquity knew a number of clerical personages named Hippolytus, thus it is not always clear which Hippolytus is the author of a particular work. Further, certain treatises are incorrectly attributed to Hippolytus, as appears to be true for the so-called *Apostolic Tradition*.

CPG 1: nos. 1737, 1870ff. * Altaner (1961) 55–56, 183–90 * Altaner (1966) 82–84, 164–69 * Bardenhewer (1908) 208–20 * Bardenhewer (1910) 183–94 * Bardenhewer (1913) 2:496–555 * Bardy (1929) 36–40 * Bautz 2:888–93 * Cross 155–67 * Goodspeed 142–51 * Hamell 80–83 * Jurgens 1:162–75 * Quasten 2:163–207 * Steidle 57–62, 268–69 * Tixeront 128–32 * CATH 5:755–60 * CE 7:360–62 * CHECL 142–49 * DACL 6.2:2419–83 * DCB 3:85–105 * DHGE 24:627–35 * DictSp 7.1:531–71 * DPAC 2:1791–98 * DTC 6.2:2487–2511 * EC 7:171–80 * EEC 1:383–85 * EEChr 1:531–32 * LTK 5:147–49 * NCE 6:1139–41 * NCES 6:858–60 * ODCC 773–74 * PEA (1991) 5:602–4 * TRE 15:381–87

31-A. Apostolic Tradition[†]

One of the most important works for our knowledge of the early Church's liturgical life is the *Apostolic Tradition*, in the past usually, though not universally, attributed to Hippolytus. This treatise, like the *Didache* (WEC 1:7), belongs to a genre of writings called "church orders," namely, a collection of various canonical and liturgical rules dealing with such topics as, among others, baptism, orders, and the Eucharist. Incorporated into a number of later documents, the *Apostolic Tradition* exerted a far-reaching influence, especially among the churches in the East.

In 1891 H. Achelis published a document, found in Ethiopic, Coptic, and Arabic, which he, for lack of a better title, simply called the *Egyptian Church Order*. Nine years later, in 1900, E. Hauler published a palimpsest manuscript, lacking a title, written in Latin sometime at the end of the fourth or during the fifth century, and conserved in the Chapter Library in Verona. Although the original Greek of the work has been lost, it has been

---

[†] Translation based on *La Tradition apostolique de s. Hippolyte*, trans. and ed. B. Botte, SChr 11 bis (Paris, 1968). Although Botte presents the Latin of the Verona manuscript, his French translation generally follows the textual traditions of the East. For an excellent presentation of the various textual traditions, see G.J. Cuming, *Hippolytus: A Text for Students*, where each section is translated from the oldest source.

possible to reconstruct the Greek original since the Verona palimpsest, although incomplete, is a quite literal translation of the original language. Sections lacking in the Latin version have been supplied from various oriental language manuscripts. In 1910 E. Schwarz claimed that this work was indeed the long-lost *Apostolic Tradition*, an assertion proved independently by R.H. Connolly in 1916.

Recent years have seen an intensification of interest in this document. Although individual scholars may differ among themselves in regard to details and sections of the work, there appears to be growing consensus in a number of areas. First, the origin of the *Apostolic Tradition* is not necessarily Rome but may also be—and some consider this far more likely—Egypt, and perhaps Alexandria. Second, the document is a compilation having several layers—two, perhaps three—some of which may be dated as early as the second century. And thus the work has no single author, if one can even speak of an "author" in this context. Some scholars also suggest that the document portrays a liturgy that was never celebrated.

EDITIONS

R.H. Connolly, *The So-Called Egyptian Church Order and Derived Documents*, Texts and Studies 8, no. 4 (Cambridge, England, 1916). * G. Dix, *The Apostolic Tradition of St. Hippolytus* (London, 1937); 2nd ed. with prefaces and corrections by H. Chadwick (London, 1968). * B. Botte, trans., ed., *La Tradition Apostolique de s. Hippolyte*, SChr 11 (Paris, 1946); 2nd ed. (1968). * B. Botte, *La Tradition Apostolique de s. Hippolyte*, LQF 39 (Münster i. W., 1963). * J.M. Hanssens, *La liturgie d'Hippolyte, ses documents, son titulaire, ses origines et son caractère*, OCA 155, vol. 1 (Rome, 1959); 2nd ed. (Rome, 1965); vol. 2 (Rome, 1970). * G.J. Cuming, *Hippolytus: A Text for Students, with Introduction, Translation, Commentary and Notes*, Grove Liturgical Study 8 (Bramcote, Nottingham, 1976).

GENERAL STUDIES

H. Achelis, *Die ältesten Quellen des orientalischen Kirchenrechts*, vol. 1, *Die Canones Hippolyti*, TU 6, 4 (Leipzig, 1891). * H. Achelis, "Hippolytus im Kirchenrecht," ZKG 15 (1895) 1–43. * H. Achelis, *Hippolytstudien*, TU, n.s., 1, 4 (Leipzig, 1897). * F.X. Funk, "Die Symbolstücke in der ägyptischen Kirchenordnung und den Kanones Hippolyts," ThQ (1899) 161–87. * A. Baumstark, "Die nichtgriechischen Paralleltexte sum achten Buche der Apostolischen Konstitutiones," OC 1 (1901) 98–137. * A. J. Maclean, *The Ancient Church Orders*, The Cambridge Handbooks of Liturgical Study (Cambridge, England, 1910). * E. Schwartz, *Ueber die pseudo-apostolischen Kirchenordnungen*, Schriften der wissenschaftlichen Gesellschaft in Strassbourg 6 (Strassbourg, 1910). * Th. Schermann, *Die allgemeine Kirchenordnung, frühchristliche Liturgie und kirchliche Ueberlieferung*, StGKA 3, Ergänzungsband, Teil 1–3 (Paderborn, 1914). * A. Wilmart, "Le texte latin de la Paradosis de s. Hippolyte," RSR 9 (1916) 62–71. * A. Wilmart, "Un règlement écclésiastique du IIIe siècle: la 'Tradition Apostolique' du s. Hippolyte," RCF 96 (1918) 81–116. * R. Devreesse, "La 'Tradition Apostolique' de s. Hippolyte," *La vie et les arts liturgiques* 8 (1921–22) 11–18. * Vigourel, "Autour de la 'Tradition apostolique,'" *La vie et les arts liturgiques* 8 (1921–22) 150–56. * P. Galtier, "La Tradition Apostolique d'Hippolyte," RSR 11 (1923) 511–27. * A. Baumstark, "Christus Jesus: Ein Alterskriterium römischer liturgischer Texte," StC 1 (1924–25) 44–55. * R. Lorentz, *De egyptische Kerkordening en Hippolytus van Rome* (Leiden, 1929). * J.A. Jungman, "Beobachtungen zum Fortleben von Hippolyts 'Apostolischer Ueberlieferung' in Palladius und dem Pontificale Romanum," ZkTh 53 (1929) 579–85. * P.O. Norwood, "The Apostolic Tradition of Hippolytus," AThR 17 (1935) 15–18. * A. Hamel, "Ueber das kirchenrechtliche Schriftum Hippolyts," ZNW 36 (1937) 238–50. * H. Engberding, "Das angebliche Dokument römischer Liturgie aus dem Beginn des 3. Jahrhunderts," in *Miscellanea Liturgica in Hon. L.C. Mohlberg*, vol. 1 (Rome, 1948) 47–71. * C.C. Richardson, "The Date and Setting of the Apostolic Tradition of Hippolytus," AThR 30 (1948) 38–44. * B. Botte, "L'authenticité de la Tradition Apostolique de s. Hippolyte," RTAM 16 (1949) 177–85. * Dix, 221–24. * B. Capelle, "Hippolyte de Rome," RTAM 17 (1950) 145–74; repr. in *Travaux liturgiques*, vol. 2 (Louvain, 1962) 31–60. * B. Capelle, "A propos d'Hippolyte de Rome," RTAM 19 (1952) 193–202; repr. in *Travaux liturgiques*, vol. 2 (Louvain, 1962) 61–70.* H. Elfers, "Neue Untersuchungen über die Kirchenordnung Hippolyts von Rom," in *Abhandlungen über Theologie und Kirche, Festschrift für Karl Adam*, ed. M. Reding (Düsseldorf, 1952) 169–211. * O. Casel, "Die Kirchenordnung Hippolyts von Rom," ALW 2 (1952) 115–30. * B. Botte, "Le texte de la Tradition Apostolique," RTAM 22 (1955) 161–72. * G. Kretschmat, "Bibliographie zu Hippolyt v. Rom," JLH 1 (1955) 90–95. * A. Salles, "La 'Tradition Apostolique', est-elle un témoin de la liturgie romaine?" RHE 148 (1955) 181–213. * J.M. Hanssens, *La liturgie d'Hippolyte: ses documents, son titulaire, ses origines et son caractère*, OCA 155 (Rome, 1959). * J. Jungmann, *The Early Liturgy: To the Time of Gregory the Great*, University of Notre Dame Liturgical Studies 6 (Notre Dame, 1959) 52–86. * J.M. Hanssens, "La liturgie d'Hippolyte: assentiment et dissentiments," Greg 42 (1961) 290–302. * B. Botte, "La scoperta della 'Tradizione apostolica,'" JucL 1 (1963) 65–75. * B. Botte, "La 'Tradizione Apostolica' di sant' Ippolito," JucL 1 (1963) 133–37. * J. Magne, "La prétendu Tradition Apostolique d'Hippolyte de Rome s'appelait-elle les 'Statuts de Saints apôtres'?" OstkSt 14 (1965) 36–67. * B. Botte, "A propos de la 'Tradition Apostolique,'" RTAM 33 (1966) 177–86. * M. Cutrone, "The Apostolic Tradition of Hippolytus of Rome," ABR 19 (1968) 492–514. * *Ricerche su Ippolito*, Studia Ephemeridis Augustinianum 13 (Rome, 1977). * P. Bradshaw, C. Whitaker, and G. Cuming, *Essays on Hippolytus*, Grove Liturgical Study 15 (Bramcote, Nottingham, 1978). * G. Kretschmar, "La liturgie ancienne dans les recherches historiques actuelles," LMD, no. 149 (1982) 57–90. * A.-G. Martimor, "Nouvel examen de la 'Tradition Apostolique' d'Hippolyte," BLE 88 (1987) 5–25. * A. Gelston, "A Note on the Text of the 'Apostolic Tradition' of Hippolytus," JThSt, n.s., 39 (1988) 112–17. * M. Metzger, "Nouvelles perspectives pour la prétendu 'Tradition Apostolique,'" EOr 5:3 (1988) 241–59. * P. Le Roy, "La Tradition Apostolique d'Hippolyte," PrO 84 (1991) 20–31. * A.-G. Martimort, "Encore Hippolyte et la 'Tradition Apostolique,'" BLE 92 (1991) 133–37. * M. Metzger, "A propos des réglements ecclésiastiques et de la prétendue 'Tradition Apostolique,'" RevSR 66 (1992) 249–61. * StLit, 87–89. * M. Metzger, "Enquêtes autour de la prétendu 'Tradition Apostolique,'" EOr 9 (1992) 7–36. * A. Brent, *Hippolytus and the Roman Church in the Third Century* (Leiden, 1995). * A.-G. Martimort, "Encore Hippolyte et la 'Tradition Apostolique,'" BLE 97 (1996) 275–79. * A. Stewart-Sykes, *Hippolytus: On the Apostolic Tradition*, Popular Patristic Series (Crestwood, NY, 2001). * P. Bradshaw and others, *The Apostolic Tradition: A Commentary*, Hermeneia Series (Minneapolis, 2002). * J. Baldovin, "Hippolytus and the *Apostolic Tradition*: Recent Research and Commentary," TS 64 (2003) 520–42.

INITIATION

P. Galtier, "La consignation à Carthage et à Rome," RSR 2 (1911) 350–83. * P. Galtier, "La consignation dans les églises d'Occident," RHE 13 (1912) 257–301. * P. Galtier, "Onction et confirmation," RHE 13 (1912) 467–76. * P. Galtier, "La 'Tradition Apostolique' d'Hippolyte, particularités et initiatives liturgiques," RSR 13 (1923) 511–27. * R.H. Connolly, "On the Text of the Baptismal Creed of Hippolytus," JThSt 25 (1924) 131–39. * B. Capelle, "Le symbol romain au second siècle," RB 39 (1927) 33–45. * F.J. Dölger, "Der Kuss im Tauf- und Firmungsrituel nach Cyprian von Karthage und Hippolyt von Rom," AC 1 (1929) 186–96. * B. Capelle, "Les origines du symbol romain," RTAM 2 (1930) 5–20. * B. Capelle, "L'introduction du catéchumenat à Rome," RTAM 5 (1933) 129–54. * D. van den Eynde, "Baptême et confirmation," RSR 27 (1937) 196ff. * F.X. Steinmetzer, *Empfangen vom Heiligen Geiste: eine Auseinandersetzung mit der Antike* (Prague, 1938). * H.J. Carpenter, "The Birth from the Holy Spirit and the Virgin in the Old Roman Creed," JThSt 40 (1939) 31–36. * D. van den Eynde, "Notes sur les rites postbaptismaux dans les Eglises d'Occident," Ant 14 (1939) 257–76. * B. Welte, *Die postbaptismale Salbung, ihr symbolischer Gehalt und ihre sakramentale Zugehöigkeit nach den Zeugnissen der alten Kirche*, FThSt 51 (Freiburg i. B., 1939). * H. Elfers, "Gehöt die Salbung mit Chrisma im ältesten abendländischen Initiationsritues zur Taufe oder zur Firmung?" ThGl 34 (1942) 334–41. * G. Dix, *The Theology of Confirmation in Relation to Baptism* (Westminster, 1946). * R.H. Connolly, "The Theology of Confirmation in Relation to Baptism," CR 27 (1947) 282–84. * W.G. van Unnik, "Les cheveux défaits des femmes baptisées: un rite de baptême dans l'ordre ecclésiastique d'Hippolyte," VC 1 (1947) 77–100. * P. Nautin, *Je crois à l'Esprit dans la saint Eglise pour la résurrection de la chair* (Paris, 1947). * Ph. M. Ménound, "Le baptême des enfants dans l'Eglise ancienne," VC 2 (1948) 15–26. * J.N.D. Kelly, *Early Christian Creeds* (Oxford, 1950) 113–19. * J.H. Crehan, *Early Christian Baptism and the Creed* (London, 1950) 159–71. * B. Botte, "Note sur le symbole baptismal de s. Hippolyte," in *Mélanges de J. Ghellinck*, vol. 1 (Gembloux, 1951) 189–200. * A. Salles, "Les plus anciennes liturgies du baptême," BLE 54 (1953) 240–42. * C.M. Edsman, "A Typology of Baptism in Hippolytus," SP 2, TU 64 (Berlin, 1957) 35–40. * E. Ferguson, "Baptism from the Second to the Fourth Century," ResQ 1 (1957) 185–97. * R.J.S. Werblowsky, "On the Baptismal Rite according to St. Hippolytus," SP 2 (1957) 93–105. * P.-M. Gy, "Histoire liturgique du sacrement de confirmation," LMD, no. 58 (1959) 135–45. * J. Jungmann, *The Early Liturgy: To the Time of Gregory the Great*, University of Notre Dame Liturgical Studies 6 (Notre Dame, 1959) 74–86. * A.-G. Martimort, "La 'Tradition Apostolique' d'Hippolyte et le rituel baptismal," BLE 60 (1959) 57–62. * B. Botte, "Sacramentum Catechumenorum," QLP 43 (1962) 322–30; repr. QL 80 (1999) 250–57. * T. Marsh, "The History and Significance of the Post-Baptismal Rite," ITQ 29 (1962) 175–206. * B. Neunheuser, *Baptism and Confirmation* (St. Louis, 1964) 56–59. * D.L. Holland, "The Earliest Text of the Old Roman Symbol: A Debate with Hanz Lietzmann and J.N.D. Kelly," CH 34 (1965) 262–81. * D.L. Holland, "The Baptismal Interrogation concerning the Holy Spirit in Hippolytus," SP 10 (1970) 360–65. * B. Botte, "Le symbolisme de l'huile et de l'onction," QL 62 (1981) 196–208; repr. QL 80 (1999) 269–81. * G. Cuming, "The Post-Baptismal Prayer in the 'Apostolic Tradition': Further Considerations," JThSt, n.s., 39 (1988) 117–19. * E.A. Leeper, "From Alexandria to Rome: The Valentinian Connection to the Incorporation of Exorcism as a Prebaptismal Rite," VC 44 (1990) 6–24. * C. Munier, "Initiation chrétienne et rites d'onction (IIe–IIIe siècles)," RSR 64 (1990) 115–25. * R. Gounelle,

"Le baptême aux temps patristiques: le cas de la 'Tradition Apostolique,'" ETR 70 (1995) 179–89. * W. Kinzig, C. Markschies, and M. Vinzent, *Tauffragen und Bekenntnis: Studien zur sogenannten "Tradition Apostolica," zu den "Interrogationes de fide" und zum "Römischen Glaubensbekenntnis."* Arbeiten zur Kirchengeschichte 74 (Berlin and New York, 1998). * M.E. Johnson, "The Problem of Creedal Formulae in the *Traditio Apostolica*," EOr 21 (2005) 12–18.

EUCHARIST

P. Batiffol, "Une prétendue anaphore apostolique," RBibl 13 (1916) 23–32. * S. Salaville, "Un text romain du Canon de la Messe au début du IIIe siècle," EO 21 (1921) 79–85. * R. Devreesse, "La prière eucharistique de s. Hippolyte," *La vie et les arts liturgiques* 8 (1921–22) 393–97, 448–53. * R.H. Connolly, "On the Meaning of 'Epiclesis,'" DR (1923) 28–43. * R.H. Connolly, "On the Meaning of ἐπίκλησις: A Reply," JThSt 25 (1924) 337–64. * J.B. Thibaut, *La liturgie romaine* (Paris, 1924) 57–80. * J.M. Frochisse, "A propos des origines du jeûne eucharistique," RHE 28 (1932) 594–609. * H. Lietzmann, *Messe und Herrenmahl*, Arbeiten zur Kirchengeschichte 8 (Bonn, 1935–37) 26–31. * O. Cullmann, "La signification de la sainte Cène dans le christianisme primitif," RHPR 16 (1936) 1–22. * A. Arnold, *Der Ursprung des christlichen Abendmahles*, FThSt 45 (Freiburg, 1937). * W.H. Frere, *The Anaphora or Great Eucharistic Prayer* (London, 1938). * R.H. Connolly, "The Eucharistic Prayer of Hippolytus," JThSt 39 (1938) 350–69. * G. Ellard, "Bread in the Form of a Penny," TS 4 (1943) 319–46. * G.V. Jourdan, "Agape or Lord's Supper: A Study of Certain Passages in the Canons of Hippolytus," *Hermathena* 64 (1944) 32–43. * B. Botte, "L'épiclèse de l'anaphore d'Hippolyte," RTAM 14 (1947) 241–51. * C.C. Richardson, "The So-called Epiclesis in Hippolytus," HThR 8 (1947) 101–8. * N.A. Dahl, "Anamnesis: mémoire et commémoration dans le christianisme primitif," STh 1 (1947) 69–95. * D. van den Eynde, "Nouvelle trace de la 'Tradition Apostolica' d'Hippolyte dans la liturgie romaine," in *Miscellanea Mohlberg*, vol. 1 (Rome, 1948) 407–11. * C.C. Richardson, "A Note on the Epiclesis in Hippolytus and the 'Testamentum Domini,'" RTAM 15 (1948) 357–59. * C. Callewaert, "Histoire positive du canon romain: une épiclèse à Rome?" SE 2 (1949) 95–110. * E.C. Ratcliff, "The Sanctus and the Pattern of the Early Anaphora I," JEH 1 (1950) 29–36, 125–34; repr. in *E.C. Ratcliff: Liturgical Studies*, ed. A.H. Couratin and D. Tripp (London, 1976) 18–40. * C.A. Bouman, "Variants in the Introduction to the Eucharistic Prayer," VC 4 (1950) 94–115. * B. Botte, "L'épiclèse dans les liturgies syriennes orientales," SE 6 (1954) 48–72. * J.A. Jungmann, *The Early Liturgy: To the Time of Gregory the Great*, University of Notre Dame Liturgical Studies 6 (Notre Dame, 1959) 64–73. * A. Orbe, "El enigma de Hipólito y su Liturgia," Greg 41 (1960) 284–92. * J.-D. Benoît, "Les liturgies eucharistiques de l'Eglise romaine et des Eglises de la Réforme," ETR 37 (1962) 3–39. * B. Poschmann, *Penance and the Anointing of the Sick* (St. Louis, 1964) 51–53. * B. Botte, "Tradition Apostolique et canon romain," LMD 87 (1966) 52–61. * B. Botte, "'Extendit manus suas cum pateretur,'" QLP 49 (1968) 307–8. * E. Moeller, "Le première des nouvelles prières eucharistiques," QLP 49 (1968) 219–21. * E.J. Lengeling, "Hippolyt von Rom und die Wendung 'extendit manus suas cum pateretur,'" QLP 50 (1969) 141–44. * W. Rordorf, "Le sacrifice eucharistique," TZ 25 (1969) 335–53. * M.A. Smith, "The Anaphora of *Apostolic Tradition* Re-considered," SP 10 (1970) 426–30. * L. Bouyer, *Eucharist: Theology and Spirituality of the Eucharistic Prayer* (Notre Dame, 1970) 158–82. * R.D. Richardson, "Supplementary Essay to H. Lietzmann," *Mass and Lord's Supper* (Leiden, 1979) 434–39. * B. Botte, "Adstare coram

te et tibi ministrare," QL 63 (1982) 223–26. * R. Grove, "'Terminum figat': Clari-
fying the Meaning of a Phrase in the Apostolic Tradition," OCP 48 (1982) 431–34.
* E. Mazza, "Omilie pasquali e Birket-ha-Mazon: fonti dell'Anafora di Ippolito?"
EphL 97 (1983) 409–81. * P. McGoldrick, "The Holy Spirit and the Eucharist," ITQ
50 (1983–84) 48–66. * P.G. Cobb, "The Apostolic Tradition of Hippolytus," in StLit,
213–16. * C.A. Bobertz, "The Role of Patron in the 'Cena Dominica' of Hippolytus'
'Apostolic Tradition,'" JThSt, n.s., 44 (1993) 170–84. * J. Driscoll, "Uncovering the
Dynamic Lex-orandi-lex-credendi in the Anaphora of the Apostolic Tradition of
Hippolytus," EOr 18 (2001) 327–64.

ORDERS/MINISTRY

Th. Schermann, *Ein Weiherituale der römischen Kirche am Schlusse des ersten Jahrhunderts* (Munich, 1913). * W.H. Frere, "Early Ordination Services," JThSt 16 (1915)
323–69. * C.H. Turner, "The Ordination Prayer for a Presbyter in the Church Order
of Hippolytus," JThSt 16 (1915) 542ff. * J.V. Bartlet, "The Ordination Prayers in
the Ancient Church Order," JThSt 17 (1916) 248ff. * A. Nairne, "The Prayer for
the Consecration of a Bishop in the Church Order of Hippolytus," JThSt 17 (1916)
598ff. * R.H. Connolly, "The Ordination Prayers of Hippolytus," JThSt 18 (1917)
55ff. * B. Botte, "Le rituel d'ordination des Statuta Ecclesiae antiqua," RTAM (1939)
223–41. * H.D. Simonin, "La prière de la consécration épiscopale dans la Tradition
Apostolique d'Hippolyte de Rome, trad. et comm.," VS 60 (1939) 65–86. * B. Botte,
"Le sacre épiscopal dans le rite romain," QLP 25 (1940) 22–32. * A.J. Otterbein,
"The Diaconate according to the Apostolic Tradition of Hippolytus and Derived
Documents," diss. (Washington, D.C., 1945). * B. Botte, "L'ordre d'après les prières
d'ordination," QLP 35 (1954) 167–79. * J. Lecuyer, "Episcopat et presbytérat dans
les écrits d'Hippolyte de Rome," RSR 41 (1953) 30–50. * J. Jungmann, *The Early Liturgy: To the Time of Gregory the Great*, University of Notre Dame Liturgical Studies
6 (Notre Dame, 1959) 59–64. * J.H. Crehan, "The Typology of Episcopal Consecration," TS 21 (1960) 250–55. * E. Lanne, "Les ordinations dans le rite copte, leurs réla-
tions avec les Constitutions Apostoliques et la Tradition de Saint Hippolyte," OrSyr
5 (1960) 81–106. * E. Ferguson, "Ordination in the Ancient Church," ResQ 5 (1961)
17–32, 67–82, 130–46. * R. Béraudy, "Le sacrement de l'ordre d'après la Tradition
Apostolique d'Hippolyte," BCE (July–December 1962) 38–39. * E.C. Ratcliff, "'Apostolic Tradition': Questions concerning the Appointment of the Bishop," SP, TU 93
(Berlin, 1966) 266–70; repr. in *E.C. Ratcliff: Liturgical Studies*, eds. A.H. Couratin and
D. Tripp (London, 1976) 156–60. * J. Lécuyer, "La prière d'ordination de l'évêque:
le pontifical romain et la 'Tradition Apostolique' d'Hippolyte," NRTh 89 (1967)
601–6. * A. Rose, "La prière de consécration pour l'ordination épiscopale," LMD,
no. 98 (1969) 127–42. * J.E. Stam, "Episcopacy in the Apostolic Tradition of Hippolytus," diss. (Basel, 1969). * W. Rordorf, "L'ordination de l'évêque selon la Tradition Apostolique d'Hippolyte de Rome," QLP 55 (1974) 137–50. * G. Kretschmar,
"Die Ordination im frühen Christentum," FZPT 22 (1975) 35–69. * J. Magne, *Tradition Apostolique sur les charismes et Diataxeis des Saints Apôtres: identification de documents and analyse du rituel d'ordination* (Paris, 1975). * E. Segelberg, "The Ordination
Prayers in Hippolytus," SP 13 (1975) 397–408. * K. Richter, "Zum Ritus der Bischo-
fordination in der 'Apostolischen Ueberlieferung' Hippolytus von Rom," ALW
17–18 (1975–76) 7–51. * G.H. Luttenberger, "The Priest as a Member of a Ministerial
College: The Development of the Church's Ministerial Structure," RTAM 43 (1976)
5–63. * C.-J. P. de Oliveira, "Signification sacerdotale du ministère de l'évêque dans

la 'Tradition Apostolique' d'Hippolyte de Rome," FZPT 25 (1978) 398–427. * E.G. Jay, "From Presbyter-Bishops to Bishops and Presbyters: Christian Ministry in the Second Century," SCJ 1 (1981) 125–62. * J. Stahl, "La typologie de l'ancient pontifical peut-elle encore nous instruire?" QL 66 (1985) 3–24.

DAILY PRAYER

B. Botte, "Les heures de prière dans la Tradition Apostolique et les documents derivés," in *La prière des heures*, eds. E. Cassien and B. Botte, LO 35 (Paris, 1963) 105–7. * D.Y. Hadidian, "The Background and Origin of the Christian Hours of Prayer," TS 25 (1964) 59–69. * P.L. Philips, "Daily Prayer in the 'Apostolic Tradition' of Hippolytus," JThSt, n.s., 40 (1989) 389–400.

OTHER TOPICS

R.H. Connolly, "The Prologue to the Apostolic Tradition of Hippolytus," JThSt 22 (1921) 356–61. * E. Hennecke, "Der Prolog zur 'Apostolischen Ueberlieferung' Hippolyts," ZNW 22 (1923) 144–46. * E. Jungklaus, *Die Gemeinde Hippolyts dargestellt nach seiner Kirchenordnung*, TU 46 (Leipzig, 1928). * D. Van den Eynde, "Nouvelle trace de la 'Traditio Apostolica' d'Hippolyte dans la liturgie romaine," in *Miscellanea Liturgica in Honorem L. Cuniberti Mohlberg*, vol. 1 (Rome, 1948) 407–11. * M. Richard, "Comput et chronographie chez s. Hippolyte," MSR 7 (1950) 237–68; 8 (1951) 19–51. * J.B. Bauer, "Die Fruchtesegnung in Hippolyts Kircheordnung," ZKTh 13 (1916) 71–75. * E. Hennecke, "Hippolyts Schrift 'Apostolische Ueberlieferung über Gnadengaben,'" *Harnackehrung* (Leipzig, 1921) 159–82. * K. Müller, "Kleine Beiträge zur Kirchengeschichte 6, Hippolyts Ἀποστολικὴ παράδοσις und die Canones Hippolyti," ZNW 23 (1924) 214–47. * K. Müller, "Noch einmal Hippolyts Ἀποστολικὴ παράδοσις," ZNW 28 (1929) 273–305. * J. Blanc, "Lexique comparé des versions de la 'Tradition Apostoloque' de s. Hippolyte," RTAM 22 (1955) 173–92. * B. Botte, "Les plus anciennes collections canoniques," ORSyr 5 (1960) 331–50. * B. Botte, "Un passage difficile de la Tradition Apostolique sur le signe de la croix," RTAM 27 (1960) 5–19. * R. Segelberg, "The Benedictio Olei in the Apostolic Tradition of Hippolytus," OC 48 (1964) 268–81. * B. Botte, "Christian People and Hierarchy in the Apostolic Tradition of St. Hippolytus," in *Roles in the Liturgical Assembly*, ed. A.M. Triaca, trans. M.J. O'Connell (New York, 1981) 61–72. * M.E. Johnson, "The Problem of Creedal Formulae in the 'Traditio Apostolica,'" EOr 22 (2005) 159–75.

1. Prologue

We have written down what was necessary concerning the spiritual gifts which God, from the beginning, granted the human race according to his divine will, presenting to himself the image[1] that humankind lost.   614

And now, strengthened by our love for all the holy ones, we come to what is essential in the tradition that is to exist in the churches so that those who are well-instructed may retain the tradition that has come down to the present, by following our explanation of it, and so that they might be strengthened by knowing it.   615

In light of the failure or error which was recently produced by ignorance, and was caused by ignorant people, the Holy Spirit confers perfect   616

---

1. See Gen 1:26–27.

grace on those who believe correctly so that the Church's leaders might
know how they should teach and protect all things.

2. Bishops

617   The man to be ordained a bishop is to be chosen by all the people and is
to lead a blameless life. When he has been selected and when the people
have given their consent, they gather on the Lord's Day with the presbytery and with the bishops who are present. Once all have agreed, the bishops lay hands on him, while the presbyters stand by in silence.

618   All are to remain silent, praying in their hearts for the descent of the
Spirit. Then one of the bishops present, at the request of all and while laying his hand upon the man who has been made bishop, prays as follows.

3. [Prayer for the ordination of a bishop]

619   "God and Father of our Lord Jesus Christ, Father of mercies and God
of all consolation,[2] you dwell in the highest heavens and look upon the
lowly.[3] You know all things before they come into being.[4] Through the
word of your grace you have given the decrees of your Church. From the
beginning you predestined the race of the just descendants of Abraham.
You appointed rulers and priests, and you did not allow your sanctuary to
be without ministry. From the foundation of the world you desired to be
glorified in those whom you have chosen. Now pour forth the power that
comes from you, the power of the royal Spirit[5] which you have granted
to your beloved Son Jesus Christ, which he granted to your holy apostles
who established the Church in every place as your sanctuary for the glory
and unceasing praise of your name.

620   "O Father, you know the human heart. Grant that your servant, whom
you have chosen for the episcopate, may feed your holy flock and blamelessly serve as your royal priest, doing so night and day. May he always
cause you to look mercifully upon us and offer the gifts of your holy
Church. Through the Spirit of the high priesthood may he, according to
your command, have the power to forgive sins.[6] May he distribute respon-
sibilities according to your command, and may he, through the power you
gave to your apostles,[7] free us from every bond. May he please you by
his gentleness and his pure heart. May he offer you a pleasing fragrance.
Through your Son Jesus Christ. Through him glory, power, and honor are
yours with the Holy Spirit in the holy Church, now and forever. Amen."

4. The offering

621   When he has been made bishop, all are to give him the kiss of peace,
greeting him because he has been made worthy.

622   The deacons then present him with the offering, and he, imposing his
hand upon it with the whole presbytery, gives thanks together with the

---

2. See 2 Cor 1:3.   3. See Ps 113:5–6.   4. See Dan 13:42.   5. See Ps 51:12.   6. See
John 20:23.   7. See Matt 18:18.

whole presbytery as he says, "The Lord be with you." And all say, "And with your spirit." "Lift up your hearts." "We lift them up to the Lord." "Let us give thanks to the Lord." "It is right and just." And he continues as follows:

"O God, through your beloved Son Jesus Christ we give you thanks   623
because in these last times you have sent him as Savior, Redeemer, and messenger of your will.[8] He is your inseparable Word through whom you made all things and whom, in your delight, you sent from heaven into the womb of the virgin. Having been conceived, he was made flesh and showed himself as your Son, born of the Holy Spirit and of the Virgin. He carried out your will and won for you a holy people. He stretched out his hands in suffering in order to deliver from suffering those who trust in you.

"When he was about to hand himself over to voluntary suffering, in   624
order to destroy death and break the chains of the devil, to crush hell beneath his feet, to give light to the just, to establish the rule [of faith?], and to show forth the resurrection, he took bread, gave you thanks, saying, 'Take, eat, this is my Body which is broken for you.' Likewise the cup, while saying, 'This is my Blood which is poured out for you. When you do this, you do it in memory of me.'

"Recalling his death and his resurrection, we offer you this bread and   625
this cup. We give thanks to you for having judged us worthy to stand before you and serve you.

"We ask that you send your Holy Spirit upon the offering of your holy   626
Church. Gather it together. Grant that all who share in your holy mysteries may be filled with the Holy Spirit so that their faith may be strengthened in truth.[a] And so may we praise and glorify you through your Son Jesus Christ. Through him may glory and honor be to you with the Holy Spirit in your holy Church now and forever. Amen."

5. [Offering of oil]

If anyone offers oil, the bishop shall give thanks just as he does for the   627
offering of the bread and wine, not expressing himself in the same words, but to similar effect, as he says: "O God, by sanctifying this oil you give holiness to those who are anointed with it and who receive this oil with which you have anointed kings, priests, and prophets. May it bring comfort to those who taste it, health to those who use it."

6. [Offering of cheese and olives]

Likewise, if anyone offers cheese and olives, the bishop says the fol-   628
lowing: "Sanctify this milk which has been curdled into cheese, and also gather us into your love. Grant that this fruit of the olive tree may never

---

a. Scholars do not agree as to the authenticity of this epiclesis or its primitive form.

8. See Isa 9:5.

depart from your sweetness since the olive tree is the symbol of your abundance which you made to flow from the tree to give life to those who hope in you." And in every blessing shall be said, "Glory to you, Father and Son with the Holy Spirit in the holy Church, now and always, forever and ever."

7. Presbyters

629   When a presbyter is ordained, the bishop lays his hand upon his head, while the other presbyters likewise touch him. The bishop prays as indicated above for the bishop. "God and Father of our Lord Jesus Christ, look upon this your servant and grant him the grace and counsel of the presbyterate so that he may help and govern your people with a pure heart, just as you looked upon your chosen people and just as you commanded Moses to choose elders whom you filled with the Holy Spirit who was given to your servant. And now, Lord, grant that we may always preserve in us the Spirit of your grace. Make us, once filled with this Spirit, worthy to serve you in simplicity of heart, by praising you through your Son Jesus Christ, through whom glory and power be to you, with the Holy Spirit in the holy Church, now and forever. Amen."

8. Deacons

630   When a deacon is instituted, he is selected as indicated above. The bishop alone imposes hands, as we said. At the ordination of the deacon, the bishop alone imposes the hand because the deacon is not ordained to the priesthood but to serve the bishop, to carry out the bishop's orders.

631   He is not a member of the council of the clergy, but he administers and informs the bishop as to what is necessary. He does not receive the common spirit of the presbyterate in which the presbyters share, but the spirit given him under the authority of the bishop. It is for this reason that the bishop alone ordains the deacon, whereas all the presbyters impose hands on presbyters because the same spirit is shared by all.

632   The presbyter has the authority only to receive the Spirit, not to give the Spirit. This is why he does not ordain clerics. However, at the ordination of a presbyter he seals whereas the bishop ordains.

633   The bishop says the following over the deacon: "O God, Father of our Lord Jesus Christ, you have created all things and disposed them by the Word. Father of our Lord Jesus Christ, whom you sent to carry out your will and manifest your desires, grant the Spirit of grace and zeal to your servant, whom you have chosen to serve your Church and to present in your sanctuary the offering of him who was established as your high priest, to the glory of your name. May he serve you without reproach and in purity. May he obtain a higher degree,[9] and may he praise and glorify you through your Son Jesus Christ our Lord. Through whom

9. See 1 Tim 3:13.

glory, power, and praise be to you with the Holy Spirit now and forever. Amen."

9. Confessors

If a confessor has been in chains because of the Lord's name, do not lay the hand upon him for the diaconate or the presbyterate since he possesses the honor of the presbyterate by his confession. But if he is appointed bishop, the hand is laid upon him. But if there is a confessor who has not been led before the authority, who has neither undergone arrest nor been imprisoned nor been condemned to another penalty, but who on occasion has been derided for the name of our Lord and punished in private, if he has confessed his faith, the hand is to be imposed on him for every order of which he is worthy. 634

Let the bishop give thanks as we have indicated above. It is not necessary that he recite the same words we have given, as if he is to say them by heart while giving thanks to God. Let each pray according to his abilities. If someone can pray somewhat longer and say a solemn prayer, it is good. But if someone while praying says a short prayer, do not hinder him, provided that the prayer is sound and orthodox. 635

10. Widows

When a widow is appointed, she is not ordained but designated by being called such. If her husband has been dead for a long time, she is appointed. But if her husband is not long dead, do not place confidence in her; even if she is elderly, she is to be tested for a certain period of time. Often passions grow old with the person within whom they are found. A widow is appointed by words alone, and then she joins the other widows. But the hand is not placed upon her since she does not offer the oblation and has no liturgical function. The clergy, however, are ordained because of their liturgical service. The widow, however, is appointed for prayer, which is the common task of all. 636

11. The reader

The reader is appointed when the bishop gives him the book, for hands are not laid on him. 637

12. The virgin

The hand is not placed upon the virgin; her decision alone makes her a virgin. 638

13. The subdeacon

There is no imposition of the hand for the subdeacon, but he is named a subdeacon so that he might serve the deacon. 639

14. Gifts of healing

If someone says, "I have received the gift of healing in a revelation," the hand is not imposed upon that person. The facts themselves will show whether such a person has spoken the truth. 640

15. Newcomers to the faith

641 Those who come for the first time to hear the word are to be brought to the teachers before all the people arrive. They will be asked why they are seeking the faith. Those who have brought them will testify on their behalf as to whether they are capable of hearing the word. Their state of life is also to be examined. Does one have a wife? Is he a slave? If he is the slave of a believer and if his master permits, let him hear the word. If his master does not give favorable testimony, he shall be sent away.

642 If some are possessed by a devil, let them not hear the word of instruction till they have been purified.

643 If a man has a wife or if a woman has a husband, teach them to be content, the man with his wife and the woman with her husband. If a man is not married, teach him not to commit fornication but to take a wife in accord with the law or else to remain as he is.

16. Jobs and professions

644 Inquire as to the jobs and professions of those who are brought for instruction.

645 If someone keeps a house of prostitution, that person is to cease doing so or is to be sent away.

646 If someone is a sculptor or painter, that person is to be taught not to make idols; they are to give this up or be sent away.

647 If someone is an actor or performs in the theater, that person is to cease doing so or be sent away.

648 It is preferable that those who teach children cease doing so; but if they have no other profession, they are allowed to teach.

649 The charioteer who competes or whoever takes part in the games will cease doing so or be sent away.

650 The gladiator or whoever teaches the gladiator to fight, or the man who fights with beasts in the games, or the official connected with the gladiatorial games, must give this up or be sent away.

651 Whoever is a priest or a keeper of idols must cease doing so or be sent away.

652 A subordinate soldier is not to kill. If commanded to do so, he will not carry out the order. Nor will he take an oath. If he does not agree to this, he will be sent away.

653 Whoever holds the power of the sword or is the city's magistrate who wears the purple will cease doing so or be sent away.

654 The catechumen or believer who wishes to become a soldier is to be sent away because he has shown contempt for God.

655 The prostitute, the dissolute man, the dandy, or anyone who has done unspeakable things will be sent away, for they are impure.

656 Nor is the magician to be admitted for testing.

657 The enchanter, the astrologer, the diviner, the interpreter of dreams, the charlatan, the counterfeiter, the maker of amulets must cease or they will be sent away.

Any man's concubine, if she is his slave and if she has raised his chil- 658
dren and is faithful to him alone, will hear the instruction; otherwise she
is to be sent away. The man who has a concubine will cease doing so and
marry her according to the law; if he refuses to do so, he will be sent away.

If we have omitted anything else, the occupations themselves will teach 659
you, for all of us have the Spirit of God.

17. The length of the instruction after the examination of jobs and
occupations

Catechumens will receive instruction for three years. If someone is 660
zealous and perseveres well in the matter, the length of time is not to be
judged, only that person's conduct.

18. The prayer of those receiving instruction

When the teacher has completed the catechesis, the catechumens pray 661
by themselves, apart from the faithful. The women, whether they be members of the faithful or catechumens, stand apart for prayer in the church.
After they have finished praying, the catechumens do not extend the kiss
of peace because their kiss is not yet holy.[10] The faithful are to greet one
another, the men greeting the men and the women greeting the women,
but the men are not to greet the women. All the women are to cover their
heads with a scarf and not merely with a piece of linen, the latter not
being a covering.

19. Laying the hand upon the catechumens

After the prayer the teacher, whether a cleric or a laic, and having laid 662
the hand on the catechumens, is to pray and dismiss them.

A catechumen who is arrested on account of the Lord's name is not to 663
be anxious about the witness given. For these people, undergoing violence
and suffering death, will be justified even though not receiving the forgiveness of sin. They have been baptized in their own blood.

20. Those to be baptized

Once those to be baptized have been chosen, their way of life is to be 664
examined. While they were catechumens, did they live honestly? Have
they shown respect to widows? Have they visited the sick and performed
all kinds of good works? If those bringing them testify that each has done
these things, then let them hear the Gospel.

From the moment of their selection let the hand be laid upon them each 665
day while they are exorcised. And when the day of baptism approaches,
the bishop will exorcise each person so as to ascertain that each is purified.
Anyone who is not good or not pure is to be put aside because this person
has not heard the word with faith since it is impossible that the Alien conceal himself forever.

---

10. See Rom 16:16; 1 Cor 16:20; 2 Cor 13:12; 1 Thess 5:26.

666   Those to be baptized are to be instructed that they are to wash and cleanse themselves on the fifth day of the week [Thursday].

667   If a woman is menstruous, she is to be put aside and baptized on another day.

668   Those to be baptized shall fast on the Preparation Day [Friday]. On the Sabbath [Saturday], the bishop will gather those to be baptized in one place where they will be instructed to pray and to kneel. The bishop will lay his hand on them and bid every foreign spirit to depart from them and never again to return. And when the bishop has concluded the exorcism, he will breathe on their faces, and after sealing their foreheads, ears, and noses, he will have them stand.

669   They are to pass the whole night in keeping vigil. The Scriptures are to be read; instructions are to be given.

670   Those to be baptized will bring nothing with them except what each brings for the Eucharist. It is fitting that each person who has become worthy brings the offering at that time.

21. Conferring holy baptism

671   At cockcrow pray first over the water. The water should be flowing in a fountain or flowing down into it. Unless some necessity occurs, it is to be done in this way. But if the scarcity of water is permanent and urgent, use any water that you find.

672   The candidates remove their clothing.

673   The children are baptized first. All who can, answer for themselves. The parents or family members will speak for those who cannot. Then the men are baptized. Next the women, who have unbound their hair and removed all their gold ornaments. No one is to go down into the water with any alien object.

674   At the time appointed for the baptism, the bishop gives thanks over the oil and places it in a vessel. This is called the oil of thanksgiving. Then he takes the other oil which he exorcises; this is called the oil of exorcism. A deacon takes the oil of exorcism and stands at the left of the presbyter; another deacon takes the oil of thanksgiving and stands at the right of the presbyter. The presbyter, taking aside each of those to be baptized, bids each to renounce the devil by saying, "I renounce you, Satan, and all your service and all your works."

675   And when each has said this, the presbyter anoints with the oil of exorcism while saying, "May every evil spirit depart from you." In this way he hands the candidate, who is nude, over to the bishop or presbyter standing near the water in order to baptize.

676   A deacon likewise goes down with the candidates. When the person to be baptized has descended into the water, he who baptizes says to him or her while imposing the hand, "Do you believe in God the Father almighty?" The one being baptized says, "I believe." And immediately the baptizer, laying a hand on the person's head, baptizes a first time.

Then he asks, "Do you believe in Christ Jesus, the Son of God, born 677
by the Holy Spirit of the Virgin Mary, who was crucified under Pontius
Pilate, who died, and on the third day was raised from the dead, who ascended into heaven, is seated at the right hand of the Father, and who will
come to judge the living and the dead?" Once again the person is baptized
after saying, "I believe."

Then the person baptizing will ask, "Do you believe in the Holy Spirit 678
in the holy Church?" The person being baptized will say, "I believe" and
thus will be baptized a third time.

Then, after coming up from the water, the baptized person will be 679
anointed with the oil of thanksgiving by the presbyter who says, "I anoint
you with the holy oil in the name of Jesus Christ." And after drying themselves, they put on their clothes and enter the church.

The bishop, while imposing his hand upon them, says the following 680
invocation: "Lord God, you have made them worthy to obtain the forgiveness of sins by the bath of regeneration. Make them worthy to be filled
with the Holy Spirit. Send your grace upon them so that, following your
will, they may serve you. For yours is the glory, Father and Son with the
Holy Spirit, in the holy Church, now and forever. Amen."

He pours the oil of thanksgiving on his hand and places it on the head 681
of each person. Then he says, "I anoint you with holy oil in God the almighty Father and in Jesus Christ and in the Holy Spirit."

After signing each on the forehead, the bishop gives the kiss and says, 682
"May the Lord be with you." The person who has been signed responds,
"And with your spirit." The bishop does this with each one.

Henceforth they will pray with all the people since they do not pray 683
with the faithful till all these things have occurred. And after they have
prayed together, they will share the kiss.

Then the deacons present the offering to the bishop. He gives thanks 684
over the bread so that it becomes the representation, which the Greeks call
the "antitype" of the Body of Christ, and over the cup mixed with wine
so that it become the "antitype," which the Greeks call "likeness" of the
Blood shed for all who believe in him.

He also gives thanks over the milk mixed with honey to indicate the 685
accomplishment of the promise made to our fathers, in which God speaks
of the earth flowing with milk and honey, in which Christ gave his flesh,
with which believers, like small children, nourish themselves, since the
pleasantness of the word sweetens the bitterness of the heart.

He also prays over the water presented as an offering to signify the bath 686
so that one's interior, namely, the soul, may obtain the same effects as the
body.

The bishop is to explain all these things to those who receive. When he 687
has broken the bread and while he is presenting each of its pieces, he says,
"The bread of heaven in Christ Jesus." The person receiving responds,
"Amen." If sufficient presbyters are not present, the deacons also hold

the cups. They do so in good order: the first holding the water, the second holding the milk, and the third holding the wine.

688   Those receiving Communion taste from each of the cups while the person presenting says, "In God the almighty Father." Those receiving reply, "Amen." "And in the Lord Jesus Christ." And they say, "Amen." "And in the Holy Spirit and in the holy Church." And they say, "Amen." This is done for each communicant. When these things have been done, all hasten to do good works, to please God, to conduct themselves well, and to be zealous for the Church, doing what has been taught and progressing in piety.

689   We have handed on to you, in brief, what concerns holy baptism and the holy offering, for you have already been instructed on the resurrection of the body and on other things as written. If it is fitting to recall anything else, the bishop will privately inform them after the baptism. Unbelievers are not to know till they are first baptized. This is the white stone spoken of by John, [on the white stone] "is written a new name which no one knows except the one who receives it."[11]

22. Communion

690   On Sunday the bishop, if possible, personally distributes the Eucharist to all the people while the deacons perform the breaking; the presbyters also break the bread. When the deacon takes it to a presbyter, he presents the plate. The presbyter himself takes it and distributes it to the people with his own hand. On other days people receive according to the directions of the bishop.

23. Fasting

691   Widows and virgins will fast often and pray for the Church. Presbyters are to fast when they wish; the laity do likewise. The bishop fasts only on days when all the people do so. It may happen that someone wants to present an offering; the bishop cannot refuse. If, however, he breaks bread, he always eats the bread.

24. Gifts to the sick [b]

692   The deacon, in case of necessity and when no presbyter is present, is to give the sign to the sick with zeal. When he has given all that is necessary, according as he will have received what is distributed, he will give thanks, and they will consume it there.

693   Those who receive the gifts are to serve with zeal.

694   If anyone has received gifts to take to a widow, to a sick person, or to someone involved in the affairs of the Church, this person will deliver them on the very day they are received. But if the gifts are not delivered on that day, it is to be done on the next day, and something of one's own is to be added since the bread of the poor has remained in another's possession.

b. The text in this chapter is not always clear.
11. Rev 2:17.

25. Bringing in the lamps for the community meal

Once evening has come and when the bishop is present, the deacon   695
brings in the lamp. Standing in the midst of all faithful who are
present, the bishop gives thanks. First, he gives the greeting, "The Lord
be with you." The people respond, "And with your spirit." "Let us give
thanks to the Lord." And all say, "It is right and proper; greatness and
grandeur with glory belong to him." He does not say, "Lift up your
hearts" since this is what he says at the offering.

He then prays as follows: "We give you thanks, O Lord, through your   696
Son Jesus Christ, Our Lord, through whom you have enlightened us by revealing to us the incorruptible light. We have passed through the course of
the day and have reached the beginning of night. You fill us with the light
of day which you created for our satisfaction and so, by your grace, we
do not lack the evening light; we praise and glorify you through your Son
Jesus Christ, our Lord. Through whom glory, power, and honor be to you,
now and forever and ever. Amen." And all say, "Amen."

All rise at the end of the meal and pray. The children and the virgins say   697
the psalms.

Then, when the deacon takes the mixed cup of the offering, he says one   698
of the psalms containing the Alleluia. Then, if the presbyter so bids, again
from the same psalms. And after the bishop has offered the cup, he will
say one of the psalms with the Alleluia which is fitting to the cup, and
all will say Alleluia. When the psalms are recited, all say Alleluia, which
means, "We praise the God who is;[12] glory and praise to him who has created the whole world through his word alone." After the psalm the bishop
blesses the cup and gives pieces of the bread to all the faithful.

26. The common meal

The faithful present at the meal receive from the bishop's hand a piece   699
of bread before breaking their own bread. This is a eulogy and not a Eucharist as is the Lord's Body.

Before drinking, all should take a cup and give thanks over it. Then   700
they eat and drink in all purity. The bread of exorcism will be given to the
catechumens, and each will offer a cup.

27. Catechumens are not to eat with the faithful

A catechumen is not to sit at the Lord's Supper. But during the entire   701
meal those who eat are to remember their host; this is why they were invited to enter the host's house.

28. Eat moderately and according to need

When eating and drinking, do so moderately and not to the point of be-   702
coming drunk. In this way no one can laugh at you, and your host will not

---

12. See Exod 3:14.

be saddened by your rowdiness, but may your host desire to be judged worthy of having the saints come into his house. As the Lord says, "You are the salt of the earth."[13]

703   If someone offers to all in common what in Greek is called the *apophoreton*, accept it. But if there is enough for all to share, eat so that some remains. In this way your host can send some of it to whomever he or she desires, as from what was left over from the saints, and thus the host can rejoice with confidence.

704   During the meal the guests will eat in silence, doing so without arguing. They may only speak as the bishop allows; if he asks a question, they can answer him.

705   When the bishop speaks, each person is to observe a modest silence until he asks another question. And if, in the absence of the bishop, the faithful share a meal at which a presbyter or deacon is present, they will likewise act in a becoming manner. Each person will hasten to receive the blessed bread from the presbyter or deacon. In like manner the catechumen is to receive exorcised bread. If the laity gather by themselves, they are to behave in an orderly fashion. A lay person cannot give the blessed bread.

29. We must eat with thanksgiving

706   Each person is to eat in the name of the Lord; what pleases God is that we compete, even among the pagans, in being united and sober.

30. A meal for widows

707   If anyone invites widows to a meal, may they already be of mature age, and may they be sent home before nightfall. If one cannot receive them because of a duty to be performed for the assembly, they are to be sent home after they have been given food and wine. If they prefer, they can take some of this with them.

31. Fruits to be offered to the bishop

708   All will hasten to present to the bishop the first of the harvest as the first fruits. The bishop is to receive these with thanksgiving and to bless them. He is to name those who presented them and say: "O God, we give you thanks and we offer you the first fruits which you have given us to receive. You nourished them by your word; you ordered the earth to produce fruits of every kind for the joy and nourishment of the human race and of all animals. O God, we praise you for this and for all the benefits you have given us by adorning all creation with various fruits, through your Son Jesus Christ, our Lord. Through him be glory to you forever and ever. Amen."

32. Blessing of fruits

709   The following fruits are blessed: grapes, figs, pomegranates, olives, pears, apples, mulberries, peaches, cherries, almonds, and plums; but not

---

13. Matt 5:13.

watermelons, melons, cucumbers, mushrooms, garlic, or any other vegetable. At times flowers also are presented: roses and lilies but no others.

For all that one eats, thanks is to be given to the holy God, and glory is   710
to be given to God while one eats.

33. No one is to take any food during the Pasch before the proper hour for
eating

During the Pasch no one is to eat anything before the offering has been   711
made; those who do so will not be considered to be fasting. If a woman
is pregnant or if anyone is sick and cannot fast two days, that person is
to fast only on Saturday because of necessity, being content with bread
and water. If a person is at sea or due to some anxiety has forgotten the
day of the Pasch, upon learning of it, he or she will observe the fast after
Pentecost. For the Pasch we celebrate is not the figure—which has indeed
passed, and that is why it ended in the second month—and it is necessary
to fast when one has learned the truth.

34. Deacons are to be zealous in serving the bishop

Each deacon, with the subdeacons, will zealously serve the bishop.   712
They are to inform the bishop of the sick so that he, should he so desire,
may visit them. The sick are greatly comforted when the high priest [the
bishop] remembers them.

35. Time for prayer

As soon as the faithful awaken and arise, and before going off to work,   713
they are to pray to God and then set about their labors. If there is an instruction on God's word, they will give preference to going there and to
hearing God's word for the comfort of their souls. They will be eager to go
to the church, where the Spirit flourishes.

36. The Eucharist, as often as offered, is to be received before eating
anything

All the faithful, before eating anything else, will eagerly receive the   714
Eucharist. If they receive it with faith, even though they are given some
deadly poison, nothing will harm them.

37. Keep the Eucharist with care

Each person must take care that no unbeliever eats the Eucharist, nor   715
a mouse nor any other animal. Let it not fall and be lost. It is the Body of
Christ which is to be eaten by those who believe and is not to be treated
with contempt.

38. Nothing is to spill from the cup

You receive the cup after it has been blessed in the name of God as the   716
antitype of the Blood of Christ. Spill nothing from it, as if you scorned it,
lest an alien spirit lick it up. You will be responsible for the Blood as someone who despises the price with which he or she has been bought.

39. Deacons and priests

717   Each day the deacons and the presbyters are to gather at the place determined by the bishop. The deacons shall not neglect to assemble at a regular time unless prevented by sickness. When all have gathered, they are to teach those who are in the church. And after praying in this way, they are to go to their individual work.

40. Cemeteries

718   No one is to feel financially burdened in order to bury someone in the cemeteries since the cemetery belongs to all the poor. Nonetheless, we must pay for the work of the grave digger and the price of the bricks. The bishop, out of what has been given to the Church, will provide for those who are in that place and are in charge of it, so that those who come to these places be not financially burdened.

41. Times for prayer

719   All the faithful, men and women—when they arise in the morning and before beginning their work—are to wash their hands and pray to God, and in this way they proceed to their labors. If, however, there is an instruction on the word of God, everyone should prefer to go there because they truly believe that it is God whom they hear in the instructor.

720   Whoever prays in church can overcome the evil of the day. Whoever is pious will consider it very wrong not to go to the place where the instruction is given, especially if this person can read and if a teacher comes.

721   No one among you is to be late in going to the church, the place where instruction is given. Then the teacher will say something that is useful to each one, and you will hear what you did not know, and you will profit from what the Holy Spirit will give you through the teacher. In this way your faith will be strengthened by what you have heard. You will also be told there what you should be doing at home. Therefore each person should be eager to go to the church, the place where the Holy Spirit flourishes.

722   If there is a day when no instruction is given, each person, remaining at home, is to take a holy book and read a sufficient amount as seems profitable.

723   And if you are at home, pray at the third hour and praise God. Should you be elsewhere, pray to God in your heart, for at this hour Christ was nailed to the cross. This is why the Law in the Old Testament prescribes that the shewbread be offered at the third hour as a type of Christ's Body and Blood; and the immolation of the lamb without reason is the type of the perfect Lamb. Christ is the shepherd; he is also the bread that came down from heaven.

724   Pray also at the sixth hour. For when Christ was nailed to the wood of the cross, the day was divided, and there was a great darkness. So at that hour offer a powerful prayer, imitating the voice of him who prayed and who made all creation dark for the unbelieving Jews.

At the ninth hour say a great prayer and a great blessing to imitate the 725
manner in which the souls of the just bless the truthful God, who remembers his holy ones, and who has sent his Word to enlighten them. At this
hour, then, Christ shed water and blood from his pierced side and, giving
light to the rest of the day, he brought it to evening. This is why, when he
began to fall asleep, he fulfilled the type of the resurrection by having the
next day begin.

Pray also before your body goes to rest on the bed. But arise toward 726
midnight; wash your hands with water and pray. If your wife is present,
both of you are to pray together. But if she is not yet a member of the
faithful, withdraw to another room, pray, and then return to bed. Do not
be lazy when it comes to prayer; whoever is bound by marriage is not
impure. Those who have bathed have no need of washing again because
they are pure.[14] When you sign yourself with your moist breath as you use
the saliva in your hand, your body is made holy down to your feet. For
the gift of the Spirit and the water of the baptismal bath, when both flow
from a believing heart as if from a spring, sanctify all who have faith. And
so it is necessary to pray at this hour.

The ancients, who passed down this tradition to us, taught that at this 727
hour all creation stood still for a moment in order to praise the Lord: the
stars, the trees, the water—all stop for a moment, and the whole army
of angels which serves him praises God at this hour together with the
souls of the just. This is why those who believe should be eager to pray
at this hour. Our Lord himself testifies to this: "Behold a cry is heard in
the middle of the night. They said, 'The bridegroom is coming. Rise up to
meet him.'"[15] And he continues, "This is why you are to watch, for you do
not know at what hour he will come."[16]

Rise toward cockcrow and likewise pray. For it was at this hour, at cock- 728
crow, when Israel's children denied Christ, whom we know by faith. In
the hope of eternal light we look forward to this day of the resurrection of
the dead.

And so if you, the faithful, do these things and keep their memory, if 729
you instruct one another and set an example for the catechumens, then
you will be neither tempted nor lost, for you will always have Christ in
your thoughts.

42. The sign of the cross

When tempted, always sign your forehead in a dignified manner, for 730
it is the sign of the Passion, a sign known and tested against the devil,
provided you make it with faith and not to be seen by others, yet skillfully
presenting it as a breastplate. When the Adversary sees power coming
from the heart, and when the person who has been animated by the Word
shows within and without the image of the Word, the devil is put to flight

---

14. See John 13:10.   15. See Matt 25:6.   16. See Matt 25:13.

by the Spirit who exists within you. It is to symbolize this, by the paschal lamb which was slain, that Moses sprinkled the threshold with blood and anointed the doorsteps. And so he signified the faith we presently have in the perfect lamb. When we make the sign on our foreheads and eyes, we put to flight the one who is trying to destroy us.

43. Conclusion

731   If you receive these things with thanksgiving and the proper faith, they will bring edification to the Church and eternal life to believers. The counsel I give is to be kept by all who are prudent. For if all who hear the apostolic tradition follow and observe it, then no heretic, no one at all, will be able to lead you into error. It was in this way that numerous heresies have grown because the leaders, unwilling to be instructed by the teaching of the apostles, acted as they wanted, according to their own pleasure and not according to what is proper. If we have omitted anything, beloved, God will reveal it to those who are worthy of it, for God governs the Church so that it may reach the peaceful port.

31-B. Commentary on Daniel[†]

Dating from the year 204, the *Commentary on Daniel* is the oldest Christian exegetical work known to us.

732   I.xvi. [. . .] Like the two maid servants who accompanied Susanna,[1] faith and love accompany the Church preparing oil and cleansing agents for those whom it washes. Now what is the cleansing agent unless the Lord's commandments? What is the oil unless the power of the Holy Spirit? These are used as perfume to anoint believers after baptism. All these were once prefigured through blessed Susanna so that we believers in God might not find strange what today happens in the Church. [. . .]

733   IV.xxiii. [. . .] If we calculate the time that has passed since the creation of the world and since Adam, the problem is clarified. The first coming of our Lord, his coming in the flesh, his birth at Bethlehem, took place on the eighth day of the calends of January [25 December], on Wednesday, in the forty-second year of the reign of Augustus.[a] [. . .]

31-C. Refutation of All Heresies[††]

The *Philosophuma* or *Refutation of All Heresies,* a treatise in ten books (books II and III are lost) and once thought to have been the work of Origen

---

† Translated from *Commentaire sur Daniel. Hippolyte,* trans. and ed. M. Lefèvre, SChr 14 (Paris, 1947) 84, 187.

a. Many believe that this passage is an interpolation.

1. See Dan 13:15.

†† Translated from GCS 26:249–50.

(WEC 1:43), was written after 222 to show that the various heresies (especially those of the Gnostic variety) depend upon pagan philosophy, not upon Christian revelation.

IX.12. [. . .] That imposter Callistus,[a] having dared to propose such opinions [regarding the Logos], set up a school in opposition to the Church and taught as follows. First he came up with a way to conspire with people in forgiving their sexual sins, claiming that he can forgive all their sins. Should someone be accustomed to associate with another teacher and commit sin, these—provided they remain Christians—are told that their sins will be forgiven if they join the school of Callistus. This ruling was pleasing to many since they were afflicted in conscience and were rejected by numerous sects. Some of these, however, upon being judged by us as being ejected from the Church, became followers of Callistus and filled his school. [. . .] Little wonder that the disciples of Callistus are numerous and take joy in their numbers. The reason is that Callistus tolerates sensual sins, something Christ did not do. Despising Christ, the followers of Callistus forbid no type of sin since, in their view, Callistus remits these sins to those having good will. [. . .]

734

32. NOVATIAN

A member of the Roman clergy, Novatian was disappointed with the election of Cornelius as bishop of Rome in 281. Joining a rigorist party in regard to reconciling the lapsed, he received the episcopal office from three Italian bishops and has been called the first true "antipope." Doctrinally quite orthodox, Novatian, however, rejected the forgiveness of grave sins as well as baptism conferred by heretics. It is said that he died a martyr in 257/258. His followers were active in Rome and elsewhere down to the fifth century.

CPL nos. 68ff. * Altaner (1961) 191–93 * Altaner (1966) 170–72 * Bardenhewer (1908) 220–23 * Bardenhewer (1910) 193–95 * Bardenhewer (1913) 2:559–74 * Bardy (1930) 46–48 * Bautz 6:1047–49 * Cross 181–83 * Goodspeed 179–82 * Hamell 84 * Jurgens 1:246–48 * Labriolle (1947) 1:248–57 * Labriolle (1968) 169–75 * Quasten 2:212–33 * Steidle 62–63 * Tixeront 132–34 * CATH 9:1433–36 * CE 11:138–41 * CHECL 157–59, 214–18 * DCB 4:58–60 * DictSp 11:479–81 * DPAC 2:2436–39 * DTC 11.1:816–49 * EC 8:1976–80 * EEC 2:603–4 * EEChr 2:819–20 * LTK 7:938–39 * NCE 10:534–35 * NCES 10:464–66 * ODCC 1165 * PEA (1894) 17.1:1138–56 * PEA (1991) 8:1021 * TRE 24:678–82

V. Coucke, "De errore Montanistarum et Novatianorum," CB 33 (1933) 172–78. * H. Gützow, *Cyprian und Novatian: der Briefwechsel zwischen die Gemeinden in Rom und Karthago z. Zeit d. Verfolgung d. Kaisers Decius* (Tübingen, 1975).

---

a. Callistus: bishop of Rome 217–22.

32-A. On the Shows[†]

Found among the works of Cyprian (WEC 1:27), this treatise is a rejection of paganism and its culture. The true Christian, says Novatian, finds delight in the Scriptures, not in public entertainments and theatrical productions. The work was inspired by Tertullian's book of the same name (WEC 1:26-C).

735   5. [. . .] [That sinful man], had he been able, would have dared take what is holy with him into a brothel. Dismissed from the Lord's table and still, as is customary, carrying with him the Eucharist, he hastens to the spectacle, carrying about Christ's holy Body among the impure bodies of the harlots. [. . .]

33. INSCRIPTIONS (WEST)

33-A. Inscription of Pectorius[††]

This Greek epitaph was discovered in 1839 in an ancient Christian cemetery near Autun in southern France. It consists of eleven lines, the first seven being of a more doctrinal character (references to both baptism and the Eucharist), the last four of a more personal nature as Pectorius both prays for his mother and asks others to pray for him. The initial letters of the first five verses form an acrostic—the Greek letters ΙΧΘΥΣ.

The seven fragments on which the inscription is found date from between 350 and 400.

CPG 1: no. 1369 * Altaner (1966) 98 * Altaner (1960) 96 * Cross 199 * Jurgens 1:78–79 * Quasten 1:173–75 * CATH 1:1098–99 * DACL 1:83 * DHGE 1:83 * EEChr 2:886–87 * NCE 11:49–50 * NCES 11:54–55

C.M. Kaufmann, *Handbuch der altchristlichen Epigraphik* (Freiburg i. B., 1917) 178–80. * G. Grabka, "Eucharistic Belief Manifest in the Epitaphs of Abercius and Pectorius," AER 131 (1954) 145–55.

736   O divine child of the heavenly Fish,
keep your soul pure among mortals.
Because you received the immortal
fountain of divine water
refresh your soul, friend, with the
ever-flowing water of wealth-giving wisdom.
Take from the Redeemer of the saints
the food as sweet as honey:

[†] Translated from *Sancti Cypriani Episcopi Opera*, part 3, no. 2, ed. W. Hartel, CCL 3 C (Turnhout, 1871) 8.
[††] Translation (modified) from Quasten 1:174.

eat with joy and desire, holding the Fish
in your hands.
I pray, give as food the Fish, Lord and Savior.
May she rest in peace, my mother,
so I pray to you, light of the dead.
Aschandius, father, my heart's beloved,
with my sweet mother and my brothers
in the peace of the Fish remember your Pectorius.

33-B. *Inscription in the Catacomb of Priscilla*[†]

This third-century epigraph is found in the Catacomb of Priscilla on the *Via Salaria*, one of the oldest Roman cemeteries.

Dedicated to the departed, Florentius made this inscription   737
for his worthy son Apronianus who lived
one year and nine months and five days.
As he was truly loved by his grandmother
and she knew that his death was imminent,
she asked the Church that he might
depart from the world as a believer.

[†] Translation from J. Jeremias, *Infant Baptism in the First Four Centuries*, trans. D. Cairns (Philadelphia, 1962) 42.

Chapter VI

Third Century. East

ASIA MINOR

34. LETTER TO DIOGNETUS[†]

Dating from the late second or early third century, this letter is an apology for the Christian religion. Replying to questions submitted by an unknown inquirer, seemingly a high-ranking official—the name Diognetus being a pseudonym—the letter's author remains anonymous despite numerous conjectures (e.g., St. Justin, Quadratus, Aristides of Athens, to mention a few). The thirteenth- or fourteenth-century manuscript upon which all modern editions are based was destroyed during the Franco-Prussian War when the Strasbourg Municipal Library was burned in 1870.

Chapter v gives a moving and memorable description of Christian life. Chapters xi and xii are fragments of a sermon, written by a hand different from that of the author of the preceding chapters and appended to the letter.

CPG 1: no. 1112 * Altaner (1961) 135–36 * Altaner (1966) 77–78 * Bardenhewer (1908) 68–69 * Bardenhewer (1910) 54–55 * Bardenhewer (1913) 1:290–99 * Casamassa 217–32 * Cross 27–28 * Goodspeed 105–6 * Hamell 43–44 * Jurgens 1:40–42 * Quasten 1:248–53 * Steidle 31 * Tixeront 47–48 * CATH 3:855 * CE 5:8–9 * DCB 2:162–67 * DictSp 3:993–95 * DPAC 1:969–71 * DTC 4.2:1366–69 * EC 4:1660 * EEC 1:237 * EEChr 1:332 * LTK 3:238–39 * NCE 4:875 * NCES 4:751–52 * ODCC 483–84 * PEA (1894) 5.1:786 * PEA (1991) 3:607

A.A. McArthur, *The Evolution of the Christian Year* (London, 1953) 61–64. * T.J. Talley, *The Origins of the Liturgical Year* (New York, 1986) 123–24.

v. Christians are distinguished from others neither by country nor by 738 speech nor by clothing. Nor do they dwell in cities of their own; they use no special language; their manner of life is not singular. It is not by means of the imagination or the musings of restless minds that their teaching is to be discovered; unlike so many others, they are not champions of a human teaching. According to each one's lot, they live in both Greek and non-Greek cities; they conform to local customs for clothing, food,

---

[†] Translated from *A Diognète*, trans. and ed. H.I. Marrou, SChr 33 bis (Paris, 1997) 62–65.

and manner of life, while giving evidence of the uncommon and truly paradoxical laws of their spiritual republic.[1] They live in their respective countries but do so like temporary residents.[2] They do all that citizens are required to do and endure the hardships of foreigners. Every foreign land is their home, and every home is a foreign land. Like all others, they marry; they have children, but they do not abandon their newly born. They share the same table but not the same bed. They are in the flesh, and yet they do not live according to the flesh.[3] They pass their days upon the earth, and yet they are citizens of heaven.[4] They obey established laws,[5] and their manner of life surpasses these laws. They love everyone, and yet they are persecuted by all. They are misunderstood, and yet they are condemned; they are put to death and thereby gain life. They are poor; yet they enrich many. They lack everything; yet they abound in all things.[6] They are held in disrespect; yet in this they find glory. They are calumniated; yet they are vindicated. They are insulted; yet they bless.[7] They are wronged; yet they show respect. Doing only what is good, they are punished as if they were evildoers. Punished, they rejoice[8] as if born to life. The Jews make war on them as if they were foreigners; the Greeks persecute them; and those who detest them cannot offer any reason for their hatred.

739   VI. To be brief, what the soul is to the body, so Christians are to the world. Just as the soul is spread through all the members of the body, so Christians are in cities throughout the world. The soul dwells within the body, and yet the soul is not the body; so Christians dwell in the world, and yet they are not part of the world.[9] Itself invisible, the soul is kept a prisoner in a visible body; likewise, Christians are seen to be such in the world, but their religion remains invisible. [. . .]

35. GREGORY THAUMATURGUS

Born ca. 213 to a prosperous pagan family in Neocaesarea in Pontus on the Black Sea, Theodore (Gregory) joined his brother, Athenodorus, in going to Caesarea in Palestine, where ca. 233 he became a student of Origen (WEC 1:43). Studying philosophy and theology he converted to Christianity and at baptism replaced the name given him at birth, Theodore, with that of Gregory. After spending at least five years with Origen, Gregory and his brother returned to Neocaesarea, where both were ordained bishops, Gregory being the first bishop of that city. His apostolic endeavors were such that by the time of his death (between 270 and 275) only a few pagans remained in the episcopal city. So great was his reputation that in the years to follow numerous miracles and

---

1. See Phil 3:20.   2. See Eph 2:19; Heb 11:13–16; 1 Pet 2:11.   3. See 2 Cor 10:3; Rom 8:12–13.   4. See Phil 3:20; Heb 13:14.   5. See Rom 13:1; Titus 3:1; 1 Pet 2:13.   6. See 2 Cor 6:9–10.   7. See 1 Cor 4:10, 12–13.   8. See 2 Cor 6:9–10.   9. See John 15:19; 17:11–16.

wonders were attributed to Gregory, and thus his title *Thaumaturgus* or "Wonder-Worker." Gregory of Nyssa has left us an account of Gregory's life (crediting him with being the first to experience an apparition of the Blessed Virgin); there are three other biographies, all of a fanciful nature. Although a fair number of treatises are ascribed to Gregory, only a few appear to be authentic.

CPG 1: nos. 1763ff. * Altaner (1961) 238–39 * Altaner (1966) 211–12 * Bardenhewer (1908) 170–75 * Bardenhewer (1910) 149–53 * Bardenhewer (1913) 2:272–89 * Bautz 2:338–39 * Cross 174–76 * Hamell 68–69 * Jurgens 1:251–52 * Quasten 2:123–24 * Steidle 54–55 * Tixeront 105–7 * CATH 5:258–59 * CE 7:15–16 * DCB 2:730–37 * DHGE 22:39–42 * DictSp 6:1014–20 * DPAC 2:1719–21 * DTC 6.2:1844–47 * EC 6:1157–58 * EEC 1:368 * EEChr 1:499–500 * LTK 4:1027–29 * NCE 6:797–98 * NCES 6:524–35 * ODCC 713–14 * PEA (1894) 7.2:1857–59 * PEA (1991) 4:1211–12 * RACh 12:779–93 * TRE 14:188–91

35-A. Canonical Letter[†]

Written between 254 and 258 in response to a letter from an unknown bishop, this document offers solutions to several pastoral problems that arose from the invasion of the Boradi and Goths into Pontus and Bithynia. The letter is called "canonical" because it came to be incorporated among the legal documents of several eastern Churches. Some doubt the authenticity of Canon 11 given below, considering it a later addition to the primitive text.[a]

Canon 7. As to those made captive by the barbarians and accompanying them in their captivity; forgetting that they are from Pontus and are Christians, they have so completely become barbarians as to put to death those of their own race, doing so by means of the gibbet or strangulation; they show escape routes or houses to the barbarians who otherwise would have been ignorant of these. You are to forbid such from even being hearers until some common decision about them has been made by the holy ones who have assembled and by the Holy Spirit previous to them.

740

Canon 8. As to those who have been so bold as to invade the houses of others; if they have been put on trial and convicted, they are to be considered unworthy to even be hearers; but if they declare themselves and make restitution, they are to be placed among those penitents who leave with the catechumens.

741

Canon 9. As to those who have found anything discarded by the barbarians, whether out in an open field or in their own houses; if they have

742

[†] Translated from PG 10:1039–48.
a. See Jurgens 1:252.

been put on trial and convicted, they should also be placed under the same class of penitents. But if they have declared themselves and made restitution, they should be deemed fit for prayer.[b]

743   Canon 11. Weeping is done outside the gate of the church. The sinners, standing there, are to request the faithful who are entering to offer prayers on their behalf. Hearing takes place inside the gate, on the porch where sinners should stand till the catechumens depart, and then they also leave, "for they are to hear the Scriptures and the teaching," it is said, "and then be sent out as being considered unfit for prayer."[c] Subjection is when sinners stand within the gate of the temple and leave together with the catechumens. Assembly is when a person is associated with the faithful and is not to depart with the catechumens. Finally, there is participation in the sacraments.

36. PHOS HILARON[†]

Originating in the third, perhaps second, century, this short hymn, regarded by Basil the Great (WEC 2:**67**) as ancient (*On the Holy Spirit* 73), was used to accompany the lighting of the lamps and has long been sung during the evening office in the East. The text, addressed to Christ, includes a trinitarian doxology.

CPG 1: no. 1355 * Jurgens 1:46 * Quasten 1:159 * DPAC 2:2777 * EEC 2:685 * EEChr 2:919 * ODCC 1283

R.R. Smothers, "Phos Hilaron," RSR 19 (1929) 266–83. * A. Tripolitis, "Phos Hilaron: Ancient Hymn and Modern Enigma," VC 24 (1970) 189–96.

744   Serene light of the Holy Glory
            Of the Father Everlasting
                Jesus Christ:
            Having come to the setting of the sun,
            And seeing the evening light
            We praise the Father and the Son
            and the Holy Spirit of God.
            It behooveth to praise Thee
            At all times with holy songs,
            Son of God, who has given life;
            Therefore the world does glorify Thee.

---

b. Does this refer to a prayer over the penitents, a prayer at the conclusion of the Liturgy of the Word, or to the eucharistic prayer?

c. Perhaps referring to an older canon?

† Translation (modified) from ANF 2:298.

37. INSCRIPTIONS

37-A. Inscription of Abercius[†]

Discovered in 1883 near Hieropolis in Phrygia Salutaris (today Pamukkale in Turkey) were two fragments from an ancient funeral inscription. Assisted by other material, scholars were able to arrive at the full text of the epitaph of twenty-two verses.

The author of the inscription is a certain Abercius, formerly believed by some to be a pagan but now generally acknowledged to be Abercius Marcellinus, the Catholic bishop of Hieropolis. The text is highly symbolic with veiled references, a common practice during times of persecution.

CPG 1: no. 1368 * Altaner (1961) 95–96 * Altaner (1966) 97–98 * Cross 198–99 * Jurgens 1:77–78 * Quasten 1:171–73 * Steidle 258 * CATH 1:34–35 * CE 1:40–41 * DACL 1.1:66–87 * DCB 1:5 * DHGE 1:104–6 * DTC 1.1:58–66 * EC 1:69–72 * EEChr 1:5 * LTK 1:46–47 * NCE 1:18–19 * NCES 1:2 * ODCC 5 * RACh 1:12–17

G. Grabka, "Eucharistic Belief Manifest in the Epitaphs of Abercius and Pectorius," AER 131 (1954) 145–55.

1. The citizens of an eminent city, I made this [tomb]   745
2. In my lifetime, that I might have here a resting-place for my body.
3. Abercius by name, I am a disciple of the chaste shepherd,
4. Who feedeth his flocks of sheep on mountains and plains,
5. Who has great eyes that look on all sides.
6. He taught me . . . faithful writings.
7. He sent me to Rome, to behold a kingdom
8. And to see a queen with golden robe and golden shoes.
9. There I saw a people bearing the splendid seal.[a]
10. And I saw the plain of Syria and all the cities, even Nisibis,
11. Having crossed the Euphrates. And everywhere I had associates
12. Having Paul as a companion, everywhere faith led the way
13. And set before me for food the fish from the spring[b]
14. Mighty and pure, whom a spotless Virgin caught,
15. And gave this to friends to eat, always
16. Having sweet wine and giving the mixed cup with bread.
17. These words, I, Abercius, standing by, ordered to be inscribed.
18. In truth, I was in the course of my seventy-second year.
19. Let him who understands and believes this pray for Abercius.
20. But no man shall place another tomb upon mine.

[†] Translation from Quasten 1:172.
a. Seal: namely, baptism.
b. Fish from the spring: namely, Christ.

21. If one do so, he shall pay to the treasury of the Romans two thousand pieces of gold,

22. And to my beloved fatherland Hieropolis, one thousand pieces of gold.

SYRIA

38. *DIDASCALIA OF THE APOSTLES*†

The *Didascalia Apostolorum* or, according to its Syriac translation, the *Catholic Teaching of the Twelve Apostles and Holy Disciples of Our Redeemer,* was originally written in Greek, although only fragments in that language survive. The full text is available in a Syriac translation, which perhaps was redacted in the fourth century. About two-fifths of the work exist in Latin, and are contained in a late fourth-century or early fifth-century palimpsest found at Verona. The document also exists in Arabic, Ethiopic, and Coptic translations.

The *Didascalia* most probably dates from the third century and is the work of an unknown author, certainly a bishop and perhaps a physician. The locale of its composition is generally regarded as northern Syria, perhaps in the vicinity of Antioch. Treating various members of the Church (bishops, deacons, deaconesses, etc.) and several liturgical (baptism, penance) and ascetic (fasting) practices, the author addresses Christians living in a Jewish milieu and warns them against following Jewish practices. His treatise is not theological but practical; lacking good organization, it contains doublets and even contradictions.

The author uses a familiar literary technique of the time, ascribing the work to the apostles together with Paul and James. The *Didascalia* utilizes former documents (e.g., the *Didache,* the *Acts of Paul,* the Gospel of Peter, etc.) and may have undergone several recensions; in turn, it forms the basis of books I through VI of the *Apostolic Constitutions* (WEC 2:77).

CPG 1: no. 1738 * Altaner (1961) 56–57 * Altaner (1966) 84–85 * Bardenhewer (1908) 168–70 * Bardenhewer (1910) 146–47 * Bardenhewer (1913) 2:255–62 * Bardy (1929) 65–66 * Cross 96–97 * Hamell 67 * Quasten 2:147–52 * Steidle 269 * Tixeront 214 * CATH 3:749–50 * CE 4:781–82 * DACL 4.1:800–802 * DDC 4:1218–24 * DictSp 3:863–65 * DPAC 1:948–49 * DTC 4.1:734–48 * EC 4:1565–66 * EEC 1:235 * EEChr 1:329 * LTK 3:210–11 * NCE 4:860 * NCES 4:437–38 * ODCC 479 * PEA (1894) 5.1:394

TEXTS AND TRANSLATIONS

P.A. de Lagarde, *Didascalia Apostolorum Syriace* (Leipzig, 1854). * E. Hauler, *Didascaliae Apostolorum Fragmenta Veronensia Latina* (Leipzig, 1900). * M. Gibson, *Horae Semiticae,* vol. 1, *The Didascalia Apostolorum in Syriac* (London, 1903). * M. Gibson, *Horae Semiticae,* vol. 2, *The Didascalia Apostolorum in English* (London, 1903). *

† Translation based upon the text given by F.X. Funk, *Didascalia et Constitutiones Apostolorum,* vol. 1 (Paderborn, 1906). Numbers in brackets [ ] give the numbering found in the same volume.

H. Anchelis and F. J. Flemming, *Die syriache Didascalia übersetz und erklärt*, TU 25, 2 (Leipzig, 1904) [German]. * F.X. Funk, *Didascalia et Constitutiones Apostolorum*, vol. 1 (Paderborn, 1905). * F. Nau, *La Didascalie des douze apôtres*, 12th ed. (Paris, 1912) [French]. * J.M. Harden, *The Ethiopic Didascalia Translated* (New York and London, 1920) [English]. * R.H. Connolly, *Didascalia Apostolorum: The Syriac Version Translated and Accompanied by the Verona Latin Fragments* (Oxford, 1929) [English]. * J. Quasten, *Monumenta Eucharistica et Liturgica Vetustissima* (Bonn, 1937) 34–36 [Latin]. * Tidner, *Didascaliae Apostolorum Canonum Ecclesiasticorum Traditionis Apostolicae Versiones Latinae*, TU 75 (Berlin, 1963). * A. Vööbus, *The Didascalia Apostolorum in Syriac*, CSCO 401–2, 407–8 (Louvain, 1979) [Syriac with English translation]. * S. Brock and M. Vasey, *The Liturgical Portions of the Didascalia*, Liturgical Study 29 (Bramcote, Nottingham, 1982) [English].

STUDIES

F.X. Funk, *Die Apostolischen Konstitutionen* (Rottenburg, 1891). * F.X. Funk, "La date de la Didascalie des apôtres," RHE 2 (1901) 798–809. * F.X. Funk, *Kirchenge-schichtliche Abhandlungen und Untersuchungen*, vol. 3 (Paderborn, 1907) 275–84. * E. Schwartz, *Bussstufen und Katechumenatsklassen* (Strassbourg, 1911) 16–20. * P.A. Prokoschev, *Die Didascalia apostolorum und die ersten sechs Bücher der Apostolischen Konstitutionem* [Russian] (Tomak, 1913). * F. Nau, "Le comput pascal de la Didas-calie et Denys d'Alexandrie," RBibl, n.s., 11 (1914) 423–25. * J.V. Bartlet, "Fragments of the Didascalia in Greek," JThSt 18 (1917) 301ff. * R.H. Connolly, "The Use of the Didache in the Didascalia," JThSt 24 (1923) 147–57. * F.C. Burkitt, "The Didascalia," JThSt 31 (1930) 258–65. * P. Galtier, *L'Eglise et la rémission des péchés au premiers siècles* (Paris, 1932) 191ff. * E. Tidner, *Sprachlicher Kommentar zur lateinischen Didascalia Apostolorum* (Stockholm, 1938). * W.C. van Unnik, "De beteekenis van de Mozais-che wet voor de kerk van Christus volgens de Syrische Didascalie," *Nederlandsch Archief voor Kerkgeschiednis* 31 (1939) 65–100. * B. Poschmann, *Paenitentia Secunda* (Bonn, 1940) 476–78. * J.V. Bartlet, *Church-Life and Church-Order during the First Four Centuries, with Special Reference to the Early Eastern Church-Orders* (London, 1943). * J.J. Cuesta, "La penitencia medicinal desde la Didascalia Apostolorum a s. Gregorio di Nisa," RET 7 (1947) 337–62. * P. Galtier, "La date de la Didascalie des apôtres," RHE 42 (1947) 315–51. * P. Beaucamp, "Un évêque du IIIe siècle aux prises avec les pécheurs: son activité apostolique," BLE 69 (1949) 26–47. * J. Colson, "L'évêque dans la Didascalie des apôtres," VS Supplément no. 18 (1951) 271–90. * A. Jaubert, "La date de la dernière Cène," RHE 146 (1954) 140–73. * B. Poschmann, *Penance and the Anointing of the Sick* (St. Louis, 1964) 75. * K. Rahner, "Busslehre und Busspraxis der Didascalia Apostolorum," ZkTh 72 (1950) 257–81; repr. in revised form in *Schriften zur Theologie* 11 (1973) 327–59. * J. Bernhard, "Les institu-tions pénitentielles d'après la 'Didascalie,'" Mel 3 (1967) 237–67. * A. Jaubert, "Le mercredi où Jésus fut livré," NTS 14 (1967–68) 145–64. * M. Cnudde, "La réconcili-ation des pécheurs," VS 118 (1968) 292–98. * C. Vagaggini, "L'ordinazione delle diaconesse nella tradizione greca e bizantina," OCP 40 (1974) 145–89. * J. Magne, *Tradition Apostolique sur les charismes et Diataxeis des Saints Apôtres: identification des documents et analyse du rituel d'ordination* (Paris, 1975). * A. Strobel, "Die Kalenden-traditionen der syr. Didaskalia Kap. 21," in *Ursprung und Geschichte des frühchrist-lichen Osterkalenders*, TU 121 (Berlin, 1971) 325–52. * M. Metzger, "The Didascalia and the Constitutiones Apostolorum," in W. Rordorf and others, *The Eucharist of the Early Christians* (New York, 1978) 194–219. * M. Metzger, "La pénitence dans les 'Constitutions apostoliques,'" RDC 34 (1984) 224–34. * W.H.C. Frend, "Mission,

Monasticism and Worship (337–361)," in *L'Eglise et l'Empire au Ie siècle*, ed. A. Dible (Geneva, 1989) ch. 2. * C. Munier, "Initiation chrétienne et rites d'unction (IIe–IIIe siècles)," RSR 64 (1990) 115–25. * C. Methuen, "Widows, Bishops and the Struggle for Authority in the 'Didascalia Apostolorum,'" JEH 46 (1995) 197–213.

746   IV. [I.II.] 1. As to the bishop, listen to what follows. The shepherd who is appointed bishop and leader of the presbyterate in every congregation of the Church "is to be blameless in every way, irreproachable,"[1] someone far removed from all evil, a man not less than fifty years old.[2] He is to be far distant from the behavior of youth, from the lusts of the Enemy, and from the slander and blasphemy of false brethren, which they raise against many because they do not understand what God says in the Gospel: "All who utter an idle word shall answer for it to the Lord on the day of judgment since by your words you will be justified, and in your words you will be condemned."[3] 2. If possible, he should be learned, but if he is unlettered, let him be versed and knowledgeable in God's word as well as mature in years. If, however, the congregation is small and there is no man old enough, no man concerning whom testimony may be given that he is wise and suitable to be a bishop, but someone is found there who is young and of whom those present testify that he is worthy to be a bishop and who, though young, yet by meekness and restrained conduct shows maturity—let him be tested to determine whether all can testify concerning him; if so, he is to be made a bishop. [. . .]

747   IV. [II.II.] [. . .] 3. When hands are imposed for the episcopacy, he is to be tested to determine whether he is chaste, whether his wife also is a believer and chaste, whether he has raised his children in the fear of God, whether he has admonished and taught them, whether his household fears, reverences, and obeys him. For if his household in the flesh resists him and refuses to obey him, how will those outside his household become his and subject themselves to him?

748   IV. [II.IV.] 1. May he be generous; may he love orphans, widows, the poor, and strangers. May he be quick to minister, and may he be constant in service; he should afflict his own soul and not be the one who is put to confusion. He is to know who is more worthy to receive. 2. If there is a widow who has something or is able to nourish herself with what is necessary for bodily sustenance, and if there is another who, though not a widow, is in want either due to sickness or the rearing of children or bodily infirmity, then he should extend his hand to the latter. However, should someone be dissolute or drunk or idle and is in need of bodily nourishment, this person is not worthy of almsgiving or of the Church.

749   IV. [II.V.] 1. The bishop is not to show special considerations to anyone, neither deferring to the rich nor favoring anyone improperly. He should not look down upon or neglect the poor, nor should he deem himself

---

1. 1 Tim 3:2; Titus 1:7.   2. See 2 Tim 2:22.   3. Matt 12:36–37.

superior to them. 2. His food is to be meager and plain so that he can be watchful in exhorting and correcting those who are undisciplined. He is not to be crafty, gluttonous, self-indulgent, pleasure-loving, fond of choice foods. 3. The bishop is not to be resentful but rather patient when admonishing, assiduous in his teaching, constant in diligently reading the Holy Scriptures so that he may interpret and explain them accurately. Let him compare the Law and the Prophets with the Gospel so that what is said in the former may accord with what is found in the latter. [. . .]

v. [II.ix.] 1. But if the bishop himself does not have a clear conscience and accepts persons for the sake of filthy gain[4] or because of the gifts he receives and spares an impious sinner, allowing that individual to remain in the Church, [II.x.] he has polluted his congregation before God and indeed before others as well. He destroys himself and many of the neophytes, catechumens, and youth, both male and female. 2. Seeing such an ungodly man in their midst, they too will doubt and imitate him. 3. But if sinners see that the bishop and the deacons are beyond reproach and that the whole flock is pure, then they will not dare enter the congregation because they have been reproved by their own consciences. 4. Yet if they are so bold as to come to church in their obstinacy, they will be reproved and convicted by the bishop, 5. and looking upon all present, they will find no offense in any of them, whether in the bishop or in those who are with him. Then they will be confounded and will quietly depart in great shame, weeping and groaning, and so shall the flock remain pure. Moreover, once they have left, they will repent of their sins, weeping and sighing before God, and there will be hope for them. The whole flock itself, when it sees them weeping, will fear, knowing and understanding that all who sin will perish. 750

v. [II.xi.] 1. Therefore, O bishop, strive to be pure in whatever you do, and know your position before God, namely, that you are made in the likeness of God Almighty, whom you represent. So sit in the church and teach as having authority to judge on God's behalf those who sin. For to you, O bishop, the Gospel says, "What you bind on earth shall be bound in heaven."[5] 751

vi. [II.xii.] 1. Therefore judge with authority, O bishop, as God Almighty does; and like God Almighty mercifully receive those who repent. Rebuke, exhort, and teach since the Lord God, with an oath, has promised forgiveness to all sinners. [. . .] 3. He gave hope to those who sin so that upon doing penance they may obtain salvation and may not despair of themselves, may not continue in and further increase their sins but may repent, sigh, and weep for their offenses and be profoundly converted. 752

vi. [II.xiii.] 1. May those who have not sinned remain sinless so that they have no need of weeping, sighs, sorrow, and forgiveness. 2. For how do you know, O sinner, how longer your life will continue in this world so that you may repent? You do not know when you will leave this world, 753

4. See 1 Tim 3:8.   5. Matt 18:18.

whether you may perhaps die in your sins and there be no more repentance for you, for as David said, "In Sheol who shall confess to you?"[6] [. . .] 4. Therefore, O bishop, judge as follows: first, strictly, but afterwards receive sinners with mercy and compassion when they promise to repent. Rebuke and afflict them, and then assist them [II.xiv.] because of the word spoken by David, "Do not deliver up the soul that confesses to you."[7] 2. In Jeremiah he again speaks concerning the repentance of those who sin: "Shall they who have fallen not rise up? Or shall those who have been turned away not return? Why are my people turned away with shameful perversion and held fast in their own devices as they refuse to repent and to return?"[8] 3. For this reason receive without the least hesitation those who repent. Be not hindered by those who refuse to show mercy, those who say, "It is not right that we should be defiled with these." [. . .]

754   vi. [II.xv.] [. . .] 8. It is right for you, O bishop, to judge sinners according to the Scriptures, doing so with gentleness and mercy. If someone is walking by the bank of a river and is ready to slip in, you yourself—if you allow this person to fall in—have thrown and cast him or her into the river and thereby committed murder. If someone were to slip on the brink of a river and be on the verge of perishing, quickly you would extend a hand and draw that person out so that he or she not perish. Therefore act toward the sinner in such a manner that your people may learn and understand, in such a manner that the sinner may not be totally lost.

755   vi. [II.xvi.] 1. But when you see someone who has sinned, show sternness, and order that they cast out the sinner; and when the sinner has gone forth, let them show anger, take the sinner to task, and keep him or her outside the church; then let them enter and pray for the sinner. Our Savior himself also pleaded with the Father for sinners, as we read in the Gospel: "My Father, they know not what they are doing nor what they are saying. If it be possible, forgive them."[9] 2. And then, O bishop, after ordering the sinner to enter, conduct an examination to determine whether he or she has repented. And if the sinner is worthy to be received into the church, appoint days of fasting in proportion to the offense, two or three weeks, five or seven. And so dismiss the sinner after saying whatever is fitting while admonishing and instructing; rebuke such people, saying that each should stand alone in humiliation, that each should beg and beseech during the days of fast to be found worthy of the forgiveness of sins. [. . .] 4. So you are to dismiss from the church those promising to repent of their sins for a period of time proportionate to their offenses; afterwards, receive them as would a merciful father.

756   vii. [II.xviii.] 1. The bishop is to care for every person, both the sinless— that they may continue as they are without sin—and sinners—that they may repent; he is to forgive sins as is written in Isaiah, "Loose every bond of iniquity and sever all bonds of violence and extortion."[10] 2. Therefore, O

---

6. Ps 6:5.   7. Ps 74:19.   8. Jer 8:4–5.   9. Luke 23:34; Matt 26:39.   10. Isa 58:6.

bishop, teach, rebuke, and loose with forgiveness. Know that you take the place of God Almighty; know that you have received authority to forgive sins. For to you, bishops, it was said, "All that you bind on earth shall be bound in heaven, and all that you loose shall be loosed."[11] [. . .] 7. You are to give an account for many. You are to preserve those who are healthy; you are to admonish, rebuke, and afflict those who have sinned. Afterwards, alleviate them with forgiveness. When sinners have repented and wept, receive them. And while all the people are praying for those who have sinned, impose your hands on the sinners and permit them henceforth to be in the church. [. . .]

IX. [II.xxvi.] 1. O members of the laity, being the elect of God's Church, 757 you are to hear these things. The Jewish people of old were called a "Church," but you are the Catholic Church, holy and perfect, "a royal priesthood, a holy nation, a people for inheritance,"[12] the great Church, the bride adorned for the Lord God. Listen now to what was said formerly. Set aside offerings and tithes and first fruits for Christ, the true High Priest, and for his ministers, tithes of salvation since his name begins with the Decade.[a] 2. Listen, O holy and Catholic Church of God, which was delivered from the ten plagues, which received the ten commandments, which learned the Law, which held fast to the faith, which knew the Decade, which believed in the Yod at the beginning of the Name, which was established in his perfect glory. Rather than the sacrifices of the past, now offer prayers, petitions, and thanksgivings. At that time there were the first fruits, tithes, offerings, and gifts; but today there are the oblations offered through the bishops to the Lord God for the remission of sins. 3. The bishops are your high priests,[b] but the priests and levites are now the presbyters and deacons, the orphans and the widows. 4. The levite and the high priest is the bishop. He is the minister of the word and the mediator, but to you he is a teacher and your father after God; he begot you through the water. He is your chief and your leader, your powerful king. He rules in the place of the Almighty. Honor him as you honor God since for you he takes the place of God Almighty. 5. The deacon takes the place of Christ, and so the deacon is loved by you. 6. The deaconess shall be honored by you in the place of the Holy Spirit; 7. the presbyters are to represent the apostles for you. 8. You will consider the orphans and the widows to be a likeness of the altar.

IX. [II.xxvii.] 1. Just as it was not lawful for a stranger, that is, someone not 758 a levite, to approach the altar or to offer anything without the high priest, so you also shall do nothing without the bishop. 2. But if any should act independently of the bishop, whatever is done is done in vain since it shall not

---

a. The first letter of the name of Jesus in Syriac (Y) and in Greek (I) has the value of "ten."

b. See *Didache* xiii.3 (WEC 1:190).

11. Matt 18:18. 12. 1 Pet 2:9.

be accounted as work because it is not right that anyone should do anything apart from the high priest. 3. Therefore present your offerings to the bishop, doing so either in person or through the deacons, and when the bishop has received them, he will distribute them as fitting to each. 4. The bishop is to be well-acquainted with those in distress, and he is to dispense and give to each as is fitting so that one person may not frequently receive on the same day or during the same week, whereas another receives not even a little. Those whom the priest and steward of God knows to be more in distress, these the priest is to assist as may be required of him.

759   IX. [II.xxVIII.] 1. As to those who invite widows for supper, the bishop should frequently send a widow whom he knows to be more needy. And again if someone is presenting gifts to the widows, the bishop should especially send a widow who is in need. 2. What is destined for the priest is to be separated and set apart for him as is required at the agapes or at the distribution of the gifts even though he may not be present. This is done in honor of Almighty God. 3. However much is given to one of the presbyters, double is to be given to each of the deacons in honor of Christ, but twice double to the leader for the glory of the Almighty. 4. If any wish to honor also the presbyters, let them give the presbyters a double portion as is done for the deacons; the presbyters are to be honored as apostles, as counsellors of the bishop, and as the crown of the Church, for they are the moderators and counsellors of the Church. If there is also a reader, he should receive together with the presbyters. To every order, therefore, each member of the laity gives the honor that is due, doing so with gifts and honors and with the respect given by the world. 6. May the people have very free access to the deacons and not always be troubling the leader, but through the ministers, namely, the deacons, they should make known what they require. No one can approach the Lord God Almighty except through Christ. Whatever the people desire to do they should make known to the bishop through the deacons and then do it. [. . .]

760   IX. [II.xxxIII.] [. . .] 2. Honor the bishops who have freed you from sins, the bishops who by means of water gave you rebirth, who filled you with the Holy Spirit, who nourished you with the word as with milk, who strengthened you with instruction, who confirmed you with admonition, who had you partake of God's holy Eucharist, and who made you partakers and joint heirs of the promise of God. [. . .]

761   IX. [II.xxxVI.] 4. [. . .] Do not remove yourself from the church. But when you have received the Eucharist of the offering, give whatever you have so that you may share it with strangers; for it is collected and brought to the bishop for assisting strangers. [. . .]

762   X. [II.xxxIX.] [. . .] 5. Those who have been convicted of evil deeds and falsehoods are to be treated by you "as heathens and publicans."[13] 6. Afterwards, if they promise to repent—just as when the heathen desire

---

13. Matt 18:17.

and promise to do penance, saying, "We believe"—we receive them into the assembly so that they may hear the word, but we do not allow them to receive Communion till they are sealed and fully initiated; nor do we accept them for Communion till they show the fruits of repentance. By all means let them enter if they desire to hear the word so that they may not totally perish. But they are not to share in the prayer;ᶜ rather, they should leave, going outside. For they also, when they see that they are not in communion with the Church, will submit themselves, repent of their former deeds, and strive to be received into the church for prayer. Likewise, those who see and hear them leaving like heathens and publicans will fear and take warning not to sin lest they also, convicted of sin or falsehood, be sent out of the church.

x. [II.xl.] 1. But you, O bishop, shall in no way forbid them to enter the church and hear the word; for neither did our Lord and Savior completely cast away and reject publicans and sinners; he even ate with them. This is why the Pharisees murmured against him, saying, "He eats with publicans and sinners."[14] Then our Savior responded to their thoughts and murmurings, saying, "They that are whole have no need of a physician but they who are sick."[15] 2. You, therefore, should associate with those who have been convicted of sins and are sick; be involved with them; show care for them; converse with them; comfort them; support and convert them.   763

x. [II.xli.] 1. Afterwards, as they repent and show the fruits of penance, admit them for prayer as is done for the heathens. 2. And just as you baptize and then receive a pagan, so also lay the hand upon these penitents while all are praying for them, and then bring them in and let them be in communion with the Church. The imposition of the hand shall take the place of baptism for them; it is by the imposition of the hand or by baptism that the fellowship of the Holy Spirit is received. [. . .]   764

x. [II.xliv.] [. . .] 2. The bishop and the deacons are to be of one mind; you are to diligently shepherd the people, doing so with one accord. You are to be one body, father and son, for you are in the likeness of the Lord. 3. The deacon is to make known all things to the bishop, just as Christ does to his Father. The deacon should take charge of whatever he can; as to the rest, let the bishop decide. 4. The deacon is to be the ears of the bishop, his mouth, his heart, and his soul; when both of you are of one mind, then through your agreement there will also be peace in the Church.   765

xi. [II.liii.] [. . .] 3. Our Lord and Savior also said, "If you offer your gift at the altar and there remember that your brother has something against you, leave your gift before the altar and go; first be reconciled with your brother and then come, offer your gift."[16] 4. Now God's gift is our prayer and our Eucharist. If, then, you bear any ill-will against another or another   766

c. Does the author have the eucharistic prayer in mind here?
14. Mark 2:16; Matt 9:11; Luke 5:30.   15. Matt 9:12.   16. Matt 5:23ff.

against you, your prayer is not heard, your Eucharist is not accepted, and you will be found devoid both of prayer and of the Eucharist because of your anger. 5. At all times we are to pray diligently, and yet God does not hear those who bear anger and malice toward their brethren; even though you pray three times in one hour, you will gain nothing since your hostility toward another prevents you from being heard. [. . .]

767   XI. [II.LIV.] 1. Wherefore, O bishops, so that your oblations and prayers may be acceptable when you stand in church to pray, let the deacon say aloud, "Does anyone have something against another?" Now if any are found who have a lawsuit against another or an argument with another, you should plead with them and make peace between them. [. . .]

768   XII. [II.LVII.] [. . .] 2. In your assemblies, in the holy churches, come together in an orderly way; with care and seriousness appoint places for the brethren. 3. The presbyters are to be assigned places in the eastern part of the building; 4. the bishop's throne is to be located in their midst; the presbyters are to sit with him. The laymen sit in another part of the eastern section of the building. 5. And so it is that in the eastern part of the building the presbyters sit together with the bishop. Next come the laymen and then the women so that when, standing up to pray, the leaders stand in front, after them the laymen, and then the women. You are to pray facing the east since, as you know, it is written, "Give glory to God who rides upon the highest heaven toward the east."[17] 6. One of the deacons is always to stand next to the gifts for the Eucharist; another stands outside at the door and observes those who enter; afterwards, when you are offering, all the deacons are to serve in the church. 7. If any people are sitting where they should not be, a deacon who is within should reprove them and have them stand and sit in their appropriate places. 8. Our Lord compared the Church to a farm enclosure where we see the dumb animals—oxen, sheep, and goats—lie down and get up, feed and ruminate, according to their families and not being separated from their own kind. The wild beasts also walk in the mountains with their own kind. So in the church the young should sit apart if there is room for them to do so; otherwise, they stand. And the elderly are to sit by themselves. Children stand on one side, or the fathers and mothers take their children with them; and let them remain standing. Young girls are also to sit apart; but if there is no room, they should stand behind the women. The young women who are married and have children are to stand apart; the elderly women and the widows sit apart. 9. A deacon is to see that each person, upon entering, goes to his or her place and does not sit in the wrong location. A deacon is also to see to it that no one whispers, falls asleep, laughs, or nods. With order and decorum all should be attentive while in the church, always listening to the word of the Lord.

769   XII. [II.LVIII.] 1. If someone, a brother or a sister, should come from another community, the deacon questions them and, for example, learns

---

17. Ps 67:34.

whether the woman is married, whether she is a widow who is a believer, whether she is [a child] of the Church, or perhaps whether she belongs to some heretical group; he should then escort her in and have her sit in a fitting place. 2. Should a presbyter come from another community, you, the presbyters, should welcome him into your fellowship. If he is a bishop, he is to sit with the bishop, who is to accord him the same honor as given to himself. 3. And you, O bishop, should invite him to preach to your people, for exhortation and admonition given by strangers is very profitable, especially since it is written, "No prophet is acceptable in his own place."[18] And when you offer the sacrifice, let him also speak. But if he is wise and defers this honor to you and is unwilling to offer, let him at least say the words over the cup. 4. Should someone also enter while you are sitting, whether it be a man or a woman, a person enjoying some worldly honor and coming either from the same district or from another community, then you, O bishop, if you are speaking, hearing, or reading God's word, shall not defer to such a one. You are not to suspend the ministry of the word by finding them a place; remain as you are, undisturbed, and do not interrupt what you are saying; the brethren themselves are to take care of them. 5. If there is no place for such late-comers, then one of the brethren, someone who is full of love toward his brothers and sisters and who desires to honor them, is to stand and give the tardy person his or her own place. But if, while younger men and women remain seated, an older man or woman should rise and relinquish his or her place, you, O deacon, are to look over those who are sitting to determine which man or woman is the youngest; have this person stand, and have seated the person who stood and gave up his or her own place. As to the person you had stand, this individual is to stand behind his or her neighbors. In such a way others learn to make room for those more honorable than themselves. 6. But if a poor man or woman should enter, whether from the same district or from another congregation and especially if they are quite elderly and there is no place for them, you, O bishop, with all your heart are to see that there is room for them, even if you must sit on the floor. Do not be a respecter of persons if your ministry is to be acceptable to God.

XIII. [II.LIX.] 1. When teaching, command and warn the people to be faithful in assembling in the church. They are not to absent themselves but are always to gather so as not to diminish the Church, thus causing the Body of Christ to lack a member. We are not to think only of others; rather, we should think of ourselves as well, listening to what our Lord said, "Whoever does not gather with me, scatters."[19] 2. Since you are Christ's members, do not scatter yourselves from the Church by failing to assemble. You have Christ for your Head just as he promised you: "You will share with me."[20] Do not, then, neglect yourselves; do not deprive our Savior of his members; do not rend and scatter his body. Do not make

770

---

18. Luke 4:24.   19. Matt 12:30.   20. Cf. 2 Pet 1:4.

your worldly affairs more important than God's word. On the Lord's Day leave everything and hasten to the church. 3. Otherwise, what excuse before God have those who do not come together on the Lord's Day in order to hear the word of life and to be nourished with the divine food that remains forever?

771   XIII. [II.LX.] 1. You are eager to receive the things of this world, things that last only for a day or for an hour, and yet you neglect what is eternal; you are anxious about bathing, about being fed with the meat and drink for the belly, and about other things. Yet you care not for what is eternal. You neglect your soul and show no zeal for the Church, no zeal for hearing and receiving God's word.

772   XV. [III.VIII.] 1. Widows, then, should be modest; they should be subject to the bishops and the deacons. They are to revere, respect, and fear the bishop as they would God. They are not to have authority over anyone or to do anything beyond what they have been advised to do or beyond what the bishop commands. They should not visit anyone in order to eat or drink, or to fast with anyone, or to receive anything from anyone, or to lay the hand on and pray over anyone without the bishop or the deacon instructing her to do so. Should she exceed what is commanded her, she is to be admonished for having acted without being instructed to do so. [. . .]

773   XV. [III.IX] 1. That a woman should baptize or that a person should be baptized by a woman we do not approve, since this is unlawful and a great danger both to her who baptizes and to the person who is baptized. If it were lawful to be baptized by a woman, our Lord and Teacher himself would indeed have been baptized by Mary, his mother, whereas he—just like the others from the [Jewish] People—was baptized by John. [. . .]

774   XVI. [III.XII.1.] 1. Therefore, O bishop, obtain for yourself workers of righteousness as helpers assisting you in leading the people to salvation. You shall choose and appoint as deacons those who are pleasing to you from among all the people: a man for doing many of the things that are necessary, a woman for serving the women. For there are houses to which you cannot send a deacon to the women because of the pagans, but you can send a deaconess. 2. Furthermore, in many other instances the service of the female deacon is required. First, when women descend into the water, it is necessary that those doing so should be anointed by a deaconess with the oil of anointing; where no woman is present, and especially no deaconess, he who baptizes must anoint the woman being baptized. But where there is a woman and especially a deaconess, it is not fitting that the women be seen by men; but with the laying-on of the hand anoint the head only. In times past this is how priests and kings were anointed in Israel. 3. In like manner at the imposition of the hand anoint the head of each who is baptized, whether they be men or women. Afterwards—whether you yourself baptize or have the deacons or presbyters do so—a female deacon, as we have already said, is to anoint the women. A man, however, pronounces over them the names invoking the Deity while they

are in the water. When the baptized woman comes up out of the water, the deaconess is to receive her, teach her, and instruct her as to how the baptismal seal should be kept unbroken in purity and holiness. 4. For this reason we say that the ministry of the woman deacon is especially necessary and needed. Our Lord and Savior also was served by women ministers, "Mary Magdalene, and Mary the mother of James and Joseph, and the mother of the sons of Zebedee,"[21] as well as the other women. You also need the ministry of a deaconess in many other areas: she is required to go to the houses of the pagans in which there are women believers; she is to visit the sick and minister to them in what they need; she is to bathe those who are about to recover from an illness.

xvi. [III.xiii.] 1. Deacons are to resemble the bishops in their behavior;   775
however, they are to be even more proficient. Let them "not love filthy gain,"[22] but may they minister well. Their number is to be proportionate to the number of people in the local community so that the deacons may personally know and assist each person; they are to give appropriate service to the elderly women who are weak and to those brothers and sisters who are sick. A woman is to serve women, a deacon to serve men. Ready to travel and carry out the bishop's command, the deacon is to labor and toil in every place where he is sent to serve. 2. Each is to know what he is to do and to make haste doing it. And you [bishop and deacon] are to be of one mind, one purpose, one soul dwelling in two bodies. [. . .] 7. It is required that you, O deacons, visit all who are in need and inform the bishop of them; as the bishop's soul and mind, you should closely observe all things and be obedient to him.

xx. [V.ix.] 1. [. . .] Baptism forgives the sins of those who come from pa-   776
ganism and enter the holy Church of God. [. . .] 4. Past sins are forgiven to all who believe and are baptized. 5. Even though after baptism a person has not committed a deadly sin or has not been an accomplice in such a sin but has only heard or seen or spoken of it, he or she is again guilty of sin. 6. Blessed are those who leave this world by being martyred for the name of the Lord since through martyrdom "their sins are covered."[23]

xxi. [V.x.] 1. Therefore a Christian should refrain from vain speech and   777
from foul and profane words. Not even on Sunday, a day on which we rejoice and are of good cheer, is it permitted to say anything that is silly or irreligious. [. . .] 2. We must celebrate our festivals and our rejoicing, then, with fear and trembling; certainly a faithful Christian must not sing pagan songs nor have anything to do with the laws and teachings of strange gatherings since it may happen that in their singing they might utter the name of the idols, something—God forbid!—the faithful are not to do. [. . .]

xxi. [V.xii.] [. . .] 5. Believers are not to swear, whether by the sun or   778
by any other sign in the heavens or by any of the elements; they are not

---

21. Matt 27:56.   22. 1 Tim 3:8.   23. Ps 32:1.

to speak the name of the idols or utter a curse but rather they are to say blessings and psalms and words from the dominical and Divine Scriptures, which are the foundation of our true faith. This is especially true during the days of the Pasch when all the faithful throughout the world fast, 6. as our Lord and Teacher said when they asked him, "Why do John's disciples fast but your disciples do not fast? He answered them: 'The wedding guests cannot fast while the bridegroom is with them. But the days will come when the bridegroom is taken away from them, and then they shall fast on that day.'"[24] Now he is with us by his actions, and yet he cannot be seen because he has ascended to the heavenly heights and sits at the right hand of his Father.

779   xxi. [V.xiii.] 1. Therefore when you fast, you should pray and intercede for those who are lost; this is what we did when our Lord was suffering.

780   xxi. [V.xiv.] 1. Before his passion, when he was still with us and while we were eating the Passover with him, he said to us, "'Today, in this night, one of you will betray me.' And each one of us said to him, 'Is it I, Lord?' And he answered and said to us, 'He who places his hand with me into the dish.'"[25] 2. And Judas Iscariot, who was one of us, stood up and went out to betray him. 3. Then our Lord said to us, "Truly I say to you, a little while and you will leave me, for it is written, 'I will strike the shepherd, and the lambs of his flock will be scattered.'"[26] 4. And Judas came with the scribes and with the priests of the people and handed over our Lord Jesus. This took place on Wednesday. 5. For after we had eaten the Passover meal on Tuesday evening, we went out to the Mount of Olives where during the night they seized our Lord Jesus. 6. The following day, Wednesday, he remained under custody in the house of Caiaphas, the high priest. On the same day the leaders of the people gathered and took counsel against him. 7. The next day, Thursday, they brought him to Pilate, the governor. He remained in Pilate's custody Thursday night. 8. But when Friday began to dawn, "they accused him of many things"[27] before Pilate; they could prove nothing but gave false witness against him. Requesting Pilate that he be put to death, 9. they crucified him on the same Friday. He suffered, then, at the sixth hour on Friday. Now the hours during which our Lord was crucified were considered to be a day. 10. And afterwards, again there was darkness for three hours, and this was considered to equal a night. Also, from the ninth hour till evening these three hours were reckoned a day. Afterwards, again there was the night of the Sabbath of the Passion. 11. But in Matthew's Gospel it is written, "In the evening of the Sabbath, when the first day of the week was dawning, Mary Magdalene and the other Mary came to see the tomb. There was a great earthquake, for an angel of the Lord came down and rolled back the rock."[28] 12. Again there was the day of the Sabbath; and then the three hours of the night

24. Mark 2:18–20; Matt 9:14–15; Luke 5:33–35.   25. Mark 14:30; Matt 26:21–23. 26. Matt 26:31; Mark 14:27; see John 16:32.   27. Mark 15:3.   28. Matt 28:12.

after the Sabbath, the three hours during which our Lord slept and rose. 13. And so was fulfilled what he said, "The Son of Man must spend three days and three nights in the heart of the earth,"[29] as is written in the Gospel. And again it is written in David, "Behold, you have set my days in measure."[30] It was written in this way because these days and nights were shortened. 14. During the night, therefore, "when the first day of the week was beginning to dawn, he appeared to Mary Magdalene and to Mary, the daughter (mother?) of James";[31] and on Sunday morning he went to the house of Levi;[d] and then he also appeared to us. 15. He taught us, saying, "Do you fast for my sake during these days? Have I any need that you should so afflict yourselves? But it is for your brethren that you have done this; and you are to do the same during these days when you fast, and always on Wednesday and Friday, as is written in Zechariah, 'the fourth fast and the fifth fast,'"[32] which is Friday. It is not lawful for you to fast on Sunday because this day is the day of my resurrection. 16. For this reason Sunday is not included in the number of the days of the Fast of the Passion, but the days are counted from Monday. In this way there are five days.[e] And so 'the fast of the fourth, the fifth, the seventh, and the tenth months will be for the house of Israel.'[33] 17. Fast, then, from Monday, six full days, till the night after Saturday, and you shall count this as a week. 18. The 'tenth' month is mentioned because my name begins with *Yod*,[f] in which we find the beginning of the fasts. Do not fast as did the People of old but according to the new covenant which I established for you; fast for them on Wednesday since on this day they began to impair their souls by apprehending me. 19. For Tuesday night is part of Wednesday, as is written, 'There was evening and there was morning, one day.'[34] Evening accordingly is part of the following day, 20. for on Tuesday evening I ate my Passover meal with you, and during that night they took me captive. 21. But fast for them also on Friday because on this day they crucified me during their feast of the unleavened bread, as David of old foretold, 'In the midst of their feasts they set their signs, and they knew not.'[35] 22. Be steadfast in fasting during these days, especially those among you who were pagans. Because the [Jewish] People failed to obey, it was the pagans whom I freed from blindness and from the error of idols. I received them so that—through your fasting and that of those who were formerly pagans and through your service during the days when you pray and intercede because of the error and destruction of the People—your prayer and intercession may be accepted by my Father who is in heaven, as though coming from the one mouth of all the faithful on earth and so that all they did

---

d. See Gospel of Peter 14.

e. Should it rather be "six days"?

f. See note a above.

29. Matt 12:40. 30. Ps 39:4. 31. Matt 28:1; see John 20:1. 32. Zech 8:19.
33. Ibid. 34. Gen 1:5. 35. Ps 74:4.

to me may be forgiven them. For this reason I have already said to you in the Gospel, 'Pray for your enemies'[36] and 'Blessed are they who mourn'[37] over the destruction of unbelievers. 23. Know, therefore, my brethren, that we are to fast during the Pasch because of the negligence of our brethren. Even though they hate you, nevertheless, we should call them brethren. [. . .]

781   XXI. [V.XVII.] 1. It is fitting for you, my brethren, that during the days of the Pasch you make careful inquiry and most diligently observe the fast. You should begin fasting when your brethren who are from the People observe the Passover. For when our Lord and Teacher ate the Passover meal with us, he was afterwards betrayed by Judas, and immediately we began to experience sorrow because the Lord was taken from us.

782   XXI. [V.XVIII.] 1. Therefore you shall fast during the days of the Pasch from the tenth which is a Monday; at the ninth hour you will nourish yourselves with bread, salt, and water only, doing so till Thursday. On Friday and Saturday fast completely, taking nothing.

783   XXI. [V.XIX.] 1. You shall come together, watch, and keep vigil throughout the whole night with prayers and intercessions, with readings from the prophets and the Gospel together with psalms. You will do so with fear and great reverence and with diligent supplication till the third hour during the night after Saturday. At that time you break your fast. 2. It was in this way that we also fasted when the Lord suffered as a witness of the three days; we were keeping vigil, praying, and interceding due to the destruction of the People because they, erring, did not confess our Savior. 3. You also are to pray so that the Lord may not at the end remember the deception they used against our Lord; but may he grant them an opportunity for repentance, for conversion, and for obtaining pardon of their wickedness. 4. Pilate the judge, who was a heathen and a foreigner, did not agree with their wicked deeds. No, he "took water and washed his hands and said, 'I am innocent of the blood of this man.'"[38] 5. Herod ordered that he should be crucified; and so it was on Friday that our Lord suffered for us. 6. Consequently it is most fitting that you observe the fast on Friday and on Saturday; also the Saturday vigil and watch. At this time there is the reading of the Scriptures, psalms, prayers, and intercessions for those who have sinned. All is done in the expectation and hope of the resurrection of our Lord Jesus and lasts till the third hour of the night after Saturday. 7. Then offer your sacrifices; thereafter eat and be of good cheer, rejoice, and be glad because Christ, the pledge of our resurrection, has risen. "This shall be a law to you forever unto the end of the world."[39] 8. Our Savior is dead for those who do not believe in him because their hope in him is dead; but to you who are believers, our Lord and Savior has risen because your hope in him is immortal and living forever. 9. Fast, then, on Friday because on this day the People slew themselves when they

---

36. Matt 5:44; Luke 6:27.   37. Matt 5:4.   38. Matt 27:24.   39. Exod 12:24.

crucified our Savior; fast also on Saturday because on this day our Lord was asleep. 10. It is a day on which you should especially fast. [. . .]

xxi. [V.xx.] 1. Let us now observe, my brethren, that most people when 784 mourning imitate the Sabbath; in like manner those observing the Sabbath imitate those who mourn. 2. The mourner kindles no light; the same is true for the People on the Sabbath since this is what Moses commanded them. 3. Whoever mourns refrains from bathing; the same is true for the People on the Sabbath. 4. Whoever mourns does not prepare meals; neither do the People on the Sabbath, for they prepare and set the table on the previous evening; they have a premonition of mourning, seeing that they were to lay hands on Jesus. 5. Whoever mourns neither works nor speaks but sits in sorrow; likewise the People on the Sabbath since this is what was told them regarding the mourning of the Sabbath, "You shall not lift up your feet to do any labor, and your mouth shall speak no word."[40] [. . .] 10. Wherever the fourteenth Pasch falls, so observe it, for neither the month nor the day corresponds to the same season every year but is variable. And so when the People observe the Passover, you are to fast; take care to hold your vigil during the feast of the unleavened bread. 11. Yet always rejoice on Sunday, for those who afflict the soul on Sunday are guilty of sin. 12. It is unlawful, except on the Pasch, for anyone to fast during the three hours of the night between Saturday and Sunday because this night belongs to the first day of the week; but only on the Pasch are you to fast for these three hours of the night when you gather as Christians in the Lord.

xxiv. [VI.xii.] 1. When the whole Church was in peril of becoming he- 785 retical, all of us, namely, the twelve apostles, gathered in Jerusalem to consider what action should be taken. It seemed good to us—there was agreement in this matter—to write this catholic *Didascalia* in order to strengthen all of you. In it we established and decreed that you should worship God Almighty, Jesus Christ his Son, and the Holy Spirit; and that you should use the Holy Scriptures and believe in the resurrection of the dead, and that you should give thanks when using all his creation. [. . .]

xxv. [VI.xiv.] 1. To be left in the church are those who have not sinned 786 as well as those who have done penance for their sins. As to those who are still held captive by error and are not undergoing penance, we have decreed that they be expelled from the church, that they be set apart from the faithful because they have become heretics; we have ordered that the faithful avoid them completely and have nothing to do with them, whether it be in speech or in prayer. 2. They are the enemies and oppo- nents of the Church. [. . .] 7. There are those who blaspheme the Holy Spirit, those who openly and hypocritically blaspheme God Almighty, those who refuse to accept his Holy Scriptures or receive them badly due to blasphemous deceit, those who with evil words blaspheme the Church, which is the dwelling place of the Holy Spirit—all these Christ already

---

40. Isa 58:13.

condemns by the judgment to come and before they can defend themselves. "It shall not be forgiven them."[41] It is this stern sentence of con-
demnation that precedes them.

39. ACTS OF THOMAS[†]

Claiming to have been written by Thomas himself and the only "Acts"
for which we have the complete text, the Acts of Thomas come from the
first half of the third century, perhaps from the neighborhood of Edessa.
The original text was in Syriac, with later versions in Greek, Ethiopic, Armenian, and Latin. Written in a romantic and popular style designed to
entertain as well as to instruct, the work tells the story of the missionary
adventures of Thomas, who according to popular belief brought Christianity to India. Although it would seem that the writer was a Gnostic
(Christ, for example, being the redeemer who frees souls from this world),
apparently many, but not all, heterodox elements were subsequently removed so that the work would appeal to a more orthodox audience.

Altaner (1961) 77 * Altaner (1966) 138–39 * Bardenhewer (1908) 106–8 * Bardenhewer (1910) 85–86 * Bardenhewer (1913) 1:442–48 * Cross 82–83 * Goodspeed
78–81 * Quasten 1:139–40 * Steidle 280 * Tixeront 71 * CATH 1:702 * DCB 1:30 * DTC
1.1:358–60 * EEChr 1:17–18 * LTK 9:1508 * ODCC 1613

G.P. Wetter, Altchristliche Liturgie, vol. 1 (Göttingen, 1921) 89ff. * H. Lietzmann,
Messe und Herrenmahl (Bonn, 1926) 243–47. * J. Quasten, Monumenta Eucharistica et
Liturgica Vetustissima (Bonn, 1935–37) 341–45.

787   26. King Gundaphoros and his brother Gad, having been set apart by
the apostle followed him. Not at all leaving him, they also provided for
all who were begging, giving to and assisting all. They entreated Thomas
that they also might receive the seal of the word, saying to him, "Since
our souls are at rest and are eager for God, grant us the seal; for we have
heard you say that the God whom you preach recognizes his own sheep[1]
by means of the seal." The apostle said to them: "I rejoice and entreat you
to receive this seal and to share with me in this Eucharist and blessing of
God, and to be thereby perfected. For this Jesus Christ whom I preach is
Lord and God of all. He is the father of truth in which I have taught you to
believe." He ordered them to bring in oil so that by means of it they might
receive the seal. They accordingly brought in the oil and, since it was
night, they lighted many lamps.

788   27. And so the apostle arose and sealed them. And the Lord was revealed to them through a voice saying, "Peace be with you, brethren."[2]

---

41. Matt 12:32.
[†] Translated from the Greek version as given in Acta Apostolorum Apocrypha,
vol. 2, ed. R.A. Lipsius and M. Bonnet (Leipzig, 1903) 141ff.
1. See John 10:3, 14.   2. See John 20:19, 21, 26.

They heard the Lord's voice only and did not seek his likeness[3] since they had yet to receive the added sealing of the seal. The apostle, taking the oil, poured it upon their heads, anointed and perfumed them, and began to say: "Come, holy name of Christ which is above every name.[4] Come, power of the Most High and compassion that is perfect. Come, gift of the Most High. Come, compassionate mother. Come, companion of the male child. Come, revealer of the sacred mysteries. Come, mother of the seven houses so that you may be able to rest in the eighth house. Come, elder of the five members—mind, thought, reflection, consideration, reason— communicate with these young men. Come, Holy Spirit and cleanse their reins and hearts,[5] and grant them added zeal in the name of the Father and of the Son and of the Holy Spirit." Once they were sealed, a young man appeared to them. He was holding a lighted torch so that their lamps were darkened at the approach of its light. Then he left and was no longer seen by them. And the apostle said to the Lord, "Lord, your light is too great for us; we are unable to bear it since we cannot stand looking at it." When light came and it was morning, he broke bread[6] and had them share in the Eucharist of Christ. They rejoiced and were glad;[7] many others also believed and were added to their number[8] and entered the refuge of the Savior.

29. [. . .] Having blessed them, Thomas took bread and oil, herbs and   789
salt, blessed and gave this to them. However, he continued his fast since the Lord's Day was approaching. On the following night when Thomas was asleep, the Lord came and stood by Thomas' head and said, "Thomas, rise up early and bless all of them; after the prayer and the service follow the eastern road for two [Roman] miles, and there I will reveal to you my glory. Since you are leaving, many shall flee to me to take refuge, and you shall expose the enemy's nature and power." Having risen from sleep, Thomas said to the brethren who were present: "Children and brethren, today the Lord intends to do something through us. May we pray and ask him that nothing impede us regarding him, but as always may we do what he desires and wills." Having spoken in this way, he placed his hands upon them and blessed them. He broke the bread of the Eucharist and gave it to them, saying, "This Eucharist shall be for you compassion and mercy, not for judgment and retribution."[9] And they said, "Amen."

49. Thomas laid hands on them and blessed them, saying, "The grace of   790
the Lord Jesus Christ be with you forever."[10] And they replied, "Amen." The woman begged him, saying, "Apostle of the Most High, give me the seal so that the enemy will not return to me." Then he had her come close to him. Placing his hand on her, he sealed her in the name of the Father and of the Son and of the Holy Spirit; many others were also sealed with her. And the Apostle ordered his servant to set out a table, and they set out a bench that they found there. They spread out a linen cloth and placed

---

3. See Acts 9:7.   4. See Phil 2:9.   5. See Ps 26:2.   6. See Matt 26:26.   7. See Matt 5:12.   8. See Acts 5:14.   9. See 1 Cor 11:29, 34.   10. Rom 16:20.

the bread of blessing upon it. And the apostle stood by it and said, "O Jesus, you commanded us to partake of the Eucharist of your Body and Blood; behold, we dare to approach your holy Eucharist and to call upon your holy name; come, share with us."

791   50. And he began to say: "Come, perfect love. Come, communion with all humankind. Come, all who know the mysteries of the Chosen One. Come, those who share in all the combats of the athletes. [. . .] Come and share with us in this Eucharist which we make in your name and in the love in which we are one as we call upon you." Having said this, he traced a cross over the bread, broke it, and began distributing it. He first gave some to the woman, saying, "This will be for you unto the remission of sins and of firmly rooted transgressions." He gave it to her and then to all the others who also received the seal.

About the young man who murdered the maiden

792   51. There was a young man who had committed an abominable act. He approached and took the bread of the Eucharist into his mouth. Immediately both his hands withered so that he no longer could put them into his mouth. Those who were present and saw this told the apostle what had happened. The apostle summoned the young man and said to him: "Tell me, be not ashamed, my child, what did you do? Why did you come here? The Lord's Eucharist has convicted you. This wonderful gift which comes to many heals those who approach it with fear and love. But in your case it has withered away. There is a reason for this." And the young man who had been convicted by the Lord's Eucharist came and fell at the apostle's feet and prayed to him, saying: "I have done something evil, and yet I intended to do somewhat good. I was in love with a woman who lived at an inn outside the city, and she was in love with me. After listening to you and believing that you preach the living God, I together with the others came and received the seal from you, for you said, 'Whoever shall engage in polluted intercourse and especially in adultery shall not live with the God whom I preach.' Since I loved her very much, I pleaded with her, entreating her to live with me in chastity and pure conversation as you yourself teach, but she refused. When she determined not to do so, I took up a sword and killed her since I could not bear to have her living in adultery with another man." [. . .]

793   132. And Thomas began to say in regard to baptism: "This baptism remits sins; it brings forth again the light that is shed about us; it brings to birth the new person; it mingles the spirit [with the body]; it raises up in threefold fashion a new person and makes this person share in the forgiveness of sins. Glory to you, hidden one, who are given in baptism. Glory to you, the unseen power that exists in baptism. Glory to you, renewal, whereby the baptized are renewed and with affection take hold over you." Having said this, he poured oil over their heads and said: "Glory to you, the lover of compassion. Glory to you, name of Christ.

Glory to you, power established in Christ." And he commanded a vessel to be brought in, and he baptized them in the name of the Father and of the Son and of the Holy Spirit.

133. And when they had been baptized and were clothed, he placed   794
bread on the table, blessed it, and said: "Bread of life—those who eat it will remain incorruptible. Bread that fills the hungry souls with its blessing. You vouchsafed to receive gifts so that you might be for us the remission of sins and that those who partake of you may become immortal. Upon you we invoke the name of the mother, of the unspeakable mystery of the hidden powers and authorities; we invoke over you the name of your Jesus." And he said: "May the power of blessing come and subside in this bread so that all the souls partaking of it may be washed of their sins. And after he broke, he gave to Siphorus and his wife and daughter.

158. When they came up [out of the water], he took bread[11] and a cup[12]   795
and blessed it and said: "We eat your holy Body that was crucified for us; we drink the Blood that was shed for our salvation. Therefore may your Body be our salvation and your Blood be for the remission of our sins. As to the gall that you drank for our sake,[13] may the gall of the devil be removed from us; and as to the vinegar that you drank for us,[14] may our weakness be made strong. As to the spitting you received for our sake,[15] may we receive the dew of your goodness. As to the reed they used to strike you,[16] may we receive a perfect house. And since you received a crown of thorns for our sake,[17] may we who love you put on an eternal crown. As to the linen cloth in which you were wrapped,[18] may we also be girded about with the power that is not overcome. As to the new tomb[19] and the burial, may we be renewed in soul and body. As to your rising[20] and being revived, may we revive and live and stand before you in righteous judgment. He broke and gave the Eucharist to Iuzanes and Tertia and Mnesara and the wife and daughter of Siphorus and said, "May this Eucharist be unto you for the salvation and joy and health of your souls." They said, "Amen." And a voice was heard saying, "Amen. Fear not. Just believe."[21]

40. CONFESSION OF CYPRIAN[†]

One of the most popular legends of early Christianity is that of Cyprian of Antioch and Justina, a story already familiar to Gregory of Nazianzus (WEC 2:68), who like many others confused this Cyprian with Cyprian of Carthage (WEC 1:27).

As the tale goes, Cyprian was a pagan magician and astrologer who attempted to seduce the Christian virgin Justina. Through her prayers and

---

11. See Matt 26:26.   12. See Matt 26:27.   13. See Matt 27:34.   14. See Matt 27:48.   15. See Matt 26:67; 27:30.   16. See Matt 27:29–30.   17. See Matt 27:29. 18. See Matt 27:59.   19. See Matt 27:60.   20. See Matt 28:6.   21. See Luke 8:50.

† Translation from J. Quasten, *Music & Worship in Pagan & Christian Antiquity*, trans. B. Ramsey (Washington, D.C., 1983) 70.

good example he converted to Christianity, became a priest, and then was made bishop of Antioch. Together with Justina he was martyred during the Diocletian persecution.

The story, in three books titled Cyprian's *Conversion, Confession,* and *Passion,* belongs to the literary genre of the hagiographical novel, so dear to the popular imagination. Although the supposed relics of these two martyrs are claimed to be in the baptistery of Saint John Lateran in Rome, there is no record of such saints in any of the early martyrologies.

Bardenhewer (1913) 2:452–53 * CATH 3:397 * DPAC 1:677–78 * EEC 1:211* LTK 6:549–50

796   Thereupon we went into the church [at Antioch], and [one could there] see the choir, which was like a choir of heavenly men of God or a choir of angels taking up a song of praise to God. To every verse they added a Hebrew word [as] with one voice, so that one might believe that there were not [a number of] men but rather one rational being comprehending a unity, which gave off a wonderful sound, which the dead prophets were announcing once more through the living.

41. PHILIP BARDESANE

Born of pagan and noble parents in 154, Philip Bardesane (Bardaişan) was baptized at the age of twenty-five and became attached to the court at Edessa, where he was philosopher/theologian/poet. When Edessa was conquered in 216 by the emperor Caracalla (212–17), Philip appears to have gone to Armenia, where he died in 222/223.

Bardesane supposedly composed 150 hymns to spread his teachings.

CPG 1: nos. 1152ff. * Altaner (1961) 143 * Altaner (1966) 101–2 * Altaner (1978) 101, 563 * Bardenhewer (1908) 78–79 * Bardenhewer (1910) 1:62–63 * Bardenhewer (1913) 1:364–68 * Bautz 1:368–69 * Cross 39–40 * Quasten 1:263–64 * Tixeront 57–58 * CATH 1:1245–46 * CE 2:293–94 * DACL 2.1:493–95 * DCB 1:250–60 * DHGE 6:765–67 * DPAC 1:476–78 * DTC 2.2:391–401 * EC 2:840–41 * EEC 1:110 * EEChr 1:167 * LTK 2:3 * NCE 2:97 * NCES 2:97–98 * ODCC 157 * PEA (1894) 3.1:8–9 * PEA (1991) 2:446 * RACh 1:1180–86 * TRE 5:206–12

41-A. Book of the Laws of Countries[†]

Also known as the *Dialogue on Fate,* this book was most probably composed by Philip, a disciple of Bardesane. It is a dialogue, with Bardesane appearing as the main speaker. Fate, he contends, is not absolute; one can freely choose to act either correctly or wrongly. Later Syrian orthodoxy, rightly or wrongly, had problems with many of Bardesane's teachings.

[†] Translation from *The Book of the Laws of Countries,* trans. and ed. H.J.W. Drijvers (Assen, The Netherlands, 1965) 59.

What shall we say of the new people of us as Christians, that the Messiah has caused to arise in every place and in all climates by his coming? For behold, we all, wherever we may be, are called Christians after the one name of the Messiah. And upon one day, the first of the week, we gather together and on the appointed days we abstain from food. [. . .] 797

PALESTINE

42. PSEUDO-CLEMENT. LETTER 2 TO VIRGINS[†]

Under the name of Clement two letters on virginity have come down to us. They were written by an anonymous author, who seems to have been born in Palestine. The letters, in fact, are one work, the first having no conclusion, the second having no introduction. Their date of composition is uncertain, scholars placing it anywhere from the first half of the third century to no earlier than the late fourth century.

CPG 1: no. 1064 * Altaner (1961) 103–4 * Altaner (1966) 47 * Bardenhewer (1908) 29–30 * Bardenhewer (1910) 27 * Bardenhewer (1913) 1:113–18 * Cross 14 * Hamell 27 * Quasten 1:58–59 * Steidle 12–13 * CATH 2:1207 * DCB 1:559 * DictSp 2.1:963 * EC 3:1813 * NCE 11:942–43 * PEA (1894) 4.1:16–17

vɪ. If however we should go to a place where there are no Christians and its residents keep us there for several days, we should be "as cunning as serpents and as simple as doves."[1] We are not to "be foolish but wise,"[2] fearful of the Lord, so that God may be glorified in all things through our Lord Jesus Christ because of our chaste and holy actions. Whether eating or drinking we must do all things for the glory of God. In this way whoever sees us will acknowledge that we—in all our words, in the respect we show, in our moderation, in our impartiality, and in all other things—are a blessed seed and the holy children of the living God. As believers, we are not to imitate the pagans; we are even to be completely different from them, in all things shrinking from evil so that we "do not cast what is holy before dogs or cast pearls before swine."[3] Let us rather glorify God with all self-control, knowledge, fear of God, and steadfastness of mind. 798

The worship we render to God sets us far apart from the pagans, for these blaspheme in their drunken pleasures and utter words of seduction in their godlessness. For this reason we do not sing the psalms in pagan gatherings, nor do we read the Scriptures in such assemblies. In this way we are not like ordinary musicians, whether those who play the harp or those who sing. [. . .] 799

[†] Translated from PG 1:429–32.
1. Matt 10:16.   2. Eph 5:15.   3. Matt 7:6.

43. ORIGEN

Origen (surnamed *Adamantius*, i.e., man of steel) was born in Egypt, probably in Alexandria and of a Catholic family, about the year 185. We know many of Origen's biographical details through the writings of Eusebius (WEC 2:**81**) and others. His father, Leonidas, was martyred in 202 during the persecution of Septimus Severus. With his family having lost its means of support, Origen began to teach grammar, eventually being appointed head of the catechetical school in Alexandria. Devoting himself to a highly ascetic life of poverty and self-denial, he—according to Eusebius—went so far as to mutilate himself, misunderstanding Matthew 19:12.

Origen traveled extensively, visiting, among other places, Rome and Arabia. Probably because of the persecution ordered by the emperor Caracalla, in 215 he left Alexandria and went to Palestine, where, even though a layman, he was asked to preach in the presence of several bishops. His own bishop, Demetrius, objected to this and recalled Origen to Egypt. He again visited Palestine in 230, where, despite his physical irregularity, he was ordained a presbyter. Demetrius again recalled him—apparently for disciplinary rather than dogmatic reasons, dismissed him from his teaching position, and in 231 had him deposed from the priesthood. Returning to Palestine, Origen took up residence in Caesarea (where it appears that Demetrius's sentence was simply ignored). When not journeying elsewhere, he devoted himself to preaching and writing. During the persecution of Decius in 250 Origen was imprisoned. Released after being subjected to torture, he died shortly thereafter ca. 254 at Tyre, where his tomb was long shown to visitors.

Origen was the most prolific author of Christian antiquity. Jerome (WEC 3:**145**) gives a list, albeit incomplete, of his works, totaling at least two thousand. While at Caesarea Origen had a large company of stenographers and copyists, all paid for by his friend Ambrose, whom he converted from Gnosticism. Unfortunately much of Origen's writing has been completely lost or has survived only in fragments or in Latin translation or perhaps in paraphrases.

Although early on there were numerous opponents of Origen's teachings, it was especially from the end of the fourth century to the middle of the sixth century that controversy regarding Origen's teaching was at its height, especially in regard to his philosophical excursions on the nature of the soul. From the relatively meager evidence that has come down to us, it is not always easy to determine what Origen was presenting as the faith of the Church or what he was suggesting as personal speculation or hypothesis. Be this as it may, it is especially as a biblical scholar that Origen ranks among the most important writers of the pre–Nicene Church.

CPG 1: nos. 1410ff. * Altaner (1961) 223–35 * Altaner (1966) 197–209 * Bardenhewer (1908) 136–53 * Bardenhewer (1910) 119–34 * Bardenhewer (1913) 2:68–158 * Bardy

(1929) 77–83 * Bautz 6:1255–71 * Campbell 37–43 * Cross 122–34 * Goodspeed
134–42 * Hamell 62–65 * Jurgens 1:189–215 * Leigh-Bennett 95–113 * Quasten
2:37–101 * Steidle 41–48 * Wright (1932) 317–20 * CATH 10:243–52 * CE 11:306–12
* CHECL 121–27, 211–14 * DACL 12.2:2677–78 * DCB 4:96–142 * DictSp 11:933–62
* DPAC 2:2517–32 * DTC 11.2:1489–1565 * EC 9:346–50 * EEC 2:619–23 * EEChr
2:835–37 * LTK 7:1131–35 * NCE 10:767–74 * NCES 10:653–61 * ODCC 1193–95 *
PEA (1894) 18.1:1036–59 * PEA (1991) 9:26–29 * TRE 25:397–420

PRAYER AND WORSHIP IN GENERAL
W. Gessel, "Die Theologie des Gebetes nach 'De Oratione' von Origines," diss.
(Munich, Paderborn, and Vienna, 1975). * T. Marsh, "The History of the Sacramental Concept," MilS 3 (1979) 21–56. * W. Schütz, *Die christliche Gottesdienst bei Origines*, Calwer theologische Monographien, Series B, Systematische Theologie und
Kirchengeschichte 8 (Stuttgart, 1984). * L. S. Cunningham, "Origen's On Prayer: A
Reflection and Appreciation," Wor 67:4 (July 1993) 332–39. * J. Laporte, *Théologie
liturgique de Philone d'Alexandrie et d'Origène* (Paris, 1995). * D.R. Stuckwisch, "Principles of Christian Prayer from the Third Century: A Brief Look at Origen, Tertullian and Cyprian with Some Comments on Their Meaning for Today," Wor 71:1
(January, 1997) 2–19. * J. Laporte, *Teologia liturgica di Filone d'Alessandria e Origene*,
Cammini nello spirito, Teologia 30 (Milan, 1998).

BAPTISM AND ORIGINAL SIN
A. v. Harnack, *Die Terminologie der Wiedergeburt und verwandter Erlebnisse in der
ältesten Kirche*, TU 42, 3 (Leipzig, 1918). * H. Rahner, "Taufe und geistliches Leben
bei Origines," *Zeitschrift für Askese und Mystik* 7 (1932) 205–22. * C.M. Edsman, *Le
baptême de feu* (Leipzig and Uppsala, 1940) 1–15. * Ph. M. Menoud, "Le baptême
des enfants dans l'Eglise ancienne," VerC 2 (1948) 15–26. * G. Burke, "Des Origines
Lehre vom Urstand des Menschen," ZkTh 72 (1950) 1–39. * F. Lovsky, "L'Eglise
ancienne baptisait-elle les enfants?" *Foi et Vie* 48 (1950) 109–38. * I.J. von Almen,
"L'Eglise primitive et le baptême des enfants," VerC 4 (1950) 43–47. * H. Crouzel,
"Origène et la structure du sacrement," BLE 6 S. 63 (1962) 81–104. * B. Neunheuser,
Baptism and Confirmation (St. Louis, 1964) 67–77.

EUCHARIST
E. Bishop, "Liturgical Comments and Memoranda," JThSt 10 (1908–9) 592–603. *
E. Klostermann, "Eine Stelle des Origenes (In Matth. ser. 85)," ThStKr 103 (1931)
195–98. * F.R.M. Hitchcock, "Holy Communion and Creed in Origen," ChQ (1941)
216–39. * O. Casel, "Glaube, Gnosis und Mysterium," JL 15 (1941) 164–95. *
L. Grimmelt, "Die Eucharistiefeier nach den Werken des Origines: eine liturgiegeschichtliche Untersuchung," diss. (Münster, 1942). * P.-T. Camelot, "L'Eucharistie
dans l'Ecole d'Alexandrie," Div 1 (1957) 71–92. * P. Nautin, *Lettres et écrivans chrétiens des IIe et IIIe siècles*, Patristica 2 (Paris, 1961) 221–32. * J.C.M. van Winden,
"Origen's Definition of 'eucharistica' in 'De Oratione,'" VC 28 (1974) 139–40. *
P. Jacquemont, "Origen," in W. Rordorf and others, *The Eucharist of the Early Christians* (New York, 1978) 183–93. * L. Lies, "Wort und Eucharistie bei Origenes: zur
Spiritualisierungstandenz des Eucharistieverständnisses," Innsbrucker theologis-
che Studien, diss. (Innsbruck, 1978). * H.-J. Vogt, "Eucharistielehre des Origenes?"
FZPT 25 (1978) 428–42. * L. Lies, *Origenes' Eucharisitelehre im Streit der Konfessionem:
die Auslegungsgeschichte seit der Reformation*, Innsbrucker theologische Studien 15
(Innsbruck, 1985).

PENANCE

V. Ermoni, "La pénitence dans l'histoire, à propos d'un ouvrage récent," RQH 67, n.s., 23 (1900) 5–55. * A. d'Alès, "Origène et la doctrine des péchés irrémissibles," RAp 12 (1911) 723–36, 801–16. * B. Poschmann, *Die Sündenvergebung bei Origines* (Breslau, 1912). * A. Vanbeck, "La pénitence dans Origène," RHL, n.s., 3 (1912) 544–57; 4 (1913) 115–29. * F. Cavallera, "A propos de l'histoire du sacrement de pénitence: la 'De oratione' d'Origène; la distinction I du 'De paenitentia,'" BLE 6 S. 24 (1923) 172–201. * B.F.M. Xiberta, "La doctrina de Origines sobre el sacramento de la Penitencia," *Reseña Ecclesiástica* 18 (1926) 237–46, 309–18. * C. Verfaillie, *La doctrine de la justification dans Origène* (Strasbourg, 1926). * F. Cavallera, "La doctrine de la pénitence au IIIe siècle," BLE 6 S. 30 (1929) 19–36; 31 (1930) 49–63. * P. Galtier, "Les péchés 'incurables' d'Origène," Greg 10 (1929) 117–209. * C. Fries, "Zur Willensfreiheit bein Origines," *Archiv für Geschichte der Philosophie* (1930) 92–101. * F.J. Dölger, "Origines über die Beurteilung des Ehebruchs in der Stoischen Philosophie," AC 4 (1934) 284–87. * M. Waldmann, "Synteresis oder Syneidesis? Ein Beitrag zur Lehre vom Gewissen," ThQ (1938) 332–71. * B. Poschmann, *Paenitentia Secunda* (Bonn, 1940) 425–80. * G.H. Joyce, "Private Penance in the Early Church," JThSt 42 (1941) 18–42. * E.F. Latko, "Origen's Concept of Penance," diss. (Québec, 1949). * K. Rahner, "La doctrine d'Origène sur la pénitence," RSR 37 (1950) 47–97, 252–86, 422–56. * B. Poschmann, *Busse und letze Oelung* (Freiburg i. B., 1951) 34–39. * H. Rondet, "Aux origines de la théologie du péché," NRTh 79 (1957) 16–32. * G. Teichtweier, "Die Sündenlehre des Origenes," diss., Studien zur Geschichte der katholischen Moralstheologie 7 (Regensburg, 1958). * B. Poschmann, *Penance and the Anointing of the Sick* (St. Louis, 1964) 66ff. * J. Laporte, "Forgiveness of Sins in Origen," Wor 60:6 (November, 1986) 520–27.

ORDERS, PRIESTHOOD

C. Gore, "On the Ordination of the Early Bishops of Alexandria," JThSt 3 (1901–2) 278–82. * G. Bardy, "Le sacerdoce chrétien d'après les Alexandrins," VS 53 (1937) 144–73. * M. Jourjon, "A propos du 'dossier d'ordination' d'Origène," MSR 15 (1958) 45–48. * E. Ferguson, "Ordination in the Ancient Church," ResQ 5 (1961) 17–32, 67–82, 130–46. * J. Lécuyer, "Sacerdoce des fidèles et sacerdoce ministériel chez Origène," VetChr 7 (1970) 253–64. * R. Gryson, "Les élections ecclésiastiques au IIe siècle," RHE 68 (1973) 353–404. * E. Ferguson, "Origen and the Election of Bishops," CH 43 (1974) 26–33. * J.A. McGuckin, "Origen's Concept of the Priesthood," TD 33:3 (Fall, 1986) 334–36.

OTHER TOPICS

D. Shin, "Some Light from Origen: Scripture as Sacrament," Wor 73:5 (September, 1999) 399–425.

43-A. Homilies

43-A-1. HOMILY 10 ON GENESIS[†]

800   3. [. . .] Tell me, those of you who come to church only on feastdays, are not the other days also feastdays? Are they not also days of the Lord? It is characteristic for the Jews to observe fixed and infrequent solemnities.

[†] Translated from *Homélies sur la Genèse*, intro. H. de Lubac and L. Doutreleau, trans. and ed. L. Doutreleau, SChr 7 (Paris, 1976) 264–65.

This is why God says to them, "I cannot bear your new moons and your Sabbaths and the great day, your fasting and your rest from work; my soul hates your feasts."[1] Therefore God hates those who believe that only one day is the Lord's Day. [. . .]

43-A-2. HOMILY 13 ON EXODUS[†]

3. Those of you who are accustomed to participate in the divine mysteries know that when receiving the Lord's Body you should normally take care that no particle falls to the ground, that nothing of the consecrated gift escapes you. You should rightly consider it a crime if any particle is dropped due to negligence. [. . .]   801

43-A-3. HOMILY 2 ON LEVITICUS[††]

4. Perhaps some of the Church's members are saying that the ancients   802
were better off than we since the sacrifices they offered in their various rites granted pardon of sins. Yet among us there is only one way by which sins are forgiven; it is granted at the beginning by the grace of baptism; afterwards no mercy, no pardon is granted to a sinner. Certainly a more rigorous discipline is fitting for a Christian, "for whom Christ died."[1] Sheep, cattle, and birds were slain for those living previously, who were sprinkled with their blood. The Son of God was slain for you, and do you take delight in sinning again? You have just heard how many sacrifices for sin are mentioned by the Law. And so that these accounts may encourage you to be virtuous rather than cause you to despair, listen now to the numerous ways sin is forgiven in the Gospel.

The first is when we are baptized "for the forgiveness of sins."[2] The second   803
is found in the suffering of the martyrs. The third is granted because of almsgiving since the Savior says, "Give what you have, and all will be pure for you."[3] The fourth comes from the fact that we also forgive the sins of one another. As the Lord and Savior says: "If you forgive others their sins, the Father will forgive your sins. But if you do not truly forgive the sins of others, neither will your Father forgive you."[4] And so he taught us to say in the [Lord's] Prayer, "Forgive us our sins as we forgive those who sin against us."[5] The fifth forgiveness takes place when one leads a sinner from the path of error. The Divine Scripture says that "whoever brings back sinners from the error of their ways will save the sinner's soul and cover a multitude of sins."[6] The sixth forgiveness of sins also comes through an

---

1. Isa 1:13–14, LXX.

[†] Translated from *Homélies sur l'Exode. Origène*, trans. and ed. M. Borret, SChr 321 (Paris, 1985) 386–87.

[††] Translated from *Homélies sur le Lévitique. Origène*, vol. 1, trans. and ed. M. Borret, SChr 286 (Paris, 1981) 106–11.

1. Rom 14:15.   2. Mark 1:4.   3. Luke 11:41.   4. Matt 6:14–15.   5. Matt 6:12. 6. Jas 5:20.

abundance of charity, as even the Lord says, "Truly I say to you that many sins will be forgiven the person who has loved much."[7] And the apostle says, "Charity covers a multitude of sins."[8] There is still another, the seventh, although difficult and laborious, namely, the forgiveness of sins through penance when the sinner washes his or her "couch with tears,"[9] when tears become a person's bread day and night,[10] when one does not blush to confess sin to God's priest and to request a remedy, as we read in the psalm, "I have said, I will confess my injustice against you to the Lord, and you have forgiven the iniquity of my heart."[11] In this way is also fulfilled what the apostle James says: "Are any among you sick? Let them call the priests of the Church who are to impose hands on them and anoint them with oil in the name of the Lord. And the prayer of faith will save the sick, and anyone who has committed sins will be forgiven."[12]

43-A-4. HOMILY 8 ON LEVITICUS[†]

804   3. [. . .] Every soul that takes on a body is soiled by the filth of evil and sin. [. . .] In the Church baptism is granted so that sins be forgiven; even infants are baptized according to the custom of the Church. Now if infants do not need the forgiveness of sins and if there were nothing in them that pertains to this forgiveness, then the grace of baptism would appear to be useless. [. . .]

43-A-5. HOMILY 15 ON LEVITICUS[††]

805   2. [. . .] As to serious sins, penance is granted only once. Nonetheless, sins that are common and into which we often fall always allow for penance and are always immediately forgiven. [. . .]

43-A-6. HOMILY 10 ON NUMBERS[†††]

806   1.8. [. . .] Those who are not holy die in their sins; those who are holy do penance for their sins, feel their wounds, understand why they have fallen, go to find a priest, request healing from him, and seek to be purified by the high priest.[a] This is why the Law prudently and significantly, states that the high priests and the priests do not take upon themselves the sins of any person whatsoever[1] but only those of the holy ones, since a "holy one" is a person who has cured his or her sin through the high priest.

---

7. Luke 7:47.   8. 1 Pet 4:8.   9. See Ps 6:7.   10. See Ps 42:3.   11. Ps 32:5.   12. Jas 5:14–15.

† Translated from *Homélies sur le Lévitique. Origène*, vol. 2, trans. and ed. M. Borret, SChr 287 (Paris, 1981) 20–21.

†† Translated from SChr 287:256–57.

††† Translated from *Homélies sur les Nombres*, trans. and ed. A. Méhat, SChr 29 (Paris, 1951) 278–79.

a. High priest: the bishop?

1. See Num 18:1.

43-A-7. HOMILY 16 ON NUMBERS[†]

9.2. May they tell us who are these people who are accustomed to drink   807
blood. Such were the words that the Jews who were following the Lord
heard in the Gospel. They were scandalized and were saying, "Who can
eat flesh and drink blood?"[1] But the Christian people, the faithful people,
understand the meaning of these words, welcome them, and follow him
who says, "Unless you eat my flesh and drink my blood, you will not
have life in you; because my flesh is food indeed and my blood is drink
indeed."[2] And truly he who said this was wounded for our sins; as Isaiah
says, "He was wounded for our sins."[3] But it is said that we drink the
blood of Christ not only when we receive it sacramentally [*sacramentorum
ritu*] but when we receive his words, words in which life resides, as he
himself says, "My words are spirit and life."[4] Therefore he was wounded,
he whose blood we drink, namely, whose teaching we receive. But no less
wounded are those who have preached his word to us. And when we read
their writings, namely, those of the apostles, and when we follow the life
they teach, it is the blood of those who are wounded that we drink.

43-A-8. HOMILY 2 ON JOSHUA[††]

1. [. . .] You see the pagans come to faith, churches being built up, al-   808
tars sprinkled no longer with the blood of oxen but consecrated by the
precious blood of Christ. You see the priests and levites ministering not
the blood of goats and bulls but the word of God through the Holy Spirit.
[. . .]

43-A-9. HOMILY 14 ON LUKE[†††]

5. [. . .] I use the present occasion to treat once again a question fre-   809
quently asked by the brethren. Infants are baptized unto the remission of
sins.[1] But what sins? When did they sin? Or how can one hold a similar
reason for the baptism of infants if one does not admit the interpretation
that we have just given: "No person is exempt from sin even if this person's life upon earth has lasted for only one day."[2] And because through
the mystery of baptism the filth of birth is removed, so it is that one baptizes also infants, "for no one can enter the kingdom of heaven without
being reborn by water and the Spirit."[3]

6. "When," says the evangelist, "the days for their purification were   810
completed."[4] The fulfillment of these days also has a spiritual meaning.

[†] Translated from SChr 29:262–63.

1. See John 6:52–53.   2. John 6:53–55.   3. Isa 53:5.   4. John 6:63.

[††] Translated from PG 12:833–34.

[†††] Translated from *Homélies sur s. Luc*, trans. and ed. H. Crouzel, F. Fournier, and
P. Périchon, SChr 87 (Paris, 1962) 222–25.

1. See Acts 2:38.   2. Job 14:4–5, LXX.   3. John 3:5.   4. Luke 2:22.

The soul, in fact, is not purified at birth, and on the day of birth cannot obtain perfect purity. But as is written in the Law: "If a mother bears a male child, she will be unclean for seven days and then for thirty-three days she shall be in pure blood."[5] And since "the Law is spiritual"[6] and is "the shadow of good things to come,"[7] we can understand that our true purification will come after a certain period of time. This is what I believe. Even after the resurrection from the dead we will need a mystery [*sacramentum*] so that we can be washed and purified—no one can rise without being soiled and no one can find any soul that is immediately freed from all vice. Also in the rebirth of baptism a mystery takes place. Just as Jesus according to the dispensation of the flesh was purified by an offering, so we are purified by a spiritual rebirth.

43-B. Commentary on Romans[†]

Most probably written before 244, this commentary consists of fifteen books, of which only fragments of the original Greek remain.

811   V.viii. [. . .] Perhaps you might ask about what the Lord said to his disciples, namely, that they are to baptize all peoples in the name of the Father, and of the Son, and of the Holy Spirit. Now why has this apostle employed the name of Christ alone in baptism, saying, "We who have been baptized into Christ"[1] since legitimate baptism is only given in the name of the Trinity? [. . .]

812   V.ix. [. . .] From the apostles the Church has received the tradition that also babies be baptized. For those confided with the secrets of the divine mysteries knew that the natural stains of sin existed in everyone, stains that must be washed away through water and the Spirit. [. . .]

813   X.xxxiii. *Greet one another with a holy kiss.*[2] From this expression and from others similar to it the custom has been handed down to the churches that after the prayers the brethren greet one another with a kiss. The apostle calls this kiss "holy." By means of this name he teaches first of all that kisses given in the churches are to be chaste; also that they are not feigned as were those of Judas. [. . .]

43-C. Against Celsus[††]

About the year 178 Celsus, a pagan philosopher, wrote *The True Discourse*, a treatise that is considered the first anti-Christian polemical work. Although this attack on Christianity (and Judaism) appears to have had

---

5. Lev 12:2–4, LXX.   6. Rom 7:14.   7. Heb 10:1.

[†] Translated from PG 14:1039, 1047, 1282–83.

1. Rom 6:3.   2. Rom 16:16.

[††] Translated from *Contre Celse*, vol. 2, trans. and ed. M. Borret, SChr 136 (Paris, 1968) 122–23; ibid., vol. 4, SChr 150 (Paris, 1969) 200ff.

limited circulation and impact, Origen was persuaded to write a refutation, doing so about the year 248 and in eight books. Most of Celsus's
work has been lost and yet can be reconstructed from its quotations by
Origen.

III.LI. [. . .] Christians mourn as dead those guilty of licentiousness or   814
any other sin since such guilty ones are lost, being dead to God. Yet if they
show a true change of heart, they are received back into the fold sometime
in the future—after a more extended period of time than when they were
first received—as though they were risen from among the dead.

VIII.XIII. [. . .] We adore the one God and his only Son, the Word and   815
the Image, through our supplications and requests, offering our prayers
to the God of the universe through his only Son. It is to the Son that we
first present them, asking him as the "propitiation for our sins"[1] and as the
High Priest to present our prayers, our sacrifices, our supplications to God
Most High.

VIII.XXII. Can anyone object to the fact that we are accustomed to cele-   816
brate certain days, for example, the Lord's Day, the Preparation Day, the
Pasch, or Pentecost? We must respond that to perfect Christians, to those
who do not cease to apply themselves to the words, actions, and thoughts
of God's Word who by nature is Lord, all their days are days of the Lord,
and they continually celebrate Sunday. Furthermore, the Preparation Day
continues to be celebrated by those who constantly prepare themselves for
a true life, who ward off the pleasures of this life which deceive the multitude, not nourishing the lust of the flesh but, on the contrary, punishing
the body and keeping it under control.[2] Also, when it is understood that
"Christ our Passover has been sacrificed"[3] and that this feast is to be celebrated by eating the flesh of the Word,[4] then the Passover is not kept immediately, the word Passover meaning "passing over," for by thought, by
each word, by each action we, hastening toward the heavenly city, never
cease to pass over from the affairs of this world to God. Finally, if we can
truly say, "We have risen with Christ,"[5] and also, "He has raised us up
with him and has seated us with Christ in heaven,"[6] there we continually
find ourselves observing the days of Pentecost especially when, ascending
to the upper room as did the apostles of Jesus, we devote ourselves to supplication and prayer. Doing so we become worthy of the mighty wind descending from heaven, a wind whose strength destroys human evil and its
effects. We also merit to share in the tongue of fire that comes from God.[7]

VIII.XXXIII. [. . .] Let Celsus, then, in his ignorance of God, bear witness   817
to the demons. We, however, give thanks to the Creator of all; we eat the
bread offered with thanksgiving and prayer, bread given to us, bread that

1. 1 John 4:10; 2:2; Heb 2:17; etc.   2. See Rom 8:6–7; 1 Cor 9:27.   3. See 1 Cor
5:7.   4. See John 6:51–56.   5. See Col 2:12; 3:1.   6. Eph 2:6.   7. See Acts 1:13–14;
2:2–3.

through prayer has become the holy Body and which sanctifies those who use it properly.[8]

818   VIII.LVII. [. . .] Celsus desires that we not show ingratitude toward the demons here below, believing that we owe them offerings of thanksgiving. But we, while making clear what is meant by thanksgiving, argue that we are not ungrateful if we refuse to sacrifice to beings that do us no good and contend against us. We only refuse to be ungrateful to God who has showered us with benefits since we are his creatures, the objects of Divine Providence, to God who has judged us worthy no matter what, and whom we await after this life, the fulfillment of our hope. As a token of our gratitude toward God, we have the bread we call the "Eucharist." [. . .]

819   VIII.LXVII. [. . .] According to Celsus we will better seem to give honor to the great God if we sing also to the sun and to Minerva. But we know that just the opposite is true. We sing hymns only to God on high and to God's only Son, who is God and the Word. We sing hymns to God and to God's only Son as do the sun, the moon, the stars, and the whole heavenly host.[9] Together they form but one divine choir, and with the just they sing a hymn to God on high and to God's only Son. [. . .]

43-D. On Prayer[†]

Written in 233–34 this treatise, the oldest formal explanation of Christian prayer, occupies a prominent place in the history of Christian spirituality. The work treats prayer in general (chapters III–XVII), then the Our Father (chapters XVIII–XXX), and concluding with a short appendix (chapters XXXI–XXXIII).

820   XI.5. [. . .] And so we must believe that the angels, as overseers and as God's servants, are present with those who are praying in order to join them in their petitions. To be sure, each person's angel—even those of the Church's "little ones who look upon the face of the Father in heaven,"[1]— when contemplating our Creator's divinity pray and help us insofar as possible regarding what we petition.

821   XII.2. Since doing what is enjoined by virtue or the commandments is also a part of prayer, those who combine right actions with prayer and prayer with becoming actions "pray unceasingly." Only if we consider the whole life of a holy person as one great continuous prayer can we understand the admonition "Pray without ceasing"[2] as something we can accomplish. What we ordinarily refer to as "prayer" is only part of this prayer, and it should be performed no less than three times a day. The example of David makes this clear. He prayed three times each day even though threatened by danger.[3] And "Peter, at about the sixth hour going

---

8. See 1 Cor 10:31.   9. See Ps 148:3.
† Translated from GCS 3:324ff.
1. Matt 18:10.   2. 1 Thess 5:17.   3. See Dan 6:11.

up to the roof to pray, saw a vessel descending from above, lowered by its four corners."⁴ This refers to the second of the three prayers, the prayer that David also spoke about much earlier: "In the morning you hear my prayer; in the morning I will stand before you and watch."⁵ The last is indicated by "the lifting up of my hands like an evening sacrifice."⁶ Without this prayer we cannot pass the night as we should. [. . .]

xxviii.9. [. . .] So that we may better grasp how God forgives our sins through others, let us use an example from the Law. The Law forbids priests from offering sacrifice for certain sins so that those for whom the sacrifice is made might be forgiven their sins. The Law also says that a priest who can offer sacrifice for certain voluntary or involuntary transgressions⁷ is not to offer a sin-offering for adultery, voluntary murder, or a more serious sin. And so the apostles, as well as those who have become similar to the apostles, being priests like the "Great High Priest"⁸ and having been instructed in the service of God, know from the teaching of the Spirit for what sins they are to offer sacrifice as well as when and how they are to do so. Additionally, they recognize the sins for which they are not to do so. [. . .]

822

xxviii.10. I simply do not understand how some can take upon themselves the power of the priestly office. Perhaps failing to possess the knowledge appropriate to a priest, they boast that they can even forgive idolatry, adultery, and fornication. They act as if, through their prayer on behalf of those daring to commit such sins, they can forgive even sin unto death. They fail to read, "There is sin unto death; I do not say that you should pray about that."⁹ [. . .]

823

xxxi.2. It seems to me that those about to pray should somewhat dispose and prepare themselves. [. . .] They should lift up the soul before lifting up the hands, raising up toward God the spirit before the eyes; and lifting up the mind from earthly things and directing it to the Lord of all before standing for prayer. [. . .] Of the numerous postures of the body, it is undeniable that elevating the hands and upraising the eyes should be preferred to all others since in this way the body brings to prayer the image of the qualities that are becoming to prayer. Except for special circumstances, this should be the normal position for prayer. As circumstances require, a person can at times appropriately pray while sitting, for example, due to some serious ailment of the feet, or even while lying down because of fever or some similar illness. Again, if we are traveling or if our business does not allow us to go apart to pray as we should, then we can pray without outwardly appearing to do so.

824

xxxi.3. A person should kneel when confessing before God one's own sins, when requesting healing and forgiveness; this is the attitude proper to those who humble themselves and who submit themselves. As Paul

825

---

4. Acts 10:9, 11.   5. Ps 5:3.   6. Ps 141:2.   7. See Num 15:15–26.   8. Heb 4:14.
9. 1 John 5:16.

says, "For this reason I kneel before the Father from whom every paternity in heaven and upon earth takes its name."[10] Spiritual kneeling, so named because every being submitting to God at the name of Jesus and humbling oneself before him is, I believe, signified by the apostle when he says, "At the name of Jesus every knee should bend in heaven, upon earth, and under the earth."[11] [. . .]

826   xxxi.4. As to place, we should understand that every place is appropriate for those who pray well: "In every place offer me incense,"[12] says the Lord. "And, I desire that in every place one should pray."[13] In order to pray calmly and without distraction each person should have in his or her house, if it is large enough, an appointed and selected place, a more solemn room, as it were, and pray there. In determining this location, one should ask whether anything contrary to law or right has taken place there. Neither the person nor the place of prayer is to be such that God has fled from it. [. . .]

827   xxxi.5. The place where believers assemble is both reasonable and useful as a place for prayer. It is there that the angelic powers take part in the assemblies of believers, where the power of our Lord and Savior himself lives, where the spirits of the holy ones gather, both, as I believe, those of the dead who have gone on before us and obviously those of the holy ones who are still alive, even though it is difficult to say how this happens. Regarding the angels, we have this to say: if "the angel of the Lord will encamp around those who fear him and will deliver them,"[14] if Jacob spoke the truth not only regarding himself but regarding all who are dedicated to God when he spoke about "the angel who delivers us from all evils,"[15] then it is likely, when many are gathered to give glory to Christ, that each person's angel encamps around those who fear God and that the angel is with the person whom it is to protect and guide. In this way when the holy ones are assembled, there are two churches, one that is human and another that is angelic. And if it was only the prayer of Tobit, and that of Sarah who later became his daughter-in-law by her marriage to the young Tobiah, that, according to Raphael, Tobit offered as a memorial,[16] then what occurs when many gather in the same spirit and mind and form one body in Christ? Paul says, "You have gathered together with my spirit and with the power of the Lord Jesus,"[17] meaning that the Lord's power was not only with the Ephesians but also with the Corinthians. And if Paul, still clothed with the body, believed that he was being carried away by his own body to Corinth, we must not lose hope that the blessed ones who have departed their bodies will come in spirit, perhaps more fully than the people who are bodily present in the churches. Wherefore we must not disregard prayers offered in churches since they have value for those who truly participate there.

---

10. Eph 3:14–15.   11. Phil 2:10.   12. Mal 1:11.   13. 1 Tim 2:8.   14. Ps 34:7.
15. Gen 48:16.   16. See Tob 12:12.   17. 1 Cor 5:4.

XXXII. As to the direction toward which we are to pray, I have just a few words. Since there are four directions—north, south, east, and west—who does not immediately recognize that the east evidently indicates that we should pray looking toward this direction, this being a symbol that the soul is gazing toward the rising of the true light?[18] One may prefer to pray facing the direction in which his or her house faces, regardless of the way in which its doors may open, saying that looking up toward heaven itself is more conducive to prayer than looking at a wall. Now if the house does not face in an easterly direction, we respond that the manner whereby human buildings are oriented is a matter of convention; but by reason of its very nature, however, the east takes precedence over the other directions, and what is natural is to be preferred over what is artificial. Furthermore, why should one who desires to pray out in the open pray toward the east rather than toward the west? If in this case it is reasonable to prefer the east, why not do the same everywhere? Enough said on this subject!

XXXIII.1. It seems that I should conclude this book by considering the parts of prayer. There are, in my opinion, four of them. These I have discovered throughout the Scriptures, and a person should, according to each of them, formulate one's prayer. They are as follows. At the beginning, like a prologue to prayer, we use all our ability to glorify God through Christ who is glorified with him in the Holy Spirit, who is praised with him. After that we give thanks, recalling as we do so the benefits given by God to all and to each of us in particular. Following the thanksgiving we should confess our sins and request first a healing that will deliver us from whatever customarily leads us to sin, and then the forgiveness of past sins. After the confession the fourth part is, I believe, a petition for great and heavenly benefits, both particular and universal, for our parents and friends. Prayer should conclude by glorifying God through Christ and in the Holy Spirit.

828

829

EGYPT

44. CLEMENT OF ALEXANDRIA

Clement (*Titus Flavius Clemens*) of Alexandria was born of pagan parents ca. 150, perhaps in Athens. After his baptism he traveled widely to seek further instruction in the Christian faith. Eventually he settled in Alexandria, where ca. 200 he became director of that city's noted catechetical school. Persecution forced him to leave Egypt a few years later, and he died in Cappadocia between 211 and 216.

Clement's writings show that he was very familiar not only with the Scriptures but also with profane literature as, for example, the philosophical treatises of Plato. Although organizing material was not his strong point, Clement has been called the "first Christian scholar."

---

18. See John 1:9.

CPG 1: nos. 1375ff. * Altaner (1961) 215–22 * Altaner (1966) 190–97 * Bardenhewer (1908) 126–35 * Bardenhewer (1910) 112–19 * Bardenhewer (1913) 2:15–66 * Bardy (1929) 72–77 * Bautz 1:1063–66 * Campbell 33–37 * Cross 118–22 * Goodspeed 127–33 * Hamell 60–62 * Jurgens 1:176–88 * Leigh-Bennett 77–94 * Quasten 2:5–36 * Tixeront 84–89 * Wright (1932) 312–17 * CATH 2:1203–6 * CE 4:45–47 * CHECL 117–20 * DCB 1:559–67 * DHGE 12:1423–28 * DictSp 2.1:950–61 * DPAC 1:706–12 * DTC 3.1:137–99 * EC 3:1842–57 * EEC 1:179–81 * EEChr 1:262–64 * LTK 6:126–27 * NCE 3:943–44 * NCES 3:797–99 * ODCC 364–65 * PEA (1894) 4.1:11–13 * PEA (1991) 3:30–31* RACh 3:182–88 * TRE 8:101–13

LITURGY IN GENERAL, PRAYER

H.G. Marsh, "The Use of 'Musterion' in the Writings of Clement of Alexandria with Special Reference to His Sacramental Doctrine," JThSt 37 (1936) 64–80. * G. Békés, *De Continua Oratione Clementis Alexandrini Doctrina*, Studia Anselmiana 14 (Rome, 1942). * J.D.B. Hamilton, "The Church and the Language of Mystery: The First Four Centuries," ETL 53 (1977) 479–94. * T. Marsh, "The History of the Sacramental Concept," MilS 3 (1979) 21–56. * C. Riedweg, "Mysterienterminologie bei Platon, Philon und Klemens von Alexandrien," diss., Untersuchungen zur antiken Literatur und Geschichte 26 (Berlin and New York, 1987).

INITIATION

C. Caspari, "Hat die alexandrinische Kirche auf Zeit des Clements ein Taufbekenntnis bessen?" *Zeitschrift für kirchlichen Wissenschaft* 7 (1886) 352–75. * A.V. Harnack, *Die Terminologie der Wiedergebut und verwandter Erlebniss in der ältesten Kirche*, TU 42, 3 (Leipzig, 1920) 97–143. * T. Rüther, *Die Lehre von der Erbsünde bein Clements von Alexandrien*, FthSt 28 (Freiburg i. B., 1922). * J. Héring, *Etude sur la doctrine de la chute et de la préexistence des âmes chez Clément d'Alexandrie*, Bibliothèque de l'Ecole des Hautes Etudes 38 (Paris, 1923). * A. Oepke, "Urchistentum und Kindertaufe," ZNW 29 (1930) 81–111. * F.J. Dölger, "Das Lösen der Schuhriemen in der Taufsymbolik des Klemens von Alexandrien," AC 5 (1936) 87–95. * H.A. Echle, "The Baptism of the Apostles," Tra 3 (1945) 365–68. * H.A. Echle, "Sacramental Initiation as a Christian Mystery: Initiation according to Clement of Alexandria," in *Vom christlichen Mysterium: Gesammelte Arbeiten zum Gedächnis Odo Casels* (Düsseldorf, 1951) 54–64. * A. Orbe, "Teologia bautismal de Clemente Alejandrino, según Paed. I, 26, 3–27, 2," Greg 36 (1955) 410–48. * H. Rondet, "Aux origines de la théologie du péché," NRTh 79 (1957) 16–32. * B. Neunheuser, *Baptism and Confirmation* (St. Louis, 1964) 64–67. * C. Nardi, *Il battesimo in Clemente Alessandrino: interpretazione di Eclogae propheticae 1–26*, Studia Ephemeridis "Augustinianum" 19 (Rome, 1984). * E.A. Leeper, "From Alexandria to Rome: The Valentinian Connection to the Incorporation of Exorcism as a Prebaptismal Rite," VC 44 (1990) 6–24.

EUCHARIST

A. Scheiwiler, *Die Elemente der Eucharistie*, FLDG 3, 4 (Mainz, 1903) 55–66. * F. Wieland, *Der vorirenäische Opferbegrifff* (Munich, 1900) 106–21. * J. Brinktrine, *Der Messopferbegriff in den ersten zwei Jahrhunderten*, FThSt 21 (Freiburg i. B., 1918) 105–10. * P. Batiffol, *L'Eucharistie: la présence réelle et la transubstantiation*, 9th ed. (Paris, 1930) 248–61. * F.R.M. Hitchcock, "Holy Communion and Creed in Clement of Alexandria," ChQ 129 (1939) 57–70. * P.-T. Camelot, "L'Eucharistie dans l'Ecole d'Alexandrie," Div 1 (1957) 71–92. * A.H.C. van Eijk, "The Gospel of Philip and Clement of Alexandria: Gnostic and Ecclesiastical Theology on the Resurrection,"

VC 25 (1971) 94–120. * C. Mondesert, "L'Eucharistie selon Clément d'Alexandrie," PP 46 (1971) 302–8. * A. Méhat, "Clement of Alexandria," in W. Rordorf and others, *The Eucharist of the Early Christians* (New York, 1978) 99–131. * A.L. Pratt, "Clement of Alexandria: Eucharist as Gnosis," GOTR 32 (1987) 163–78.

PENANCE

V. Ermoni, "La pénitence dans l'histoire, à propos d'un ouvrage récent," RQH 67, n.s., 23 (1930) 5–55. * Th. Spacil, *La doctrina del purgatorio in Clemente Alessandrine ed Origene* (Besa, 1919) 131–45. * J. Hoh, "Die Busse bei Klemens von Alexandrien," ZkTh 56 (1932) 175–89. * J. Hoh, *Die kirchliche Busse im zweiten Jahrhundert* (Breslau, 1932) 115–29. * B. Poschmann, *Paenitentia Secunda*, Theophaneia 1 (Bonn, 1940) 229–60. * H.A. Echle, "The Terminology of the Sacrament of Reconciliation according to Clement of Alexandria," diss. (Washington, D.C., 1949). * H. Karpp, *Probleme altchristlicher Anthropologie*, Beiträge zur historischen Theologie 44, 3 (Gütersloh, 1950) 92–103. * B. Poschmann, *Busse und letze Ölung* (Freiburg i. B., 1951) 32–34. * A. Méhat, "'Pénitence seconde' et 'péché involontaire' chez Clément d'Alexandrie," VC 8 (1954) 225–33. * B. Poschmann, *Penance and the Anointing of the Sick*, 6th ed. (St. Louis, 1964) 63–66. * E. Junod, "Un écho d'une controverse autour de la pénitence: l'histoire de l'apôtre Jean et du chef des brigands chez Clément d'Alexandrie (Quis dives savetur 42, 1–15)," RHPR 60 (1980) 153–60.

OTHER TOPICS

G.W. Butterworth, "Clement of Alexandria and Art," JThSt 17 (1915–16) 68–76. * C. Mondésert, "Le symbolisme chez Clément d'Alexandrie," RSR 26 (1936) 158–80. * G. Bardy, "Le sacerdoce chrétien d'après les Alexandrins," VS 53 (1937) 144–73. * W.M. Green, "Ancient Comment on Instrumental Music in the Psalms," ResQ 1 (1957) 3–8. * J.-P. Broudéhoux, *Mariage et famille chez Clément d'Alexandrie*, Théologie historique 11 (Paris, 1970). * R. Mortley, "The Theme of Silence in Clement of Alexandria," JThSt, n.s., 24 (1973) 197–202.

44-A. The Tutor of Children (Paidagogos)[†]

Generally addressed to those who have already accepted the faith, this work is an exhortation to live as faithful Christians in a world filled with pagan vices and customs.

I.vi.25. [. . .] Now if he [Jesus Christ] were perfect, then why did he,   830 the perfect one, have himself baptized? It is, they say, so that the promise concerning the human race might be fulfilled. This is indeed true. Did he become truly perfect when he was baptized by John? Apparently yes. Did he learn anything more from John? In no way. He, then, was made perfect by baptism alone and sanctified by the descent of the Holy Spirit. So it is. But the same holds true of us—whose exemplar is the Lord; baptized, we are enlightened; enlightened, we are adopted as children; adopted, we are made perfect; becoming perfect, we receive immortality. It is written,

---

[†] Translated from *Le Pédagogue*, vol. 1, trans. M. Harl and ed. H.I. Marrou, SChr 70 (Paris, 1983) 158–59; ibid., vol. 2, trans. C. Mondésert, SChr 108 (Paris, 1965) 48ff.; ibid., vol. 3, trans. C. Mondésert and C. Matray, SChr 158 (Paris, 1970) 152ff.

"I say, 'you are all gods and children of the Most High.'"[1] Numerous are the names for this: grace, illumination, perfection, bath. It is a "bath" by which we are purified from our sins; it is "grace" that takes away the punishment merited by our sins; it is "illumination" within which we gaze upon the beautiful and holy light of salvation, namely, the light that allows us to see God; it is "perfection" in that nothing is lacking.

831   II.ii.20. Wine is mixed with water, and the Spirit is united with man. One nourishes unto faith; the other leads to incorruptibility. In turn, the mixture of the two, namely, the drink and the Logos, is called the Eucharist, a grace that is praised for its beauty. Sharing in it when done with faith sanctifies both body and soul. [. . .]

832   II.iv.41. [. . .] It is against this kind of feast [i.e., a non-Christian feast] that the Spirit opposes a divine service that is worthy of God when it says in the psalm, "Praise him with the sound of the trumpet";[2] in fact, it is with the sound of the trumpet that the dead will be brought back to life.[3] "Praise him with the harp"[4] because the tongue is the harp of the Lord. Also, "Praise him with the cithara"[5] because in our understanding the word "cithara" means the "mouth" which the Spirit has vibrate as if being struck by a plectrum. "Praise him with the timbrel and dance";[6] here the Spirit desires that the Church think of the resurrection of the flesh when it hears the timbrel's skin vibrate. "Praise him with stringed instrument and organ."[7] The body is called an organ and its nerves are the strings by which it has received a harmonious tension and which expresses itself by human sounds when touched by the Spirit. "Praise him with clashing cymbals";[8] the mouth's cymbals are the tongue which moves when the lips are set into motion. And so the Spirit calls out to all people, "May each breath praise the Lord"[9] because the Lord has extended his protection to each breath he has created. In truth, the human being is a peaceful instrument whereas those who have preoccupations [other than peace] desire to invent war instruments which enflame desire, stir up lust, or arouse anger. In fact, in their wars the Etruscans employ trumpets; the Arcadians use the shepherd's pipe; the Sicilians have the harp. [. . .] We, however, have the Word alone, the one instrument of peace, as we honor God. We no longer employ the ancient psaltery, trumpet, timbrel, or flute. [. . .]

833   II.ix.79. It is necessary that we be always ready to rise from sleep. Scripture, in fact, says, "May your loins be girt and your lamps be lit; you are to be like those who await their master when he returns from the marriage feast so that they may open the door for him as soon as he arrives and knocks. Happy are those whom their master, upon arriving, finds waiting."[10] Someone who is sleeping is useless. The same holds true for a person who is dead. This is why during the night we are often to rise and

---

1. Ps 82:6.   2. Ps 150:3.   3. See 1 Cor 15:52.   4. Ps 150:3.   5. See ibid.   6. Ps 150:4.   7. Ibid.   8. Ps 150:5.   9. Ps 150:6.   10. See Luke 12:35–37.

bless God. Blessed are those who watch for him; they make themselves like the angels whom we call the "watchers." [. . .]

II.xi.79. [. . .] When going to the assembly it is necessary that both women and men be decently clothed, that they walk in a simple fashion, that they seek peace and quiet, and that they be full of "sincere love,"[11] chaste in body and soul, and ready to address God in prayer.[12] Furthermore, women, except when at home, should always be veiled; doing so conforms to modesty and protects her from being looked at. She will never fall if she maintains before her eyes modesty and her veil; nor will she lead another to sin by uncovering her face. It is the wish of the Word that she be veiled when she is at prayer.[13]

834

III.xi.81. [. . .] If we are called to the kingdom of God, let our conduct be worthy of this kingdom[14] by our love for both God and neighbor.[15] However, the criterion of love is not the kiss[16] but showing kindness. The people I have in mind are those who do nothing other than have the assemblies resound with the noise of their kiss without possessing love within themselves. Even more, their continual abuse of the kiss, which is to be a "mystical" action, has given rise to shameful suspicions and calumnies. [. . .]

835

44-B. Carpets (Stromata)[†]

The word *Stromata* refers to patchwork quilts or carpets and is used to designate a literary form common in antiquity, namely, a potpourri or work treating various topics. The treatise has eight books, the last being unfinished.

I.xix.96. [. . .] Wisdom evidently says to the heretics, "Place your hand full of joy upon the bread of mystery and upon the stolen water which is sweet."[1] When the Scripture here uses the words "bread" and "water," it has in mind nothing other than those heretics who use bread and water in the offering, doing so contrary to the rule of the Church. The same holds true for those who celebrate the Eucharist with pure water. [. . .]

836

I.xxi.146. The followers of Basilides[a] celebrate the day of [Christ's] baptism as a feast, passing the night before with readings. [. . .]

837

---

11. Rom 12:9; see 2 Cor 6:6.   12. See Matt 5:8.   13. See 1 Cor 11:5–6.   14. See Phil 1:27; 1 Thess 2:12.   15. See Matt 22:37, 39.   16. See Rom 16:16; 1 Cor 16:20; 2 Cor 13:12; 1 Thess 5:26.

† Translated from *Les Stromates*, vol. 1, intro. C. Mondésert, trans. and ed. M. Caster, SChr 30 bis (Paris, 2006) 120ff.; ibid., vol. 2, trans. C. Mondésert, ed. P.Th. Camelot, SChr 38 bis (Paris, 2006) 79ff.; ibid., vol. 7, trans. and ed. A. Le Boulluec, SChr 428 (Paris, 2006) 108ff.

a. Basilides: a theologian of somewhat Gnostic tendencies who taught at Alexandria during the second century.

1. Prov 9:17.

838   II.XIII.56. Whoever has received the pardon of sins should sin no more. In addition to the first and sole penance for sins—surely the sins of those who formerly led a pagan life, namely, a life in ignorance—penance is offered to those who have been called, a penance that purifies the soul from errors so that the faith may take deep root there. The Lord, having "knowledge of hearts"[2] and knowing the future in advance, has always foreseen human fickleness and the devil's craftiness; the Lord knew how the devil, jealous of the human race because of the pardon granted to sins, raised up for God's servants occasions of sin, doing this by means of mischievous designs in order that they also might fall with him.

839   II.XIII.57. God, then, in his great mercy granted a second penance to those who, although possessing the faith, fall into some error. This is so a person who is tempted after being called and who is overtaken by violence and deceit might still obtain a penance not to be repented of.[3] "In fact, if we willingly sin after having come to the knowledge of the truth, there is no more sacrifice to offer for our sins; all that remains is to fearfully await the judgment and the raging fire that will devour those who rebel."[4]

840   VII.V.29. [. . .] If what is sacred is understood in two ways, namely, God himself and the building constructed in his honor, then would we not have to properly call the Church holy, made so though knowledge for the honor of God, an edifice sacred to God, great in value, not built by human work, not constructed by the hand of a charlatan, but a Church intended by God to be a temple? For it is not the place but the gathering of the elect that I call the Church. Such a temple is more apt for receiving the greatness of God's dignity. [. . .]

841   VII.VI.31. [. . .] But if God rejoices in being honored, even though by nature he needs nothing, we do no wrong to honor God by prayer; this is the best and most holy sacrifice that we rightly send up, giving him honor through the Word of all righteousness, by whom we receive knowledge and by whom we also give glory for what we have learned. And so our altar of sacrifice, the altar we have here below, is the earthly gathering of those devoted to prayer, those having one voice and being of one mind. [. . .]

842   VII.VII.35. We are commanded to revere and honor the Word, convinced as we are by faith that he is the Savior and governor, and through him the Father. We are not to do so just on selected days as is done by others, but continually, throughout all one's life and in every way possible. In fact, the chosen race,[5] justified according to the commandment,[6] says, "I have praised you seven times a day."[7] Also, this is to happen not in a determined place nor in a chosen sanctuary nor on certain feasts or selected days but throughout a person's whole life. In this way the [true] Gnostic[b]

---

b. The *true* Gnostic, Clement contends, is the person who has attained a harmony of faith and knowledge.

2. Acts 15:8.   3. See 2 Cor 7:10.   4. Heb 10:26–27.   5. See 1 Pet 2:9; Isa 43:20.
6. See Ps 119:172.   7. Ps 119:164.

honors God, namely, shows gratitude for his or her knowledge of how to live. This is to be done everywhere, whether one is alone or with others who share the same faith. [. . .] And so throughout our whole life we keep festival, convinced that God is present everywhere; we cultivate our fields while offering praise; we travel on the sea while singing hymns; and we live according to the rules. [. . .]

VII.vii.40. And so we lift our heads and extend our hands toward heaven; we stand on tiptoes as we give the acclamation that concludes the prayer. [. . .] Now if some appoint particular hours for prayer, for example, the third, the sixth, the ninth hour, nonetheless the [true] Gnostic prays throughout all his or her life, hastening to be with God by means of prayer and, to be brief, leaving behind all that will not be useful when this is attained since now the perfection of a person acting out of love is received. But the distribution of the hours according to three moments, each solemnized by an equal number of prayers—this is known by those who are acquainted with the blessed triad of the holy dwelling places.

843

VII.vii.43. [. . .] When we pray we face the morning sun. The most ancient temples faced the west, this teaching the people who are standing before the images to turn toward the east. "May my prayer rise like incense before you, the lifting up of my hands as an evening sacrifice,"[8] says the psalm.

844

VII.vii.49. [. . .] And so the [true] Gnostic will also pray in the company of those with whom the faith is shared, but only for actions where collaboration is required. One's entire life is a festival. His or her offerings consist of prayers and the giving of praise, reading the Scriptures before meals and before retiring at night, and also by praying during the night. Doing so, one is joined to the heavenly choir. [. . .]

845

VIII.xii.78. [. . .] The [true] Gnostic even prays with the angels as someone who is already equal to them. Never beyond their keeping and even though praying alone, he or she is always part of the choir of angels.

846

44-C. Excerpts from Theodotus[†]

This appendix to Clement's *Carpets* contains various extracts from the writings of Theodotus, a Valentinian Gnostic, although at times it is difficult to distinguish which material is that of Theodotus whom Clement is refuting and which material is that of Clement himself.

D.82. The bread [of the Eucharist?] and the oil [of the baptismal anointing?] are sanctified by the *dynamis* of the NAME [of God]. They are the same outwardly as when they were taken. Yet by the *dynamis* they have been changed into a "pneumatic *dynamis*." The same is true for the water

847

---

8. Ps 141:2.

[†] Translated from *Extraits de Théodote*, trans. and ed. F. Sagnard, SChr 23 (Paris, 1948) 206–7.

which becomes an exorcised water, a water then used for baptism. This is not only changed within but also obtains sanctification.

848   D.83. Baptism is usually celebrated with joy; but since impure spirits often descend [into the water] at the same time that certain [neophytes] do, accompanying the baptized and being sealed with them—thus making these spirits obstinate in the future—fear is then mixed with joy. Consequently only a person who is pure can go down into the water. For this reason there are fasts, supplications, prayers, [the laying on of] hands, so that the soul might be preserved "from the world"[1] and from the "mouth of lions."[2] [. . .]

45. DIONYSIUS THE GREAT OF ALEXANDRIA

If one is to believe Eusebius of Caesarea (WEC 2:**81**), and not all do, Dionysius was a pupil of Origen (WEC 1:**43**) and ca. 233 became head of the catechetical school at Alexandria. Ordained bishop in 248, he fled the city in 250 due to persecution. Two years later he returned, only to leave again in 257 during the persecution of Valerian. Nonetheless, he directed his flock from places of exile, a practice not without its critics. Returning to Alexandria in 264, Dionysius died shortly thereafter.

He was a prolific writer on a variety of topics, both theological and pastoral. Unfortunately most of his writings survive only in excerpts preserved in the works of others, including Eusebius (WEC 2:**81**) and Athanasius (WEC 2:**90**). Although his orthodoxy had been questioned by Basil the Great (WEC 2:**67**), Dionysius exerted great influence in the East. Eusebius called him "the Great" (*Church History*, VI.xxix.3).

CPG 1: nos. 1550ff. * Altaner (1961) 237 * Altaner (1966) 210–11 * Bardenhewer (1908) 153–57 * Bardenhewer (1910) 134–38 * Bardenhewer (1913) 2:167–91 * Bardy (1929) 84–85 * Bautz 1:1318–20 * Cross 169–71 * Goodspeed 153–57 * Hamell 65–66 * Jurgens 1:250 * Quasten 2:101–9 * Steidle 49–50 * Tixeront 97–99 * CATH 3:614–16 * CE 5:11–13 * DCB 1:850–52 * DHGE 4:248–53 * DictSp 3:243 * DPAC 1:980–81 * DTC 4.1:425–27 * EC 4:1661–62 * EEC 1:238 * EEChr 1:333–34 * LTK 3:241–42 * NCE 4:876–77 * NCES 4:755 * ODCC 484 * PEA (1991) 3:646 * TRE 8:767–71

F. Nau, "Le comput pascal de la Didascalie et Denys d'Alexandrie," RBibl, n.s., 11 (1914) 423–25. * L.E. Phillips, "The Proof Is in the Eating: Dionysius of Alexandria and the Rebaptism Controversy," in *Studia Liturgica Diversa: Essays in Honor of Paul F. Bradshaw*, ed. M.E. Johnson and L.E. Phillips (Portland, 2004) 31–43.

45-A. Letter to Bishop Basilides[ta]

849   Canon 1. [. . .] You [. . .] inquire as to the correct hour for concluding the fast at the Pasch. You say that some of the brethren believe that this should

---

1. John 17:14.   2. Ps 22:21.
† Translated from PG 10:1271–74, 1275–78, 1281–82.
a. Basilides: bishop of the parishes in Pentapolis, a district west of Egypt along the Mediterranean Sea.

be done at cockcrow. Others, however, maintain that it should occur in the evening. The brethren in Rome, as they say, wait till cockcrow. And as you stated, those here do so earlier. You desire to have the hour explained exactly and with great calculation. To do this is certainly difficult and risky. All will admit that those who have been mortifying their souls by fasting should begin their festal joy immediately after the time of the Lord's resurrection. But in what you have written to me, you have clearly shown—and with an understanding of the holy Scriptures—that nothing precise is given by these books as to the hour when he arose. The evangelists describe differently those who came to the tomb at various times, all of whom said that the Lord had already risen. [. . .]

As things now stand, this is what we have to say to those who desire 850 to consider more accurately and precisely at which hour or half-hour or quarter hour it is fitting to begin rejoicing because our Lord rose from the dead. Those who are too hasty and break the fast before midnight we blame as contemptuous and intemperate. [. . .] Those who persevere and resolutely fast till the fourth watch, a time when our Savior appeared to those at sea when he walked on the water,[1] we acknowledge as being generous and industrious. Let us not, however, be too annoyed with those who being urged or of their own volition break their fast since all do not observe the six days of fasting equally or alike. Some fast every day; others two days; others three, others four, and still others none. As to those who have labored greatly in observing these fasts and, having grown weary, are almost exhausted, they are excused should they take food earlier. There are also those who not only refuse to fast for any long period of time but evade fasting completely. During the first four days they eat luxurious and rich meals, and then on the last two days—that of the Preparation and that of the Sabbath—they observe a strict fast, believing that they are doing something great and admirable if they continue to fast till the morning. I do not believe that these are equal to those whose fast has lasted several days previously. [. . .]

Canon 2. May women enter the house of God during their time of 851 withdrawal?[b] This, it seems to me, is an unnecessary question. I do not believe that they, if they are godly and faithful, will at such a time dare approach the holy table or receive the Lord's Body and Blood. For the woman who for twelve years had been suffering from hemorrhages did not touch the physician himself but only the hem of his garment.[2] No matter the condition in which people find themselves, to pray, to remember the Lord, and to request the Lord's help—these are not to be censured. However, a person who is not completely pure in both soul and body is forbidden to approach the holy of holies.

---

b. Namely, menstruation.
1. See Matt 9:20; Luke 8:43.   2. See Matt 14:25.

46. APOSTOLIC CHURCH ORDER[†]

Also known as the *Ecclesiastical Canons of the Apostles* (*Canones ecclesiastici apostolorum*) or as the *Ecclesiastical Constitution of the Apostles*, the *Apostolic Church Order* comes from Egypt—a few suggest Syria—and was redacted in the third or perhaps the fourth or even the early fifth century. The unknown author (or authors) uses a common literary device of the time, namely, ascribing to individual apostles the directives contained in the work; among these Peter and Cephas, interestingly enough, appear as two distinct individuals. So popular was the document that it became part of various canonical collections in the East, e.g., the Sinodos in Egypt.

The work contains two main sections preceded by an introduction: the first part (4–14) is based on the *Didache* 1–4 and gives a number of moral directives; the second section (15–21) treats the ordination or appointment of bishops, deacons, readers, etc.

Only one manuscript containing the original and complete Greek text of the work has come down to us. There is a fragment in Latin. Translations also exist in Arabic, Coptic, Syriac, and Ethiopic.

CPG 1: no. 1739 * Altaner (1961) 57 * Altaner (1966) 254–55 * Bardenhewer (1908) 160–62 * Bardenhewer (1910) 147–49 * Bardenhewer (1913) 2:262–69 * Hamell 66 * Quasten 2:119–20 * Steidle 269 * Tixeront 214 * CATH 1:478–79 * CE 1:635–36 * EEC 1:259 * EEChr 1:92 * NCE 1:689 * NCES 1:580–81 * ODCC 90

Texts and Translations
Greek
J.W. Bickell, *Geschichte des Kirchenrechts*, vol. 1 (Giessen, 1843) 107–32. * P.A. de Lagarde, *Reliquiae Iuris Ecclesiasticae Antiquissimae Graecae* (Leipzig, 1856) 74–79. * J.B. Pitra, *Iuris Ecclesiastici Graecorum Historia et Monumenta*, vol. 1 (Rome, 1864) 75–88. * Th. Schermann, *Die allgemeine Kirchenordnung, frühchristliche Liturgien und kirchliche Ueberlieferung*, vol. 1, StGKA 3, Ergänzungsband (Paderborn, 1914) 12–34.

Latin (fragment)
E. Hauler, *Didascaliae Apostolorum Fragmenta Veronensia Latina: Accedunt Canonum qui Dicuntur Apostolorum et Aegyptiorum Reliquiae*, fasc. 1 (Leipzig, 1900) 99–101. * E. Tidner, *Didascaliae Apostolorum, Canonum Ecclesiasticorum, Traditionis Apostolicae Versiones Latinae*, TU 75 (Berlin, 1963) 107–13.

Syriac (Octateuch)
J.P. Arendzen, "An Entire Syriac Text of the 'Apostolic Church Order,'" JThSt 3 (1902) 59–80. * A. Baumstark, Στρωμάτιον ἀρχαιολογικόν, *Mitteilungen dem internationalen Kongress für christlichen Archäologie zu Rom gew. vom Kollegium des deutschen Campo Santo* (Rome, 1900) 15–31 (with German translation).

Coptic (Sinodos)
H. Tattam, *The Apostolic Constitutions or Canons of the Apostles in Coptic with an English Translation* (London, 1848; reimpr. New York, 1965). * P. de Lagarde, *Aegyptiaca*

[†] Adapted from a translation based upon the Ethiopic as given in G. Horner, *The Statutes of the Apostles or Canones ecclesiastici* (London, 1904) 131–38.

(Göttingen, 1883; 1972) 239–48. * G. Horner, *The Statutes of the Apostles or Canones Ecclesiastici* (London, 1904) 295–306.

ARABIC (SINODOS)

G. Horner, *Statutes*, 233ff. * J. Périer and A. Périer, *Les "127 canons des Apôtres": texte arabe en partie inédit publié et traduit en français d'après les manuscrits de Paris, de Rome et de Londres*, PO VIII (Paris, 1912; Turnhout, 1971) 573–90.

ETHIOPIC (SINODOS)

G. Horner, *Statutes*, 1ff. (text), 127ff. (translation).

STUDIES

A. Harnack, *Die Lehre der zwölf Apostel*, TU 2, 1–2 (Leipzig, 1884–93) 193–241. * A. Harnack, *Die Quellen der sog. Apostolischen Kirchenordnung*, TU 2, 5 (Leipzig, 1886). * F.X. Funk, *Didascaliae et Constitutiones Apostolorum*, vol. 2 (Paderborn, 1903), Proleg. XLII–XLIV. * W.H.P. Hatch, "The Apostles in the New Testament and in the Ecclesiastical Tradition of Egypt," HThR 21 (1928) 147–61. * J.M. Hanssens, *La liturgie d'Hippolyte. documents et études* (Rome, 1970) 62–65. * A. Faivre, *Naissance d'une hiérarchie*, Théologie historique 40 (Paris, 1977) 143–53. * A. Faivre, "Le texte grec de la 'Constitution ecclésiastique des apôtres' et ses sources," RevSR 55 (1981) 31–42. * A. Faivre, "Apostolicité et pseudo-apostolicité dans la 'Constitution ecclésiastique des apôtres': l'art de faire parler les origines," RevSR 66 (1992) 19–67. * M. Metzger, "A propos des règlements ecclésiastiques et de la prétendue 'Tradition apostolique,'" RevSR 66 (1992) 249–61. * L. Bernadette, "Etude de la notice sur l'évêque dans la 'Constitution ecclésiastique des apôtres,'" QL 80 (1999) 5–23.

14. Concerning the ordination of a bishop. If a district should have only a few members of the faithful—not enough people to gather with the bishop, not even having twelve members—they shall send a message to the neighboring churches where there are many believers, requesting these churches to bring three members of the faithful, holy and chosen men of that area. They shall carefully examine these men concerning their suitability for the good work [of being bishop]: they are to determine whether he is a man who has a good reputation among the people, whether he is sinless, without anger, and a lover of the poor; whether he is kind, not a drunkard, not an adulterer, not a man who desires the greater share for himself; not a railer, not someone who is unfair, not anything of such sort. It is also good that he be unmarried, although if he married one wife before being ordained bishop, he shall live with her. He should be someone who adheres to solid doctrine and who can explain the Scriptures; yet if he is unable to do so, he should be humble and abound in love for all. The bishop should be condemned in nothing whatever, nor is he to be reproved in anything.   852

John said: If the bishop who is to be ordained knows how to keep himself and loves God, two approved presbyters shall be appointed to be with him. And they all said: "Not two but three because there are twenty-four presbyters, twelve on the right hand and twelve on the left hand." John said: Well it is that you have reminded me, my brethren. Behold, those on the right take the cups from the archangels, and they offer these to the   853

Lord. Those on the left have authority over all the angels. It is proper that the presbyters be like elders who have passed the time of having intercourse with their wives. They shall share in the mystery with the bishop, helping him in everything and gathering around him with love for their shepherd. The presbyters on the right shall carefully assist at the altar. May they be worthy of this honor and reject all that deserves rejection. The presbyters on the left shall attend to all the people, seeing that they are quiet, that they are not causing any disturbance, that they are fully controlled and obedient.

854   15. Concerning the appointment of the reader. James said: A reader shall be appointed after he has first been tested. He shall not be someone of many words, not a drunkard, not a scoffer. He shall be of good character and a lover of what is good; a person who daily hastens to the church, who remembers there the judgment; he shall be obedient, a person who reads well, and who knows that the duty of the reader is to act according to what he reads. Isn't a person who fills the ears of others with words called upon to act according to what is read? If one fails to do so, then will not this [i.e., the reading] be charged against this person as a sin before God?

855   16. Matthew said: Deacons shall be ordained as it is written: two or three witnesses will bear testimony. They [i.e., the candidates] shall be examined concerning all their service, with all the people bearing witness that they live with one wife, have reared their children in purity, are merciful and humble, are not murmurers, are not double-tongued, are not wrathful because wrath corrupts the wise. They shall not respect the person of the rich, not act unjustly toward the poor, not drink much wine; they shall work hard for the hidden mystery and the beauty of the consolation. They shall encourage those of the faithful who have something, to give to those who have nothing, and in this way they also shall share in the giving. They shall honor every person, doing so with all respect, humility, and fear; they shall keep themselves completely pure. Some they shall teach, some they shall question, some they shall reprove, and some they shall console. As for the rejected, they shall expel them immediately, knowing that those who oppose, who revile, who reject, are your enemies.

856   17. Concerning the widow. Cephas said: Three widows shall be appointed, two of them devoting themselves to prayer for all who are suffering; sufficient daily sustenance shall be given these widows. One of them shall stay with those women who are ill so that she may further their recovery, be watchful, and inform the presbyters by sending word to them. She shall not be a lover of gain, nor shall she be a drunkard lest she neglect her work of being watchful and praying during the night. If one of them wishes to do a good work, may she do it according to the commandment so that she may comfort the heart of the sorrowful because God's goodness has been made known to her first.

857   18. Concerning deacons: they should do good works. Andrew said: Deacons shall do good works by night and by day, for everyone and in

every place; and they shall not exalt themselves over the poor and the needy nor respect the person of the rich; they shall care for those who have nothing and provide for them from what is surplus; they shall encourage almsgiving on the part of those who have something to give; in this way they carry out the words of the Lord, who said, "I was hungry and you fed me."[1] Those who serve well, doing so without fault, shall inherit a place of rest.

19. Concerning the laity. Philip said: The laity shall cheerfully do what is commanded them; they shall obey those who devote themselves to the altar; and all of them shall please God in what God has given them and ordered them to do. You shall not learn to hate one another because of what is commanded you; rather, all shall hasten to do what God has given them to do; they shall not hate anyone nor cause a neighbor to be hated by making accusations. Even the angels do not overstep what is defined for them. 858

20. Concerning the reminder that the oblation is the Body of Christ and what comes after it. Andrew said: We have already ordered what was said concerning the oblation, namely, it is the Body of Christ and his precious Blood, something we declare to you with certainty. And John said: Have you forgotten, my brethren, that on the day when our Lord offered up the bread and the wine, he said, "This is my Body" and "This is my Blood"?[2] He did not command that they should treat these as common things. And Martha said in regard to Mary, "See her laughing." Mary replied, "That is not why I laughed, for our Lord said to us, 'It is good that the sick be healed by the whole.'" 859

21. Cephas said: It is not fitting for women to speak aloud while they are standing in church; rather, they should prostrate themselves with faces toward the earth. James said: How can they order for women a ministry of the mystery except the ministry they have in assisting the needy? Philip said: My brethren, as to the acts of charity that people perform, by doing them they store up for themselves a rich treasure in the kingdom of heaven; a good deed is credited to one by God, who continues it forever. Peter said: My brethren, you know that we are not placed over anyone by compulsion, but we give you a command from God. We beseech you to hear and keep the commandments; add nothing to them, take nothing away from them, all in the name of our Lord Jesus Christ to whom be honor and praise forever and ever. Amen. 860

47. OXYRHYNCHUS HYMN[†]

In 1897 the beginnings of what would eventually prove to be an extremely rich treasure of papyri were discovered at Oxyrhynchus (today the village

---

1. Matt 25:35.   2. Matt 26:26, 28; Mark 14:22, 24; Luke 22:19–20; 1 Cor 11:24–25.

[†] Translation from *The Oxyrhynchus Papyri*, Part XV, ed. B.P. Grenfell and A.S. Hunt (London, 1922) 21–25 (no. 1786).

of al-Bahnasa or Behnesa in middle Egypt, about 110 miles up the Nile from Cairo). The site was an ancient town dump where all types of written rubbish were deposited. The many thousands of retrieved pieces, dating from the first to the seventh centuries A.D. and to a large extent in fragmentary form, include not only literary works (about 10 percent of the total) but also inventories, bills of sale, and the like. Discovered and published over the years, today most of the papyri are preserved in Oxford, where modern technology (e.g., multispectral imaging) is helping to decipher cases of illegible lettering. As to religious texts, fragments from both the Old and the New Testaments are found; also selections from various apocryphal works as well as a number of hitherto unknown writings, e.g., an ecclesiastical calendar for 535–36.

In 1922 a papyrus fragment was discovered with a grain invoice on one side and on the opposite side the text and notes for what is most probably the conclusion of a longer Christian hymn text. The text itself is in Greek, and the melody appears in Greek vocal notation. The date of the hymn is usually thought to be toward the end of the third century.

Quasten 1:159–60 * EEChr 2:842–43 * LTK 7:1240 * NCE 10:847 * ODCC 1206 * PEA (1991) 9:123

Th. Reinach, "Un ancêtre de la musique de l'Eglise," *Revue musicale* 3 (1922) No. 9. * H. Abert, "Ein neuentdeckter frühchristliche Hymnus mit antiken Musiknoten," *Zeitschrift für Musikwissenschaft* 4 (1922) 524ff. * H. Abert, "Das älteste Denkmal der christlichen Kirchenmusik," *Antike* 2 (1926) 282–90. * R. Wagner, "Der Oxyrhynchos-Notepapyrus XV Nr. 1786," *Philologus* 79 (1923) 201–21. * C. del Grande, "Inno cristiano antico," *Rivista Indo-Greco-Italica* 7 (1923) 173–79. * O. Ursprung, "Der Hymnus aus Oxyrhynchos, das älteste Denkmal christlicher Kirchen," Musik Bulletin de la Société "Union *Musicologique*" 3 (1923) 129. * O. Ursprung, "Der Hymnus aus Oxyrhynchos in Rahmen unserer kirchmusikalischen Frühzeit," ThGl 18 (1926) 390ff. * J. Quasten, *Music & Worship in Pagan & Christian Antiquity* (Washington, D.C., 1983) 71.

861   All noble [ones] of God together . . . shall not be silent, nor shall the luminous stars lag behind . . . All the rushing rivers shall praise our Father and Son and Holy Spirit, all the powers shall join in saying: Amen, amen, power [and] praise . . . to the only giver of all good things. Amen, amen.

Index to Volume One

Numbers in bold and within parentheses are subhead numbers, which indicate particular authors/documents in this volume. All other numbers refer to marginal paragraph numbers.

funerals. *See* burial, procession during

general intercessions. *See* Word, Liturgy of: petitions
genuflecting. *See* kneeling/prostrating/genuflecting
gifts, bringing/presenting of. *See* Eucharist, Liturgy of: bringing/presenting/distributing/praying over gifts
Gnostic, 842–46
godparents. *See* baptism/initiation: sponsors/godparents
Good Friday
    fasting on. *See* fasting/fasts: on Good Friday
    observance of, 185
    refraining from the peace on, 474
Gregory Thaumaturgus (ca. 213–ca. 270), 740–43 (**35**)

Hallel (Jewish Passover), 80, 114
hands, holding, 301
hand(s), imposition/laying on of,
    baptism, after, 493, 602–3, 680
    baptism, before, 495, 662, 665, 668, 774, 848
    diaconal ordinations, during, 630
    episcopal ordinations, during, 617
    healers, not upon, 640
    presbyteral ordination, during, 631
    readers, not upon, 637
    reconciliation, during, 531, 589, 599, 604, 764
    subdeacons, not upon, 639
    virgins, not upon, 638
    widows, not upon, 636
hands, upraised, 239, 304, 471, 824, 843
Hanukkah, feast of, 20
hearers, 486–87
heathens. *See* pagans
heretics, reconciliation of, 585
Hermas, Pastor. *See* Pastor Hermas
Hippolytus (ca. 170–ca. 236), 614–734 (**31**)
Holy Spirit
    anointing and, 263. *See also* baptism/initiation, liturgy of: anointing(s), postbaptismal
    apostles, descended upon, 264, 470

baptism and, 287, 450, 457, 459, 461, 577, 584, 587, 593, 601–6, 608, 732. *See also* baptism/initiation, liturgy of: anointing(s), postbaptismal
    Christ, promised by, 265
    Church, present in, 721
    Pentecost and, 816
Hours. *See* Office, Daily (cathedral)—east; Office, Daily (private/early beginnings of)
hymn
    sung by Christians on a fixed day, 292, 444
    sung while holding hands, 301
hymns
    God, sung only to, 819
    married couples, sung by, 484
    pagan, 777
    singing of, 306, 481

Ignatius of Antioch (ca. 35–ca. 107), 203–25 (**9**)
imposition of hands. *See* hand(s), imposition/laying on of
infants, baptism of. *See* children/infants: baptism of
Irenaeus of Lyons (ca. 130–ca. 202/203), 254–87 (**15**)
Israel, 21–109 passim, 142, 148–50, 162, 163, 166, 172, 177, 321–410 passim

Jerusalem, 21–126 passim, 168, 172, 197, 315, 355, 383, 404–5, 603
Jesus Christ
    baptism by John, 262, 455, 461
    chrism and, 458
    as "daily bread," 472
    eucharistic command of, 250
    fish as symbol of, 736
    forgiveness of sins and, 509
    Holy Spirit promised by, 265
    penance and, 195
    prayers offered through, 759, 815
Jewish prayers, 1–177 (**1–6**)
Jewish rituals, Christians not to observe, 497
Jews
    "Church," once called a, 757
    darkness, remaining in, 522